RELIGION IN AMERICAN LIFE

RELIGION IN AMERICAN LIFE

A Short History

Updated Edition

JON BUTLER, GRANT WACKER,
and RANDALL BALMER

UNIVERSITY PRESS

2008

OXFORD

UNIVERSITY PRESS

Oxford University Press, Inc., publishes works that further
Oxford University's objective of excellence
in research, scholarship, and education.

Oxford   New York
Auckland   Cape Town   Dar es Salaam   Hong Kong   Karachi
Kuala Lumpur   Madrid   Melbourne   Mexico City   Nairobi
New Delhi   Shanghai   Taipei   Toronto

With offices in
Argentina   Austria   Brazil   Chile   Czech Republic   France   Greece
Guatemala   Hungary   Italy   Japan   Poland   Portugal   Singapore
South Korea   Switzerland   Thailand   Turkey   Ukraine   Vietnam

First published in hardcover as Jon Butler, *Religion in Colonial America* (2000);
Grant Wacker, *Religion in Nineteenth-Century America* (2000); Randall Balmer,
Religion in Twentieth-Century America (2001); Jon Butler, Grant Wacker, and
Randall Balmer, *Religion in American Life: A Short History* (2003)

Published by Oxford University Press, Inc.
198 Madison Avenue, New York, NY 10016

www.oup.com

Oxford is a registered trademark of Oxford University Press

Library of Congress Cataloging-in-Publication Data
Butler, Jon
   Religion in American life: a short history / Jon Butler, Grant
Wacker, and Randall Balmer
      p. cm.
   Includes bibliographical references and index.
   ISBN 978-0-19-533329-9 (pbk.)
   1. United States—Religion. I. Wacker, Grant II. Balmer,
Randall Herbert. III. Title.

BL2525.B88 2002
200'.973—dc21   2002014481

Frontispiece: Presbyterian Mission School employees and their children head
home after Sunday church in Oklahoma.

9   8   7   6   5   4   3   2   1

Printed in the United States of America
on acid-free paper

CONTENTS

CONTENTS

CONTENTS

PREFACE

Religion—beliefs in supernatural powers, forces, and beings—powerfully shaped the peoples and society that would become the United States. That this happened in a society lacking any official national church after American independence in 1776 is one of the central themes of *Religion in American Life: A Short History*. This book offers a succinct and vivid account of religion's astonishing interaction with America's peoples, society, politics, and life from European conquest and colonization to the beginning of the twenty-first century. In America, religion would be pursued by an amazing variety of individuals and groups whose successes and failures across three centuries not only defined religion in America but America itself.

The story of religion in America thus stands at the heart of the story of America itself. It is not the story of just a few. Quite the contrary. It is a story of natives and immigrants, of the wealthy, the poor, and those in between, of women, men, and children in families and out, of powerful political movements and parties to highly introspective individuals, of dreams realized and aspirations disappointed, of bigotry, yet also of often tender generosity, kindness, and mutual esteem.

Religion in America, therefore, usually stands with the grain of American secular history, not against it. In America, religion has been intertwined with immigration from the sixteenth to the twenty-first centuries. It deals with the American Revolution and the Civil War, with abolitionism and the corruptions of the Gilded Age, with American Progressivism, the rise of big business, and the response of the labor movement, with racism, anti-Catholicism, and anti-Semitism as well as with the civil rights crusade of the 1950s, 1960s, and 1970s, with protest against the Vietnam War and with the rise of a new American conservatism and the elections of Ronald Reagan and George Bush.

Above all, the narrative of religion in America is a story about people. It is the story of women—Anne Hutchinson, Phoebe Palmer, and Dorothy Day—as well as the story of men—Tenskwatawa, George Whitefield, Isaac Mayer Wise, and Billy Graham. It is the story of efforts to instruct children not only in formal religious teachings but also in morals and ways of behaving, from the Puritans to nineteenth-century Protestant temperance crusaders, to Buddhist immigrants honoring a traditional infant presentation ceremony. It is a story of failed preachers—the evangelist Jimmy Swaggart—and of subtly religious laity—Abraham Lincoln. And it is the story of men and women and, sometimes, children, not only as individuals but gathered together in that famous American institution, the "voluntary organization"—religious congregations plus countless religiously directed groups—the Women's Christian Temperance Union, Hadassah, the Moral Majority, Sunday Schools, the list is nearly endless.

The story of religion in America, then, is not an aberrant story. In a society so remarkably secular in so many ways—the American pursuit of wealth, the quest for international leadership, the love of science and technology—religion frequently stood at the heart of the American experience itself, guiding it, underscoring its central themes, providing its often most idealistic—and sometimes its most difficult—expressions. Indeed, religion's centrality to twenty-first-century America—especially its complexity and intricacy—is a virtual invitation to understand the rich and fascinating evolution of religion in the American past. In a brief compass, this is the history that *Religion in American Life: A Short History* seeks to tell.

RELIGION IN
COLONIAL AMERICA

CHAPTER ONE

Worlds Old and New

The French Jesuit Pierre de Charlevoix was fascinated by the religious customs of the Algonquian-speaking Indians of southern Canada and northern New York and New England. In his two-volume *Journal of a Voyage to North-America* (1761), Charlevoix related many stories about Algonquian religion that seemed both wonderful and strange. Charlevoix was especially intrigued by Algonquian dreaming and its dramatic effect among traditional Algonquian believers. He was particularly taken by a story told to him by French Jesuit missionaries working among the Algonquian Indians. An Algonquian man dreamed that he had been a prisoner held by Algonquian enemies. When he awoke, he was confused and afraid. What did the dream mean? When he consulted the Algonquian shaman, the figure who mediated between humans, the gods, and nature, the shaman told him he had to act out the implications of the dream. The man had himself tied to a post, and other Algonquians burned several parts of his body, just as would have happened had his captivity been real.

For Algonquian-speaking Indians and other eastern wood-lands Indians, dreams and visions gave signals about life that must be followed. The dreams and visions exposed dangers, revealed opportunities, and explained important principles. Dreams demonstrated that the souls of men and women existed separately from the body. The souls of others spoke to the living through dreams, including the souls of the dead. When Algonquians dreamed about elk, they felt encouraged because the elk was a symbol of life. But when Algonquians dreamed about bears, they became afraid because the bear signified the approach of death.

The Algonquian dream episodes signaled the compelling interrelationship between the Indians' religious life and their day-to-day existence. Dreams and visions allowed spirits to communicate with Indians who revealed eternal values. Dreams and visions evoked ordinary emotions and everyday circumstances to explain how the world worked. They described where each individual fit in a universe that otherwise seemed so often disconcerting and confusing. For Indians, dreams revealed how thoroughly religion was not merely "belief," but an intimate and interactive relationship among humans, the supernatural, and nature. As Charlevoix put it, "in whatever manner the dream is conceived, it is always looked upon as a thing sacred, and as the most ordinary way in which the gods make known their will to men."

Judith Giton did not want to go to America. She was a French Protestant, or "Huguenot," in the village of La Voulte in Languedoc in southern France. But in 1682 the French king, Louis XIV, began using soldiers to enforce restrictions on Protestant worship in La Voulte, sometimes with violence. As Judith Giton wrote years later in a memoir, the village "suffered through eight months [of] exactions and quartering...by the soldiery, with much evil." With her mother and two brothers, Pierre and Louis, she decided "to go out of France by night, and leave the soldiers in bed." The Gitons fled to Lyon and Dijon, then on to Cologne, Germany, where they met other refugee Huguenots. Judith, Louis, and their mother fervently believed they should settle thirty miles from Cologne with another brother. But Pierre had read a pamphlet advertising a colony in America—South Carolina, a place with many opportunities as well as freedom of religion. Pierre had "nothing but Carolina on his thoughts," Judith wrote.

Pierre won the argument. He took Judith, Louis, and their mother to Amsterdam and then London to book passage for South Carolina. The voyage to the New World turned out to be a disaster. Mother Giton died of scarlet fever. Their ship's captain left the three Giton children in Bermuda, where they had to find another ship for South Carolina. Louis died of a fever eighteen months after arriving in South Carolina. Although Judith and Pierre survived, she remembered the ordeal as extremely difficult. She experienced much "sickness, pestilence, famine, poverty [and] very hard work. I was in this country a full six months without tasting bread." Later she married another Huguenot refugee in South Carolina, Pierre Manigault. "God has had pity on me, and has changed my lot to one more happy," she wrote. "Glory be unto him."

Sometime in late 1723, the Protestant bishop of London, who had informal responsibility for Church of England affairs in America, received a wrenching petition from slaves in Virginia. It was unsigned, written by a mulatto slave "baptized and brought up in the way of the Christian faith." He described how the masters were harsh with him and all other slaves, "as hard with us as the Egyptians was with the children of Israel. . . . To be plain, they do look no more upon us than if we were dogs." Masters kept the slaves "in ignorance of our salvation . . . kept out of the church, and matrimony is denied [to] us." The slaves begged the bishop for opportunities to learn "the Lord's Prayer, the creed, and the Ten Commandments." They hoped that their children could "be put to school and learned to read through the Bible."

The Africans feared for their lives in writing this petition. If their masters were to discover the document "we should go near to swing upon the gallows' tree." But they wrote anyway. They hoped that the bishop, "Lord King George, and the rest of the rulers will release us out of this cruel bondage, and this we beg for Jesus Christ's his sake, who has commanded us to seek first the kingdom of God and all things shall be added unto us."

These slaves need not have worried about the effects of their petition. It was ignored in London and remained unknown in Virginia despite many rumors about slave dissatisfaction and rebellions in that colony throughout the 1720s. After being received in London, the petition was misfiled with papers on Jamaica; it was discovered by historians only in the 1990s, its author unknown now as then. And the petition's eloquent pleas remained unfulfilled, in Virginia as in the other British colonies. Through most of the colonial period, religion never disturbed the advance of slavery.

Nathan Cole had been bothered by religious questions for some time. Twenty-nine-years old, a carpenter and a farmer, Cole lived in Kensington, Connecticut. In 1739 he heard that the British revivalist George Whitefield had arrived in the colonies. When Cole wrote many years later about his experience hearing Whitefield, he remembered the event vividly.

Now it pleased God to send Mr. Whitefield into this land....I longed to see and hear him, and wished he would come this way. I heard he was come to New York and the Jerseys and great multitudes flocking after him...next I heard he was at Long Island, then at Boston...Then of a sudden, in the morning about 8 or 9 of the clock there came a messenger and said Mr. Whitefield preached at Hartford and Wethersfield yesterday and is to preach at Middletown this morning at ten of the clock. I was in my field at work, I dropped my tool that I had in my hand and ran home to my wife telling her to make ready quickly to go and hear Mr. Whitefield.

On high land I saw before me a cloud or fog raising. I first thought it came from the great [Connecticut] river, but as I came nearer the road, I heard a noise something like a low rumbling thunder....It was the noise of horses feet coming down the road and this cloud was a cloud of dust made by the horses feet....When we got to Middletown['s] old meeting house there was a great multitude, it was said to be 3000 or 4000 people assembled together....The land and banks over the river looked black with people and horses....I saw no man at work in his field, but all seemed to be gone.

When I saw Mr. Whitefield come upon the scaffold he looked almost angelical; a young, slim, slender, youth before some thousands of people...He looked as if he was clothed with the authority from the Great God...and my hearing him preach gave me a heart wound. By God's blessing, my old foundation was broken up, and I saw that my righteousness would not save me...all that I could do would not save me.

Within a year, Nathan Cole had undergone a "born again" experience, feeling guilt because of his sins but placing all his faith in God's forgiveness. He later joined an evangelical congregation that limited its membership to men and women who had had similar experiences, then left that congregation to join an evangelical Baptist church that limited the rite of baptism to believing or converted adults. Cole belonged to that congregation for another forty years until he died in 1783 at the age of seventy-two.

How thoroughly religion affected individuals and society in early America can be difficult to understand. We have been taught to believe that our ancestors, especially our colonial ancestors, were remarkably pious, and indeed many were. Yet religion's importance for individuals and societies also produced numerous differences and antagonisms that leave a confusing picture of early American religion. In Europe, Catholics and Protestants opposed each other and then divided among themselves as a consequence of the Protestant Reformation that began in the 1520s, thirty years after Columbus's discovery of the Americas. National rivalries separated French Catholics from Spanish Catholics and Protestants in England from those in the Netherlands. In turn, theological differences caused many internal divisions among Catholics and Protestants. In Africa, language and cultural differences reinforced religious disagreements between different societies, while within the same society individuals often disagreed about the expression and practice of religion. The importance of nature in American Indian religions never guaranteed that all native groups would honor nature in similar ways; the contrasts in their religious customs produced discord between individuals and rivalries between societies.

As a result, religious expression was complicated throughout America. In Catholic France and Protestant England, among the Ibo and Ashanti peoples of Africa, and amid the Micmacs and Catawbas of America, religious expression emerged in many different ways. What and how these men and women thought about religion was important to them as individuals and to their societies. In crucial ways, their religious beliefs and practices often accounted for the distinctiveness of their societies. These differences and similarities—individual and national, linguistic and theological—became the foundation of the diverse, historically evolving experiences of religion that characterized the entire American experience, both before and after the American Revolution.

What did religion mean to men and women on the eve of European colonization in America? Many things, it turns out.

When the British writer Henry Fielding published his comic novel *Tom Jones* in 1749, the Reverend Mr. Thwackum, Fielding's ludicrous Church of England, or Anglican, clergyman, became one of Fielding's most memorable characters. Thwackum's fussy description of "religion" exemplified the narrow-mindedness of Britain's mid-eighteenth-century Anglican establishment that Fielding detested: "When I mention religion, I mean the Christian religion; and not only the Christian religion but the Protestant religion; and not only the Protestant religion, but the Church of England."

Unfortunately for Thwackum, reality was—and long would be—far more complex in Britain and throughout Europe, Africa, and America. In Europe, state-supported churches formally monopolized public worship and gave each nation an appearance of unanimity in religion. Clearly, politics played a major role in determining both national and local religious commitments, as symbolized in the phrase "whose Prince, whose Church." Because King Henry VIII willed it, England became Protestant, and all English men and women legally became members of the Church of England once it had separated from the Roman Catholic Church. But then England switched back to Catholicism under Mary I, after which Elizabeth I brought the nation back to Protestantism. France and Spain remained Catholic because their monarchs not only remained Catholic, but used their faith to expand the power of the state in both religious and secular life. The numerous German principalities presented a patchwork of faiths. Most of the northern princes, including the king of Prussia, chose Protestantism, whereas many of their southern counterparts, including the rulers of Saxony, chose Catholicism.

In England, the royal command that created the Church of England fanned further religious debate. Elizabeth I controlled demands for wider reform of the Church of England better than any of her successors did. She eliminated practices that seemed Catholic yet vigorously suppressed radical Protestants. In the 1580s, she simply forbade meetings by Protestant "schismatics" who sought to split off from the official church, the Church of England, and enforced her orders with remarkable success.

Elizabeth's successor, King James I, who had previously been King James VI of Scotland, experienced greater frustration in matters of religion. By his reign reformers were demanding more changes in the Church of England. As their numbers multiplied under James, opponents decried them as "Puritans"—rigorous, overly demanding religious zealots. By the time King James asked the archbishop of Canterbury, William Laud, to suppress the Puritans in the 1620s, they were too numerous to put down easily. The effort, often poorly planned and clumsily executed, initiated debates in the 1630s that ultimately produced major parliamentary confrontations, the English Civil War of the 1640s, and the beheading of James's son, Charles I, in 1649.

As a result, by the 1690s England possessed a seemingly endless array of religious groups, which helps explain Thwackum's prissy bitterness about the meaning of the term *religion*. Most English men and women formally remained Anglicans, or members of the Church of England. But many others were Congregationalists, Presbyterians, Baptists, and Quakers—all Protestants, as were the Anglicans—and some even remained Catholics despite the century-long attack on their church and the social and political penalties that English Catholics endured. In addition, England also contained a small number of Jews, concentrated mostly in London and the port towns, not unlike the urban pattern of Jewish residence throughout the European continent. The 1689 Toleration Act grudgingly recognized this

diversity. Although the act did not legitimize Catholics or Jews and required officeholders to be Anglicans, it permitted at least some dissenting Protestants to worship, including Congregationalists, Presbyterians, and Quakers, and thus marked an important step toward modern religious freedom.

Important as religious identity was, however, actual participation in public worship in fact varied greatly, not only in England but throughout Europe. In England, for example, religion sometimes seemed only the indulgence of "enthusiasts." While Puritan reformers or Quakers pursued religious truth and the most adamant Anglicans sought to suppress them, many English men and women seldom participated in worship. A minister in Hertfordshire, England, complained in 1572 that on Sunday "a man may find the churches empty, saving the minister and two or four lame, and old folke; for the rest are gone to follow the Devil's daunce." This apathy was not confined to England. In the 1590s in Toulouse, France, only 2 to 5 percent of the laity (as opposed to priests and nuns) attended weekly mass, even though more than 90 percent of adults took Easter communion. A 1584 census of Antwerp, Belgium, revealed both significant religious diversity and considerable apathy: About 9 percent of household heads said they were Lutheran, 21 percent said they were Calvinist, some 30 percent claimed to be Catholic, and about 40 percent failed to specify any religious affiliation.

Individual beliefs also varied. Although open atheism was uncommon, a surprising number of people expressed not only criticism of specific groups but also doubt about religion altogether. Doing so proved to be dangerous. As late as 1697, Scottish authorities hanged a boy for denying the truth of the Bible. Some men and women denied the existence of God, of heaven and hell, and of heavenly rewards for good behavior. At least one woman believed in the Devil but not in God: "She thinks the Devil doth tempt her to do evil to herself and she doubteth whether there is a God." A man in Yorkshire called preaching "bibble babble" and said that he would "rather hear a cuckoo sing."

Many Europeans believed in magic. Magic invoked the supernatural without any necessary reference to God or Christianity, and Europeans everywhere knew thousands of magical practitioners. Some were learned scholars, including John Dee, whom Queen Elizabeth hired to cast horoscopes—astrological forecasts based on the alignment of the planets and stars— and William Lilly, who told fortunes and cast horoscopes for more than 4,000 well-paying London clients in the 1640s and 1650s.

"Wise men" and "wise women," usually illiterate, practiced cruder forms of magic for the common people. One official in Lincolnshire described them as using books that contained occult or magical information, "old mouldy almanacks, and several sheets of astrological schemes, all drawn false and wrong." Nevertheless, throughout Europe, they attracted men and women who wished to know the future, find lost or stolen objects, know good days on which to conceive children, or who hoped for cures from diseases of themselves, their children and relatives, and valuable animals they owned.

Europeans sometimes mixed magic and Christianity—to the dismay of the Christian clergy. One seventeenth-century skeleton recovered in a modern archaeological excavation bore a neck charm with the inscription "Jesus Christ for mercy sake, take away this toothache." One Anglican minister recorded in his diary how he mixed the two himself when, in desperation, he gave an insane women an amulet with "some verses of John I written in a paper to hang about her neck, as also certayn herbes to drive the Devil out of her."

Amid this variety and confusion, traditional institutional religion—Catholicism, Protestantism, and Judaism, especially—provided reassurance to believers and important formal religious structures for society. Above all, traditional institutional religion dominated the visual landscape. The European countryside, towns, and cities teemed with religious buildings, ranging from small chapels to immense cathedrals and, in the Jewish ghettos of cities and towns, synagogues. Many sixteenth- and seventeenth-century church authorities complained that the buildings outnumbered their priests, ministers, and rabbis and that they could not staff all the possible pulpits.

Public Christian worship also commanded more sustained and cohesive loyalty from laypeople than did private practices, including magic, despite complaints by clergymen about the influence of magic and popular religious indifference. Throughout Europe, large numbers of men and women served the state-supported churches. In Catholic France and Spain, priests, monks, and nuns often accounted for as much as 10 to 15 percent of the adult population. Even though Protestants abolished monasteries, an enormous number of clergymen were needed to serve Protestant interests. As European colonization began in America, thousands of Protestant clergymen were working throughout Europe, from Germany to England and Scotland. Because most of them served the churches supported by their governments, their influence extended far beyond their individual endeavors.

Above all, institutional religion explained how and why the world was the way it was and told believers what they could expect in this life and the next. Catholics found both order and relevance in the authority of the pope, in the timeless truth of the seven sacraments (especially the Mass, in which wine and bread became Christ's blood that had been sacrificed so that all believers could live forever), and in the panoply of the saints whose shrines dotted Europe and whose miraculous healing of the sick and injured testified to Christianity's truth and power.

Protestants celebrated the sovereignty of God and God's exclusive grant of salvation, which could not be earned with money or human labor. They believed they had reconstructed the worship and theology of the early church, and placed great stress on the sermon that replaced the ritual of the Catholic Mass as the central feature of worship. Whereas Catholics stressed miracles in the cure of disease and injury, Protestants stressed prayer, although some Protestants, such as the Englishman George Fox, the founder of Quakerism, performed miracles to demonstrate the truth of his new religion.

Jews honored God's commandments set out in the Torah for God's chosen people. These beliefs, duties, and rituals were further elucidated by centuries of Talmudic scholarship, the ancient Jewish rabbinical writings, that explicated biblical commandments for modern men and women. The study of the Talmudic writings, developing Jewish theology, and interchanges among different Jewish communities and with Christians shaped Jewish life across Europe from Russia to Spain in a continuing diaspora now almost 1,500 years old.

The New World provided fresh territory for Old World religious traditions. For Catholics and Protestants alike, the New World offered millions of "heathen" souls to be converted. Spanish and Portuguese Catholics saw the native peoples of South America and Mexico as God's challenge to Christian missions. They destroyed as many examples of native culture as they could (some Aztec and Inca buildings proved impossible to demolish) and imposed the Mass everywhere they could, thus giving the areas they conquered the new name of "Latin" America, because the Mass was observed in Latin.

England's James I chartered the Virginia Company to bring Christianity to Indians living "in darkness" and in "miserable ignorance of the true knowledge and worship of God." As a result, the New World presented new arenas for religious and national contests that had become all too familiar in the Old World. Who would win the souls of the New World's peoples, and who would conquer the territory they occupied?

For Jews, the New World represented something quite different: another place of exile in the face of persistent and renewed persecution. In 1492, the year Columbus discovered America, Queen Isabella ordered all Spanish Jews to leave the country or convert to Christianity, a climax to several centuries of Spanish Christian persecution of Jews. Some Jews fled the country; others (called Marranos, meaning Jews forcibly converted to Christianity) converted publicly but practiced Judaism secretly. Not surprisingly, throughout the colonial period some Jews also emigrated to America, hoping not merely for survival but for freedom as well, as would be true of many seventeenth- and eighteenth-century Christian emigrants to America.

Understanding African and American Indian religion before European colonization is difficult, because the literary sources that provide a broad profile of European religion are seldom available for precolonial African and American societies. Moreover, the archaeological evidence usually is insufficient to portray the vast array of individual and group differences in religion within societies that were known to exist in America before 1800. Yet we know that religious expression in these societies was rich and complex. Anthropologists and historians have long demonstrated that the religions of preliterate societies were exceptionally sophisticated, easily rivaling Christianity, Judaism, Islam, and other major world religious systems.

Certainly, the Africans and Europeans of the colonial period shared beliefs in a finite earthly life and an infinite afterlife. They also believed that supernatural figures and forces shaped both lives. Jean Barbot, a European traveler in western Africa in the 1670s, argued that many Africans believed in a supreme being who determined when people were born and when they died, who caused events to happen, and who ruled the afterlife. A Dutch traveler named William Bosman observed that Africans understood the "idea of the True God and ascribe to him the Attributes of Almighty, and Omnipresent," not unlike the Christians. At the same time, these Africans did not always offer sacrifices or even prayers to this god, because the god "is too high exalted above us, and too great to condescend so much as to trouble himself or think of Mankind."

West Africans believed in a great variety of spirits that determined what happened in this life and the next. Some believed that the "high god" or "creator of the world" constructed the lesser spirits or gods. Many of these gods had specialized characteristics. The Ga peoples of western Africa, for example, honored no "high god," and each Ga village was protected by a god senior to all other Ga deities. The Yoruba peoples honored Olorun as their high god and performed sacrifices in this deity's name to a panoply of minor gods. Gods of the rain, of thunder or lightning, and of the waterways shaped secular and human events. And like the spirits that inhabited or governed animals, they also sometimes competed with each other.

Africans fashioned remarkable varieties of religious expression. For example, many societies believed in and practiced augury or divination, the predicting of things to come. Religious leaders of considerable stature discerned revelations in the arrangements in plants or rocks and interpreted dreams and visions. In Mbundu society in the area of modern Angola, it was thought that events might be predicted by understanding the behavior of animals, the arrangement of leaves, bird calls, or the configuration of the stars. Although the process might have been similar to some forms of European magic, the specific details were unique to each society. In the Yoruba culture, in the area of modern Nigeria, a priest practicing Whydah threw cowry shells on a board and asked the spirits to make the shells land in such a way as to allow him to predict events.

Africans also believed in religious revelations communicated by supernatural beings to humans. These beings intervened in human events to teach people important religious lessons. Africans received religious revelations through spirit "mediums" who passed on messages from supernatural powers and gods. Indeed, revelations were everyday occurrences in many African societies. They were not relegated to ancient times, as in the Christian Old Testament and Jewish Torah. Many revelations predicted modern events. For example, the king of Allada in West Africa believed that his vision of a new white childlike god predicted the later arrival of Europeans.

Other Africans communicated with the souls of the dead, especially dead ancestors. For example, Africans visited a *ngombo*, a spirit medium, when they wanted to know what had made them sick and what would cure their diseases. They also frequently believed in spirit possession, in which an evil spirit possessed the body of a person or animal to make them sick. Spirit possessions afflicted humans as well as animals and demonstrated the power of the spirit or god to others, just as early Christians performed miracles to demonstrate the validity of their faith. Finally, late-seventeenth-century European travelers reported the existence of occasional atheists and doubters who cast aside particular religious traditions or rejected religion in general and lent individual variety to the societies in which they lived.

African religions underwent substantial historical change in the centuries before American colonization. As in Europe, in Africa wars and peaceful emigrations produced substantial alterations in the religions and religious practices of the African peoples. Islam, long a powerful religious force in eastern Africa, extended its influence into the western part of the continent in the centuries before the European colonization of America and the growth of the slave trade. Mosques could be found in western Africa in the seventeenth century, and Christian travelers were sometimes stunned by the devotion of African Muslims. "Foolas and Mandingoes attend to the ceremonial duties of their religion with such strictness as well might cause Christians to blush," wrote one seventeenth-century traveler. The kingdoms of Ghana, Mali, and Songhay became principal centers of Muslim influence in north central Africa as European colonization developed in the New World.

Christians also began proselytizing in West Africa in the sixteenth century but with only limited success. Portuguese Catholics were among the most insistent missionaries. In the 1530s they converted the principal king of the Kongo, Nzinga Mbemba, and baptized him as Dom Affonso I. The Portuguese also won converts in the small "creole" or mixed societies of Europeans and Africans that developed on the West African coast in the seventeenth and eighteenth centuries as a consequence of the slave trade, although major success in Christian missions in Africa did not occur until the mid-nineteenth century.

In all, then, African religions were as dynamic and shaped by human actions in different ways and different times as were European religions. The African religions evolved substantially in the thirteenth, fourteenth, and fifteenth centuries, even before the arrival of European missionaries, slave traders, and conquerors. African religious practices changed as European encounters with both Africa and America accelerated in the 1500s. The arrival of Christians only complicated the changes that had already been occurring in African religious beliefs for centuries, just as the Protestant Reformation brought out tensions that had long existed within European Catholicism for centuries before the Reformation.

America's Indians also proved to be deeply religious. It is not easy to untangle the preconquest religious life of America's native peoples from romantic myths and self-serving criticisms of missionaries and other European observers throughout the colonial period. Still, archaeological evidence, astute travel and descriptive narratives, and artifacts collected from the earliest days of European settlement create a dramatic and nuanced view of the religious practices and beliefs among American Indians on the eve of European contact, conquest, and colonization.

America's Indians had created breathtaking numbers of different cultures and religions by the late sixteenth century. Most U.S. historians now estimate that at least 500 independent cultures, and perhaps more, existed in the area of the modern United States on the eve of European contact, but it is impossible to count with complete accuracy. Indeed, the area of modern California alone probably contained more than 200 different linguistic and cultural groups. Yet these late-sixteenth-century Indian groups exhibited striking similarities in their religious beliefs and practices despite their many differences in language, economy, and society.

Many Indian religious systems believed that the world was one whole: They did not separate life into the secular and the sacred. The Indians often believed that they shared the world with supernatural beings and forces who rewarded and punished them and whom they encountered directly and indirectly through nature. Thus, for them religion was not a separate entity in their lives, something to turn to in times of difficulty or joy, but a part of daily existence. As they moved through the forests and deserts they talked to spirits, performed rites to honor them, saw them in visions and dreams, felt their reprobation in bee stings or nettle scratches, or found themselves cut down by the competing gods of alien nations sent to kill and conquer. For the Native Americans religion connected with all of life, from the seemingly trivial to the most consequential.

The Indians' religion often centered on maintaining intimate relationships with nature. The various Indian tribes typically viewed nature as powerful, all encompassing, and sacred. For example, the Micmacs of modern-day Nova Scotia and eastern Canada developed a religious system in which the beaver stood at the center of their cosmos, not as a god but as a symbol of the deeply spiritual relationship between the Micmacs and nature. One European missionary described hunting, especially for beaver, as a "holy occupation" among the Micmacs. The rules for hunting required strict adherence to honor that people's special relationship to nature. As a result, beavers were to be hunted in particular ways, with certain rituals. When beavers were trapped, for example, their blood was to be drawn in a public ritual that expressed the Micmacs' respect for the animal. Beaver bones could never be given to dogs, because the Micmacs believed that doing so would cause beavers to lose their sense of smell. And as one Frenchman observed, beaver bones never could be thrown away, "lest the spirit of the bones...would promptly carry the news to the other beavers, which would desert the country in order to escape the same misfortune."

Shamans, who also acted as medicine men and women, interpreted the intimate relationship between humans and nature for the Native Americans. Shamans were individuals set aside by themselves or the community to serve as intermediaries among humans, nature, and the supernatural. Their societies' complex, difficult world needed the skills of sensitive, intelligent guides who understood the foibles of human beings as well as the mysterious ways of nature and the supernatural. In some Indian societies, such as the Mohawks, women served as shamans, in others only men served, and in still others both women and men served. Shamans often received guidance through dreams or visions. They demonstrated their status through cures that combined physical skill and training, such as setting broken bones, with prophetic and revelatory powers that provided the force behind secret medicines, prayers, and magical practices. Thus, American Indians, not unlike Africans as well as European Jews, Catholics, and Protestants, used religion not only to shape the way believers thought about the world but also to defend against injury and sickness brought on by both human and supernatural causes.

The religious concerns of Europeans, Africans, and Native Americans did indeed have certain elements in common; moreover, this was already apparent to some men and women of that time. One of these was William Moraley, a British emigrant who came to America in the 1720s. Moraley could not accept the Indians' rejection of the Christian God. Yet he had come to understand many, if not all, of the functions of Native American religions:

> As to their notions of Religion, they are very wild, having none establish'd among them; but believe there is a God, Creator of all Things, endowed with Wisdom, Goodness, and Mercy; and believe they shall be judged, punished, and rewarded, according as they observe the moral Precepts instilled into them by the Light of Nature, and the Tradition of their Fathers.

What Moraley understood about the American Indians could be fairly well applied to both Europeans and Africans at the time. What he did not understand well, however, was the dramatic change that was transforming religion among all those peoples even as he wrote. For Europeans, Africans, and Native Americans, the colonial period from 1580 to 1776 would witness major upheavals and transformations in the nature and expression of religion among all of them. European Catholics, Protestants, and Jews witnessed major growth and spread of their religious traditions in ways not even the most pious of them could have foreseen on the eve of the European settlement of America. Africans found many traditional religious beliefs and practices shattered by the ordeal of New World slavery. Yet they discovered crucial ways to sustain and practice both new and old religious convictions under the most difficult circumstances. American Indians suffered under immense difficulties as European-induced sickness and warfare destroyed whole societies and cultures. Their traditional ways of life were undermined by the work of Christian missionaries. Yet in the eighteenth century they emerged with new religious configurations that proved to be as crucial to their own future as had been the religious changes undergone by Europeans and Africans.

Throughout the era of European colonization, religious practices and beliefs in America were modified in response to changing circumstances. In turn, changing religious traditions altered the ways Europeans, Africans, and Native Americans experienced life. These powerful interactions made religion a major force everywhere in colonial American life.

CHAPTER TWO

Religion and Missions in New Spain and New France

The Spanish, Portuguese, French, and English conquerors, who so ferociously subjugated the "New World" after Columbus discovered America in 1492, were startled by America's native inhabitants. Natives worshiped gods the Europeans found incomprehensible but displayed goods the Europeans found irresistible—gold, crops, plants, and animals. Natives were no less startled by the Europeans. Europeans brought new gods—in competing versions of Christianity—as well as goods that natives found irresistible—tools, clothing, weapons, and foods. Europeans and natives proved as serious about their gods as about their goods, and the interchanges among the Spanish, French, and North American natives that began in the early 1500s, which were often deadly, became the foundation for two centuries of changing religious patterns in northern Mexico, Florida, and Canada.

The Spanish proselytized heavily in the Caribbean and in the area of modern Mexico, while the Portuguese established missions in Brazil throughout the 1500s, a full century before the English successfully established their permanent settlement along North America's eastern shore, in Virginia in 1607. Then, between 1600 and 1800, the Spanish established missions in the areas of modern Florida, southern Georgia, Alabama, and Mississippi and in southwest Texas, New Mexico, Arizona, and California, while the French established missions among natives along Canada's eastern shores and the Saint Lawrence River.

Natives everywhere simultaneously resisted and accommodated to the European presence and demands. Many rejected demands to convert to Christianity by ignoring, openly opposing, and sometimes killing missionary priests. Other natives converted, but sometimes retained many vestiges of traditional culture, so that priests worried about the genuineness or depth of their conversions.

Christians argued among themselves about missions. Did the missions truly serve religious purposes or were they agents of secular control? How should natives be taught? Could missionaries use force when converting Indians? Should Indian converts be treated equally with Europeans?

Indians also argued about the interchange with Christianity. Was conversion legitimate? Could they receive European goods but reject Europe's gods? Did the conversion of one Indian group endanger religion and culture among neighboring groups?

These questions bedeviled Indians and Europeans in America long after the British had conquered French Canada (in 1763), after the American Revolution of 1776, and into the early nineteenth century, when the final control of Florida, Louisiana, and northwestern Mexico, including California, still remained unsettled.

Spanish and Portuguese efforts to Christianize Indians in America stemmed from two overweening drives: a traditional Christian missionary impulse that now eagerly extended to the

New World, and deep concerns about creating a uniform version of Christianity in their societies, whether Old World or New. Heroism and tragedy among both Europeans and Indians often accompanied the results.

Spanish religious policy in the New World emerged as the new monarchs of Castile and Aragon, the two kingdoms within Spain, sought to transform their own pluralistic societies into a purely Christian kingdom. Muslims ("Moors") invaded the area of Castile in 711, and then fought a losing struggle to maintain their place in Spain against Christians until the 1400s; Jews had lived in Christian and Muslim Spain for centuries, not without difficulty, yet in surprising peace. However, in 1492, Ferdinand and Isabella ordered the expulsion of Muslims and Jews from their kingdoms of Aragon and Castile unless they converted to Christianity. Hundreds of thousands of Muslims and Jews fled Spain, and those who remained underwent a forced conversion, a feat Christians regarded as a "success" that earned its sponsors, Ferdinand and Isabella, the title "los reyos católicos," the Catholic Monarchs.

The pursuit of Christian conversion of Indians in America by Spanish explorers and conquerors in America mirrored Ferdinand and Isabella's campaigns to turn all residents of Aragon and Castile into Christians. Columbus sailed to America on the *Santa Maria* under the flag of the Virgin Mary and described his purpose: "to see the said princes and peoples and lands" and to determine how to effect "their conversion to our Holy Faith." Papal "bulls," or decrees, entitled *Inter caetera* ("Among Other Things") issued by Pope Alexander VI in 1493, divided the New World territories, which were still almost completely unknown, between the kingdom of Castile and the Portuguese. The pope hoped that this division of responsibility would create even more opportunities "to bring [natives] to the Catholic faith."

To counteract the mistreatment of natives by Spanish explorers, soldiers, and settlers in America, Pope Paul III proclaimed in a 1537 bull, *Sublimis Deus* ("Most High God"), that all of the New World's peoples were fully human; Christians were obligated to attempt to convert natives to Christianity as well as treat them as humans who, like themselves, had been created by God.

Catholic authorities quickly established an institutional structure in America to advance the Church and support missionary efforts with Indians. Pope Julius II established the archdiocese of Yaguata, headquartered near Santo Domingo in the island of Hispaniola in 1504. Among the earliest priests present in the Caribbean were those from "mendicant orders," priestly communities supported by contributions and even begging, especially Franciscans from the religious order named after St. Francis of Assisi and Dominicans, members of the order of St. Dominic, which stressed public preaching and university teaching. They were followed by Jesuit priests, members of the rapidly growing Society of Jesus founded by the Spanish nobleman Ignatius Loyola in 1540. Between 1500 and 1800, as many as 15,000 European priests arrived in the Americas controlled by Spain and Portugal, some "diocesan" clerics under the control of bishops and archbishops (called "diocesan" priests because they ministered under the authority of local diocesan officials), and many from the Franciscan, Dominican, and Jesuit orders. More than 8,000 Franciscans alone arrived in America before the colonical period ended, and all of them spread throughout the Caribbean, Mexico, and finally Peru, to teach Christianity to the Indians.

The earliest efforts to Christianize Indians in New Spain proved disastrous. If Columbus was indeed serious about converting Indians, and he was, this scarcely precluded tensions among European Christians themselves or guaranteed common sense or decency in treating Indians. Columbus argued with priests who accompanied his second voyage to America, in 1493, over everything from authority on the ship to the behavior of Columbus and his crew. Columbus's rough treatment of native inhabitants left many Caribbean Indians dead. Columbus and his brother, Bartolomo, burned Indians at the stake when they rejected and destroyed statues of Christian saints the explorers brought to America. The combination of open slaughter and European diseases, especially smallpox and venereal diseases, left only a few thousand Indians still living in the Caribbean by 1600. Many Indians converted to Christianity by necessity, not choice.

Deaths from attack and disease, the collapse of the Aztec empire in Mexico and the Inca empire in Peru, and the continuing arrival of priests and construction of missions in the Caribbean, Florida, and Mexico transformed the religious landscape of New Spain between 1492 and 1800. In areas under Spanish control, Indians could no longer practice their diverse traditional religions openly or vigorously. Spanish authorities destroyed traditional religious objects and sites when they could (the great pyramid at Tenochtitlán in Mexico City, for example, proved indestructible, although the Spanish destroyed the great Aztec city that supported it), built Catholic churches on traditional Aztec sites, and prohibited the practice of traditional Indian rituals. These Spanish practices differed sharply from those in British America, where the general British indifference to Indians and conversion gave Protestants little interest in appropriating Indian religious sites and rituals, either for their own use or in converting Indians to Christianity.

Amidst this carnage, the Spanish created religious, educational, and medical institutions that would last into the modern era. The conqueror Hernando Cortés founded the

Hospital de Jesús in Mexico City (he is buried there), and by the end of the late 1500s, most major towns in central Mexico had a hospital staffed by priests. Dominican, Franciscan, and Jesuit missionaries developed exceptional language skills to assist in proselytizing among Indians. But Spanish landowners, fearful of rebellion from Indians who might hold the belief that conversion to Christianity might give them rights against Europeans, opposed teaching Indians how to read and write, whether in Spanish, Latin, or in native languages, much as slaveholders in Great Britain's colonies later rejected teaching Africans how to read and write in the century before the American Revolution.

Two important figures demanded that Indians receive humane treatment at the hands of European conquerors and established the outlines of the debate that would swirl around the question of conquest and Christian conversion. In 1511, a Dominican priest, Antonio de Montesinos, challenged the Spanish laity to whom he spoke: "Tell me, by what right or justice do you hold these Indians in such cruel and horrible slavery?... Are they not men? Do they not have rational souls? Are you not bound to love them as you love yourselves?"

Then, in 1514, another Dominican, Bartolomé de las Casas, reversed his own course—Las Casas had managed a plantation using Indian labor for almost a decade—to take up the cause of the Indians. Working first with Montesinos, Las Casas sought to develop a program of both colonization and Christianization that ended the exploitation of Indians. When politics in both Spain and in the Americas frustrated his plan, Las Casas turned to words and history. He wrote a massive *History of the Indies*, another work called the *Apologetic History*, and a treatise on converting unbelievers to Christianity. Las Casas catalogued the virulent abuses of Indians by their European conquerors;

his accounts, buttressed by many documents he collected, often constitute the earliest written descriptions of Indian life at European conquest. Las Casas demanded respect for the Indians' intellect and capacity to learn Christian doctrine, and argued that Christianity itself demanded respect for traditional Indian culture. As a result of Las Casas's efforts, the Spanish Crown proclaimed the New Laws in 1542, which forbade Indian enslavement and tributary labor and demanded humanitarian treatment of Indians.

Yet Las Casas won only momentary backing for his ideas. Spanish landholders exploited Indian labor through meager wages and miserable working conditions, and missionary priests often exploited force in converting Indians. Then in 1585, the bishops of New Spain forbade the ordination of Indians to the priesthood. This decision not only created a centuries-long gulf between the Christian church with its wholly European clergy and the natives it sought to Christianize, but it made the creation of schools, even for an elite who might become priests, unnecessary and undesirable. As a result, the new university, founded in Mexico City in 1541, served only Europeans, while the Jesuits' many colleges and seminaries created in the colonial era likewise served Europeans, not natives.

The shrine of Our Lady of Guadalupe just outside Mexico City, now visited by more than six million Roman Catholics from around the world each year, suggests how the Old and New Worlds interacted even in a difficult setting. A small shrine and devotion, or religious prayers dedicated to the Virgin Mary, apparently was built at this site, though whether by priests or Indians is not known. An Indian claimed to have been cured at the site in a Christian miracle. But some Spanish priests worried that Indians actually used the shrine as a cover to worship traditional Aztec goddesses even as the Spanish watched.

In the 1600s, a new local tradition at Guadalupe emerged that traced the shrine back to visions of an Indian, Juan Diego, in 1531. Although no mention of either Diego or the visions exists in any documents of the sixteenth century, an account in the Nahuatl language of Aztec descendants first published in 1649, *Nican Mopohua*, traced the Guadalupe shrine to visions of the Virgin Mary by Juan Diego at Guadalupe in 1531; this account became the basis for the modern religious devotion at Guadalupe. In 1754, Pope Benedict XIV officially recognized the feast day of Our Lady of Guadalupe in Mexico, December 12, as the devotion assumed growing importance among Indian worshipers in Mexico. In 1810, the priest Miguel Hidalgo invoked the tradition of Our Lady of Guadalupe in support of Mexican independence from Spain, and the Mexican land reformer and revolutionary Emiliano Zapata did the same in supporting peasant uprisings during the Mexican Revolution of 1910. Pope Pius XII named Our Lady of Guadalupe patroness of the Americas in 1945, and Pope John Paul II canonized Juan Diego during his 2002 visit to Mexico.

Spanish missions in Florida and Mexico, which then extended as far north into California as modern San Francisco, revealed extraordinary instances of missionary failure and success between 1500 and 1800 as well as remarkably resilient Indian efforts to preserve traditional worship, despite inordinate religious and secular pressures toward Christian conversion.

Substantial Spanish missions emerged in Florida only after the peninsula absorbed a permanent Spanish settlement at what now is Saint Augustine in 1563, and the earliest missions proved futile. The nomadic character of Indian settlement in Florida, Indian ferocity in opposing the Spanish, and the sparseness of the missionary ranks cost many missionaries their lives, mostly Jesuits. Franciscans replaced Jesuit missionaries in 1573 but were nearly extinguished by a 1597 revolt of Guale Indians in Georgia who protested Christian opposition to monogamous marriage and killed many Franciscan priests.

Franciscan missionaries experienced greater outward success in Florida in the seventeenth century. Larger Spanish garrisons in Florida enabled priests to call upon better defenses when Indians revolted, as happened in 1647 and 1656. Several priests lost their lives in these revolts, but Spanish authorities crushed the Indian dissidents with considerable ruthlessness. The Franciscans taught Christianity to Indians who came to the mission compounds for both religious instruction and trade, but who largely continued to live in nearby villages, in contrast to the practice of French Jesuits in Canada who generally lived with Indians in their villages. Between 1580 and 1690, the Franciscans established more than thirty missions in Florida, where they claimed to be teaching Christianity to as many as 25,000 Indians. The lack of substantial immigration to Florida by Spanish settlers meant that the Franciscans actually occupied often isolated and vulnerable garrisons dependent for protection on Spanish troops, while the Indians controlled the nearby countryside.

The Franciscan efforts in Florida succumbed to both Indian opposition and increasing British attacks on the Spanish enclaves in Florida. Guale Indians increasingly spurned Florida's Franciscan missions after 1680 as British settlers moved into South Carolina and then into Georgia; resistant Indians ridiculed baptism with such expressions as "Go away water! I am no Christian!" British attacks all but destroyed Florida's Franciscan mission network by 1720, and when Florida became a British province in 1763 by terms of the Treaty of Paris, the demise of the remaining Franciscan missions had little effect on native religion among Florida's Indians because their commitment to

Catholicism had been fragile at best. Even though the Franciscan missions in Florida had been numerous and deeply staffed between 1580 and 1680, their swift demise bespoke the exceptional difficulties of the entire mission enterprise.

It is hard to imagine more romantic images than those of the Franciscan friars constructing beautiful adobe chapels nestled along California's undulating coast or in the Sonoran desert. Helen Hunt Jackson memorialized the California missions in her romantic 1884 novel *Ramona*, with its sentimentalized friars and gently paternalistic Spanish landholders, and photographs of the Sonoran missions have graced American photo albums for more than a century.

The mission experience in what Spanish authorities soon called Nuevo Mexico proved more stark. The earliest years of exploration and conquest proved just that. The expeditions of Hernando de Soto from Florida into the area of modern Kansas from 1539 to 1542, and those of Francisco Vásquez de Coronado into the area of modern New Mexico from 1540 to 1542, did not find the golden cities from which the Aztecs were reputed to have come, and they won few Christian converts. Instead, the more serious and dubiously successful mission efforts came with the arrival of Franciscan missionaries in the 1590s and early 1600s. They established Santa Fe as their base and worked to Christianize Indians living in the pueblos or interconnected communal dwellings typical of the nearby Acoma, Hopi, and Zuni Indians.

The earliest stages of Franciscan activity in Nuevo Mexico proved exceptionally violent. In 1598 the military commander Don Juan de Oñate led soldiers and priests into northern Mexico to demand obedience and conversion from pueblo leaders. If Indians accepted baptism and Christianity, Oñate promised that the Indians "would go to heaven to enjoy an eternal life of great bliss in the presence of God." If they rejected Christianity, "they would go to hell to suffer cruel and everlasting torment." When Indians at the Acoma pueblo revolted after Spanish soldiers raped young Acoma girls, Oñate attacked the pueblo, killed more than 800 Acoma Indians, amputated one foot from each man more than twenty-five years old, and gave Indian children under twelve to the Franciscan friars to use as servants.

Throughout the seventeenth century, Franciscans supported by Spanish troops battled with pueblo leaders for the Indians' spiritual loyalties. They attempted to reduce the number of pueblos and concentrate Indians into fewer and larger settlements, an acknowledgment of the friars' feats that Christian conversion would succeed only by controlling Indian settlements. They rejected Indian practice of premarital and extramarital sex, and they objected to the Indians' sharp division between men and women that gave Indian women—"corn mothers"— an exceptional authority in pueblo households far beyond any authority Christian women enjoyed in Spanish households.

The friars became well known for their dogged persistence in converting Indians. They successfully converted many children by removing them from their pueblo homes and teaching them in Franciscan schools, and by introducing Indians to trade with the Spanish, they drew them inside a larger world of imperial commerce. As a result, the Franciscans experienced substantial success in pueblos along the Rio Grande River and in the smaller settlements around Santa Fe. Perhaps as many as 20,000 Indians in these pueblos formally converted to Christianity, altering their societies and lives in subtle and profound ways. As one Indian lamented the result, "when Padre Jesús came, the Corn Mothers went away."

However, in larger pueblos inhabited by the Acoma, Hopi, and Zuni, resistance to Christianity erupted into armed conflict. Small revolts occurred in the 1630s, 1640s, and 1650s and resulted in the murder of several Franciscan priests. Franciscans reported that within the pueblo, Indians practiced traditional religion and even adapted Christian crucifixes and medals for their own purposes, despite their outward adherence to Christianity.

In 1680, following economic problems caused by drought and increasing anti-Christian resistance, a massive Indian revolt against the Franciscans occurred in the northernmost pueblos. It was led by an Indian named Popé with support from major pueblo leaders and nearby Navajos and Apaches. Indians killed more than thirty priests outright as well as almost 500 of their Indian and mestizo or mixed Indian-European supporters. Indians forced one priest to ride naked on a pig before beating him to death. They burned chapels, destroyed bells and icons, and, as one priest wrote, dove "into the rivers and wash[ed] themselves with...a root native to the country" to remove the stain of baptism.

The Spanish reconquest of the pueblos in the 1690s and early 1700s caused substantial changes in the religion of New Mexico and Arizona. The Spanish population itself increased dramatically from fewer than 2,000 in 1700 to more than 10,000 in the 1770s, and many Franciscan priests turned their attention toward Spanish settlers and away from Indians, whose population also continued to decline as a result of European diseases and malnutrition. In the meantime, Hopi Indians continued to reject Christianity and did so well into the twentieth century, particularly Hopis who continued to live in the large pueblos.

But Indians in smaller pueblos, as well as many remaining Franciscan priests, increasingly tolerated a mix of Christianity and traditional Indian religion. After the Spanish reconquest of the 1690s, New Mexico political authorities warned about "idolatrous Indians and witch doctors," and Franciscans bemoaned pueblo Indians who received baptism and took communion yet seemed to retain many traditional non-Christian religious practices, ranging from ceremonial dancing to burial rituals. Yet even the Franciscans themselves tacitly permitted Indian dancing and allowed natives to use Indian rather than Christian names, although the priests complained about the practice. One Franciscan dismissed them as "neophyte" Christians who often "have preserved some very indecent, and perhaps superstitious, customs."

The result was a kind of standoff in the large pueblos. As both New Mexico civil authorities and Franciscan priests turned more attention to Spanish settlers, who were far wealthier than the Indians, a kind of peculiar latitude emerged in these northern reaches of Mexico. Some Indians, especially the Hopi, resisted Christianity wholesale, and from the eighteenth to the late twentieth century, Catholicism won little following in the Hopi pueblos. Yet other Indians mixed elements of traditional worship and Christianity in ways that increasingly seemed palatable on both sides; priests accommodated a Christianity that seemed more Indian than Spanish, and Indians practiced a Christianity that still preserved some Indian customs. Meanwhile, Indians throughout New Mexico increasingly found themselves outnumbered by Europeans and pressed by new territory as they fled United States settlers moving west from Texas and south from the middle plains.

The history of California's Spanish missions repeated many elements found in New Mexico save one—successful, widespread Indian resistance. California's Indians indeed resisted Christianity, sometimes as violently as in New Mexico. But their resistance occurred amidst a devastating Indian population decline that far outstripped Indian population decline in

New Mexico. Between 1600 and 1850, more than 100 different Indian peoples and cultures simply became extinct in California, the very years in which Indian-European contact increased and Franciscans established their missions along the California coast. Thus, as Spanish, and then Mexican, power advanced in California down to the 1830s, Indian resistance generally failed as many Californian Indian groups became extinct and others were almost wholly absorbed inside California's Spanish mission complexes.

The Franciscan missions in modern-day California, called Alta California—literally upper or northern California—in the late Spanish colonial period, did not appear until the 1760s and 1770s. They were set up because of increasing Spanish concern over British, French, and even Russian expansionism in North America and imperialistic concerns to increase Spanish power in western North America. But as in New Mexico, the desire to bring Indians to Christianity and the Franciscans' strong influence with Spanish authorities in Mexico promoted the development of missions along the California coast supported by garrisons of Spanish troops.

Father Junípero Serra, a Franciscan priest, founded the first nine Franciscan missions in California between 1769 and his death in 1784. By the 1820s, the Franciscan mission system in California included twenty-one missions stretching from Serra's first mission, at San Diego de Alcala, to the northern missions at San Rafael and San Francisco Solano established by Serra's successors in the 1810s and 1820s. Slowly, the missions became linked by trails later romantically called El Camino Real, or the King's Highway. These were mainly horse paths providing the only routes from mission to mission, each about a day's ride from the next and the principal means of land communication among Spanish authorities in Alta California.

Serra proved as controversial in his own time as he has proved to be in modern times. An intense, devout man, Serra dedicated his life to the conversion of California Indians. He directed the establishment of missions with a single-minded purpose and promoted them before secular authorities with exceptional skill. Although not always well during his years in California (he was already in his late fifties when he founded San Diego de Alcala in 1769), he demonstrated his own unworthiness before his Indian subjects through vigorous self-flagellation, beatings with a small rope or chain. During a sermon, one listener reported how Serra "drew out a chain, and...let his habit fall below his shoulders." After exhorting his audience to the penance, Serra "began to beat himself so cruelly that all the spectators were moved to tears" at the punishment Serra inflicted on his own body. Serra and his Franciscan successors also recorded punishments inflicted on Indians who rejected Christianity. One priest informed Serra that Indians, who rejected his sermons, had died in an epidemic but that the priest's Indian listeners were spared, a lesson Serra believed demonstrated the validity of Christianity.

The California missions quickly became major economic enterprises. They followed out the aims of the *encomienda*, a system in which the Spanish conquerors demanded tributary labor from Indians but also instructed them in Christianity and protected them. The encomienda, originally used in conquered Moorish territories in Castile, did not work well in the Caribbean, in part because enslaved African labor so quickly replaced the all-but-extinguished native population. But it became an effective model for the Franciscan missions in California, because enough Indians survived, who also became dependent on the missions as their own societies withered. The Franciscan missions developed extensive agriculture using Indian labor.

They introduced cattle farming on a scale far beyond anything previously present in California. They developed citrus farming and grapes for both wine and juice that foreshadowed California's modern agricultural patterns.

The missions' growing need for labor, combined with the Franciscans' hierarchical understandings of society and their convictions about converting Indians, coincided with and reinforced, but did not cause, the precipitous population decline that devastated so many California Indian societies in the eighteenth and early nineteenth centuries. Especially after 1800, Spanish and Mexican authorities used troops to secure mission laborers. Troops scoured the countryside for Indians to work at the missions, sometimes for food, sometimes under conditions that verged on enslavement. Franciscans beat the worshipful as well as recalcitrant Indians, sometimes ritually, sometimes forcibly. The ritual flagellation followed centuries of European Roman Catholic penitential tradition and only appeared cruel to Indians. Indians from the many California native societies, threatened by smallpox, dysentery, venereal disease, and malnutrition, yet fearful of Spanish military power, clustered around the missions; some converted to Christianity while others vacillated.

Serra and his Franciscan priests withstood open Indian resistance that sometimes escalated into violence. Serra barely escaped an armed rebellion by Indians at San Diego de Alcala in 1769, the year the mission opened. Just as Serra was about to perform his first infant baptism at the mission, Indians grabbed the child from Serra and ran back to the Indian town, ridiculing both Serra and Christianity. Five years later, in 1774, after Spanish troops raped several Indian girls, 800 Indians attacked San Diego de Alcala, burning the mission buildings, destroying statues of the Virgin Mary and St. Joseph, and murdering one priest and several Indian workers. Serra rebuilt the mission but uncovered a design for another attack in 1778 that he thwarted by arresting and executing four Indian chiefs involved in the planning.

By 1800, perhaps 20,000 Indians lived in and around the nearly twenty Franciscan missions in Alta California. Many were survivors of California Indian groups decimated by European diseases. Some had been forced by Spanish troops into the missions to work. Increasingly, others were second- and then third-generation Indian converts, loyal to Serra, the Franciscans, and Christianity.

The divide, evident by 1800, over the Franciscan missions and the fate of California's Indians continued not merely into the nineteenth century but as late as the 1990s. A movement in the 1980s to beatify Junípero Serra, the first step in the path toward Roman Catholic sainthood, drew both strong support and intense criticism. Detractors, including Catholic and non-Catholic Indian activists, charged Serra and the Franciscans with participating in and even leading the destruction of California's Indians in the 1700s and 1800s through their forced labor, violent punishment, and intolerance. Supporters saw in Serra a flawed but beneficent protector of Indians who acted within eighteenth-century Catholic tradition and Spanish hierarchical values, however paternalistic and lacking in modern sensibilities. Pope John Paul II postponed a beatification ceremony for Serra originally scheduled for a 1987 visit to the United States, but a year later beatified Serra at the Vatican.

Religion in France's New World possessions echoed themes common to New Spain but developed two new ones as well. Interaction between Roman Catholic missionary priests and Indians proved quite different and generally more successful than in New Spain, but it was scarcely peaceful. And the church paid greater attention to the substantially larger numbers of

French immigrants who arrived in Canada and Louisiana after 1700 and who far outnumbered Spanish immigrants to Florida or northern Mexico and California.

France's New World settlements were found in three markedly different areas of North America—the Caribbean, Canada, and Louisiana. The quickly changing character of France's small Caribbean settlements directly shaped the efforts of the Roman Catholic efforts there. The perceived attraction of the West Indies, buttressed by a strong desire to compete with both Spain and Britain, encouraged French incursions into the Caribbean in the 1630s. By the 1680s, the French had established a presence on as many as ten islands in the Caribbean. The French established small settlements on St. Christopher, Martinique, and Guadeloupe, but became best known for the colony of Saint Domingue on the island of Hispaniola, which the French divided with the Spanish, a division now represented by modern Haiti and the Dominican Republic.

In fact, France's Caribbean colonies quickly became the home for thousands of African slaves rather than model communities of Christianized Indians. The few Indians still living in France's Caribbean territories even by 1650 met the same fate experienced by native populations on the Caribbean islands controlled by the Spanish, British, and Danish: almost wholesale extinction. The French then turned to imported slaves from Africa to work large sugar plantations just as the Spanish and British did or would do, and African slaves not only displaced any remaining Indians but quickly outnumbered the small population of French immigrants on the islands.

Roman Catholic efforts to Christianize Africans in the French Caribbean remained largely the work of mendicant orders, such as Capuchins, Carmelites, Dominicans, and Jesuits, all of whom established missions in the French Caribbean. None were known for their successes with either enslaved Africans or with local French residents. One French Jesuit, Antoine La Vallette, simply pursued business, just like the laymen in his congregation. But he scandalized the Jesuit order when the British seized two French trading vessels in 1755 and gleefully exposed La Vallette's heavy involvement in merchant trades, embarrassing his Jesuit superiors in France and forcing them to close the Jesuit missions in the Caribbean in 1762.

New France—the name customarily applied to France's sprawling colony in Canada—demonstrated how differently French Jesuits proselytized among Indians than did Spain's Franciscans in Mexico. The history of New France also revealed how the rising importance of European settlement in Canada after 1700 shifted Roman Catholic activity in the colony in markedly different directions.

Although France claimed the area of modern Canada from the late 1520s, a substantial French presence there did not begin until the 1620s, and the territory did not become a royal province until 1663. New France prospered primarily on the fur trade well into the 1730s and encouraged very little settlement by French immigrants. This pattern resembled the pattern of Spanish occupation of the Caribbean, Florida, and Mexico before 1800, but it stood in sharp contrast to Britain's development of its mainland colonies from Maine to Georgia that so strongly encouraged British immigration to all its mainland North American colonies.

Not surprisingly, French missions to Indians proved the principal activity of Roman Catholic enterprise in Canada from the 1620s into the 1730s and 1740s. French dependence on the fur trade, which prospered on extensive knowledge of native cultures, provided an opportunity for Jesuit missionaries, and the Jesuits in Canada approached their task much differently than had the Franciscans and other mendicant orders in Spanish America.

France's Jesuits generally proselytized from within traditional Indian cultures and societies in Canada, whereas Spain's Franciscans lived in their own settlements and brought Indians into them. The Jesuits adapted the approach taken in 1 Corinthians 9:22, "I became all things to all men, that I might save all," and adapted themselves to many aspects of Indian culture in Canada. They learned Indian languages (whereas Franciscans often demanded that Indians learn Spanish). The Jesuits moved directly into Indian villages, especially among the Hurons along Lake Erie, rather than living apart. They allowed Christianized Indians to retain traditional dress, and they learned and appropriated Indian rhetorical traditions and even religion. They sometimes described Jesus as a superior version of the trickster so common in Indian mythology or cast the Christian God as a superior version of the Indians' own divine figures. The priests also challenged Indian shamans or healers with humor, ridicule, and anger and not only stressed Christianity's superiority in theology but in curing illness and attaining miracles.

The earliest Jesuit missionaries in Canada achieved substantial success among Canada's Huron Indians as early as the 1630s. Led by Fathers Jean de Brébeuf and Gabriel Lalemant, Jesuits moved in among the Hurons, ministered daily, and won numerous converts to Christianity, despite the Hurons' anger about rising death tolls from European sicknesses, increasing Indian use of alcohol, and tension over the lure and consequences of the rapacious fur trade that drained the forests of precious animals that were as valuable and important to Indians spiritually as they were economically. Brébeuf, Lalemant, and the Jesuits encouraged Hurons to settle in a ring of villages in eastern Ontario, ultimately called Huronia, including one named Ste. Marje. Brébeuf's instructions to the missionaries stressed the importance of accommodating Indian mores: "You must never keep the Indians waiting at the time of embarking." "Eat the little food they offer you, and eat all you can." "Do not ask many questions; silence is golden." "Do not be ceremonious with the Indians." "Always carry something during the portages." The Jesuits' detailed reports of their work in Huronia, called the *Jesuit Relations*, have been among the most important sources of information on native culture in early Canada since their original publication in the 1630s and 1640s.

The near undoing of the Jesuits' mission among the Hurons occurred in 1649 and stemmed not so much from missionary failure as from intertribal tensions, including tensions over religion and Christianization. In March 1649, Iroquois Indians burned the settlements in Huronia, killed hundreds of Hurons to avenge Huron incursions into Iroquois territory and the Hurons' increasing adoption of Christianity, and captured several of Huronia's Jesuit missionaries, including Jean de Brébeuf and Gabriel Lalemant.

Angry at Brébeuf and Lalemant for their proselytizing and France's incursions into Indian territory, the Iroquois subjected the priests to particularly gruesome tortures. Christianized Hurons later reported that the Iroquois "baptized" the priests with boiling water. They placed red-hot hatchets under the priests' armpits and hot metal collars around their necks. They stripped flesh from the missionaries' legs and skulls, which the Iroquois cooked and ate as Brébeuf and Lalemant watched. Then, "seeing that the good Father [Brébeuf] would soon die, [they] made an opening in the upper part of his chest, and tore out his heart [when Brébeuf was still living], which [they] roasted and ate." Other Jesuit missionaries later rescued Brébeuf's and Lalemant's remains, and in 1930 Brébeuf, Lalemant, and six other Jesuits who had been killed by Indians in the seventeenth century were canonized by Pope Pius XI.

Despite the 1649 Iroquois attack on Huronia, Jesuits resumed their Huron missions and even added missions to the Iroquois, who were themselves weakened by new intertribal tensions. But from the 1680s to the British takeover of Canada in 1763, Jesuits exchanged breadth for depth in their Canadian missions. Jesuits established outposts at St. Ignace, where Lake Huron meets Lake Michigan, and at Green Bay in Wisconsin, and Jesuit missionaries traveled as far south as southern Illinois and west to the Mississippi River. But after 1700, the numbers of Jesuit missionaries in Canada declined and their older missions to the Hurons and Iroquois thinned, patterns that paralleled France's weakened position in the fur trade, increased British competition on Canada's frontiers, and increasing neglect by French authorities, secular and religious alike.

The eighteenth-century Jesuit missions in Canada were not without their successes. In 1676, Kateri Tekakwitha, a Mohawk orphan in northern New York, accepted baptism at age twenty from Jesuit missionaries despite strong family opposition, then moved to the Jesuit mission at St. Francis Xavier du Sault in Quebec for protection. There she developed a scrupulous devotional life and began a small convent for women in 1679. When she died the next year, Tekakwitha became the focus of a Roman Catholic devotion that expanded steadily among both Canadian and United States Native American Catholics throughout the nineteenth century, and Pope John Paul II beatified Kateri Tekakwitha in 1980.

Roman Catholic practice among the relatively small French immigrant population in Canada experienced the difficulties often common to underdeveloped colonial societies. In 1674, the pope appointed a bishop to administer Roman Catholic affairs in Quebec, rather than have them administered by a bishop in France. But the paucity of French immigrants—fewer than 20,000 in 1710 and only 42,000 in 1740 (compared with 250,000 English settlers in New England)—and French Canada's relative impoverishment gave the Church few resources with which to work. Worse, Roman Catholic bishops and priests struggled with each other over church authority and finances as they worked to bring a vigorous spiritual life to Canada's French immigrant population.

Still, when the British acquired Canada by terms of the Treaty of Paris in 1763, Roman Catholic religious life among Canada's immigrant French residents bore two notable traits. First, Canada's small and often isolated French populace increasingly sustained a dependable parish life despite ecclesiastical struggles and financial problems. The small seminary established at Quebec in 1663 trained priests both for immigrant French parishes and as missionaries to the Indians. By 1740, more than eighty parishes serving French immigrants had been established along the Saint Lawrence River served by priests from the Quebec seminary as well as members of several religious orders, not only Jesuits, who had domineered the early Indian missions. These other orders included Sulpicians, a French order of priests founded to support seminary directors; Recollects, a branch of the Franciscan order; and Ursulines, a religious order dedicated to educating young girls. The Ursuline order maintained an extensive system of schools for girls, and in 1737 Montreal women led by a widow, Marguerite d'Youville, established the Sisters of Charity, later called the "Grey Nuns," notable for their work among the sick and the poor.

Thus, the British encountered a relatively healthy Catholicism among the French settlers of Canada when they assumed control of Canada in 1763. Anti-Catholic Protestants in the lower British mainland colonies protested Britain's pledge to allow Canada's Catholics to exercise their religion without harassment or limitation, but the British really had no choice; the British could defeat the French military, but they could not remove the French settlers. Some of these objections exaggerated the strength of Roman Catholic institutions in Canada in the 1760s. But they unwittingly tapped into another important theme: for French settlers chafing under British rule in occupied Canada in future decades, Catholicism would become a principal vehicle for asserting French identity and ethnic solidarity after their British conquest. And when the British divided Canada in 1791 into two provinces—Lower Canada (largely French-speaking with guarantees for Catholic religious practice in what is now modern Quebec) and Upper Canada (increasingly settled by British Protestants in the eastern territory of modern Ontario)—Britain's formally Protestant government effectively guaranteed the preservation and extension of Roman Catholicism in French-speaking Canada from the nineteenth century to the present.

Far to the south, French Catholicism also emerged with an increasingly visible presence in the French territory of Louisiana, which the French controlled until 1763, and which the Spanish controlled between 1763 and the purchase of the Louisiana territory by the United States in 1803.

The earliest entrance of Catholicism into the lower Mississippi River valley came from the extension of French exploration and early missionary ventures in the upper Mississippi in the 1680s and 1690s. Systematic French settlement along the Gulf Coast from modern New Orleans east to modern Biloxi, Mississippi, did not begin until after 1700. Nor did this settlement have a successful, or often peaceful, political or religious history. As late as 1760, only a few thousand

Europeans lived in the Louisiana territory. Settlement was hampered by intrigues among the officials and merchants who were fearful of British incursions from the north and east and Spanish incursions from the south and west. Missionary work among natives depended on a succession of generally unsuccessful Jesuits, Quebec seminary priests, Carmelites, and finally Capuchins, whose work with Indians in the lower Mississippi never really prospered.

Still, the small French settlements in Louisiana, especially at New Orleans, slowly developed a basic parish life after 1720, including, as in Canada, intriguing developments among women. Ursulines arrived in New Orleans in 1727 to teach and staff a hospital for soldiers. Three years later, a small group of French laywomen formed a confraternity, the Children of Mary, a society of laywomen who would honor the Virgin Mary by relieving the sick and teaching the poor, including enslaved Africans increasingly arriving in Louisiana. Working with the Ursuline nuns, the women of the confraternity helped prepare Africans for baptism by instructing them in Christianity. By the mid-1740s, the Catholic laywomen in the Children of Mary and the city's Ursuline nuns had helped prepare almost 100 of the 300 Africans baptized in previous years. Yet, as in the Caribbean and other French and Spanish settlements throughout the Americas, most Africans remained unchristianized, and unlike the Ursulines and Children of Mary in New Orleans, most Europeans remained unconcerned about the Africans' spiritual fate.

By about 1800, then, many elements of the European experience in America had already been laid down in the colonies established by Spain and France since Columbus's fateful discovery of America—bitter, often violent secular and religious struggles with Indians, the reestablishment of traditional patterns of worship among Spanish and French immigrants, and a highly varied record of proselytizing among increasing numbers of Africans in the Spanish and French colonies in America. However different the Roman Catholicism of the French and Spanish and the Protestantism of most English settlers in Britain's mainland colonies, the French and Spanish experiences often anticipated the English religious experience in America more than the frequently dramatic differences might suggest was possible.

CHAPTER THREE

Religion in England's First Colonies

The English settlers of New England intended to make religion the focus of their settlement. These first immigrants were alienated English Puritans called separatists, who had already fled England for the Netherlands because of their inability to achieve further reformation in the Church of England at home. They originally received a charter for land in Virginia but landed instead near Plymouth, Massachusetts, in December 1620. They renegotiated their charter with London authorities and celebrated the famous first Thanksgiving with nearby Indians in October 1621.

A far larger body of settlers arrived in 1630 to establish a separate outpost, the Massachusetts Bay colony, north of the Plymouth colony. Facing continued persecution in England and led by the Cambridge-educated Puritan lawyer John Winthrop, these Puritans began to leave England in large numbers in 1630. By the end of 1630, eleven ships with more than 1,000 Puritan immigrants had landed in Salem, the first town established in the new colony. They then proceeded to establish

a second town, Boston, named for Boston in England, a major
Puritan center. By 1635, more than 5,000 additional Puritans
had arrived in Massachusetts Bay.

John Winthrop, who soon became the governor of the
Massachusetts Bay Company, described a powerful religiously
centered vision for the new colony. Speaking aboard the *Arbella*,
the flagship of the small Puritan fleet, as it rested in Salem harbor before the settlers disembarked, Winthrop gave what would
become one of the most renowned sermons in American history, a lay homily that he entitled "A Model of Christian Charity." These were not just alienated Puritans fleeing England,
perhaps hoping to return, but men and women with a vision for
the future in America. In his sermon Winthrop set down what
he believed his followers should intend for this New World now
that they had left England, that "sinful land."

Winthrop believed the Puritans should settle together in
a city or town where large and small farmers and merchants
alike would form a community housing their church, their government, and their defenses against enemies, whether Indian or
European. He believed it would be a "city of God" and a "city
upon a hill." The Puritans would worship as the Bible intended
them to. Men and women would aid each other and, as a consequence, serve God. They would not satisfy individual desires
at the expense of the community. "We must be knit together
in this work as one man," Winthrop wrote. "We must entertain each other in brotherly affection. [W]e must delight in
each other, make others' conditions our own, rejoice together,
mourn together, labor and suffer together, always having before
our eyes our commission and community in the work, our community as members of the same body."

The importance of religion in New England was not unique
among England's American colonies. In 1619, the initial meeting

of the first colonial legislative assembly, the Virginia House of Burgesses, took up religion as a major task. The Burgesses opened its first meeting with a prayer by the Rev. Richard Buck. "Men's affairs do little prosper where God's service is neglected," the Burgesses wrote. They then passed laws to uphold "God's service" in the New World wilderness. Ministers would preach every Sunday and all colonists would be required to attend. The laws banned idleness, drunkenness, gambling, and fancy dress. Reports of "all ungodly disorders," such as "dishonest company keeping with women and such like," would be presented by ministers and church wardens to the colony's churches, which would excommunicate offenders and confiscate their property.

Buck — "God's Service" in America

An emphasis on religion and moral order had been present in Virginia since its first settlement in 1607. The original charter of the Virginia Company declared that the company existed to propagate the "Christian religion to such people [Indians], as yet live in darkness and miserable ignorance of the true knowledge and worship of God." A 1610 tract advertising the colony insisted that it had Indian missions as its "principal and main ends...to recover out of the arms of the Devil, a number of poor and miserable souls, wrapped up unto death, in almost invincible ignorance."

Virginia Company ↓ missionary

It was not surprising, then, that the company sent twenty-two ministers to America before the colony went bankrupt in 1624. In 1616, the colony had no fewer than four ministers for only 350 settlers, a far higher ratio of clergymen to laity than could be found anywhere in England. The Virginia Company constructed a church in Jamestown with a cedar chancel and a black-walnut communion table. After Virginia became a royal colony in 1624 it legally established the Church of England and levied taxes to pay for churches and ministers "as near as may be to the Canons of England both in substance and circumstance."

Anglican

Maryland & Catholic

Maryland, first settled in 1634, had similarly religious intentions but ones of a different persuasion. The colony was granted to the English Catholic convert George Calvert, Lord Baltimore, by King Charles I in 1632 and was understood to be a haven for persecuted English Catholics. Catholics had always formed a minority of the colony's settlers, and Calvert was sensitive to the realities of English public life. He instructed his brother Leonard, the colony's first governor, "to preserve unity and peace amongst all the passengers" to America. Maryland's Catholics would worship privately and were "to be silent upon all occasions of discourse concerning matters of religion." The governor was to "treat the Protestants with as much mildness and favor as justice will permit."

Silence & peace between Religions

In the first decade, Maryland's Catholics established chapels for public worship, where Jesuit priests regularly performed Mass and held confession. The priests overcame fears of Indian reprisals among both the Catholic and Protestant settlers and began to carry out a systematic mission program among Maryland's Patuxent Indians. At the same time, Calvert resisted Jesuit pressure to increase their legal powers in the colony and allow them to purchase lands from the Indians independently, without the governor's explicit permission. In the end, Calvert won his arguments with the Jesuits, largely because they recognized that they were a minority in the colony and that the uneasy religious peace prevailing there might easily be short-lived.

missions w/ Native Am.

By 1649, however, the year of John Winthrop's death in Massachusetts, the religious practices of the earliest English settlers everywhere in America diverged strongly from their founders' intentions. In New England, the Puritans disagreed with each other, ignored new settlers, and lost their own religious intensity while becoming increasingly intolerant. In Virginia and Maryland, the religious leadership failed, churches fell

within 15 years, religion changed in all areas

into disuse, Protestants attacked Catholics, and worship became so uncommon that many colonists observed it only occasionally. As a result, seventeenth-century American religious practices bore a surprisingly mottled face. In New England, their early strength masked internal discord and then remarkable apathy. In the Chesapeake region, the early religious fervor gave way to a spiritual lethargy that lasted well into the 1680s.

We are liable to misunderstand the Puritans partly because so many myths have come down to us about them: that they created a theocratic society—one ruled by ministers; that their religion stimulated unusual economic success; that they were mean and vindictive; and that they were perpetually unhappy. The early-twentieth-century social critic H. L. Mencken, who disliked the Puritans intensely, claimed they were driven by "the haunting fear that someone, somewhere, may be happy."

One way to grasp Puritanism is to understand what it was not. It never was a theocracy where ministers ruled a cowed laity. And Puritanism seems to have spurred no special economic gains. Except for the earliest years of settlement, New England probably was somewhat poorer than the Chesapeake region. Puritanism as a religion extended far beyond New England, to Presbyterians and Baptists in the middle and southern colonies. New England itself was not uniformly Puritan. By 1650, many New Englanders were paying little attention to Puritan demands and theology. Nor was Puritanism necessarily anti-intellectual and unbending. The Puritans danced and sang, and on occasion they even joked.

Puritanism was a rarefied form of Calvinism, the theology of the sixteenth-century Genevan reformer John Calvin. He stressed God's omnipotence, salvation by God's grace alone, and predestination, the idea that God has already determined who is to be saved and who not saved. Calvin's followers, including the English Puritans, added important ideas to Calvin's original formulations. In England, they emphasized the quest for group discipline among believers organized into congregations, subjecting individuals to the censure of the congregations when they adopted wrong beliefs or behaved in immoral ways. In America, they stressed the need for religious direction in the ongoing history of whole towns and communities, much in the way that John Winthrop had outlined in "A Model of Christian Charity."

Winthrop's ideals often played themselves out in the history of the New England towns, but not always in ways he imagined. Puritans settling there often signed "town covenants" that fused individual and community aims. The settlers of Dedham, Massachusetts, for example, established their community not merely as a place where individuals happened to purchase land but "in the fear and reverence of our Almighty God." They promised to "profess and practice one truth according to that most perfect rule, the foundation whereof is everlasting love." This covenant also meant that they agreed to exclude dissenters—a requirement that would soon be a problem—and to "receive only such unto us as may be probably of one heart with us."

In theory, the closed community advocated by Winthrop and established in towns like Dedham gave tremendous power to Puritan congregations. In 1631, the Massachusetts government, headed by Winthrop, required all voters to be members of the local Puritan congregation. As the Massachusetts assembly put it, the "body politic" would be synonymous with church members, and the civil government would be moral and virtuous, because it would be elected by good and right-minded citizens, all of whom belonged to Puritan churches. These congregations, which accepted the authority of no higher ecclesiastical body— hence their later labeling as "Congregationalist"—exercised the local management of congregational affairs. They did not form a democracy. Women could not vote at all in them, and power and authority within them tended to be held largely by wealthy, well-known men. But they became one of several different foundations of later American democracy.

not democratic but religious

The Puritans also worshiped—at great length—in ways that summarized their objections to the Church of England, England's state church. Puritans had two principal criticisms of Church of England, or Anglican, worship. First, Puritans objected to the many ceremonies, processions, and ornate music that characterized Anglican worship. Puritans searched the Scriptures but could find no specific warrant for these practices. (Catholics and Lutherans, in contrast, believed that such practices glorified God and were not specifically prohibited by the Scriptures.) Puritans therefore stripped their services of these age-old ceremonies and elaborate music. They emphasized prayer, Bible reading, psalm singing, and a sermon, which they believed constituted the only essential elements of early Christian worship. The Puritan objection to ornate music did not, however, preclude the singing of psalms to simple tunes without an organ or instrumental accompaniment. One person sometimes sang a line first—a technique called lining out—and the congregation followed. In a society where illiteracy was high, singing psalms was an important way to teach biblical lessons.

criticism of CofE

Second, Puritans objected to Anglican theology and doctrine, which was "Arminian" in character. It followed the theology of the sixteenth-century Dutch theologian Jacob Arminius, who modified Calvin's emphasis on predestination by stressing that men and women indeed made free choices that affected their salvation, although God knew about these choices in advance. In contrast, Puritans stressed the complete dependence of men and women upon God for salvation and rejected the idea that

no free choice

they could do anything on their own to achieve salvation. Men and women worshiped God because they were dependent upon God and obliged to do so, not because they could win salvation by it.

In New England, as in England itself, Puritan worship was lengthy. It typically consisted of an opening prayer, a reading from the Bible, psalm singing, a sermon, another singing of a psalm, a prayer, and a concluding blessing. The entire service might last three to four hours. Although the opening prayer was relatively short, perhaps fifteen minutes, the concluding prayer often lasted an hour, and in 1680 a Dutch traveler reported that one Massachusetts minister prayed for a "full two hours in length." The sermon, which also lasted an hour or more, customarily examined the biblical text read at the opening of the service.

Because of the intimacy of Puritan worship and community, some New England towns became "communities of saints." Congregations determined the values Christians should follow and watched, judged, and condemned those who strayed. In 1639, the Boston courts fined a Puritan merchant named Robert Keayne for profit gouging. Supplies from England were scarce, and Keayne had raised his prices to take advantage of market shortages. Rather than make "others' conditions our own," as Governor Winthrop had urged, Keayne had sought to profit from them, and the courts fined him for doing so. But Keayne then faced even more serious censure from his congregation. That body conducted an "exquisite search" of Keayne's behavior and condemned him again in front of his fellow church members. This judgment humiliated Keayne for the remainder of his life. It also illustrates the Puritans' affinity for censure and, sometimes, vindictiveness.

What especially distinguished New England's Puritans, at least briefly, was their willingness to attempt to do good even *"do -g good"*

though they believed men and women were sinful and depraved. For a time, seventeenth-century New England Puritanism thrived on the tension produced by these conflicting aims and views. Michael Wigglesworth, a tutor at Harvard, struggled for years with his impulses and what he called his "carnal" habits: "I am often slothful and lay down the weapons of my warfare and do not fight, cry [and] strive as I should against them." Yet if anything he enjoyed this self-reproach, because it measured his labor as a sinful man trying to do good. Congregations acted similarly. It was not that these bodies were healthy because no one sinned. Rather, Puritanism's success depended on the way a congregation's members accepted censure, advice, and consolation, much as Robert Keayne had done. Only in this way could sinful Puritans be models for others and their communities.

In the end, Puritanism failed most notably when the men and women of New England drifted away from the discipline of the congregation and slowly, almost imperceptibly, abandoned the quest for a godly life that Puritan doctrine told them they were unlikely to achieve yet whose pursuit honored God even when it failed.

Puritans failed - theologically had to motivate self.

Puritanism also brought turmoil even within its own ranks. As early as 1636, less than a decade after the Puritans' arrival in Massachusetts, Boston witnessed an extraordinary trial that resulted in charges of heresy among the town's clergy and the expulsion of a prominent merchant and his wife from the community. The case centered on Anne Hutchinson, the wife of William Hutchinson, who had landed in Boston in 1634, fresh from the continuing persecution of Puritans in England. Before emigrating she had, for more than a decade in the 1620s and early 1630s, listened tenaciously to the sermons of the reforming minister John Cotton, who had already become a legend among England's Puritans. Cotton did away with much Church

trials

John Cotton read.

of England ritual and stressed preaching, concentrating on the idea that only God's grace, not paltry human works, led to salvation. Cotton fled England for America in 1633 after spending a year hiding from Archbishop William Laud, who threatened to imprison him for his reforming activities. This episode left Cotton's followers like Anne Hutchinson fearful and worried about their safety and religion. Now, safely arrived in Massachusetts, she felt she could continue Cotton's instruction in America.

Hutchinson's freedom in America soon dissolved, however, into argument, banishment, and death. By 1636, only two years after she arrived in Boston, most ministers were aghast at her behavior. Hutchinson had begun speaking about religious doctrine to groups of sixty to eighty men and women. She interpreted the Scriptures. Worse, she said that many Boston clergymen possessed "no gifts or graces." In 1637, the Boston authorities charged her with civil offenses, including "traducing [maligning] the ministers and their ministry." Her followers defended her by ridiculing the ministers and their English university training. Hutchinson, they said, "preaches better Gospel than any of your black-coats that have been at the Ninneversity."

Anne Hutchinson's trial demonstrated how assertive a Puritan woman could be. She directly challenged Governor John Winthrop when he interrogated her, saying, "What law have I broken?" She attacked "legal" preachers who stressed religious rules and regulations rather than God's free grace and salvation. She upbraided ministers who criticized her use of biblical citations when she defended her teaching: "Must I show my name written therein?" She claimed that men and women who were saved by God were not bound by the civil law as others were but obeyed it only as an example to the unsaved. And, most disastrously, she claimed that she spoke directly to God and possessed powers of "immediate revelation...by the voice of [God's] own spirit to my soul!" She needed no intermediaries, no unfit clergymen.

Hutchinson paid for her boldness. The Boston court banished her from Massachusetts for undermining the civil order. She moved to Rhode Island, where her husband died in 1642. A year later, Hutchinson and all but one of her six children were killed by Indians after she moved to north of New York City. Although Thomas Welde, a member of the court that convicted Hutchinson in Boston, later gloated that "God's hand" could be seen in Hutchinson's death, the affair cast a pall over Puritan New England. It demonstrated that a wide variety of beliefs could in fact be found among the Puritans and that achieving religious uniformity in Puritan New England might come at a very high price.

More serious problems stemmed from mundane causes. Although the number of Puritan congregations increased as towns grew up in the countryside, the percentage of church members in the towns began to decline, especially after about 1660. Many congregations turned inward, leaving new settlers outside the church. Spiritual vitality sagged. Second- and third-generation children lacked the experience with God and the knowledge of theology known to first-generation settlers. As a result, they were not admitted to the congregations, because they could not give a public accounting of "God's dealings" with them.

In the 1660s some, but not all, congregations adopted a "halfway covenant" to solve the membership problem. This agreement allowed the children of lagging second-generation parents to be baptized so that they would have a kind of "halfway" membership in their grandparents' congregations. But only the old settlers benefited from this innovation; new settlers who arrived from other towns or England never took up membership in the congregations.

Boston indeed became a "city on a hill," but not a city John Winthrop would have liked. By 1649, when Winthrop died only twenty years after the Puritans settled there, Boston was more modern than Puritan. More than half the town's adults ignored its churches and did not ask to belong to them. In Plymouth, to the south, children of the original settlers so often went away to pursue new lands and opportunities that the town minister, William Bradford, described Plymouth as "an ancient mother grown old and forsaken of her children." The town unity that Winthrop and Bradford so valued had fallen victim to individual economic enterprise.

Other towns took more relaxed views on the question of church membership and politics. Some allowed the unchurched and the landless to vote despite the colony's laws on the subject. Some of the other towns had as many unchurched residents as Boston. Still more never "owned" a town covenant or, if they did, plunged into bitter quarrels in which economics competed with religion. When the Rev. Edmund Brown led one faction against another in land allocation disputes in Sudbury, Massachusetts, the town officers finally warned him in the 1640s not to "meddle." They called his lobbying a "dishonor to God ... a prejudice to his ministry" and "a hindrance to the conversion and building up of souls." Indeed, one resident simply told Brown that "setting aside your office, I regard you no more than another man." In short, Brown might be a clergyman, but many parishioners thought he had too much interest in land.

By the 1690s churches still were important in New England, and church members still dominated local and provincial politics. But society had changed. Many second- and third-generation New Englanders had lost their religious fervor. The new immigrants, from England, Scotland, and even France, did not join the older Puritan congregations. By 1690 many

New England settlers did not belong to a Puritan congregation. Church membership that had been as high as 70 to 80 percent in the 1630s and 1640s plummeted to half those rates by the 1670s. In Salem, Massachusetts, only about 30 percent of the taxpayers belonged to the town's Puritan congregations in 1690, and in four Connecticut towns—New Haven, New London, Stonington, and Woodbury—only about 15 percent of the towns' men belonged to its churches by the 1680s.

New England also became more spiritually diverse. When the president of Harvard College, Henry Dunster, became a Baptist in 1654, leaders of the college forced him to resign. By 1670 Baptist, Presbyterian, and Quaker congregations all could be found in New England, often in competition with the old Puritan Congregational churches. French Protestant, or Huguenot, refugees settled in Rhode Island and Boston in the 1680s and shocked some Puritans, because these newcomers celebrated Christmas, which the Puritans did not. The Huguenots' arrival heralded more immigration by non-English settlers, such as the Scots, Scots-Irish, and Welsh. And by 1695, even the hated old Church of England had established a congregation in Boston, although the town authorities had used every possible legal means to stop its formation.

[handwritten margin note: immigration of various religious groups]

News about the practice of magic also circulated in New England. An East Haven, Connecticut, a man claimed he could "raise the Devil" and drew horoscopes for his neighbors. A wealthy Massachusetts woman claimed she had learned fortune-telling by reading William Lilly's astrological textbook *Christian Astrology*, published in London in 1643. By 1689, Cotton Mather acknowledged that disturbing numbers of New Englanders were employing magical practices to cure diseases, even though they knew, or should have known, that in doing so they were invoking the aid of the Devil.

[handwritten margin note: magic worries began here]

Little wonder, then, that New England's authorities were increasingly prosecuting witches in the late seventeenth century. These trials culminated in the infamous Salem witch trials of 1692, in which 20 people were executed, another 150 arrested, and many more privately accused and gossiped about. Whereas witch trials were uncommon in England after 1645, in New England the number of witch trials rose dramatically between 1660 and 1690, prompted in part by a need for scapegoats to explain the decline of "traditional" Puritan values, the rise of religious diversity, and people's resorting to magic. Surely the Devil had brought these upon New England.

The Salem witch trials of 1692 capped the rise of witch trials in New England after 1660 but then brought the trials and some Puritan supporters into disrepute when public reaction turned against the execution of alleged witches. The episode in question began when local girls accused an Indian slave, Tituba, of casting spells. This accusation, pursued by the local minister, Rev. Samuel Parris, escalated after Tituba named several local women as witches. Then the afflicted girls identified more women and several men as witches based on "spectral evidence"—evidence that came from the "specters" or ghostly apparitions of accused witches that appeared in dreams of the afflicted.

Some of the girls' behavior was merely innocuous, if odd. Twelve-year-old Ann Putnam, for example, called out to Reverend Parris in the church, "There is a yellow bird sitting on the minister's hat, as it hangs on the pin in the pulpit." But other accusations were vicious, involving curses and suggestions of sexual impropriety and desire. According to Reverend Parris and other New England ministers, such as Boston's Cotton Mather, the accused witches made bargains with the devil, luring the young girls with promises of punishing their enemies or finding them wealthy husbands. The witches seemed to exemplify the threat to New England's Christianity, its society, and its values.

In fact, personal tensions and social cleavages played important roles in the accusations. Reverend Parris was a weak, ineffective minister who used the witchcraft accusations to assert his own power and explain his failings. Some of the accused men owned large tracts of land desired by competing families, and some of the accused women had long been disliked in the community. Despite adamant denials by the women and men indicted at Salem, by September the courts had hanged fourteen women and five men for witchcraft and pressed one man to death with stones because he challenged the court's authority and refused to plead guilty or innocent to witchcraft charges.

The excesses of the trials proved their own undoing, however, and probably saved lives later, if not in 1692. Initially, the convictions and hangings brought only more accusations. By October 1692, more than 150 people stood accused of witchcraft. But now the accusations reached people who seemed unlikely to be witches yet who had been seen as witch "specters" in dreams. Longstanding criticism of spectral evidence that had been pushed aside in the first trials suddenly seemed more relevant. Boston's Rev. Increase Mather, whose son Cotton Mather had earlier backed the witch trials, disavowed spectral evidence and called for an end to the trials. Governor William Phipps disbanded the special court he had established to conduct the trials, and no further witch trials and executions for witchcraft occurred in New England.

Over the next fifteen years, Puritan leaders grappled with their failures at Salem. By 1696, the Boston judge Samuel Sewall, who had sat on the Salem court, publicly confessed his errors. In 1700, a Boston merchant named Robert Calef denounced

61

Cotton Mather and the New England clergy in his book *More Wonders of the Invisible World*. In it he accused them not only of vanity but of stupidity. After all, he argued, if the devil was so clever, couldn't he inflame wrongful accusations as well as entice women and men into witchcraft? In 1714, the Massachusetts assembly reversed the convictions of those accused and executed at Salem and called upon the colony to repent for its delusions.

If the Puritans never succeeded in creating a peaceful established religion in New England, they did produce an important preaching style that resonated through America well into the nineteenth century, the so-called jeremiad sermon. Broadly speaking, the theme of the jeremiad, which was styled after the laments and prophecies of doom in the Old Testament's "Lamentations of Jeremiah," was the decline of spiritual fervor among the citizenry, the community's flirtation with disaster, and its dramatic recovery. Although no golden age of Puritanism ever existed in New England, as Anne Hutchinson's troubles in the 1630s demonstrate, ministers used this kind of sermon to promote church membership, though with limited success.

Long after the Puritans had disappeared, however, the jeremiad style provided an important rhetorical form invoked in times of crisis to decry the country's sins and call down judgment upon them. By claiming in his second inaugural address in March 1865 that slavery was "one of those offenses" that God "now wills to remove" and quoting Psalm 19 that "the judgments of the Lord are true and righteous altogether," President Abraham Lincoln invoked the jeremiad style of sermonizing to shame Americans into greater resolve and purpose in pursuing the Civil War.

Religion fared quite differently in the Chesapeake region. For a time in the 1620s and early 1630s, Virginia's ministers and congregations tried to maintain vigorous worship and moral discipline in the colony. The Virginia House of Burgesses established many parishes, some of which constructed church buildings. The ministers published public notices of marriages ("banns"), and church wardens cited settlers for not observing the Sabbath, such as "Thomas Farley, Gentleman," who missed worship for three months. They shamed women convicted of sexual misdeeds by ordering them to dress in white gowns, hold white wands, and stand on chairs or stools during public worship. In some congregations, worshipers publicly confessed their sins and sought forgiveness much as they did in New England.

other areas – different successes

Indeed, Puritan-style congregations emerged in the area south of Jamestown, in Nansemond and Lower Norfolk counties, in the 1640s. In 1641, more than seventy men and women signed a letter to the New Haven Puritan minister John Davenport pleading for Puritan clergymen to move to Virginia to serve their congregations. Three New England ministers did in fact arrive to serve the Virginia congregations, but they were gone by 1650. Governor William Berkeley saw them as a threat to the established Church of England and not only forced them to leave Virginia but made many of their supporters move across the Chesapeake Bay to Maryland.

Church of England

Yet the greatest threat to Virginia's Church of England in particular and Christian worship in general was organizational shortcoming, not Puritan competition. The Church of England failed to sustain working parishes and congregations despite its establishment as the colony's official church. Most Virginia counties never added congregations as their populations expanded, and as early as the 1650s many Virginians did not live within easy reach of a congregation with regular services. The congregations that did exist often did not keep their church buildings in repair, and many churches lacked ministers. Worshipers sometimes met in homes and barns, but this worship was not always sustained. A 1656 description of Virginia depicted the colony's Anglican ministers as drunkards who "battle in a pulpit, roar in a tavern,...[and] by their dissoluteness destroy rather than feed their flocks." Perhaps it was just as well, then, when a 1661 pamphlet claimed that only ten of Virginia's fifty parishes actually had resident clergymen.

A few of the clergy struggled on against the rising tide of parish vacancies and ministerial sloth. In Accomack County, on Virginia's eastern shore, Thomas Teackle served several parishes, apparently well, for more than forty years between his arrival before 1652 and his death in 1695, making him the longest-serving minister in seventeenth-century Virginia. He argued about his salary with several parish vestries, the board of laymen who managed parish affairs, and when he died he was one of the wealthiest clergymen in colonial America, worth 337 pounds sterling, not counting his land and slaves (he owned eleven at his death). Teackle preached regularly, not only Sabbath after Sabbath but for funerals as well: in 1679, one settler asked not only that his friends refrain from drunkenness at his funeral but that "Mr. Teackle if possible preach my funeral sermon."

Little wonder. Teackle could draw upon an enormous library when writing his sermons, the largest known in seventeenth-century Virginia and far larger than most Puritan libraries—more than 300 books on biblical commentary, Puritanism, Anglicanism, medicine, and humor, as well as many occult titles that mixed highly learned or speculative magic with Christianity. But Thomas Teackle ministered to only one small part of Virginia, and no one else duplicated his life and achievement in the colony before 1690.

The situation in Maryland was little better, despite the colony's seemingly promising start as a haven for persecuted

English Catholics. Owned by George Calvert, Lord Baltimore, England's most prestigious Catholic nobleman, Maryland attracted practicing Catholics who saw in America a chance to remain English yet practice a faith forbidden at home. Priests accompanied these settlers; by the early 1640s, Catholicism offered the principal form of public Christian worship available in the colony, with four Catholic church buildings erected there by 1650.

But English anti-Catholicism quickly destroyed public Catholic worship in the colony. Political disturbances and revolts in 1645, 1654, 1676, and 1689 arose as major outbreaks of anti-Catholic violence by non-Catholic settlers contesting Lord Baltimore's power in the colony. They attacked Catholic church buildings and forced priests to return to England. In one episode, anti-Catholic rioters threw prayer books out of a barn while yelling, "Burn them Papists' Devils," equating the pope with the Devil. From the 1650s until the eve of the American Revolution, Maryland's Catholics usually worshipped privately in homes rather than publicly in church buildings, and only a few Catholic priests conducted worship in the colony between 1660 and the 1740s.

Little Protestant worship supplanted the disappearing Catholic services until the 1690s. A quarter century before the settlement of Quaker Pennsylvania, a female Quaker preacher, Elizabeth Harris, preached in Maryland in 1655, and slowly several Quaker meetings were formed there. But as late as 1690, the Quakers probably counted fewer than 500 adherents in the colony. Some Virginia Puritans exiled to Maryland by Governor Berkeley in 1650 established a Presbyterian congregation in the colony, but it seems to have disappeared quickly. By the 1670s, then, Maryland probably knew only one or two Catholic priests and, at best, one or two Protestant clergymen in the colony. It is no wonder that in the 1680s a Church of England minister, John Yeo, wrote that Maryland was a place where "the Lord's day is profaned, religion despised, and all notorious vices committed…it is become a Sodom of uncleanness and a pest house of iniquity."

By the 1680s, the Virginia and Maryland colonies had become remarkably indifferent in matters of religion. Settlers there seldom participated in public Christian worship and many children grew to adulthood without Christian baptism. Some 85 percent of the children born in Charles Parish, Virginia, between 1649 and 1680 never received baptism in the Church of England, and since no dissenting Protestants were active in the parish, it is doubtful that they were baptized anywhere else. In Maryland's Kent County, only five baptisms occurred among 115 white children born between 1657 and 1670. A French Jesuit reported that English settlers in Maryland had gone so long without receiving the rite of baptism that they had stopped complaining about it.

Funerals in Maryland bore an especially secular character between 1640 and 1690. Owing to the lack of ministers, priests, and church buildings, raucous banquets became the dominant public ceremony surrounding death. Meats, fowl, breads, cakes, cider, and as many casks of brandy, rum, and beer as the deceased's estate could afford were spread among surviving friends in drunken parties that lasted two or three days. In 1662, the Charles County court complained that it was not "Christian like" when neighbors turned "their bousing [drinking] Cups to the quantity of three barrels of beer" worth "nine hundred pounds of tobacco." The neighbors should instead have showed "a mournfulness for the loss of their friend," the court observed. But few heeded the plea.

Magic came to the Chesapeake as it had to New England. In 1626, the Virginia courts investigated magical acts performed by Goodwife Wright. She allegedly used magic to help neighbors turn curses back upon those who had pronounced them, predicted the deaths of neighbors, made a woman and her newborn infant sick, caused a hunter to miss when shooting deer, and made a servant girl "dance stark naked." One woman with a mean husband was consoled by Wright's advice to "be content, for thou shall shortly bury him." (In fact, the man died soon afterward.)

Other Virginians nailed horseshoes over their doors to protect themselves from alleged witches. Some claimed that witches ruined their tobacco; one man described to a Virginia court how a witch "had rid him along the Seaside and home to his own house." Even the clergyman Thomas Teackle owned books about the occult arts. These works described magic, alchemy (in which magic was used to try to transform base metals like lead into gold), and astrology, sometimes to cure diseases. One of the books in Teackle's library, Marin Cureau de la Chambre's *The Art How to Know Men*, published in London in 1675, employed astrology, chiromancy (palm reading), and metoposcopy (forehead reading) to analyze human passions.

By the 1690s, the religious future of British America worried many observers. Puritan writers like Boston's Cotton Mather— although they tended to exaggerate the achievements of the earliest Puritan settlers—believed that their own generation was not living up to the models set by their parents and grandparents. Settlers in Maryland and Virginia found themselves bereft of spiritual guidance and leadership and seldom could carry on worship on their own. The next century, however, would see the rise of new patterns of religious activity, including new

[handwritten margin note: fear of magic in these colonies too]

religious groups and beliefs. Not only would religious life be transformed in New England and the Chesapeake region—a new religious order would be created everywhere in British America, extending as far as the many new settlements that strengthened the European presence throughout the land.

A PURITAN LEADER SPEAKS TO EARLY AMERICAN EMIGRANTS

Before landing in Massachusetts in the spring of 1630, the English Puritan layman John Winthrop spoke to the assembled passengers on the ship Arbella, *explaining his view of what America could become. His thoughts, written in the essay "A Model of Christian Charity," did not always guide the Massachusetts Bay Colony, even though he served as its governor for most of the years between his arrival in 1630 and his death in 1649. The settlers disagreed about religion, land, and politics in ways that distressed Winthrop. But his idealism remained a powerful beacon long after his death. His words have been invoked by Americans, including many presidents, again and again because they seem to capture the elusive meaning of community, even if later readers and listeners followed Winthrop's injunctions no better than the Puritans.*

Now the only way to avoid [a] shipwreck and to provide for our posterity is to follow the counsel of [the prophet] Micah, to doe justly, to love mercy, to walk humbly with our God. For this end, we must be knit together in this work as one man, we must entertain each other in brotherly affection. [W]e must delight in each other, make others' conditions our own, rejoice together, mourn together, labor, and suffer together, always having before our eyes our commission and community in the work, our community as members of the same body.... We shall find that the God of Israel is among us, when ten of us shall be able to resist a thousand of our enemies, when he shall make us a praise and glory. [Then] men shall say of succeeding plantations: the Lord make it like that of New England.

For we must consider that we shall be as a city upon a hill. The eyes of all people are upon us, so that if we shall deal falsely with our God in this work we have undertaken and so cause him to withdraw his present help from us, we shall be made a story and a by-word through the world....If our hearts shall turn away so that we will not obey...we shall surely perish out of the good land [even if] we pass over this vast sea to possess it. Therefore let us choose life, that we, and our seed, may live, by obeying his voice, and cleaving to him, for he is our life, and our prosperity.

CHAPTER FOUR

The Flowering of Religious Diversity

Thomas Dongan was perplexed. In 1683, he had become governor of New York, the old Dutch colony that the British had conquered in 1664. Dongan was a Roman Catholic who keenly felt the desirability of religious tolerance. But he had never encountered such religious diversity as he had found in New York. When he arrived from England in 1683, he expected to find one or two ministers of the Dutch Reformed Church, the Protestant state church of the Netherlands, and a Church of England minister preaching to the small but growing English population in New York.

Instead, Dongan encountered a religious blend so rich and confusing that he hardly knew what to make of it. The Dutch Reformed Church was indeed the town's largest congregation; Dongan observed that there were "not many of the Church of England, [and] few Roman Catholics." But New York teemed with other groups. It harbored an "abundance of Quaker preachers and women [preachers] especially." It contained "singing Quakers" and "ranting Quakers" who did not always see eye to eye. "Sabbatarian" and "Antisabbatarian" Baptists disagreed about which day was the true Sabbath; some worshiped on Saturday, others on Sunday. New Englanders who had already migrated to New York divided themselves between the traditional Puritans and the Baptists. Jews from Curaçao in the Dutch West Indies gave the town a distinctive non-Christian element. Yet most New Yorkers did not belong to a religious congregation at all, despite the wide variety of available choices. They were like the religiously indifferent in Europe, though they seemed more visible in New York. In short, Dongan wrote, "of all sorts of opinion there are some, and the most part [are] of none at all."

New York prefigured the religious future of eighteenth-century America. In colonial America many religions, not just one or two, quickly came to typify the immigrants' spiritual life, and much of this diversity emerged between 1690 and 1770. Congregational statistics measured the growth of religious diversity in the colonies. Before 1690, 90 percent of all congregations in colonial America were either Congregationalist (as in Puritan New England) or Anglican (as in Virginia). But by 1770 this was no longer true. Congregationalism and the Church of England indeed remained strong on the eve of the American Revolution. About 20 percent of all colonial congregations were Congregationalist and about 15 percent adhered to the Church of England. But by 1770 Scottish and Scots-Irish Presbyterians made up 18 percent of all colonial congregations, English and Welsh Baptists about 15 percent, and Quakers, German Lutherans, and German Reformed each claimed 5 to 10 percent of the colonial congregations. Non-English congregations by then accounted for at least 25 percent of all colonial congregations, although they had been rare before 1690, and by 1770 no single religious body could claim more than 20 percent of all the colonial congregations.

The "middle colonies" of New York, New Jersey, Pennsylvania, and Delaware proved especially diverse and, ultimately, good prophets of America's religious future. By the Revolution, the middle colony congregations were divided among the Presbyterians, German Lutherans, German Reformed, Quakers, Dutch Reformed, Anglicans, Mennonites, Moravians, Catholics, German Baptists, and the newest and smallest of all the groups, English Methodists. At most, Presbyterians claimed 20 percent of the middle colony congregations, with the many additional denominations dividing the remaining 80 percent. By the time of the American Revolution, then, religious diversity had become one of the region's most distinctive features and, in fact, a major component of colonial life everywhere.

Three causes stimulated European religious pluralism in the American colonies after 1690: the immigration of Europeans from many different religious groups, the expansion of religious groups already present earlier but in only small numbers, and a surprising persistence of beliefs in magic and occultism long after the infamous Salem witch trials of 1692. These three causes together produced a religious diversity unmatched in any Old World society.

Protestants from France, or Huguenots, became the first significant non-English Protestants to arrive in the colonies at the end of the seventeenth century. They fled France in the 1680s when the French king, Louis XIV, revoked the Edict of Nantes, proclaimed in 1598, that had given the Huguenots limited freedom to worship. More than 100,000 Huguenots left France, and between 2,000 and 2,500 finally reached the British colonies in America between 1680 and 1700. Most Huguenots came to America because they could not return to France and because their life in Europe's Huguenot refugee centers was frequently miserable. In London, for example, Huguenots had little work, few possessions, and poor prospects.

In America, the Huguenots settled primarily in Boston, New York, and South Carolina. But after forming new congregations they quickly assimilated or mixed with English and other European settlers. They usually took up occupations similar to those of the settlers around them. In Boston, New York City, and Charleston the Huguenots became merchants and artisans. In rural New York and low-country South Carolina, they became farmers and planters. In their rural settlements they quickly embraced slaveholding, whether in northern farming villages like New Rochelle, New York, or in rural South Carolina. Even though they had fled France to preserve their own freedom, they could not resist the economic opportunities offered by the cheap labor of enslaved Africans.

The Huguenots also assimilated into their surrounding culture in matters of family life and religion. They married non-Huguenots quickly. As early as 1710, only twenty years after they had arrived, more than half of all Huguenots took non-Huguenot wives and husbands. They joined other religious congregations, becoming Congregationalists in Boston and Anglicans, Dutch Reformed, Presbyterians, and Quakers in New York, and Anglicans and sometimes Baptists in South Carolina. By 1750 only two small Huguenot congregations still existed in the colonies, in New York City and Charleston, and both closed at the time of the American Revolution.

The German-speaking immigrants, who accounted for the largest number of settlers arriving from continental Europe, came out of at least six different religious traditions: Lutherans, German Reformed, Mennonites, Moravians, German Baptists, and Catholics. These Germans settled principally in Pennsylvania, but substantial numbers of other German immigrants also

74

resided in New York, Maryland, western Virginia, and North Carolina. In all, as many as 75,000 Germans probably immigrated to the British colonies between 1700 and 1776.

The German Lutherans and German Reformed immigrants claimed the largest proportion of the German immigrants to America. The Lutheran Church was the largest German immigrant church, especially in Pennsylvania. Lutheranism was the principal state-supported Protestant church in many of the German states and had a larger following than any other Protestant denomination in German-speaking Europe. This meant that in most northern German parishes children would be baptized as Lutherans as a matter of course, even if their parents were not especially loyal church members.

Several Lutheran congregations were formed among the German immigrants in New York and Pennsylvania in the 1690s. These added to the two or three Swedish Lutheran congregations in Delaware that remained there from the short-lived colony of New Sweden. (Settled in 1638, New Sweden had been captured by the Dutch in 1655.) More German Lutheran congregations were organized in the 1710s and 1720s as German immigration increased. But little leadership was present until minister Henry Melchior Muhlenberg arrived in Philadelphia in 1742. Guided by the motto "Ecclesia plantanda" ("Let the church be planted"), Muhlenberg traveled about Pennsylvania for three decades, organizing congregations, chastising religiously indifferent immigrants, and disciplining wayward clergymen in an effort to overcome low attendance and loose manners among immigrants, most of whom had come to America for secular rather than religious reasons.

The German Reformed Church constituted the second-largest church of German-speaking immigrants in America. German Reformed immigrants were Calvinists who, like the

75

English Puritans, believed in predestination—that God had pre-ordained some men and women to go to heaven and others to hell and that individuals could not earn their own salvation. Yet the German Reformed Church never formed the strict, demanding congregations that emerged in New England. At the same time, the social conditions of many German Reformed immigrants inhibited their religious participation. Most German Reformed immigrants arrived from the Palatinate, an area along the Rhine River where the Reformed tradition was strong. But they came as "redemptioners," indentured servants who had contracted to work for a Pennsylvania merchant or farmer to "redeem" the cost of their ship passage, usually over a term of four years. Their labor for strangers, who were often English, and the absence of strong family and kinship ties among many such immigrants hindered their religious activity in the New World.

Several German "sectarian" groups also arrived in the colonies after 1690. The sects kept to themselves, restricted marriage to other members of the sect, and avoided close contact with nonmembers, whether German or English. They stressed a contemplative life, emphasized personal piety and spiritual reflection, rejected political involvement, and were pacifists who refused to fight in wars. Mennonites were present in the earliest German immigration to Pennsylvania in the 1680s. Followers of a sixteenth-century religious leader, Menno Simons, they settled first in Germantown, just outside Philadelphia, but after 1710, they established themselves largely in Lancaster Country in central Pennsylvania, later called Pennsylvania Dutch country, a corruption of the word *Deutsche* or German. There, between 1720 and 1740, they were joined by followers of a Mennonite dissident from Switzerland, Jacob Amman, who demanded greater discipline and shunned those who rejected it, calling themselves the Amish in honor of their founder.

76

German "Dunkers," or members of the Church of the Brethren, originated as a dissident group within the German Reformed Church. They were called Dunkers in derision because they believed in baptism by full immersion in water, often in a river. The printer Christopher Sauer was the best-known Dunker in Pennsylvania. Sauer printed the first German-language newspaper in Pennsylvania in 1739 and produced an edition of Martin Luther's Bible in 1743, the first Bible printed in the American colonies. Another offshoot of the German Baptists established an ascetic perfectionist community at Ephrata in Lancaster County in the 1740s. This community separated men and women, observed Saturday as the Sabbath, and enjoyed considerable prosperity and success until internal disputes weakened it in the 1770s.

A German-speaking group usually called Moravians, because they originated in Moravia, the central region of the modern Czech Republic, also emigrated to the British colonies in the eighteenth century. Formally known as the Unitas Fratrum, or Renewed Church, of the United Brethren, they were led by the aristocratic Count Nicholas Zinzendorf, who arrived in Pennsylvania in 1741. In Pennsylvania the Moravians established the communities of Bethlehem and Nazareth, and in the 1760s they established a similar community in Salem, North Carolina. Zinzendorf was an idealist who hoped to unite all Protestants into a single denomination, but his campaign failed among both the German and English Protestants. From the 1750s forward, Moravians lived quietly in their semicommunal settlements, where they farmed land jointly and sponsored extensive missionary activity among American Indians.

Jews permanently entered the American colonies in the 1680s and 1690s. The first Jews in the American colonies, who arrived in New Amsterdam in 1654, came from Brazil.

They were refugees who had fled that country after the Portuguese had captured the Dutch colony there. However, most of these immigrants left New Amsterdam within a few years. More permanent Jewish settlers arrived in the 1680s, and by 1695, they formed the first permanent synagogue in New York City, later called Shearith Israel (Remnant of Israel).

By the 1720s, New York City (as New Amsterdam was now called) contained at least twenty Jewish families, who constituted about 2 percent of the town's population. In 1730, services at Shearith Israel moved from a rented building to the first permanent Jewish synagogue building in the colonies. Jews subsequently settled in Philadelphia, Charleston, Savannah, and Newport, Rhode Island, where the famous Touro Synagogue building, dedicated in 1763, has become the oldest surviving synagogue in the United States.

The colonial Jewish communities were small, located entirely in urban areas, and sometimes proved fragile. Most early Jewish immigrants were "Sephardic" Jews, who spoke Spanish or Portuguese and observed the traditions of worship of Spanish and Portuguese Judaism. Others were "Ashkenazic" Jews, German- or Yiddish-speaking Jews who observed the somewhat different rituals of northern and eastern Europe. Their small numbers made colonial Jews especially vulnerable to anti-Semitism, which came in various forms, from legal prohibitions against voting to public derision and occasional violence. Yet this kind of anti-Semitism was mild by comparison to that in Europe. European legal restrictions on Jews were far more severe and Jews were openly persecuted, not only in Spain and Portugal (from which they were expelled in 1492) but throughout Britain, France, and Germany.

Sometimes, however, it was difficult to preserve one's Jewish identity in the colonies. Abigail Franks was devastated when her daughter, Phila, secretly married Oliver DeLancey, son of a wealthy Huguenot merchant named Stephen DeLancey, in New York City in 1743. (The DeLanceys had already left the Huguenot Church and joined the Church of England.) She wrote her oldest son, then in London, "My spirits was for some time so depressed that it was a pain to me to speak or see anyone....My house has been my prison ever since. I had not heart enough to go near the street door." In fact, between 80 and 90 percent of colonial Jews married other Jews. But the Franks family intermarried with non-Jewish colonists so frequently that by the 1790s it had disappeared as a Jewish family in America.

The Methodists were the last new English religious group to arrive in the colonies. John and Charles Wesley began the Methodist reform movement in the Church of England in the 1740s. The movement drew its name from the Wesleys' emphasis on a "method" of regular prayer, devotional reading, and contemplation that drew participants closer to God and led to a personal experience of religious conversion. The Wesleys were Arminians, followers of the sixteenth-century Dutch theologian Jacob Arminius. They stressed the completeness of Christ's sacrifice for all men and women, rejecting Calvin's views about human depravity and his concept of predestination. Methodists believed that a combination of God's grace and human endeavor could pull believing Christians toward God. The Wesleys were influenced by Moravian missionaries working in England, and in 1738, John Wesley sought spiritual guidance from the Moravian leader Count Nicholas Zinzendorf in Germany.

The Wesleys first sent missionaries to the American colonies in 1769, even as the colonists' political contests with Parliament were still simmering. The early missionaries, led by Francis Asbury, worked in Maryland and Delaware as well as in New York City. The Methodists formed small "classes," usually involving a dozen or so believers, who used their meetings to deepen their spiritual life and commitment. Despite early success in attracting followers, especially poorer farmers in the countryside and laborers in cities like Annapolis, Philadelphia, and New York, the movement halted abruptly with the issuing of the Declaration of Independence in 1776. The Wesleys still worked within the Church of England, were politically conservative and deeply sensitive to charges of radicalism in their movement, and vigorously backed the Crown in its struggle with the colonies. In 1776, Wesley recalled all the Methodist missionaries in the colonies, and all of them except Francis Asbury returned to England. By the start of the Revolution, then, the first Methodist success in America seemed wasted.

The period from 1690 to 1770 also witnessed the dramatic growth of English, Scottish, and Welsh religious groups that had been present earlier in the colonies only in small numbers. The Quakers were among the most prominent and distinctive of these groups. The Society of Friends originated in England in the 1650s. They were derisively called Quakers because, as they said themselves, they "trembled at the Word of the Lord" and sometimes shook or "danced" during their religious services. Quaker services contained no hymns, formal sermons, or traditional liturgy and processions. Instead, individual Quakers described God's dealing with their souls and their struggles with moral and religious problems.

Led by George Fox, the Quakers believed that Christian revelation did not stop with the writing of the Bible and could be obtained in modern times. They believed that each individual possessed an "inward light" that, properly cultivated, might lead to religious truth. Attacked by both the government and other religious groups, the Quakers also became pacifists and refused to resist these assaults physically or fight in wars.

France's Catholics actively pursued the conversion of Indians in America, including the Hurons of Canada, whose modes of dress and housing were illustrated in this book supporting the missionary effort.

Seventeenth-century men and women often ridiculed effete and fussy clergymen. This cartoon compared clergymen in politics to monkeys in toy shops: Both "may do much Mischief, but cannot possibly do any Good."

Leaders of the Spanish Inquisition of the late sixteenth century prosecuted heretics and alleged witches and forced Jews to convert to Catholicism or burn at the stake, although Jews had previously lived in Spain with considerable but not perfect freedom.

THE PURITAN.

"To Banbury came I, O profane one!
Where I saw a Puritane... one
Hanging of his cat on Monday
For killing of a Mouse on Sunday."

The Puritans' emphasis on morals often brought them considerable criticism. One anti-Puritan verse criticized a Puritan for hanging his cat on Monday because it killed a "mouse on Sunday."

A late-eighteenth-century German Lutheran minister in Pennsylvania baptizes a baby surrounded by its parents and sponsors. Religious rituals such as baptism helped cement a sense of community among the participants.

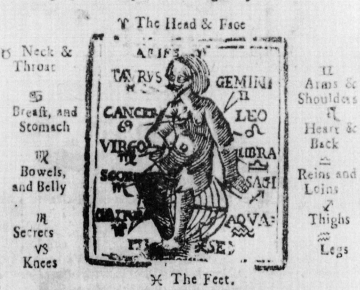

1 7 2 9.

The Anatomy of Man's Body, and what part thereof is Reprefented by the 12 Signs of the Zodiack.

♈ The Head & Face

♉ Neck & Throat

♊ Breaft, and Stomach

♍ Bowels, and Belly

♏ Secrets

♑ Knees

ARIES ♈
TAURUS ♉
GEMINI ♊
CANCER ♋
LEO ♌
VIRGO ♍
LIBRA ♎
SCORPIO ♏
SAGI ♐
CAPRI ♑
AQUA ♒
PISCES ♓

♊ Arms & Shoulders

♌ Heart & Back

♎ Reins and Loins

♐ Thighs

♒ Legs

♓ The Feet.

The Blackmoor may as eas'ly change his Skin,
As Men forfake the ways they'r brought up in ;
Therefore I've fet the Old Anatomy,
Hoping to pleafe my Country men thereby,
But where's the Man that's born & lives among,
——— Can pleafe a Fickle throng ?

The Vulgar Notes of this Year, 1.7 2 9.
Golden Number ——— 1 ? 5 Epact ——— 1
Cycle of the Sun ———2 5 ? Dominical Letter——— C

☞ *Note,* The Planet ♀ *Venus* is Occidental or Evening
Star to the Third day of *June,* and from thence
Oriental or Morning Star to the Years End.

Astrological beliefs persisted throughout the eighteenth-century British colonies. Nathaniel Ames's 1729 Almanac included the "anatomy" that showed the different parts of the body controlled by various signs of the zodiac.

The Ten Commandments adorn the wall of this reconstruction of the interior of Touro Synagogue in Newport, Rhode Island, built in 1763. In the New World, colonial craftsmen, following eighteenth-century British design, could create elegant places of worship.

John Eliot published his Massachusett translation of the New Testament in 1663. More of the books probably were given to Eliot's English supporters than to Indians.

MAMUSSE
WUNNEETUPANATAMWE
UP-BIBLUM GOD
NANEESWE
NUKKONE TESTAMENT
KAH WONK
WUSKU TESTAMENT.

Ne quoshkinnumuk nashpe Wuttinneumoh *CHRIST*
noh asoowesit

JOHN ELIOT·

CAMBRIDGE:

Printeuoop nashpe *Samuel Green* kah *Marmaduke Johnson,*

1 6 6 3.

Black and white Moravians worship together in Johann Valentin Haidt's 1747 painting Erstlingsbild (The First Fruits). *The unique success of Moravian proselytizing among West Indian slaves contrasted sharply with English Protestant failures in converting mainland colonial Africans.*

Philadelphia's Christ Church, constructed in 1744 by the Church of England, typified the ornate church buildings erected by many Protestant denominations in colonial cities before the American Revolution.

Around 1775, when she was sixteen, Prudence Punderson made this needlepoint, depicting a young colonial woman's view of life from birth (on the right) to death (on the left). In fact, Punderson died only a decade later, at age twenty-six.

Paul Revere's commitment to the colonists' cause led him to engrave this satirical cartoon lampooning the Crown's support for Catholicism in French Canada in the Quebec Act of 1774. The Devil is overlooking the proceedings.

The settlement of Pennsylvania, acquired by the wealthy Quaker William Penn in 1681, transformed the Quaker presence in America. In fact, Quakers had begun seeking converts in the American colonies as early as the late 1650s. Successful Quaker preaching in Massachusetts, Rhode Island, and Maryland attracted small numbers of followers there and encouraged George Fox to visit Maryland, Virginia, and North Carolina in 1672 and 1673 and establish more meetings. These trips were difficult. In Maryland, Fox was "dirtied with getting through bogs," as he wrote in his journal. But his efforts always brought rewards—he won over, for example, "several magistrates with their wives, many Protestants of divers sorts, and some Papists [Catholics] and persons of chief account in the country."

Penn's acquisition of Pennsylvania, stimulated by earlier Quaker migration to New Jersey, turned Quakerism into a powerful religious force in the middle colonies. By 1685, only a few years after Pennsylvania began to be settled, so many thousands of Quakers had fled England to settle in Penn's new American territory that some Quaker authorities in England criticized his venture. Quaker churchmen in Wales complained in 1698 that "runnings to Pennsylvania" were stripping their meetings of members, and Quaker preachers became discouraged and found "cause to complain" about Penn's all-too-successful American colony.

In Pennsylvania and parts of New Jersey, Quakers dominated both government and society, in sharp contrast to their status in England as a persecuted minority. Although Pennsylvania became famous as a haven for many different religious and ethnic groups, the Quakers probably remained the colony's largest religious group into the 1720s. For decades they were Pennsylvania's most powerful and important merchants and farmers. They controlled the colony's politics until the mid-1750s, even though they were pacifists who opposed fighting, and this became a difficult principle to uphold when western settlers wanted protection from Indian attacks. The Quakers invented the first modern political party in the American colonies and through the famous "Quaker party" ran candidates for public office, including the Pennsylvania Assembly.

By the 1750s, however, the Quakers had become a minority in Pennsylvania, outnumbered by recent German, Scottish, and Scots-Irish immigrants. They also lost much of their own discipline as Quakers married non-Quakers; others traded in slaves and even in guns and munitions. Quaker politicians found it difficult to resist demands to meet Indian attacks on the Pennsylvania frontier with force. Reformers within the Quaker movement challenged Friends, including Quaker politicians, to return to older values. The reformers forced many, but not all, Quakers to withdraw from elective politics. They also increased the discipline in Quaker meetings and disowned Quakers with non-Quaker spouses or those who traded in slaves and guns. After 1750 the Quakers still remained important in Pennsylvania and New Jersey, but they no longer dominated these two colonies as they had for the previous half century.

English and Welsh Baptists and Scottish and Scots-Irish Presbyterians also energetically increased their presence in the British colonies after 1690. Baptists from Wales and England emigrated to Pennsylvania and New Jersey in substantial enough numbers between 1680 and 1740 that soon they greatly outnumbered the few Baptist congregations that had emerged in New England between 1640 and 1690.

Ethnic identity defined membership in most of the Pennsylvania and New Jersey Baptist congregations. Most were Calvinists who accepted the doctrine of predestination but also reserved the rite of baptism for adults, like Baptists elsewhere.

The Baptist congregation in Philadelphia contained mostly English settlers; in contrast, many rural Baptist congregations were Welsh. By 1710, more than twenty Baptist congregations existed in Pennsylvania and New Jersey, and by 1740, there were more than 60 Baptist congregations throughout the colonies from New England to Virginia and North and South Carolina.

Church government, rather than theology, separated Presbyterians from Baptists and Congregationalists. All three were Calvinist in theology, but the Presbyterians, unlike the Baptists, baptized children. Equally important, the Presbyterians stressed a hierarchical church government that the New England Congregationalists rejected. Their "presbyteries" and "synods," controlled by clergymen, exercised authority over individual congregations. Presbyteries governed congregations in several regions, and a synod supervised the presbyteries.

Presbyterians quickly outnumbered Baptists throughout the British settlements on the North American continent. Before 1690, no more than a handful of Presbyterian congregations existed in the colonies. But by 1710, almost thirty Presbyterian congregations had been formed, and by 1740 the number had reached more than 130. English settlers made up some of these congregations, especially in the cities of Boston, New York, and Charleston. In New Jersey several old Congregationalist churches founded by emigrants from New England affiliated with the Presbyterians after losing touch with their Congregationalist origins.

Most new Presbyterian congregations were filled with immigrants, however. Many were Scots-Irish—the children and grandchildren of Scottish men and women who had settled in northern Ireland in the seventeenth century to aid the English in their subjugation of the Irish. The Scots-Irish who moved on from Ireland to America settled throughout the colonies, from

New England to North Carolina. More new Presbyterians were immigrants from Scotland itself. Not all of them had been Presbyterians at home. Late-seventeenth- and early-eighteenth-century Scotland contained many different religious groups, not only Presbyterians but Quakers as well as adherents of the Church of Scotland, which was allied with the Church of England. But in both Scotland and America, active missionary efforts and effective organization by the Presbyterians won many Scots over to Presbyterianism. As a result, by 1740 the misnomer *Scotch Presbyterian* (the term *Scotch* properly refers to the alcoholic drink) actually described the religious affiliation of most Scots in America (and in Scotland), although this Presbyterian identity had not been as secure a half century earlier on either side of the Atlantic.

Finally, groups old and new began to splinter in America, a process that later typified many nineteenth- and twentieth-century U.S. religious groups. For example, in the 1670s dissident Baptists in Rhode Island led by John Rogers established a separate religious movement called the Rogerenes. They worshiped on Saturday, not Sunday, and apparently rejected the use of medicine in healing, depending exclusively on prayer to cure diseases and heal injuries. Although they won substantial numbers of followers in their early years, the Rogerenes' strength never extended far beyond Rhode Island and eastern Connecticut, and the group declined after 1740.

Quakers led by the Scottish Quaker intellectual George Keith split the movement in Pennsylvania in the 1690s so seriously that the church's authorities in Philadelphia hauled him into court to silence him. But Keith never overcame the power of the Quaker authorities, and his followers soon divided into Keithian Quakers, then Keithian Baptists. Some returned to the Quakers, others became Baptists, and George Keith himself became a Church of England minister who toured the colonies preaching against the Quakers in the early 1700s.

The survival and surprising strength of magical practices further complicated the British American religious landscape after 1690. Historians formerly thought that most magical beliefs and practices died out in the colonies over the 1692 Salem witch trials. New studies have shown, however, that this was not necessarily true. On at least two occasions authorities held additional witch trials in the colonies after 1692. Virginia authorities tried a woman named Grace Sherwood for witchcraft in 1705 and used the so-called dunking test to prove the charge. If she floated in water, she was guilty; if she sank, she was innocent—albeit dead by drowning. Unfortunately, the court records are incomplete, and Sherwood's fate remains unknown.

In 1706, the chief justice of South Carolina, Nicholas Trott, wrote a learned treatise demanding that the Charleston grand jury prosecute witches. Trott supported his demand with quotations from many authorities advocating the prosecution of witches, including the Puritan clergyman Increase Mather. But the grand jury refused to do so and apparently called witchcraft illusory, not real. This decision dismayed one local clergyman. He worried that "the Spirit of the Devil should be so much respected as to make men call open witchcraft" merely "imagination and no more." No more attempts to prosecute witches are known in the colonial period, although rumors about witchcraft popped up in Massachusetts and Virginia in the 1720s and 1740s.

European immigration after 1690 introduced new sources of magical and occult beliefs that still circulated throughout Europe. The prominent Lutheran clergyman Henry Melchior Muhlenberg conducted a one-man crusade against magic and occultism among German immigrants in the 1740s and 1750s.

He complained that Pennsylvania contained "more necroman-cers," or practitioners of magic, "than Christians," and that old people in Germany harbored especially "superstitious and godless notions." Yet Muhlenberg worried about Pennsylva-nia's younger immigrants as well: "Their heads, too, are full of fantastic notions of witchcraft and Satanic arts." In response, Muhlenberg publicly ridiculed ghost stories as "hocus-pocus" and a sin against God. When he learned that an immigrant named Simon Graf "dealt in witchcraft and exorcism of dev-ils," he excluded Graf from his congregation until Graf "burned his books and publicly confessed his offense before the congre-gation." Graf repented, and at his death Muhlenberg used the story of Graf's repudiation of magic to make a "good impression upon the congregation," because it knew about Graf's former practice of magic.

"Cunning people" who found lost objects and cured dis-eases also remained in the colonies after 1690. A man in Tiver-ton, Massachusetts, cast horoscopes and reportedly located lost objects for seamen using magical means, and a woman in New-port, Rhode Island, made urine cakes for use in predicting the future. Much to his disgust, the Reverend Ebenezer Parkman reported in 1755 that after extensive searches and prayers had failed to locate a child lost in the woods near Wachusett, Massa-chusetts, neighbors resorted to a blacksmith and "wise man" to find the child by using magic. An astrologers' society in Penn-sylvania briefly taught magical arts to inquiring students in the 1690s, and in 1723, Pennsylvania Quaker leaders renewed an earlier denunciation of wise men and women who "pretend to discover things hiddenly transacted, or tell where things lost or stolen may be found."

Almanacs contained the most important sources of magical and occult information available to colonists after 1690. Up to the time of the American Revolution, many almanacs included a picture called the "anatomy," a crude figure of a man circled by the signs of the zodiac—representations, that is, of the principal planets, moon, and sun, which were said to control various parts of the body. Even men and women who could barely read could use such an illustration to match occult medicines to their diseases or injuries and seek cures.

Almanac makers sometimes complained about pressure to include astrological or occult information in them. Samuel Clough's *New York Almanac* for 1703 included a poem that carped about readers' demands to see such material in every almanac:

> The anatomy must still be in,
> Else the almanac's not worth a pin,
> For country-men regard the sign,
> As though it were oracle divine.

Although these magical beliefs survived in the eighteenth-century colonies, they certainly declined among the educated elite. The president of Yale, Ezra Stiles, admitted in the 1780s that magic "subsists among some almanac makers and fortune tellers." But he believed that "in general the system is broken up, the vessel of sorcery shipwrecked, and only some scattered planks and pieces disjoined floating and scattered on the ocean of…human activity and bustle." Still, even its remnants increased the already spectacular religious diversity of eighteenth-century colonial America.

Not everyone responded positively to colonial religious diversity. Many settlers found such religious variety puzzling, or even disturbing. This was well demonstrated in the experience of Charles Woodmason, a Church of England minister who preached in the backcountry of North Carolina in the 1760s. Most of Woodmason's listeners belonged to no church, although they heard many different preachers. They were rough and untutored. Woodmason had to remind them how to behave in church: "Bring no dogs with you. They are very troublesome.... When you are seated, do not whisper, talk, [or] gaze about.... If you are thirsty, pray drink before you enter."

But often, Woodmason's listeners simply did not know what to make of the religious choices swirling around them. Nothing in Europe had prepared them for it, and the results were not always attractive, at least not in Woodmason's mind. He wrote in his journal after a visit to Lynch's Creek, North Carolina, in 1767, that the residents "complained of being eaten up by itinerant teachers, preachers, and impostors...Baptists, New Lights, Presbyterians, Independents, and a hundred other sects, so that one day you might hear this system of doctrine, the next day another." People were so confused that they simply could not choose. Woodmason described the result succinctly: "By the variety of tailors who would pretend to know [how]...Christ's coat is to be worn, none will put it on." Many colonists enjoyed the religious freedom that had emerged in America. But not everyone grappled easily with the confusion it produced.

A MOTHER LAMENTS HER
DAUGHTER'S FAITHLESSNESS

The ethnic pluralism and relatively open religious toleration of colonial New York saw many colonists take brides and grooms from other religious faiths. Huguenots married Anglicans, Dutch Reformed married Quakers, and English Baptists married English Presbyterians. Yet mixed marriages could also cause anguish.

In this remarkable letter from Abigail Franks, wife of New York City merchant Jacob Franks, both of whom were Ashkenazic or German Jews, Abigail reports to her son Naphtali (whom she calls by the affectionate nickname Heartsey) in London the shocking news of her daughter Phila's secret marriage to wealthy Anglican Oliver DeLancey in New York City sometime in January 1743.

Flatbush Tuesday June 7th 1743

Dear Heartsey

I am now retired from Town and would from myself if it were possible to have some peace of mind from the severe affliction I am under on the conduct of that unhappy girl [Phila]. Good God what a shock it was when they acquainted me she had left the house and had been married six months. I can hardly hold my pen whilst I am a writing it. It's what I never could have imagined especially after what I heard her so often say that no consideration in life should ever induce her to disoblige such good parents.

I had heard the report of her going to be married to Oliver DeLancey, but as such reports had often been of either of your sisters I gave no heed to it further than a general caution of her

[handwritten marginal note:] Mixed marriages

conduct, which has always been unblemished. And is so still in the eye of the Christians who allow she has disobliged us but has in no way been dishonorable being married to a man of worth and character.

My spirits was for some time so depressed that it was a pain to me to speak or see anyone. I have overcome it so far as not to make my concern so conspicuous, but I shall never have that serenity nor peace within I have so happily had hitherto. My house has been my prison ever since. I had not heart enough to go near the street door. It's a pain to me to think of going again to town, and if your father's business would permit him to live out of it, I never would go near it again....

Your Affectionate Mother

Abigail Franks

CHAPTER FIVE

African and American Indian Religion

In the mid-1600s, Mohegans living in eastern Connecticut interred several bodies at their principal burial ground, near modern-day Norwich. Along with the body of Lucy Occum, who had been converted to Christianity yet was also a medicine woman, the Mohegans had placed a bowl inlaid with wampum, the brightly colored cylindrical beads often used as currency in Indian transactions. With Hannah Wequot, the daughter of Chief Uncas, a seventeenth-century Mohegan leader, they had buried a bowl carved from a pepperidge tree knot and decorated with the figure of an owl. With a third, unknown Mohegan they had included a small "Hobbomocko" doll used to ward off evil spirits.

In 1868, looters invaded the Mohegan burial mound, scattering skeletons and removing hundreds of items buried with them, including the Hobbomocko doll and the bowls buried with Lucy Occum and Hannah Uncas. The looters sold most of the items they retrieved to collectors, and some later found their way to museums. In 1990, however, Congress passed the Native American Graves Protection and Repatriation Act, which required museums to return burial objects to the surviving tribes for reburial. This act honored a spiritual reality crucial to Native American life, that burial objects, like the dead themselves, carried immense religious meaning. Such relics were not art for homes and museums but spiritual objects that were to accompany the dead in new lives and journeys. Since the passage of the law in 1990 thousands of items, ranging from sacred objects to skeletons, have been returned to their original sources and reburied. Yale University's Peabody Museum, which acquired the three Mohegan objects through purchase in the early twentieth century, returned them to the Mohegan nation in 1998, and they were reburied at the Royal Mohegan burial ground 350 years after they had been placed there, some 130 years after their theft.

In the 1990s, a remarkably different kind of exhumation cast new light on African-American religious life in New York City between 1690 and 1794. In 1991, archaeologists examining ground in lower Manhattan prior to the construction of a $276 million federal office building unexpectedly uncovered more than 400 graves of African Americans. The site was later determined to have been the "Negro Burial Ground" used from the 1690s until its closure in 1794, then later forgotten when graveyard markers were obliterated and buildings were constructed on the site.

Analysis of this site, together with additional archaeological evidence from other African burial sites on the eastern seaboard, provides important clues to understanding African-American religious practices in the colonial era. Skeletons often bespoke the horrific conditions of New World slavery. Many of these, which were of children, were in numbers that suggested the difficulties that African Americans faced in sustaining family life in the colonial era. The remains of adults frequently showed broken bones, most likely sustained in work or from punishment.

The archaeological evidence also suggests that African Americans tried to follow traditional Old World African burial customs in the colonial settlements. The New York authorities, among others, did not make this easy. By law, no more than a dozen African Americans were allowed to attend a slave funeral, and coffins could not be covered, for fear that slaves would conceal weapons under the pall. Yet as early as the 1710s, a Church of England minister acknowledged that most New York slaves were buried without Christian services and that "heathenish rites are performed over them." What these rites were is impossible now to say. But beads, shells, and polished stones often accompanied the remains found in the New York burial site and in eighteenth-century African-American burials in Virginia and Maryland. They suggest that traditional African religious customs persisted in the face of obstacles that were quite unknown to the adherents of European religions.

The story of Native American religion during the British colonial period is simultaneously a tale of disappearance, change, and resilience. Enormous numbers of Native American religions simply disappeared, because so many of the cultures and societies that sustained them became extinct. Native American religions also often changed, sometimes adopting and adapting to Christianity, at others taking on new elements that also honored traditional concerns. As Native American cultures evolved, the Indians often found new ways to express old ideas and develop new ones, processes that also have been central to Christianity and Judaism throughout their engagement with Western civilization.

The outright disappearance of many distinctive Indian societies, and of the religions that sustained them, constitutes one of the most distressing facts of early American religious history. Between 100 and 200 Indian societies disappeared by the time of the American Revolution, and more became extinct in the nineteenth century. Most fell victim to devastating diseases, like cholera and smallpox, that had been introduced by Europeans, and the small size of many Indian societies, sometimes as few as 500 or 1,000 people, made disease among them unusually devastating. In the southeastern United States alone, groups that became extinct included the Chilucan and Oconee of Florida; the Tacatacuru, Yufera, and Yui of Georgia; the Chawasha of Mississippi; the Cape Fear and Chowanoc of North Carolina; the Sewee, Shakori, and Waxhaw of South Carolina; and the Manahoac, Monacan, Moneton, Nahyssan, and Occaneechi of Virginia. Some, like the Ais, Guacata, and Jeaga Indians of Florida, fled to Cuba, probably about 1763, at the end of the French and Indian War, where they were absorbed into the native population. As these cultures disappeared, so too did their religions.

The Indians who survived responded in a variety of ways to Christian missionary endeavors. The efforts at conversion in Virginia brought few results. The early Virginians proved more adept at attacking Indians than at converting them. The early missionary efforts by the first ministers in Virginia quickly evaporated, and most Indians rejected the Christian gospel even when it was offered. An Indian uprising in 1622, which resulted in 300 deaths among the English settlers—almost a quarter of the colony's population—brought an end to the missionary efforts and turned the English toward even more aggressive expansion. The Virginians fought a major war against the Indians in 1676 that reduced the colony's Indian population to less than 1,000.

The seal of the Massachusetts Bay Company, which held the charter to the colony of Massachusetts, featured an Indian carrying a bow and arrow standing between two pine trees and saying, "Come over and help us." The Puritans' missionary efforts among the Indians, unlike the Virginians', achieved some success. The Puritan minister John Eliot spent his entire career in Massachusetts seeking conversions among the Indians. The Puritans published more than twenty religious books in the Massachusett language between 1654 and 1690, including a complete translation of the Bible, with enough copies printed to distribute one to every 2.5 Indians. Converted Indians themselves preached among other Indians. By 1674 more than thirty so-called praying towns of Christian Indians dotted Massachusetts. All told, about 1,600 Christian Indians lived on the mainland and on Martha's Vineyard.

Yet the Puritan success was not what it seemed. Few Indians could read Eliot's translated Bibles because like many Puritans themselves, Indians seldom learned to read. Indeed, Eliot's Bibles may have been published mainly for English promoters of Indian missionary work. Fewer than 20 percent of the Indians in the "praying towns" received Christian baptism, and the Massachusett leader Metacom, known to the English as Philip, never converted to Christianity. Eliot demanded that the Indians abandon their traditional Indian religion completely, including its age-old medical customs and reliance upon the shamans, or medicine men and women, who practiced it. At the same time, the English settlers and the Indians squabbled frequently about property rights and English expansion into formerly Indian territory.

The so-called King Philip's War of 1675–76 effectively ended Eliot's work. In 1675, Indians led by Metacom attacked English settlements. They devastated 25 English villages, destroyed more than 1,000 English homes, and killed at least 2,000 English men and women and 8,000 cattle. The English counterattacked vengefully, killing Metacom and upward of

7,000 Indians, some in battle, others by starvation and disease. They reduced the "praying towns" to four, several of which quickly disbanded. They sold many Indians as slaves in the West Indies and put others out as servants in Massachusetts. If the war ended the Indian threat to New England, it also stopped any extensive effort at establishing Puritan Indian missions for decades. Many Indians were dead or gone, English sympathies for setting up missions evaporated, and John Eliot, now more than seventy years old, was too frail to carry on.

By comparison, the Jesuits who brought Catholicism to the Indians in Canada proved substantially more successful. The Jesuits worked more patiently and learned more about native customs and life, not just the native language. They introduced Christian physical objects like rosaries, crucifixes, and rings that superficially resembled physical objects used in Indian worship like medicine clubs and sticks. They offered richly appointed altars with burning candles. Catholic visual images helped strengthen the Indians' regard for Christianity. The Jesuits refrained from explaining the concept behind the sacrament of Christian communion, in which bread and wine are believed to be transformed into Christ's body and blood, fearing that it would be thought of as cannibalism, and described it instead as a commemorative service.

Even more than the Puritans, the Jesuits were superb logicians whose understanding of the Indian way of life made them better able to refute Indian objections to Christianity. Most importantly, as one Jesuit put it himself, to win converts they used "mildness and force, threats and prayers, labors and tears." They understood that conversion was an emotional as well as a logical process. As one Jesuit put it, "In order to convert these peoples, one must begin by touching their hearts, before he can convince their minds."

The Jesuits met with considerable success among the Hurons in southern Canada and northern New York. By 1648, they counted twenty-two Jesuits working in numerous Huron villages with almost fifty native assistants. But an unexpected attack from the Iroquois had murderous effects on the Hurons and brought much Jesuit work to a stop. The Iroquois killed thousands of Hurons, destroyed many of their villages, and killed the principal Jesuit missionary to the Hurons, Jean de Brébeuf. The Iroquois were so impressed with Brébeuf's bravery that they ate his heart and drank his blood to absorb his strength. The Jesuits retained the allegiance of the remaining Hurons, and thousands more Hurons underwent Christian baptism after the Iroquois war ended. But the Huron nation remained a pale reflection of its former self after the Iroquois attacks, and the Jesuits' missionary efforts toward them suffered with it.

More denominations became involved in missions to the Indians in the eighteenth-century British colonies, though not always with great success. The Church of England sponsored a mere handful of missions among the Indians and succeeded with even fewer. The Congregationalist minister Eleazar Wheelock trained Indians at a special school in Lebanon, Connecticut, and later at what would become Dartmouth College, in New Hampshire. He separated Indian students from their native communities so he could train and discipline them without interference. Samson Occom, a Mohegan, who became Wheelock's greatest success story, ministered to the Indians in Long Island, New England, and New York City. But Wheelock and Occom won relatively few converts, and Wheelock's school was generally considered a failure.

Moravian missionaries in New York and Pennsylvania experienced greater success. Like the Jesuits, the Moravians made a point of learning much about the native cultures and exhibited considerable patience in awaiting conversions. They also distanced themselves from aggressive government policies on English settlement and warfare. But most importantly, Moravian theology fit the realities of the conversion process and important themes in traditional native beliefs. The Moravians stressed piety and the love of Christ, both of which could be learned by example. Unlike the Puritans, they did not stress doctrine. The Moravians lived among the Indians and used native language in day-to-day conversation, not merely in translated books. Like the Native Americans, they discussed how dreams could communicate religious truths and moral lessons. A Presbyterian observer in Pennsylvania commented enviously, "The Moravians appear to have adopted the best mode of Christianizing the Indians. They go among them without noise or parade, and by their friendly behavior conciliate their good will."

Few Indians ever converted to Christianity, yet there was substantial change throughout the Indian religious world during the British colonial era. This was not surprising. Just as Christianity changed drastically after it became the official religion of the Roman Empire, the native religions of North America changed greatly as contact with Europeans drastically altered native cultures. The changes in nature and ecology produced by European colonization greatly threatened many native religions. The extraordinary slaughtering of animals that came in with the Europeans undermined the beliefs that assigned crucial supernatural roles to animals, for example. The Micmacs of far eastern Canada found their special relationship with the beaver imperiled by unchecked harvesting of beaver skins, a trade the Micmacs themselves indulged. The spirits residing in nature no longer spoke. Later, in the mid-eighteenth century, the Micmacs tore out the eyes of beavers and other animals they killed as a way of blinding the animals to the treatment the animals were now receiving.

Other Indian groups demonstrated remarkable resilience in the face of multiple threats to their political, cultural, and spiritual universe. One form this took was to incorporate the material goods that the Europeans brought into their own existing religious milieu. This "syncretism," or fusing of different beliefs and cultures, stimulated the survival of native cultures and beliefs and demonstrated the creative adaptability of native cultures and religions. A Micmac medicine woman used Catholic rosary beads as the centerpiece of her Micmac healing practice. As an unhappy Jesuit priest described it, "These she carefully preserved, and gave them only to those who were her friends, protesting... that the gift which she gave them had come originally from heaven."

New cultures and new religious systems emerged among the Indians as European expansion continued. A new "Catawba" nation emerged between 1700 and 1740 from an array of endangered separate peoples in North and South Carolina, among them the Eno, Cape Fear, Cheraw, Congaree, Cusago, Keyauwee, Santee, Saponi, Sissipahaw, Sugeree, Waccamaw, Wateree, Winyaw, and Woccon Indians. The new Catawba culture created a new Indian society. Its religious expressions mixed elements from the older Indian societies as well as Christianity, which some Indians had learned through missionaries. One Catawba, a former Saponi Indian named Ned Bearskin, described for the Virginia planter William Byrd the Catawba belief in a single supreme being who punished goodness and badness.

This was not, however, the Christian God of a Christian world. Bearskin described a sacred world where deer and turkey meat could not be mixed, where the "regions of bliss" after death contained beautiful women and men, abundant game, and plentiful crops, and where "regions of misery" brought cold, hunger, and constant sexual aggressiveness. New ceremonies bound Catawbas together in life and death. Their rituals commemorated harvests and honored the dead. In shaping these new spiritual expressions the Catawbas, like other Native Americans, wrested meaning from endangerment and cleared the way for survival into modern times.

African religions also experienced exceptional difficulties under British slavery that were at least as severe as those experienced by American Indian religions and far beyond any difficulties known to Christianity and Judaism. Ultimately, no African religions survived whole in the British colonies of North America. Thus, the religions from the Ashanti or Ibo societies on Africa's west coast, for example, were no longer practiced on the North American continent in the broad, expansive fashion they had been observed in Africa. This made the story of African religions in British America remarkably different from the history of all the other immigrant religions in America. No other Old World peoples suffered such wholesale destruction of their traditional religions as did Africans enslaved in Britain's North American colonies. Yet despite the odds against them, Africans reconstructed in America some key elements of their traditional religious practice and slowly reconfigured Christianity according to their own needs; in the process, they would leave their imprint upon the wider Christian world.

The destruction of the traditional African religious systems in the British colonies stemmed from two primary causes: the religious havoc caused by capture and New World enslavement, and the repressiveness of British slavery. The African slave trade disregarded the individual slaves' spirituality. Slave traders were interested in workers, not spiritual leaders. Africans who exercised special religious leadership in their home societies arrived in America only by accident, not intent. Worse, the variety of African religions reduced the spiritual guidance one person might give to many captured Africans. The Akan, Ashanti, Dahoman, Ibo, and Yoruba societies were as religiously and culturally distinct as were the Scottish, Welsh, English, French, and Spanish societies of Europe. As a result, a religious figure from one African society would have found it difficult to provide spiritual leadership for the many enslaved Africans from other societies.

Slaveholders in America suppressed public African religious practice in almost all areas except burials and, possibly, marriages or betrothals. Planters, farmers, and merchants who owned slaves worried most about Africans' use of religious meetings as places to hatch resistance and rebellion and actively opposed African religious gatherings. An Anglican minister in South Carolina acknowledged that he readily suppressed African "feasts, dances, and merry meetings upon the Lord's day." The laws in most colonies prohibited meetings of Africans for any reason. Finally, since large-scale slaveholding in America was rare, most enslaved Africans lived in small groups on small farms widely separated from other Africans. These conditions made the public and collective practice of traditional African religion extraordinarily difficult in America.

English efforts to convert slaves to Christianity met with little success before the American Revolution. In fact, many slaveholders actively resisted attempts to convert the Africans. They worried that Christian baptism would undermine the concept of enslavement and encourage Africans to regard themselves as the equals of their owners. One South Carolina slaveholder told his minister that he would "never come to the [communion] table while slaves are received." Another asked, "If any of my slaves go to heaven...must I see them there?" The Reverend Francis Le Jau tried to appease his South Carolina parishioners by forcing slaves to take an oath that they did not seek baptism "out of any design to free yourself from the duty and obedience you owe to your master while you live." The effort satisfied few owners, and most slaves remained unbaptized.

Between 1690 and 1750, few Africans converted to Christianity. Anglicans conducted most of the occasional efforts at slave conversion before 1750. They operated schools for slaves in New York City in the early decades of the eighteenth century, but they never produced large numbers of converts. Rural Anglican clergymen ministering where most Africans lived reported few converts there, and most eventually abandoned serious work among Africans. Presbyterians preached to enslaved Africans in Virginia and North Carolina in the 1750s and 1760s but won few converts. The Presbyterian minister Samuel Davies preached among Africans but denied baptism to them because he worried, like Le Jau, that they sought an "equality with their masters."

In contrast, several specific African rites did survive capture and enslavement despite the harshness of British slaveholding. South Carolina planters complained about "rites and revels" carried out among recently arrived Africans. Some owners recognized the validity of marriages among Africans that were not sanctioned by colonial law or by other owners. More importantly, Africans recognized these marriages among themselves and gathered to celebrate them. A rare eighteenth-century picture, probably from South Carolina, most likely depicts one of these marriage celebrations. The slave owner's home is in the far background, only Africans are depicted, the musical instruments are African, and the dancing suggests the joy of a major occasion, such as a marriage, perhaps of the woman seated to the left and the man in the white coat kneeling next to her.

Africans also consulted conjurers who invoked traditional African magic and medical knowledge to cure disease and harm enemies, whether slaves or owners. An African "sorcerer" reputedly supplied magical powder to shield Africans from European weapons before launching a bloody but unsuccessful revolt in New York City in 1712. Two Africans won public recognition from whites for cures, a Virginian whose medicine reputedly healed "the Yawes, Lame Distemper, Pox, Dropsy etc." and a South Carolinian who discovered a cure for rattlesnake bites. Both were most likely African "conjure men" who possessed formidable knowledge of herbs, plants, and African magical lore. At least one South Carolina poisoning case offered evidence that the African perpetrator had obtained poison from a conjurer and that several victims had employed other conjurers to ward off the poison.

Funeral rites among slaves sometimes employed African burial rituals. Slave owners appear to have been more tolerant of at least some African ceremonies at death than of other African religious practices. Several African burial sites from eighteenth-century Maryland contain corpses buried with beads, bracelets, wreaths, and large numbers of seeds. The Africans interred in one Maryland site lacked clothing or shrouds, as though the dead were to be born again in a new life. It is unclear, however, whether Africans were left to bury their fellows as they saw fit; it may be that they performed rites of their own following a Christian ceremony. A Scots traveler in North Carolina reported in 1774 that after the Christian funeral of an African woman "the Negroes assembled to perform their part of the funeral rites, which they did by running, jumping, crying and various exercises."

After 1760, enslaved Africans were exposed to new missionary efforts by Baptists and Methodists. These efforts led to the founding of the many African-American Christian churches that flowered in the nineteenth century. The Baptist and Methodist preaching among Africans that developed in the 1760s and 1770s differed considerably from earlier Anglican and Presbyterian efforts at Christian conversion. The Anglicans and Presbyterians stressed ritual and doctrine, not experience. The Anglicans never accorded Africans congregational membership, and the Presbyterians often refused to baptize Africans. The Anglican revivalist George Whitefield evangelized among enslaved Africans and criticized slaveholders in his first trip to America in 1739 and 1740. But Whitefield also accepted slavery, and regularly purchased slaves to work on the plantation that he had begun for orphans in Bethesda, Georgia, in the 1740s.

In contrast, evangelical Baptists and Methodists stressed the conversion experience and encouraged shouting, trembling, and ecstatic singing in their services. They often promoted millennialist beliefs that Christ would return to earth for a 1,000-year reign and emphasized the transformation of personal life that came with Christian conversion. They evangelized among poorer whites and quickly began preaching among enslaved Africans as well. By the early 1770s, both the Baptists and the Methodists had baptized hundreds of Africans, in the southern colonies especially. Most importantly, some Baptist preachers, such as Elhanan Winchester, openly condemned slavery and slaveholding.

Africans who became Baptists and Methodists quickly exercised a religious leadership unknown among either the Anglicans or Presbyterians. Africans often became members of Baptist congregations, and some African Baptists began preaching, at least to fellow Africans. George Liele, born into slavery in Virginia to a master who was himself a convert to the Baptist movement, began preaching to his fellow slaves in the 1770s.

After Liele was freed by his master in 1777, he moved to Savannah, Georgia, where he founded the town's first separate African Baptist congregation, the First African Church of Savannah.

Enslaved and free Africans alike quickly became prominent in the early Methodist movement. The Methodists evangelized heavily in the British West Indies among enslaved Africans, and in the southern colonies they won converts among both the poorer whites and enslaved Africans. Methodist itinerant preachers such as Freeborn Garrettson freely described Maryland Methodist gatherings as racially mixed: "I suppose about twelve whites and blacks were present. The power of the Lord came among us." Sometimes the power or the message or the preacher proved dangerous for the Methodists, however. David Margate, an African trained by Methodists in England, preached to slaves in South Carolina in 1775. But when he claimed that he was a second Moses and had been "called to deliver his people from slavery," the Methodist authorities returned him to England, fearful of his rhetoric and intentions.

The Revolution interrupted these developments, if only for a moment. When it ended, the example of African preaching among Baptists and Methodists created new opportunities and, eventually, new religious movements for enslaved and free Africans in America. After the Revolution, African Baptist preachers worked regularly from Pennsylvania to South Carolina. A Williamsburg, Virginia, court tried to stop the preaching of an African Baptist named Moses because he drew such large crowds. Another African Baptist, Gowan Pamphlet, formed a separate African Baptist congregation in Williamsburg that was admitted to the local white Baptist association in 1791. By 1800, at least a dozen independent African Baptist congregations existed in the United States, most of them formed by free or enslaved African preachers.

Africans also claimed important places within the post-Revolutionary Methodist movement. "Black Harry Hosier" preached regularly with Methodist leaders Francis Asbury, Thomas Coke, and Freeborn Garrettson despite white objections to his race. Other African Methodist preachers campaigned in Virginia and Maryland. Sometimes tensions resulted when Africans followed African preachers. On one occasion, a white Methodist who was preaching to a racially mixed congregation lost his African listeners when an African Methodist preacher joined him. When the African began preaching, the African listeners "immediately flocked around, while I myself could be suffered to preach and pray in the church." In Philadelphia, free Africans who had previously worshiped with whites formed two congregations of their own in 1794. One, led by an African American named Absalom Jones, was first called simply the African Church but was later renamed St. Thomas's. The other, led by Richard Allen, emerged from within the Methodist movement and was later called Bethel African Methodist Episcopal Church.

The African preaching among Methodists and Baptists in the late colonial era laid a foundation for post-Revolutionary religious activism among both enslaved and free Africans and for the great African-American Christian denominations formed in the nineteenth century. After 1810 the Baptists created a substantial bloc of independent African congregations up and down the East Coast and in the American West. The Methodists formed two important denominations, the African Methodist Episcopal Church, organized in 1816, and the African Methodist Episcopal Zion Church, founded in 1821.

Folk religious customs drawn from a variety of African traditions in the colonial era also blossomed in the nineteenth century. In the early-nineteenth-century South the tradition of "conjurers" and African medicine men and women occasionally glimpsed in the British colonies emerged into the widespread appearance of "Obeah men," a common African name for sorcerers who were consulted by both blacks and whites in the South. Indeed, even in the early twentieth century the tradition still could be seen in New York City's Harlem, where a variety of "African medicine men," "herb doctors," and "spiritualists" healed and cured among the African-American population.

Despite important differences, then, the religious experiences of American Indians and Africans bore striking similarities in the colonial period. Unlike European immigrants to America, Indians and Africans faced immense difficulties continuing or extending their traditional religious practices in settings that European colonization made new for everyone. Indians and Africans employed religion in new and vital ways in colonial America. They shaped meaning and sustained community life across two extraordinarily difficult centuries, and the new religious expressions they created became central to Indian and African-American identity in the centuries that followed.

The Reverend David Brainerd, a Presbyterian missionary to Native Americans in New Jersey and Pennsylvania in the 1740s, was fascinated by their religion. Brainerd wrote that they were "brutishly stupid and ignorant of divine things" and "obstinately set against Christianity." But Brainerd also recorded traditional Indian religious beliefs with surprising sensitivity in a report he published in Philadelphia in 1746, Mirabilia Dei inter Indicos; or, The Rise and Progress of a Remarkable Work of Grace Amongst a Number of the Indians in the Provinces of New-Jersey and Pennsylvania.

I have taken much pains to inquire of my Christian people [Indians converted to Christianity], whether they, before their acquaintance with Christianity, imagined there was a plurality of great invisible powers.... So far as I can learn, they had a notion of a plurality of indivisible deities, and paid some kind of homage to them promiscuously, under a great variety of forms and shapes. And it is certain, those who yet remain Pagans pay some kind of superstitious reverence to beasts, birds, fishes, and even reptiles; that is, some to one kind of animal, and some to another. They do not indeed suppose a divine power essential to, or inhering in these creatures, but that some indivisible beings...communicate to these animals a great power, either one or other of them, or perhaps sometimes all of them, and so make these creatures the immediate authors of good to certain persons.

They seem to have some confused notion about a future state of existence, and many of them imagine that the *chichung,* (i.e., the shadow), or what survives the body, will at death go southward, and in an unknown but curious place, will enjoy some kind of happiness, such as, hunting, feasting, dancing, and the like....I remember I once consulted a very ancient, but intelligent Indian upon this point, for my own satisfaction; asked him whether the Indians of old times had supposed there was anything of the man that would survive the body? He replied, Yes. I asked him, where they supposed its abode would be? He replied, "It would go southward." I asked him further, whether it would be happy there? He answered, after a considerable pause, "that the souls of good folks would be happy, and the souls of bad folks miserable." I then asked him, who he called bad folks? His answer (as I remember) was, "Those who lie, steal, quarrel with their neighbors, are unkind to their friends, and especially to aged parents, and, in a word, such as are a plague to mankind."

They give much heed to dreams, because they suppose these invisible powers give them directions at such times about certain affairs, and sometime inform them what animal they would chuse to be worshipped in. They are like-wise much attached to the traditions and fabulous notions of their fathers, who have informed them of diverse miracles that were anciently wrought among the Indians, which they firmly believe, and thence look upon their ancestors to have been the best of men.

CHAPTER SIX

Reviving Colonial Religion

In "Rip Van Winkle," Washington Irving's 1819 short story, Rip awakens from a twenty-year sleep to find himself a stranger to almost everything he had known. The story contains nothing about religion. But if it did, and if Rip had slept ninety years starting in 1680, his astonishment would have been even greater. Upon awakening in 1770, he would have discovered that America was now awash in extraordinary religious pluralism; but he might have been even more startled by how religious activity itself had changed in crucial ways. All the religious denominations, old and new, formed more congregations and constructed far more church buildings in those years than they ever had in the seventeenth century. Revivalism, an intense campaign for religious renewal, changed the style of colonial religion. And women became increasingly prominent in colonial religious activity, even if men still exercised the authority in most religious groups. These changes, made hand in hand with the growth of religious pluralism, gave colonial religion much of the flavor characterizing it as uniquely American.

110

So many new congregations constructed so many new church buildings between 1680 and 1770 that they completely altered the colonial religious landscape as the American Revolution approached. More than 85 percent of the approximately 1,200 religious congregations in the colonies on the eve of the Revolution were founded after 1680. As a result, only a tiny portion of the Revolutionary-era congregations could trace their origins to the seventeenth century.

The expansion of colonial congregations occured in two separate bursts, each with its own characteristics. The first occurred between 1680 and 1710. In this period both the New England Puritans, by then generally called Congregationalists, and the Church of England considerably expanded and strengthened their hold on important portions of the population. In New England, the Congregationalists established at least sixty new congregations between 1680 and 1710. Many of them served new towns established when younger New Englanders migrated to these settlements and as further immigrants continued to arrive from England. These new congregations carried forth New England's "state church" tradition into the eighteenth century in that they all received tax monies for their support. This financial support helped forestall the formation of competing congregations. A Baptist, for example, would have to pay taxes to support the legally established Congregational church in town, then also contribute to the Baptist congregation he or she might want to join.

The Church of England, the state church of that country, expanded dramatically between 1680 and 1710 throughout Britain's North American colonies. The Anglicans accomplished this feat in two ways. They strengthened the weak laws that had originally established the Church of England as the government-supported church in Virginia, and they won the legal

111

establishment of new churches in South Carolina, North Carolina, and Maryland. As a result, all four colonies witnessed the creation of dozens of new Anglican parishes in the two decades after 1680.

In addition, Anglicans in England created the Society for the Propagation of the Gospel in Foreign Parts (SPG). The SPG raised money to support the Church of England in colonies where it lacked a legal basis and to support newly formed Anglican parishes in colonies where the Church of England was legally established. The SPG provided these churches ministers, salaries, and books, and sometimes helped construct buildings for them.

The results of both efforts were impressive. The Anglicans established almost ninety congregations in the colonies between 1680 and 1710 alone. In Maryland, which was notorious for its lack of public Christian worship before 1680, Anglicans established nearly thirty working parishes by 1710, almost all with new church buildings, two-thirds of them being staffed with resident clergymen.

A second great burst of congregational expansion occured between 1740 and 1770. Some of it resulted from revivalism that appeared sporadically in the colonies from New England to South Carolina in this period. Eighteenth-century colonial revivalism typically stressed a "new birth" in Christ and encouraged believers to purify their lives and rejuvenate their congregations. Activist ministers led revivals in their own congregations and traveled through the countryside, preaching in friendly congregations or in the open air where local ministers opposed their work. The revivalist ministers insisted that listeners acknowledge their own depravity and seek safety in Christ. Listeners sometimes responded emotionally, occasionally shrieking and fainting when their feelings of sinfulness overcame them. The Congregationalists, Presbyterians, and Baptists benefited most from this revivalism, although a third or more of the congregations established through revivalism survived for less than a decade.

However, most congregations formed in the eighteenth century stemmed from efforts to expand religious denominations that did not necessarily support revivalism. The SPG, for example, established nearly 150 Anglican congregations throughout the colonies between 1740 and 1770. At least 400 Presbyterian and Baptist congregations were formed in this period, only some of them through revivalism. When added to the congregations formed by the Quakers, German Lutherans, German Reformed, and the Mennonites and Moravians, the era from 1740 to 1770 emerged as the single most fruitful era of congregational expansion in the entire colonial period.

After 1680, many denominations formed annual meetings, or administrative councils, to supervise church affairs in the colonies, most of them modeled on Old World institutions. Many were located in Philadelphia, which became the informal capital of colonial American Protestantism for decades. The Quakers' Philadelphia Yearly Meeting, which was modeled on the London Yearly Meeting, first met in 1685, three years after the Quaker settlement of Pennsylvania. The prominence of its leaders and the Quakers' dominance of early Pennsylvania quickly made it the most important Quaker meeting in the colonies.

The Presbytery of Philadelphia, a meeting of Presbyterian ministers and some lay elders modeled on presbyteries in Scotland and northern Ireland, first met in 1706 to supervise the Presbyterian congregations multiplying rapidly between New York and Maryland. In 1716, the Presbyterians added further regional presbyteries and created the Synod of Philadelphia to supervise the new presbyteries. By 1740, the synod had six regional presbyteries and more than fifty ministers and seventy congregations.

In 1707, the Baptists formally organized the Philadelphia Baptist Association, led by Baptists with ministerial responsibilities. It superseded the informal meetings that had been held among Baptist congregations in Pennsylvania and New Jersey since the 1680s. In 1747, German Reformed ministers established a Coetus, or assembly of ministers, in Philadelphia to manage affairs among the German Calvinists, and in 1748, German Lutherans established the Lutheran Ministerium of Pennsylvania to guide Lutheran congregational life in that colony and Maryland.

Ironically, the Church of England remained the only European religious group failing to transfer its traditional form of church government to the colonies. Political infighting in England prevented naming a bishop to supervise Anglican affairs in America. Dissenters like the Congregationalists and the Baptists feared that an Anglican bishop in America would have too much political power, and other Anglican bishops and leaders in England worried about competition from the new bishop. In the wake of this failure, Anglican officials had to depend upon ineffective "commissaries," or representatives of the bishop of London, to oversee church affairs in America, or on the SPG, which provided ministers and money but lacked authority to govern America's Anglican churches.

These denominational institutions directed the expansion of Quaker, Presbyterian, Baptist, Lutheran, and Reformed congregations and did much to keep colonial Protestantism from exploding into chaos. They approved and sometimes directed the establishment of new congregations, provided preachers, settled disputes within and between congregations, established standards for ministerial conduct, and disciplined wayward ministers and members. For example, when the Baptist congregation at Piscataway, New Jersey, discovered that its minister, Henry Loveall, was a bigamist and an impostor, the Philadelphia Baptist Association helped the congregation select a new minister approved by the Association, noting that Loveall seemed to have chosen an appropriate name for himself.

The denominational institutions also settled—and sometimes heightened—doctrinal and theological disputes. When the Quakers divided over matters of doctrine in the 1690s, the Philadelphia Yearly Meeting settled the affair, and when the Presbyterians debated the merits of revivalism in the 1740s pro-revivalists marched out of the Synod of Philadelphia to form their own Synod of New York.

Authority in the denominations flowed down from the top, not up from the bottom. Ordained ministers conducted the proceedings of all the denominational sessions except the Quaker meetings, because the Quakers did not ordain clergymen. Yet even there, men who were designated to preach publicly dominated the yearly meetings. Lay men and women seldom took part in or even attended denominational meetings. The Presbyterians did not allow a congregation to send a lay representative to these meetings unless the congregation's minister was present, and few congregations sent lay representatives to presbyteries or the Synod of Philadelphia. At the same time, congregations found that they could exercise their own power over clergymen through controlling their ministers' salaries. Because most of these ministers were paid by their listeners rather than by the government, they risked losing their salaries if they displeased their congregations.

On the whole, the denominational institutions in America proved to be far more vigorous than their counterparts in Europe. Through their emphasis on effective leadership they *democracy affected by committees*

made an important contribution to the ultimate rise of democracy in America. All of them were modeled on similar institutions in England or Germany—the Quakers' London Yearly Meeting, the London Baptist Association, the numerous presbyteries in England and Scotland, and the organizations of Lutheran and Reformed ministers in the German states. But the number of Baptists and Presbyterians declined in England, and the Quakers' ranks there only held steady, partially drained by the Quaker emigration to Pennsylvania. In Germany, Lutheran and Reformed ministers disagreed about doctrine, revivalism, and the degree to which the churches should have government support.

In America, however, the denominational institutions that were established in the colonies, especially those that grew up in and around Philadelphia, enabled many European religious groups to expand significantly. Colonial Quakers, Presbyterians, Baptists, German Lutherans, and German Reformed denominations increased without colonial governmental support. Between 1680 and 1770 all of them substantially increased the number of congregations affiliated with their groups and raised the membership in their individual congregations.

The expansion of congregational life after 1680 transformed the visual landscape of colonial American religion for all Protestant denominations as well as Catholic and Jewish congregations. The best measure of this transformation is the simplest: Only one or two of the colonial church buildings still seen on the East Coast were constructed before 1680; all the rest were built between 1680 and 1770.

tons of new churches/ synagogues

Most churches built before 1680 were small and crude. Few were larger than 20 by 40 or 50 feet, and most featured wood construction, not the stone or brick used in England. For example, the first church constructed in Sudbury, Massachusetts, in 1643, had a thatched roof and measured only 20 by 30 feet. Not until the town's third church was built in 1688 did Sudbury claim a church with a permanent roof and a finished exterior.

Colonial church architecture changed dramatically after 1680 as colonial society expanded dramatically, the economy boomed, and the society became more diverse and sophisticated. Church buildings grew larger and accommodated more people in far more ornate and plush settings. This was true everywhere in the colonies. New England still constructed wooden church buildings, but now they were built on deeper foundations by master craftsmen who raised buildings to staggering heights, often to striking visual effect. The roof in the Old Ship Meeting House in Hingham, Massachusetts, constructed in 1681, spanned a length unimaginable forty years earlier, and New England churches constructed over the next several decades only grew larger. Churches constructed in the middle and southern colonies after 1680 were equally large, although usually they were brick or stone or had stucco finishes laid over a wood frame.

architecture

largeness of wooden churches.

Regional variations in church architecture also developed after 1680. Maryland and Virginia churches constructed after that year tended to be long and narrow with English and Flemish brickwork that sometimes created zigzag patterns in exterior walls. In contrast, South Carolina's craftsmen more often erected square stucco buildings, like the parish church constructed at St. James Goose Creek in 1706. Before 1740, most rural church buildings could not afford steeples or bells. Congregations that acquired bells usually placed them in wooden stands on the ground and frequently did not build a steeple to house the bells for several decades.

The churches constructed after 1680 typically underwent substantial renovation in the next half century. The Anglican church at St. James Goose Creek may have had a relatively plain interior when it was built in 1706. But by the 1740s, it contained a coat of arms of George II, who ascended the British throne in 1727, decorative carved cherubs in gilt paint, a cantilevered pulpit with a mahogany sounding board that amplified the minister's voice, and carefully laid out box pews constructed of fine, polished woods. New England church buildings were no less ornate and featured smoothly polished pews, finely carved pulpits, mahogany baptismal fonts, and silver communion cups.

Synagogues followed similar patterns. New York City's Shearith Israel Synagogue had a women's balcony with high arched windows when it was built in 1730, and Touro Synagogue in Newport, Rhode Island, dedicated in 1763, contained an ornate carved wood interior and finely wrought pews that easily compared with any Christian congregation in the colonies. The Jewish silversmith Myer Myers crafted numerous ceremonial objects, including circumcision instruments and sets of silver Torah ornaments used at Congregation Shearith Israel in New York and Congregation Mikveh Israel in Philadelphia.

Between 1690 and 1770, the colonial cities became centers of ecclesiastical splendor. Although New York City lacked a single church steeple in 1680, four pierced the skyline by 1720 and more were added in the next decades. In Philadelphia, Anglican, Presbyterian, Baptist, German Lutheran, and German Reformed churches constructed between 1720 and 1750 transformed the skyline of a city previously known only for its quiet Quaker meetinghouses.

By the 1750s, Charleston offered the most spectacular example of resplendent church architecture in the American colonies. St. Philip's, the city's first large Anglican church, was constructed in 1720. Then in 1751, an even larger Anglican church, St. Michael's, was built only six blocks to the south of St. Philip's. Both churches had an organ, steeples, bells, hanging lamps, embroidered seat cushions, finely carved pews, and massive columns. If they reflected the wealth gained through slaveholding and trade, they also bespoke the rising power of the European denominations in the eighteenth-century colonies.

Revivalism among evangelical Protestants challenged and reinforced traditional organized religion in the eighteenth-century colonies. Distinguished by frequent emotional outpourings and promoting a "born again" religious experience in which participants declared their rebirth as believing Christians, revivals were as controversial in the eighteenth century as they have been since. Critics found them crude, overly emotional, and anti-intellectual. Supporters viewed revivals as unparalleled opportunities to refresh denominations that were expanding numerically yet lacked inner conviction and fervor.

Controversy of revivalisms

The colonial revivals had important European origins. They were a far distant expression of the European "pietist" movement that stressed personal religious introspection and individual transformation. This movement originated in Prussia and other German principalities in the 1690s and early 1700s, then extended to the Netherlands and England. It stressed personal religious experience and encouraged individuals to look within to determine their true adherence to Christianity. Aspects of this European revivalism appeared in the 1690s in Northampton, Massachusetts, where the Congregationalist minister Solomon Stoddard sponsored revivals for more than a decade. In the 1720s, similar pietist sentiments supported an intense revivalism in the New Jersey Dutch Reformed congregations led by Theodorus Frelinghuysen. Then, in the 1740s, revivalism seemed to spring up in many places, especially among middle colony Presbyterians and New England Baptists, as well as in the preaching of powerful transatlantic figures like the Anglican revivalist George Whitefield.

& origins

(margin note: Whitefield Anglican revivalist → critical of his own church)

Two especially powerful clergymen typified eighteenth-century colonial revivalism. The Anglican minister George Whitefield became a model for the modern evangelist. This Church of England minister bitterly criticized his own denomination. Other Anglican clergymen treated him as a virtual enemy, yet Whitefield never left the Anglican Church. He was regarded as unusually handsome but had crossed eyes that followers sometimes regarded as a sign of divine promise. And he possessed an actor's voice and an extraordinary sense of public relations that made him the first modern celebrity in America.

Whitefield made seven tours of the British colonies between 1739 and his death in Newburyport, Massachusetts, in 1770. He attracted enormous crowds in the colonial cities. Some 10,000 people reputedly flocked to hear him preach in Philadelphia in 1741. Even the skeptical Benjamin Franklin found Whitefield engaging and discovered himself contributing to Whitefield's cause during the evangelist's Philadelphia visit. Whitefield's preaching was distinguished by the simple question he asked over and over: "What must I do to be saved?" This question dominated Whitefield's preaching for thirty years and was central to much of American revivalism for the next two centuries.

(margin note: more oral tradition than written)

Whitefield made major changes in colonial preaching. Before he arrived in America, many colonial preachers wrote their sermons on small pieces of paper that they held close to their eyes when they preached, often reading the sermon in a dull drone for more than an hour. Whitefield gave ministers a new standard. He memorized his sermons and spoke without notes. He varied his voice. He gestured, sometimes calmly, at others in agitation. He held audiences in awe and created the model for modern American revivalists, from Charles Finney in the nineteenth century to Billy Sunday and Billy Graham in the twentieth century.

Jonathan Edwards of western Massachusetts offered another model for the colonial revivalists. Whitefield had little interest in theology, but Edwards became the most important English theologian on either side of the Atlantic in the eighteenth century. He produced an enormous range of published works that made him internationally known by the time of his death in 1758, the most famous being his books *Freedom of the Will* (1754) and *Original Sin* (1758).

Edwards's importance in the colonial revivals reveals their complexity. In the 1730s, Edwards believed that the revivals he was leading and experiencing in Northampton, Massachusetts, reflected the operation of God in human history. He thought the revivals prefaced the second coming of Christ and would usher in a new millennium, or thousand-year reign of Christ on earth. Edwards's most famous revival sermon, "Sinners in the Hands of an Angry God," which he preached in 1741 at the height of the revivals, established the stereotype of the angry, vindictive revival preacher. In it, Edwards so vividly described the destruction of those who were not saved that he had to stop preaching several times because his frightening words convulsed the audience: "Your wickedness makes you as...heavy as lead. [You will] tend downwards with great weight and pressure towards hell, and if God should let you go, you would immediately sink and descend and plunge into the bottomless gulf."

But Edwards also became doubtful about revivals as they progressed. He worried that enthusiastic preachers could too easily lead lay men and women into irresponsible, even blasphemous behavior. For example, James Davenport, a Presbyterian minister who had been trained at Yale, promoted emotional displays of revival activity, encouraged laymen to preach, and burned books and luxury goods in New London, Connecticut, in 1743 as a sign that his followers had adopted a new life.

Edwards rejected such radicalism and encouraged ministers to be more careful in their preaching and especially in encouraging emotional outbursts from their listeners.

The revivals, which historians have called the Great Awakening, never were consistent in theology. Early revivalists like the Presbyterian Gilbert Tennent encouraged listeners to reject unconverted ministers. In a well-known sermon he preached in 1740 titled "The Danger of an Unconverted Ministry," Tennent attacked perfunctory, lifeless ministers who knew church doctrine but could not claim a conversion experience. Tennent urged congregations to follow other preachers, including itinerants. But George Whitefield and Jonathan Edwards rejected such views, and Tennent soon changed his own mind. By 1742, Tennent, like Edwards, had come to view itinerant and lay preaching alike with suspicion. He thundered that "ignorant young converts" who preached introduced "the greatest errors and the greatest anarchy and confusion."

Theological diversity also characterized the revivals. Calvinists still believing in predestination dominated the New England revivals. The Dutch Reformed revivals in New Jersey in the 1720s stemmed from pietistic influence from Germany. The Presbyterian revivals in the middle colonies were strongly affected by the charismatic leadership of that denomination's ministers Gilbert, John, and William Tennent. They intimated that they bore special signs of divine favor or even supernatural possession. Gilbert Tennent described how his brother William had once been raised from the dead, and John Tennent was known for his frequent flights of ecstatic, mystical religiosity: "He often took the Bible in his hand, and walked up and down the room, weeping and moaning over it."

Despite the notoriety cast upon them by opponents, the eighteenth-century colonial religious revivals often were shortlived, tied to local circumstances, and modest in their social and political consequences. Upheavals and schisms, or splits, within churches occurred almost everywhere revivals appeared. In New England the revivals began in the 1730s and ended about 1750. They split the Congregationalists and Baptists into the "New Lights" who backed the revivals and the "Old Lights" who opposed them. English and Scottish Presbyterians carried on most of the revivals in the middle colonies, but the Baptists were almost completely unaffected by revivals in those colonies. These revivals split the middle colony Presbyterians, just as they had New England's Congregationalists and Baptists. Proponents of revivals walked out of the Synod of Philadelphia and formed a rival Synod of New York in 1745. The revivalists demanded higher standards for ministers in personal life and guarantees that their ministers were indeed "born again." Only moral and regenerate ministers could preach with conviction, they argued. The breach between the two synods was not healed until 1758.

Revivals in the southern colonies produced confrontations between the Church of England and evangelical Baptists and Methodists. Unlike revivals in most other colonies, those in Virginia and Maryland exploited social and political tensions in the colony. Baptists, and later Methodists, openly appealed to poorer, often illiterate farmers and to enslaved Africans. They directly attacked the Church of England, whose large, ornate churches by then symbolized the powerful status they had achieved in both colonies. In contrast, the Baptists and Methodists often preached outdoors or in private homes. Their crude, plain churches only heightened their differences with the Anglicans.

Women's roles changed in colonial religion as the denominations expanded and as revivalism rose and fell. These changes

were subtle rather than dramatic. But they held important implications for American religion well into the nineteenth century.
These changes quietly altered the overwhelming power of men
in colonial religion. In both the seventeenth and eighteenth centuries women could not be ordained as ministers in any colonial
religious group, and in all groups except the Quakers women
could conduct no formal meetings or hold regular offices in
colonial congregations and denominations. This meant that it
was extremely difficult for women to influence colonial congregational life directly in ways available to men. Such conditions
were not unexpected, because they paralleled women's status
in secular life. In the eighteenth century women could not
vote. Women lost their property rights when they married, and
women often had to have men manage property for them even
when they had inherited it or purchased it themselves.

One fact made women's situation in colonial religion
unusual, however: after 1680 women made up between 55 and
70 percent of the membership in most Congregational, Baptist,
and German Lutheran congregations and probably constituted
the majority of listeners in the remaining congregations. This
was true from New England to South Carolina and from east to
west. Just why women outnumbered men in the colonial congregations is not clear. One observation explains at least part
of the pattern, however: Women joined congregations at much
younger ages than men, often in their early twenties, while men
frequently delayed joining until their thirties and forties. As
a result, women sometimes outnumbered men two to one in
many colonial congregations.

Colonial Quakers and Baptists, however, gave women more
direct roles in their denominations and presaged the rise of
women's religious activity in nineteenth- and twentieth-century
America. The Quakers in England and America created special

women's meetings within their overall form of denominational government. They were the only English denomination to do so. It was the Quakers' theology that made this possible. George Fox, the founder of the Quaker movement, wrote that after the fall of Adam, "man was to rule over his wife." But "in the restoration by Christ," which the Quakers believed they were accomplishing, "they are help-meets, man and woman, as they were before the fall."

wow!

In this role as "help-meets," Quaker women regularly handled two important issues in their women's meetings: charity and marriage. The women's meeting made arrangements to take care of the elderly poor of both sexes, cared for widows, found homes for orphaned children, and gave cash to the destitute. They disciplined not only women members but men as well when they violated Quaker marriage regulations. In fact, most Quaker discipline cases focused on marriage to non-Quakers, or marrying "out of unity with Friends," as the Quakers put it. When these marriages reached epidemic proportions in Pennsylvania in the early 1750s, the women's and men's meetings cooperated to disown wayward Quakers. The women's meetings initiated the disownments, and the men's meetings reviewed and regularly upheld them. The Quaker women's meetings were not independent of the men's meetings, but the men's meetings recognized and honored the authority of the women's meetings. By the early nineteenth century, the women's meetings and the women who conducted them had become the foundations of an extraordinary activism among Quaker women that helped create the American tradition of social activism and humanitarianism.

charity & marriage

✱

The Baptists sometimes allowed women to vote in congregational matters, especially in New England and sometimes in Pennsylvania. "New Light" Baptist congregations formed in New England during the revivals of the 1730s and 1740s often

Baptist

allowed women members to vote on congregational affairs. In doing so, women spoke publicly about a variety of issues important to congregational life, including the disciplining of sinful members for sexual misconduct, "pridefulness," theft, and unorthodox preaching. Women also voted to help select ministers and participated in the process of the "washing of feet," a ritual adopted in some Baptist congregations to symbolize the equality of all believers.

When challenged, women defended their right to vote. Once, when men in the Philadelphia Baptist Congregation tried to prevent women from voting in congregational matters in 1764, the women responded vigorously. One of them, Joanna Anthony, wrote that if the women had "thought their privilege or their practices contrary to the word of God they would or ought to have kept themselves separate from them." For the moment, at least, Philadelphia's Baptist women retained their voting rights.

This Baptist experiment in congregational government did not last, however. After the American Revolution, Baptist congregations stopped allowing women to vote, perhaps because the Baptists became more conventional as they moved farther away from their eighteenth-century revivalist enthusiasm. Yet like the example of the Quakers, the mid-eighteenth-century Baptist example looked forward to greater women's activism and assertiveness in nineteenth-century American religion. Belief in the outright religious equality of men and women, symbolized in a willingness to ordain women to the ministry, did not occur until the late twentieth century in most American religious groups.

Women also played interesting, and sometimes vital, roles in other colonial churches where they could not vote or lacked special meetings. Their centrality in home life gave them important roles in funerals, baptisms, and weddings, many of which were performed in the home and were often managed by women, although men conducted the services. Women frequently managed the religious education of children, especially because there were no special services for children and the Sunday school would not be created until the 1820s. Finally, women were frequently extremely well informed on religious issues, and men and women often discussed religious issues in each other's company. Not all these conversations went well. Ann Carter sometimes so irritated her husband, a wealthy Virginia planter named William Byrd, with her contrary religious views that Byrd skipped his own nightly prayers when they argued.

Yet the predominance of women in most colonial congregations and the late age at which men joined congregations gave rise to two situations. Rightly or wrongly, men often thought of women as more "naturally" religious. And women persistently informed themselves on religion and theology despite their exclusion in most denominations from the pulpit and formal church business.

In all, the decades between 1680 and 1770 changed American religion in fundamental ways. The number of individual congregations greatly multiplied, and the various denominational institutions expanded. Revivals that were markedly different in theology and style tore some religious groups apart and thrust others into bitter interdenominational contests. While women lacked authority and power in most denominations, they continued to constitute a majority of church members in virtually all denominations. Within two denominations, the Quakers and Baptists, eighteenth-century women created important models for increased religious activity in the nineteenth century when women managed philanthropic and reform groups and demanded the right to preach. In these ways, the eighteenth century witnessed the birth of important distinctive traits—denominational aggressiveness, revivalism, and women's religious activism—that typified American religion in the next three centuries.

JONATHAN EDWARDS
ROUSES A CONGREGATION

Jonathan Edwards preached this sermon, "Sinners in the Hands of an Angry God," during a revival in Enfield, Massachusetts, in 1741. He sought to impress his listeners with a simple, terrifying idea: that only God and nothing else kept them from eternal damnation. The sermon was far more negative and frightening than any of Edwards's other sermons, but it has long been his most famous writing.

Natural men are held in the hand of God over the pit of hell; they have deserved the fiery pit, and are already sentenced to it; and God is dreadfully provoked, his anger is as great towards them as to those that are actually suffering the executions of the fierceness of his wrath in hell....

You probably are not sensible of this; you find you are kept out of hell, but don't see the hand of God in it, but look at other things, as the good state of your bodily constitution, your care of your own life, and the means you use for your own preservation. But indeed these things are nothing; if God should withdraw his hand, they would avail no more to keep you from falling, than the thin air to hold up a person that is suspended in it.

Your wickedness makes you as it were heavy as lead, and to tend downwards with great weight and pressure towards hell; and if God should let you go, you would immediately sink and swiftly descend and plunge into the bottomless gulf, and your healthy constitution, and your own care and prudence, and best contrivance, and all your righteousness, would have no more influence to uphold you and keep you out of hell, than a spider's web would have to stop a falling rock.

SARAH OSBORN LEADS
AFRICAN-AMERICAN RELIGIOUS REVIVALS

In the colonial period, very few women were allowed to exercise religious leadership in Christian congregations, although they usually made up 60 to 70 percent of the congregational membership. Sarah Osborn challenged this pattern in Newport, Rhode Island, in the mid-1760s. A white schoolteacher who supported her family when her merchant husband went bankrupt, Mrs. Osborn began leading religious "exercise" in 1766–67 among the town's numerous African slaves. Initially, she faced vigorous criticism for her work and acted cautiously to win support, as she reported in this letter to a supporter, Reverend Joseph Fish of Stonington, Connecticut. Within several months, Osborn, who was also leading religious meetings among Newport whites with as many as 500 people in attendance.

I will begin with the great [work] respecting the poor Blacks on Lord's day evenings, which above all the rest has been exercising to my mind. And first let me assure you sir, it would be the joy of my heart to commit it into superior hands did any arise for their help. My reverend pastor and brethren are my witnesses that I have earnestly sought, yea in bitterness of soul, for their assistance and protection. [I] would gladly be under inspection of pastor and church and turn things into a safe channel. O forever blessed be my gracious God that has Himself vouchsafed to be my protection hitherto by putting his fear into my heart and thereby moving me as far as possible in this suprising day....I only read to them, talk to them, and sing a psalm or hymn with them, and then at eight o'clock dismiss them all by name as upon list. They call it school, and I had rather it should be called almost any thing that is good than [the word] meeting, I [am so reluctant to be the] head of any thing that bears that name.... The poor creatures attend with so much decency and quitness you might almost hear as we say the shaking of a leaf when there is more than an hundred under the roof at once.

I know of no one in the town now that is against me.... Every intimate brother and friend intreats and charges me not to dismiss [the meetings] so long as things rest as they are, telling me it would be the worst days work that ever I did if I should, as God Himself has thus employed me. If any disturbance or disorder should arise either to the breaking of public or family peace, that would immediately make the path of duty plain for dismissing at once, but on the contrary ministers and magistrates send their servants and approve.

S. Osborn

February 28, 1767

CHAPTER SEVEN

Religion and the American Revolution

At its heart, the American Revolution was a profoundly secular event. The Declaration of Independence said little about religion. Instead, it discussed disputes over English parliamentary authority, the rights of colonial legislatures, and foolish mistakes made by English politicians.

Yet religion played interesting, occasionally surprising, and sometimes contradictory roles in the American Revolution. Moreover, the Revolution deeply affected religion in America far beyond 1776. By 1791, the first U.S. Congress passed the Bill of Rights, or the first ten amendments to the new federal Constitution, including the First Amendment, which prohibited any governmental establishment of religion and guaranteed freedom of worship in the new republic.

The First Amendment looked in two directions simultaneously. It confirmed the diverse and vigorous religious expressions created in the colonial period and guaranteed that government would not engage in religious activity itself. For the future, it freed religion from government, and government from religion, in unprecedented ways never proposed by any society, Old World or New.

Both paths were novel. Some people believed they were dangerous. But few doubted that they embodied the essence of colonial American religious development—the evolution of a lively, multifaceted, multiracial, multiethnic religious world brought forth mainly by independent groups and individuals rather than by the state.

Religion affected the American Revolution, but religion did not cause the Revolution. The Declaration of Independence, signed on July 4, 1776, best expresses the secular character of the Revolution. Religion entered into the Declaration only in the phrase "the laws of nature and nature's God," and in references to "Divine Providence" (on which Americans would rely for protection) and to "the Supreme Judge of the world" (who would judge the "rectitude of our intentions"). Nowhere did Thomas Jefferson, its principal author, refer simply to "God" alone or to Christ. He did not invoke Christian doctrine in support of the Revolution. Not a single religious issue found a place in the long "history of repeated injuries and usurpations" at the end of the Declaration where Jefferson described the misbehavior of the British.

This seeming omission is surprising, because at least one religious issue played an interesting role in fostering anti-English feeling in the colonies. This was the so-called bishop question. This term referred to a proposal made several times in the 1710s, the 1750s, and then again in the 1760s to name a bishop to preside over the Church of England in the colonies. The Boston Congregationalist minister Jonathan Mayhew preached against the appointment of an Anglican bishop in 1750. He stressed the danger of "imperious bishops" and used the word "tyranny" four or five times on a single page to describe Anglican intentions.

The controversy escalated in 1761, when a new Anglican minister in Cambridge, Massachusetts, built a large mansion for himself that was seemingly beyond the reach of a mere parish clergyman. Congregationalist opponents of the Church of England dubbed it the "bishop's palace." They claimed that the Anglicans were on the verge of naming a bishop who would destroy religious liberty, convene ecclesiastical courts to try colonists for religious offenses, and use government funds to promote Anglican causes. Actually, Anglicans sought the appointment of a "suffragan" bishop who, by law, could administer Anglican church matters but had no authority to convene ecclesiastical courts or exercise governmental power.

No Anglican bishop was ever appointed, but the "bishop question" became a part of anti-English agitation for the next decade. In 1763 and 1764, the possible appointment of an Anglican bishop joined colonial protests against stamps and taxes. In 1774, colonists linked the bishop question to protests against the Quebec Act in which the English government recognized the Catholic Church in the conquered French territories of Canada, where most settlers were Catholic. But in the old British mainland colonies, the Quebec Act conjured up fears that Catholics and a tyrannical Church of England would steal America's religious freedom.

The Boston silversmith and engraver Paul Revere graphically exploited these fears in a 1774 cartoon. In it, the Devil hovers over Anglican bishops and members of Parliament plotting to achieve their long-secret objective of catholicizing the American colonies. In fact, the bishop question became a major issue only in New England and New York. In other colonies, where the Anglican presence was larger, especially those from Maryland down to South Carolina, the bishop question held little interest. Delegates to the Continental Congress did not mention it in the Declaration of Independence adopted in July 1776.

Before the Revolution, religion reinforced popular arguments about the need for virtue and morality in society and politics. In politics, this was called Whiggism, because it overlapped the rhetoric of England's eighteenth-century Whig political party. Several important political tracts widely distributed in the colonies supported this view, especially *Cato's Letters*, written in the 1720s by two English authors, John Trenchard and Thomas Gordon.

A wide variety of colonial clergymen reinforced Whig political ideals. Throughout the eighteenth century, the public discussion of virtue and morality came most often from clergymen. Laymen and clergymen alike assumed that political liberty depended on having a virtuous public. The ministers emphasized virtue, responsibility, and the importance of moral choices. In doing so, they created important standards that colonists used to criticize English actions in the 1760s and 1770s.

For example, when the Maryland Anglican clergyman John Gordon preached against tyranny and in favor of virtue and morality in government in the mid-1740s, his text bristled with allusions to Whig political literature. Gordon and other clergymen from Massachusetts to South Carolina stressed the work necessary to sustain private morality and virtue in public life and politics. As Thomas Cradock, another Maryland Anglican minister, put it, "Virtue is a rich prey rescued narrowly out of the fire." Virtue had to be maintained by the "purchase of labor and sweat of care and vigilance. We are too liable to lose it by our own sloth and treachery."

These standards came into play even before the British began to tinker with the empire after 1763. Many colonists were repelled by the behavior of British "regulars" sent from

England to fight in the so-called French and Indian War of 1758–63. Colonial ministers were not silent on the topic. John Cleveland of Ipswich, Massachusetts, who served as a chaplain, or minister, to solidiers during the war, complained that "profane swearing seems to be the naturalized language of the regulars." Their "gaming, robbery, [and] thievery" epitomized the immorality and corruption that colonists feared was rampant in English society.

Between 1763 and 1776, especially in New England, some ministers discussed colonial politics and protests in their sermons as the level of colonial political protest escalated. A few ministers who supported the colonial cause argued that the colonists' own immorality brought them God's wrath in the form of English tyranny. One New England minister proclaimed that "it is for a people's sins when God suffers this evil to come upon them."

Other ministers supported the colonists more enthusiastically. The Massachusetts loyalist Peter Oliver laid the blame for New England's anti-British sentiment on "black coated mobs," clergymen who preached anti-English sermons from their tax-supported pulpits. One observer claimed that Philadelphia's ministers "thunder and lighten every sabbath" with anti-English sermons. The wealthy Virginia planter Landon Carter reported that his own Anglican parish minister, who might have been expected to support the Crown, exhorted listeners "to support their Liberties—and in the room of 'God save the king,' he cried out 'God preserve all the just rights and liberties of America.' "

But most colonial ministers remained silent about politics during the upheavals of the 1760s and 1770s. The Presbyterians exhibited a particularly mixed record on the Revolution. John Witherspoon, a Presbyterian minister who was president of the College of New Jersey (later renamed Princeton), wrote against the English and attended the Continental Congress as a delegate. Several other Presbyterian ministers also supported the colonists in the 1760s and 1770s and described the Revolutionary War as a battle between Christ and Antichrist, with Christ supporting the colonists, of course.

Yet most Presbyterian clergymen remained aloof from revolutionary fervor as late as 1775. The Synod of Philadelphia reflected their ambivalence about the war. The 1775 synod acknowledged that it was "well known...that we have not been instrumental in inflaming the minds of the people." Many of the ministers were Scots. They worried that any possible war would be like the bloody civil war that had ravaged Scotland in the 1740s, which they warned was "carried on with a rancor and spirit of revenge much greater than [wars] between independent states." Presbyterians expressed their "attachment and respect to our soverign King George" and to the "person of the prince." They believed he may have been misled in his actions toward the colonies. But they also rejected "such insults as have been offered to the sovereign" by many colonial protesters.

German Lutheran and Reformed clergymen in Pennsylvania also exhibited misgivings about the Revolution. They were a minority in the colony, and their occasional disputes with Pennsylvania's leading politicians, who now led anti-English protests, dampened their enthusiasm for independence. They also worried about the possible effects of the upheavals on both Christianity and America. In May 1775, the German Reformed Coetus, the organization of Reformed ministers, warned lay men and women about the "precarious times" in which they lived, "the like of which...has never been seen in America." In 1777, the Coetus still described the Revolution as a "sad war" that had uprooted "the keeping of the Sabbath day and Christian exercises in the families at home."

Open loyalism to the king was evident most obviously in the Church of England. Anglicans, both ministers and lay men and women, supported the Crown for the simplest of reasons: The king was the head of the church, and the church, like all other churches, had long taught obedience to constituted authority. Similar loyalism also cropped up among some New England Congregationalists and occasional Presbyterians and Baptists, although these expressions proved rare.

A second kind of loyalism stemmed from longstanding antagonism between dominant religious groups and minorities, especially in backcountry settlements. Scots and Scots-Irish Presbyterians in the western Carolinas, English Baptists in Virginia, German Lutherans and German Reformed groups in Pennsylvania, and Anglicans in New England all had experienced antagonism from the dominant religious groups in their regions. They often found the patriots' antiparliamentary protests hypocritical. Some groups, especially Virginia's Baptists, who had struggled for a decade with the colony's Anglican church, supported the Revolution nonetheless. But many of the others either remained neutral or openly supported the Crown.

Of course, most colonists supported independence. In doing so, religion followed politics rather than leading it. Yet religion offered important rhetoric in support of the Revolutionary cause. A New York Presbyterian, Abraham Keteltas, called the Revolution "the cause of heaven against hell." A South Carolina Baptist, Elhanan Winchester, described English actions as motivated by "Rome and Hell."

Some clergymen added a new dimension to Revolutionary rhetoric in the form of millennialism. Millennialist beliefs asserted Christ's imminent return to earth to carry out a thousand-year reign, and they had surfaced occasionally in the colonial period, especially in the revivals of the 1740s. But the political turmoil between 1763 and 1776 recharged these beliefs. According to this way of thinking, the Revolution was a matter of religious, not just secular, significance. One Connecticut clergyman, Ebenezer Baldwin, believed that Christ's return to earth was imminent and that the Revolution was "preparing the way for this glorious event." A New Hampshire minister thought the Revolution fulfilled certain second-coming predictions in the Old Testament book of Isaiah.

Most clergymen and lay men and women looked upon such beliefs with skepticism. Yet the rise of millennialist thinking during the Revolution had two important consequences. For one, it initiated a pattern common in American wars, from the Civil War to the Vietnam War, that associated God with America's cause. Secondly, it sometimes interpreted these wars as signs of Christ's return to earth. To some people these views demonstrated the Revolution's links to religion, even though only a tiny minority of Revolutionary-era Americans ever embraced millennialism.

The Revolutionary War proved difficult for some denominations. Predictably, the Church of England suffered the most. The colonial protests and the Revolutionary War destroyed the patient work that had enlarged the Anglican following in the previous century. About 75 percent of the Church of England congregations lost their clergymen. Anglican ministers in parish after parish left because they supported the Crown and could not endure continued abuse by local patriots. And the physical destruction loosed on Anglican churches was similar to that against Catholic churches in seventeenth-century Maryland. Revolutionaries ripped out royal coats of arms from the walls of many Anglican churches and murdered an Anglican minister in Rye, New York.

Baptists also experienced substantial problems during the Revolution. The war disrupted local congregational life and activity. In 1776, the Philadelphia Baptist Association counted forty-two congregations with 3,000 members. But in 1781, the association's rolls had declined to twenty-six congregations with only 1,400 members. Many congregations disbanded, and the surviving ones lost significant membership, with the average congregation declining from seventy-one to fifty-five members.

The Quakers split over the Revolution, especially in Pennsylvania. One group called the Free Quakers backed independence and rejected the traditional Quaker pacifism. Quaker leaders viewed the call to arms and the violence of the Revolution as abhorrent to Quaker principles. Friends found themselves hunted down in the very colony they had founded. In May 1776, a stone-throwing mob forced Philadelphia Quakers to observe a fast day declared by the Continental Congress. A patriot mob in Berks County shackled and jailed a Quaker preacher until he posted a $10,000 bond that guaranteed his "good" behavior, meaning that he would stop encouraging Quakers not to fight. Philadelphia leaders exiled seventeen Quakers to Virginia for two years so they would not interfere with revolutionary activities.

Presbyterians suffered at the hands of the British, who burned three Presbyterian churches in New York, two in Connecticut, and five in New Jersey, including the church led by pro-Revolutionary Presbyterian clergyman John Witherspoon. At Huntington, New York, English troops headquartered themselves in the local Presbyterian church and used tombstones as the floor for an oven that left funereal inscriptions on the bread they baked.

Even ministers who supported the Revolution bemoaned the immorality it seemed to foster. During the war years, the Synod of Philadelphia spoke of "gross immoralities," an "increasing decay of vital piety," a "degeneracy of manners," and a "want of public spirit." Baptists in Virginia, South Carolina, and New England decried what they saw as spreading sin and immorality amid the Revolution.

Revolutionary War chaplains frequently experienced highly mixed reactions to their work. Some chaplains found soldiers receptive to their preaching. Religious soldiers appreciated the chaplains' sermons in part because they were reminders of the spiritual rituals they knew at home. But other chaplains encountered apathy and even open rejection from their soldiers. "It don't seem like Sabbath day,...none seem to know or think any thing about it," wrote one chaplain near Albany, New York. A Rhode Island chaplain "made out miserably" when he preached to battle-weary wounded soldiers. A New England chaplain responded with resignation about his task: "Encourage [the soldiers] when doing their duty, attend and pray...with them when sick, and bury them when they die."

The difficulties many religious groups experienced during the Revolutionary War did not prepare Americans for the marked resurgence in religious activity that occurred after the war ended in 1783. All the denominations, including even the old Church of England, renewed themselves with remarkable vigor. America's religious groups saw their mission as even more important in the new republic than it had been in the old British empire. The freedom promised by independence required even more moral and spiritual guidance. The new republic depended by definition on "a virtuous people," a phrase that circulated throughout all forms of political discussion in the 1780s. Who better to create that "virtuous people" than America's religious denominations?

American religious groups acted quickly to support the new society and government as the patriots' success mounted despite earlier doubts about political revolution and the effects of war. Between 1783 and 1800, clergymen preached hundreds of sermons commemorating the war, praising America's soldiers, and directing its government toward moral and spiritual ends. Fasting and thanksgiving day sermons continued and even increased. Everywhere, ministers proclaimed the fusion that came out of American independence and organized religion, especially Christianity.

Denominational growth resumed after independence. The Presbyterian Synod of Philadelphia expanded from 153 to 215 churches between 1774 and 1788. The Baptists in South Carolina doubled their congregations between 1775 and 1790 and even experienced some congregational expansion during the Revolutionary War itself. In 1785, the Church of England became the Protestant Episcopal Church headed by a bishop elected by American ministers, who was loyal to America, not to England or the British king. Although internal squabbles and lingering resentment over Anglican opposition to independence slowed the Episcopalian recovery, under new leaders the church experienced substantial expansion after about 1810.

Catholicism and Judaism also expanded after the war. John Carroll of Maryland became "superior of the missions" in the former colonies in 1784, replacing London's Vicar Apostolate as the coordinator of Catholic efforts in America. In 1790, Carroll became the first Roman Catholic bishop in the United States, supervising some 65 congregations.

Jewish congregations also grew in number, but not always in size. The congregation in Newport, Rhode Island, declined as the city's economic fortunes withered. However, Jews in Savannah, Georgia, organized a congregation there in 1791, Jews in Philadelphia and Charleston built synagogues in those cities in 1782 and 1794, and New York's Jews reorganized their congregation in 1790 and rebuilt their synagogue in 1817.

The Methodists sustained unusually dramatic growth after the Revolutionary War. In the 1770s, the Methodist movement was seriously hobbled by the loyalist Toryism of John Wesley, its leader. Wesley, who firmly supported the king in the revolutionary struggle, recalled the Methodist preachers in the colonies to England, and all but one complied. Francis Asbury, however, continued preaching in the colonies and supported independence. After the war, Methodism boomed. New ministers arrived from England, others were recruited in America, and the Methodist "circuit" system managed by Asbury and others attracted thousands of new followers through highly coordinated preaching tours. In 1784 the Methodists had scarcely 15,000 followers. By 1790, the movement counted almost 60,000 members. By 1810, the Methodists had nearly 150,000 members.

Baptists became the largest single religious group in America after the Revolution. The Baptists never used the strong central organization that the Methodists perfected. Baptist congregations remained relatively independent, joined in loosely affiliated associations modeled on the Philadelphia Baptist Association formed in 1707. But like the Methodists, the Baptists also preached to poor whites and enslaved and free Africans. The fervency of the Baptists' modestly educated preachers, not their formal learning, drew extraordinary crowds. In turn, the Baptist associations quickly drew new congregations into their midst, secured pastors, and created a sense of belonging without imposing an overbearing, centralized church government. Baptist membership skyrocketed. The denomination numbered 35,000 members in 1784, 65,000 in 1790, and more than 170,000 in 1810.

The growth in church membership in the several decades after the Revolution signaled a slow rise in church membership in America that reached its peak in the twentieth century. As the Revolutionary era ended, probably no more than 20 percent of America's adults were church members, although occasional church attendance pushed contact with Christian congregations a little higher. Among whites, South Carolina had the highest rate of church membership; about a third of its white adults belonged to Christian congregations. The percentage of adult whites who were church members ranged from 10 percent in Vermont, the lowest, to about 20 percent, the average. The vast majority of enslaved and free African Americans belonged to no Christian congregation, but neither did most whites. This situation changed over the next two centuries. Denominational evangelizing initiated after the Revolution brought church membership in the United States to between 30 and 40 percent by the 1840s. This figure finally topped 50 percent sometime in the early twentieth century, then slowly climbed to about 65 percent in the 1950s, where it largely remained to the end of the twentieth century.

The involvement of government in religion declined as the denominations expanded. The experience of colonial religious diversity, the failures of the old religious establishments, the association of the Church of England with the king and Parliament, and the principles of the Declaration of Independence all encouraged Americans to rethink the relationship between government and religion as the Revolution proceeded. The old Anglican Church lost most in this reevaluation. Between 1776 and 1785 the legal establishments it had won eighty years earlier in colonies from New York to Maryland, Virginia, and North and South Carolina all collapsed.

Originally, the First Amendment, which banned any state-supported religion, applied only to the federal government. As a result, many states experienced important struggles over government establishment of religion in their own locales. New

England dissenters had earlier attacked the establishment of the Congregational Church in Massachusetts and Connecticut, but their battle against governmental involvement in religion generally took much longer. In part, this happened because the newly formed state legislatures removed some of the immediate discontent by exempting Presbyterians, Baptists, Quakers, and Episcopalians from parish church taxes. But the new constitution approved by Connecticut voters in 1818 eliminated the old church establishment. Massachusetts finally abolished its weakened religious establishment in 1833. As in Connecticut, it had become ineffective and stimulated endless lawsuits when established churches splintered and their members bickered over who would retain the church's tax revenues.

The most momentous contest over the establishment of religion occurred in Virginia between 1779 and 1785. This debate centered on two issues: "multiple establishment," or government support for several Protestant groups, and complete disestablishment. In 1779 and again in 1784, Virginia's proponents of multiple establishment, including some Presbyterians and the fiery Revolutionary leader Patrick Henry, introduced bills to provide government support and tax funds for several, but not all, Protestant groups. Henry and the supporters of multiple establishment also proposed limited freedom of worship for all those who recognized one God, believed in future punishment and reward, and supported public worship.

In contrast, Thomas Jefferson offered a bill in 1779 "for Establishing Religious Freedom." It prohibited tax levies for "any religious worship, place, or ministry whatsoever" and also upheld freedom of worship for all religious groups. As the act put it, "All men shall be free to profess, and by argument to maintain, their opinions in matters of religion." Both sides struggled over these issues from 1779 to 1785 without resolution.

A great public debate in 1784–85 effectively stopped the call for multiple establishment, prohibited direct government funding for religious activity, and promoted full religious freedom. James Madison vigorously attacked any government aid for religion in his famous petition "Memorial and Remonstrance against Religious Assessments," which he sent to Virginia's House of Burgesses in 1785. In it he called religion an "unalienable right" of each individual that no government could usurp. Petitions containing more than 10,000 signatures opposed multiple establishment and government aid to select Protestant groups. Baptists especially opposed government aid to religion. Rockbridge County, Virginia, petitioners argued that "religion and all of its duties...ought not to be made the object of human legislation." A Cumberland County petition argued that the early Christians had prospered "for several hundred years without the aid of a civil power" but that corruption had followed after Christianity became the official religion of the Roman Empire. What did this history teach? The Cumberland County petitioners had a simple answer: "Religious establishment has never been a means of prospering the Gospel."

The debate completely altered public opinion in Virginia. George Washington's turnaround symbolized the transformation. At first, Washington supported multiple establishment. He initially thought it was a fine idea to give government aid to some Protestant groups. But as the debate proceeded he changed his mind and turned against the proposal. Multiple establishment, Washington commented, seemed so innocuous and natural but would "rankle, and perhaps convulse the state." As a result, in 1786, the Virginia legislature rejected Patrick Henry's bill for multiple establishment. Overwhelming opposition to it came from Baptists, Methodists, Episcopalians, and some Presbyterians. The legislature then approved by a vote of 74 to 20

Thomas Jefferson's bill "for Establishing Religious Freedom." It outlawed government aid to religion and guaranteed freedom of worship to all religious in the state, not just Protestants or even Christians.

The Virginia debate speeded the decline of the multiple-establishment proposals that had at first seemed attractive in other states. South Carolina's 1778 constitution had authorized government aid to several Protestant groups. But its 1790 constitution abandoned multiple establishment and guaranteed "the free exercise and enjoyment of religious profession and worship, without discrimination or preference." Within a year, the state had chartered Charleston's Jewish congregation, Beth Elochim. Multiple-establishment bills failed in Georgia in 1782 and 1784. Government aid to several Protestant groups was approved in 1785 but was never implemented, and in 1789, a new Georgia constitution eliminated multiple religious establishment. The post-Revolutionary Maryland constitution permitted multiple establishment, but the state's legislature never approved such aid. It rejected funding for Protestant groups by a 2-to-1 margin in 1785 and in 1810 eliminated multiple establishment through an amendment to the state constitution.

In New Hampshire, government aid to local Protestant congregations slowly collapsed because of the local disputes it caused. By 1815, half the state's towns were no longer collecting taxes for religious congregations, and in 1819, the legislature repealed the statute allowing the remaining towns to do so. In this regard, then, the failure of Connecticut and Massachusetts to repeal their establishment of the Congregational Church until 1818 and 1833 remained exceptions to the larger post-Revolutionary trend in religion to reject government aid and involvement.

The Virginia debate also affected the First Amendment to the federal Constitution, passed in 1791. The First Amendment used only sixteen words to outline the relationship between religion and the new federal government: "Congress shall make no law respecting an establishment of religion, or prohibiting the free exercise thereof." Their meaning has, understandably, raised much debate over the years. In fact, the amendment reflected the nature of colonial American religious development even as it proposed an unprecedented course for society and religion in the new nation.

The First Amendment prohibited "an establishment of religion," not just of churches, by the new federal government. Commentators have long described the First Amendment as being about "church and state." Thomas Jefferson did so himself when he described the First Amendment as creating a "wall of separation between church and state" in a letter to the Danbury Baptist Association of Connecticut in 1802. But the First Amendment banned government activity in religion generally, not just the establishment of a national church. In debating the First Amendment, Congress specifically rejected changes that would have limited the amendment to issues such as "religious doctrine," "articles of faith or modes of worship," or merely prohibiting aid to "one religious sect or society in preference to others."

The First Amendment thus meant what it said and said what it meant. The federal government should not legislate on religious matters and should leave individuals alone in their pursuit of religion and religious truth. As Congressman Samuel Livermore of New York summarized the intentions of those who approved it, "Congress shall make no laws touching religion, or infringing the rights of conscience."

The First Amendment caught the essence of colonial America's religious development. It recognized the extraordinary, almost unimaginable diversity of religion that emerged in colonial America, a spiritual pluralism unlike that found in any society on either side of the Atlantic or Pacific. It guaranteed that government would not itself seek to change this diversity by intervening in religion or by supporting one or more religious groups. And it guaranteed that the federal government would uphold "free exercise" of religion for all groups, not just some.

No other government in Western civilization had ever before made such pledges. These pledges, together with the history of religion in the American colonies and the growth of religious diversity and activity in the next centuries, determined not only the health of religion in the United States but much about the character of its people.

During the political crisis with England between 1763 and 1776, some American ministers consistently supported the colonists' cause. Most, however, said nothing, and the Revolution split groups like the Quakers, some of whom abandoned their traditional pacifism to fight for independence.

In May 1775 Presbyterians who had gathered in their yearly synod or administrative council in Philadelphia devoted much of their annual "pastoral letter" to the dispute with England. The ministers concluded with a commitment to settling the dispute on "constitutional principles." But their experience in the 1740s with violent civil war in Scotland between Scots loyal to Britain and others supporting James II, the Catholic pretender to the Scottish throne, led the ministers to warn their congregations about the dangers and violence of the coming contest.

Very Dear Brethren:

The Synod of New York and Philadelphia... have long seen with concern, the circumstances which occasioned, and the gradual increase of this unhappy difference. As ministers of the gospel of peace, we have ardently wished that it could, and often hoped that it would have been more early accommodated. It is well known to you... that we have not been instrumental in inflaming the minds of the people, or urging them to acts of violence and disorder. Perhaps no instance can be given on so interesting a subject, in which political sentiments have been so long and so fully kept from the pulpit....

We think it of importance, at this time, to recommend to all of every rank, but especially to those who may be called to action, a spirit of humanity and mercy. Every battle of the warrior is with confused noise, and garments rolled in blood. It is impossible to appeal to the sword without being exposed to many scenes of cruelty and slaughter; but it is often observed, that civil wars are carried on with a rancour and spirit of revenge much greater than those between independent States. The injuries received, or supposed, in civil wars, wound more deeply than those of foreign enemies[;] it is therefore the more necessary to guard against this abuse, and recommend that meekness and gentleness of spirit, which is the noblest attendant on true valour. That man will fight most bravely, who never fights till it is necessary, and who ceases to fight as soon as the necessity is over....

We conclude with our most earnest prayer, that the God of heaven may bless you in your temporal and spiritual concerns, and that the present unnatural dispute may be speedily terminated by an equitable and lasting settlement on constitutional principles.

Signed in the name, presence, and by appointment of the Synod.
Benjamin Hait, Moderator.
New York, May 22d, 1775

RELIGION IN NINETEENTH-
CENTURY AMERICA

CHAPTER EIGHT

Prophets for a New Nation

My country, tis of thee, sweet land of liberty,
of thee I sing; land where my fathers died,
land of the pilgrims pride,
from every mountainside let freedom ring!
—*Samuel F. Smith, "America" (1832)*

Things looked grim. When the guns at the Yorktown, Virginia, battlefield fell silent in the fall of 1781, ending the Revolutionary War, the young nation found itself in disarray, as did its churches. At most, one person in ten, and perhaps only one in twenty, counted themselves a member of any organized religious body. Many ministers had abandoned their pulpits, either to serve as chaplains or to fight the enemy. Sometimes they battled as Tories, loyal to the British Crown, sometimes as patriots, and sometimes they refused to fight for either side, an independence for which they paid dearly. Revival meetings designed to rekindle religious zeal had flourished off and on for the better part of fifty years. Yet those too finally sputtered. For the past decade, people had been preoccupied first with political matters and then with the war for independence. Apathy reigned.

At the beginning of the war, many patriots believed that Christ himself would return to earth, first to defeat the British redcoats, and then to establish his reign of peace and righteousness for a thousand years. But now, with that hope dashed, what remained?

Things looked darker for some groups than for others. The Church of England, which had dominated the southern colonies and remained strong in the urban centers of the North, now faced the crisis of its life. Virtually all of its clergy outside New England had fled the country. Those who remained were now required by their vows to swear allegiance to the king. But how could they do so, since the colonies had just revolted from England and proclaimed themselves an independent nation? The Church of England eventually solved this problem by reorganizing itself in 1789 as the Protestant Episcopal Church in the U.S.A. But it would be many decades until that body would achieve the kind of strength and stability it had enjoyed before the Revolution.

The Methodists too faced hard times. They had started in England in the 1730s as a reform movement within the Church of England. Methodist preachers came to the colonies in the 1760s. There they tried to build their followers' enthusiasm in Church of England gatherings, just as they had done at home. But their founder, John Wesley, had strongly opposed the Revolution, making Methodist sympathizers in the colonies suspect at best. All but one of Mr. Wesley's preachers, as they were called, returned to England during the war.

Thus, after the Revolution the Methodists in the United States too faced a major decision. Should they just let their movement die? Ought they to try to carry on as a revival impulse in the crippled Church of England in America? Or should they form their own sect (upstart group)? The denomination's leaders, meeting in Baltimore on a wintry Christmas Eve in 1784, decided to embrace the last option: to form their own sect. The infant denomination, which they called the Methodist Episcopal Church, grew rapidly. Indeed, for most of the following century the new sect would rank as the largest Protestant body in the nation.

Most of the other major religious groups in the colonies also had to struggle to get back on their feet. The Congregationalists (or Puritans) and the Presbyterians did best, partly because they had supported the winning side during the Revolution. The Lutherans experienced more problems, for precisely the opposite reason: many had failed to support the patriots. And the Quakers, once very strong, faced even more severe problems. As pacifists, most had refused to fight at all. Many Americans doubted the Quakers' loyalty to the new nation and shunned them.

Altogether, then, great stretches of the religious landscape looked bleak: meeting houses destroyed, people apathetic, ministers gone, long-established denominations in disarray. The churches all found themselves wondering how to reorganize in the face of a new nation with new laws and new expectations.

But appearances proved to be deceiving. In fact, many found the prospects exhilarating. In 1782, for example, J. Hector St. Jean de Crèvecoeur, a French farmer in upstate New York, declared that the new land contained the embryos of all the arts, sciences, and ingenuity that flourished in Europe. In America one beheld "fair cities, substantial villages, extensive fields, an immense country filled with decent houses, good roads, orchards, meadows, and bridges, where an hundred years ago all was wild, woody and uncultivated!" This vision proved intoxicating: "[We] are the most perfect society now existing in the world." De Crèvecoeur summed up his feelings in words that would be quoted repeatedly by subsequent generations:

The American is a new man, who acts upon new principles; he must therefore entertain new ideas, and form new opinions. From involuntary idleness, servile dependence, penury, and useless labour, he has passed to toils of a very different nature.... This is an American.

This appreciative Frenchman perceived, albeit dimly, that the young nation was beginning to forge a dramatically new way to organize religion as part of its new independent identity. Today we take for granted that people may worship any time and anywhere they want as long as they do not disturb their neighbors. Or they may not worship at all, if they prefer. We also take for granted that the government will not help religious groups in any systematic or significant way, except for incidental help, such as, for instance, in putting out a fire. But in the 1780s and 1790s, religious liberty and the separation of church and state were largely new ideas in the Western world. How did this immense change come about?

Most of the colonies assumed that everyone living in a given colony should belong to the same religious tradition. They also assumed that this tradition should receive support from the state, either through tax money or through laws forcing people to attend the primary church, or both. This arrangement was called the established religion. Even Pennsylvania and Maryland, two colonies that had allowed substantial religious freedom in the beginning, presented a mixed record regarding religious tolerance. At one time or another Roman Catholics found themselves barred from public office in both places.

By the time of the Revolution the idea of having one established religion had come under sharp criticism. Thoughtful men and women raised three arguments against it. Thomas Jefferson, author of the Declaration of Independence, governor of Virginia, and the third president of the United States, offered the first one. Jefferson insisted that people should be free to choose their own religion, or no religion at all, just as they should be free to choose where they lived or what kind of job they held. Freedom of religion was a natural right, he argued, one that people held simply because they were human. Besides, Jefferson added, what people imagine to be true about God does no harm one way or another. "[I]t does me no injury for my neighbor to say there are twenty gods, or no god. It neither picks my pocket nor breaks my leg." Coercion by the state in matters of religion simply did not work, he said. The result was "to make one half the world fools, the other half hypocrites."

The second argument against established religion found a strong voice in Isaac Backus, a Baptist pastor in Massachusetts in the Revolutionary era. Backus believed that it was not fair for the government to support one religious group but not others. It was not the government's job to decide which one was right, he argued. And supporting all the different religious groups would not solve the problem either. Backus worried that state support for religion would do more harm than good. When Christians (or anyone else, for that matter) took money from the state for the support of their churches, sooner or later they would have to pay the price.

To be sure, the Baptists worried about the prevalence of "Gaming, Dancing, and Sabbath-Day Diversions," as one of their opponents put it. But the Baptists felt that government coercion offered no solution. Backus himself paid a steep price for his views. The authorities repeatedly fined and jailed him for refusing to pay taxes that would go to the support of a rival group. But Backus's ideas gradually won wide respect. Later generations would regard him as a lonely pioneer of the Baptist conscience in America.

James Madison voiced the third argument against establishment. Madison followed Thomas Jefferson as president. Though only a wisp of a man and constantly worried about his health,

Madison exerted immense influence upon American religion. He believed that the young nation had become too diverse for the government to support one religion over another. Things might be different if everyone held the same views, he supposed, but in fact they did not. The young republic harbored dozens of competing sects, each jostling the others for a place in the new American sun. Madison's position might be called the practical argument against established religion: it just did not work.

In the 1780s, these three reasons for opposing a religious establishment—reasons based on principle, on conscience, and on practicality—flowed together and informed the writing of the Constitution and the First Amendment. (Madison served as the main author of both.) Article 6 of the Constitution states that "no religious Test shall ever be required as a Qualification to any Office of public Trust under the United States." The Constitution does not mention God or say anything else directly about religion, thus making it one of the most secular (nonreligious) documents of the modern world.

Madison and the other signers of the Constitution did not mean to say that religion was unimportant. What they sought was to remove religion from national politics. They tried to say, in other words, that religion was one thing, politics another, and people should not mix them up. The First Amendment to the Constitution, ratified in 1791, contained the following words about the federal government's relation to religion: "Congress shall make no law respecting an establishment of religion, or prohibiting the free exercise thereof." This sentence aimed to reinforce the main point of article 6 in the Constitution: that government should stay out of the religion business, neither helping nor harming the religious institutions of the land.

But there was more to the story. Although the founders did not want the federal government to help religion in formal or official ways, they had no qualms about its rendering incidental assistance, and they certainly saw no reason that government officials should hide their personal commitments. President George Washington, for example, set aside November 26, 1789, as a national day of prayer, repentance, and thanksgiving to God. John Adams, the second president, continued Washington's prayer day tradition. Adams boldly called himself a "church-going animal," and in his inaugural address specified a "decent respect for Christianity" as a recommendation for public service.

Jefferson, the third president, not only attended church regularly while president but also generously supported the construction of meetinghouses of various sects in the Washington area. For more than a half century, from 1800 through the 1860s, believers regularly used the House of Representatives for worship. Episcopalians, Congregationalists, Baptists, Methodists, Quakers, Unitarians, and even Catholics each had their turn. Throughout the period, other federal buildings also saw use for worship, including the sacrament of Holy Communion and old-fashioned revival services.

The Constitution and the First Amendment applied only to the federal government, however, leaving the states free to do as they wished regarding the establishment of religion. Some people worried that the federal government might be making a terrible mistake. Connecticut, New Hampshire, and Massachusetts thus continued to support the Congregational church with tax money for many years: Connecticut until 1818, New Hampshire until the following year, and Massachusetts until 1833. Patrick Henry, the Revolutionary War orator who won lasting fame for his "Give me liberty or give me death" speech, wanted his beloved Virginia to continue to support all religions equally. South Carolina even wrote that aim into its constitution.

But most Americans disagreed. Virginia, the home of Jefferson and Madison, moved swiftly to eliminate state support for religion, abolishing taxes for the livelihood of the clergy in 1776 and guaranteeing religious freedom for everyone nine years later. Sooner or later most of the other states followed Virginia's path, sometimes grudgingly, at other times eagerly. The invigorating breeze of political liberty inspired them to desire religious liberty as well.

The closing years of the eighteenth century saw the birth of another pattern that remains strong today. That trend went by various names. Some philosophers called it political religion. Benjamin Franklin dubbed it "Publick Religion." After World War II many called it civil religion. By whatever name, political or public or civil religion stemmed from a desire to give religious meaning to the nation itself. It represented more than patriotism or love of country. Rather, it symbolized a desire to place the United States in a larger framework of significance, an attempt to say that America occupied a special or even unique place in God's plan for the world. In civil religion, in other words, religious language blurred with political language so that the two became almost indistinguishable.

Even today, civil religion hangs in the atmosphere like a fine mist. We pledge allegiance to the flag (a political statement) but, in the same breath, go on to say that the nation stands "under God" (a religious statement). Memorial Day and the Fourth of July are more than political celebrations. They prompt bowed heads and moist eyes as flags flutter over courthouses and churches alike. Each year thousands of tourists file past the looming statue of Abraham Lincoln at his memorial in Washington, D.C. They whisper, with caps removed, as if they were in a cathedral. We treat some political figures, especially in death, as if they were saints. Abraham Lincoln and

John F. Kennedy come to mind. At the same time, we permit some religious figures to speak about political matters with the authority of Old Testament prophets. Consider, for example, Martin Luther King, Jr., and Billy Graham. In sum, in the United States, church and state have been legally separated for some 200 years. But in practice our national civil religion short-circuits that arrangement. Going to church is optional; honoring the flag is not.

In the young republic, two streams flowed together to form the broad river of civil religion. Historic Christianity was one of them. Delegates to the Constitutional convention spent six years trying to come up with a design for the Great Seal of the United States by using images from the Old and New Testaments. Benjamin Franklin (who was not a Christian by any conventional definition of the term) wanted the seal to depict Moses dividing the Red Sea. Jefferson wanted it to show the Israelites trekking through the wilderness.

The other stream of the religious tradition was the religious and cultures of ancient Greece and Rome. The architectural style of Greek and Roman temples turned up everywhere in the new republic, especially in the bustling new town of Washington, D.C. Thus John Adams wanted the Great Seal to bear a Roman image of the god Hercules torn between Virtue (pointing upward) and Sloth (aimed downward).

The design on an early dollar bill offered a clear example of the way that Christian and classical (Greek and Roman) themes entwined. One side of the design displayed a pyramid with an eye at the top. Latin inscriptions stood above and below the pyramid. One said "Annuit Coeptis" (He has ordered our way): in other words, God Himself would guide the new nation. The other read "Novus Ordo Seclorum" (New order of the ages): in other words, the young republic would mark the beginning of a fresh age of human history. This hope stemmed from the New Testament Book of Revelation, but also from the Greek and Roman notion that history ran in cycles. Thus, the American experiment represented the rebirth of the beauty and advanced civilization of ancient Greece and Rome.

The twisting of Christian and classical strands found its clearest expression in the veneration bestowed upon President George Washington. During his lifetime people clamored for locks of his hair, named babies after him, and spoke of his uncanny abilities as a military general. In 1779, twenty years before his death, a Pennsylvania German–language almanac called him the father of the country. People duly noted that Washington's mother was named Mary and his wife Martha. Could these names, which loomed large in the New Testament stories about Jesus, be a mere coincidence? Americans likened him to Moses, who had freed the Israelites from slavery, and to Joshua, who had fought bravely for the Lord. At the same time, they also compared Washington to the Roman military general Cincinnatus, who preferred farming to fighting. After the president's death, people solemnly noted that an eagle, the national bird, had flown over his tomb. And when Washington's body was moved in 1837 to a new marble coffin, reports said that the body showed almost no decay.

The theory and practice of civil religion waxed and waned throughout the nineteenth century. It proved to be particularly conspicuous in times of war or national stress when the people needed assurance that their nation was favored by the Almighty. The esteem bestowed upon the fallen—some said martyred—President Lincoln in 1865 rivaled the attention given Washington and many of the saints of the church. It was no accident that some of the songs Americans came to love best—"America," "The Battle Hymn of the Republic," and "America the

Beautiful"—mixed religious and patriotic themes line by line. (Indeed, Samuel F. Smith, a Baptist pastor in New England, penned the first in 1832, Julia Ward Howe, a Unitarian activist and abolitionist, dashed off the second in 1861, and Katherine Lee Bates, daughter of a Congregationalist minister, wrote the last in 1904.)

After the Revolution, many Americans not only embraced civil religion but also resisted traditional forms of authority, especially the oppressive weight of historic Christianity. Today television evangelists commonly talk about the deep Christian faith of the founding fathers. In truth, most of those preachers would almost certainly be horrified if any of the first four Presidents of the United States—Washington, Adams, Jefferson, or Madison—turned up in their congregations and said what they really thought about Christianity. All were courageous and high-minded men, but none was a Christian in any conventional way.

Consider George Washington. The first president believed in a creator God, held the Bible in high esteem, and respected the teachings of Jesus. He served as a leader in his local Episcopal church and went out of his way to show respect for Christianity in public. When he first took the oath of office, for example, he laid his hand on a Bible and added "So help me God," a practice followed by all subsequent presidents. But Washington always referred to God in distant, impersonal terms such as Providence, Almighty Being, Great Author, or Invisible Hand. He worshiped irregularly, rarely took Holy Communion, refused to kneel to pray, and regarded Jesus as a fine man but did not consider him divine. Privately, Washington probably remained skeptical about the main doctrines of Christianity.

Thomas Jefferson proved to be even more radical about religion than Washington. Like Washington, Jefferson believed that a supreme God existed and that Jesus' ethical teachings offered useful guidelines for daily life. He never disparaged religion in public. Jefferson defended the doctrine of the strict separation of church and state because that arrangement allowed citizens to worship or not worship as they pleased. But his God was tangible, like the deities of pagan Greece and Rome. The miracles attributed to Jesus struck Jefferson as so absurd that he went to the trouble of putting together his own version of the New Testament, popularly called the Jefferson Bible, with all the supernatural elements scissored out. The Virginian's strongest grievance, however, was not against Christian doctrine but against Christian priests and ministers. He felt that they persuaded people to "give up morals for mysteries" and that they took advantage of people by cheating them of their hard-earned dollars.

The ideas of individuals like Washington and Jefferson often received the label Deism, which might be defined as the belief that God created but did not involve himself in the world thereafter. How common was Deism? The short answer is, not very. In matters of religion, the founders spoke for an influential and well-educated elite, but not many others. Even so, they merit study, since they shaped the church-state patterns of the young republic. Those patterns persist today remarkably intact.

At the beginning of the nineteenth century, another group of antitraditionalists won more support, especially among the college educated and the rising middle class. They called themselves Unitarians. The creed of the Unitarians, outsiders quipped, affirmed the fatherhood of God, the brotherhood of man, and the neighborhood of Boston. The quip held considerable truth, for the Unitarians did believe in God's essential unity. For them, Jesus Christ ranked high as a uniquely moral man, possibly even divine in some sense, but not equal to God the father. The Holy Spirit referred not to the third person of the Trinity but to God's actions in history.

Unitarians also thought that humans, who were born without original sin, could learn to live productive lives through education. With effort and foresight human history could become a story of moral progress rather than an unending cycle of war and suffering. As for Boston, most Unitarians did in fact live in New England, and many attended or taught at Harvard, but their ideas extended far and wide. Unitarian ideas powerfully stirred nineteenth-century writers such as Henry David Thoreau (author of *Walden*) and Ralph Waldo Emerson (who wrote *Nature*), as well as reformers like Dorothea Dix (who helped establish asylums for the insane) and Julia Ward Howe (who fought slavery).

Other Americans forged their own nontraditional paths to religious truth. The Secret Society of Freemasons, commonly known as the Freemasons, or just Masons, provided one of the most common options. The Masons traced their origin to ancient Egypt, symbolized by the pyramid on the dollar bill. That notion reflected mostly wishful thinking, but it offered the security of connecting Americans with a source of wisdom in the distant past. The Masons actually started in England in the twelfth century as an all-male fraternity of craftsmen. The first Masonic lodge in the colonies opened in Philadelphia in 1731. Rapid growth followed. Almost all the signers of the Declaration of Independence were Masons, as were many members of the Continental Congress.

Masonry (and hundreds of similar orders, such as the Odd Fellows, Knights of Pythias, and Prince Hall Masons) flourished in the nineteenth century, among blacks as well as whites. They offered men a form of fellowship different from ordinary religion, one rich with rituals, special clothes, and secret passwords. The Masons emphasized brotherhood and fair dealing. While some embraced Christianity, many others felt that people should outgrow that religion in favor of a more rational and useful one like theirs. The Masons saw God as a grand architect who designed the universe according to natural law. Their symbols centered upon the carpenter's square and the compass, building tools that suggested firmness of character (square dealing) and high ideals (aiming high, as the compass pointed toward the sky). Just as the sun provided light for the physical universe, reason, the internal sun, supplied light to the human universe. Thus the eternal eye of God, symbolizing reason, peered from the top of the pyramid on the dollar bill.

Many citizens of the new republic who resisted traditional Christianity still considered themselves Christians. Jefferson, for example, called himself a Christian to the end. Many Masons attended their own lodge meetings on Saturday, then church on Sunday. Beyond these patterns, thousands of rank-and-file Christians perpetuated the religious practices of their ancestors. They used divining rods to find water, amulets to ward off evil spirits, and special potions to stir affection in the opposite sex. They consulted the stars to learn their future. They sought to heal through the use of white magic and to curse through the use of black magic (terms that may have held racial overtones). Some clergymen worried about all this mixing and matching, but most ordinary people thought nothing of it.

Most importantly, as the eighteenth century slipped into the nineteenth, thousands of Americans drifted away from traditional Christianity simply because it no longer met their needs. In the minds of many, the two largest and strongest groups before the Revolution, the Congregationalists (the Puritans) and the Church of England (the Anglicans), left much to be desired. The former seemed to overstress God's arbitrariness and the importance of a well-educated clergy. The latter seemed to overemphasize hierarchies, creeds, and liturgies.

But did that kind of religion—starchy and intellectual—represent the true message of the New Testament? Or was God's grace available to any who asked for it? Could ordinary people read the Bible for themselves and decide what it meant? Should not worship lead to heartfelt conversion and a morally rigorous life? Millions who answered these questions affirmatively drifted from the older groups. They joined new ones—new in the United States, anyway—that called themselves Baptists and Methodists and Disciples of Christ. By the opening of the Civil War, the upstarts had come to reign as the new religious insiders.

Thomas Jefferson, the third president of the United States, believed that men and women should be free to select their religious beliefs without interference, let alone coercion, from the government. He made this point often, but nowhere more forcefully than in his only book, Notes on the State of Virginia (1785).

The legitimate powers of government extend to such acts only as are injurious to others. But it does me no injury to say that there are twenty gods, or no God. It neither picks my pocket nor breaks my leg.... Reason and free inquiry are the only effectual agents against error.... It is error alone which needs the support of government. Truth can stand by itself.... [Is] uniformity of opinion desirable? No more than of face and stature.... Is uniformity attainable? Millions of innocent men, women, and children, since the introduction of Christianity, have been burnt, tortured, fined, imprisoned; yet we have not advanced one inch towards uniformity. What has been the effect of coercion? To make one half the world fools, the other half hypocrites.... Reason and persuasion are the only practicable instruments. To make way for these, free inquiry must be indulged; and how can we wish others to indulge it while we refuse it ourselves[?]

CHAPTER NINE

Awakeners of the Heart

Just as I am, without one plea,
but that thy blood was shed for me,
and that thou bidst me come to thee,
O Lamb of God, I come, I come.

    —*Charlotte Elliott, "Just as I Am, Without One Plea" (1835)*

The first half of the nineteenth century witnessed the dramatic expansion of a religious movement that had started a hundred years earlier in England and Scotland. Its supporters called it evangelicalism. The word *evangelical* came into the English language from Greek and Latin terms that meant messenger of good news, or gospel. And good news it was. Evangelists spread the word that Christ's death and resurrection had freed sinners from their shackles and reconciled them to God. They preached this message in meetings called revivals, where they proclaimed that believers' flagging faith could be revived to vigorous new life. The evangelical stirring would rank as the largest, strongest, most sustained religious movement in U.S. history.

In America revivals began in a serious way with the preaching of English itinerant George Whitefield in the 1730s and 1740s. Commonly called the Great Awakening, these revivals sputtered out during and after the Revolutionary War years, but then reappeared at the end of the century and persisted off and on through the 1830s. They cropped up again just before the Civil War and ran until its end in 1865. Later observers would call the entire era, running for the better part of seventy years, the Second Great Awakening (to distinguish it from the Great Awakening of the 1730s and 1740s). It would be inaccurate to suppose that everyone in antebellum (pre–Civil War) America considered themselves evangelicals, let alone supporters of revivals. But never again would a single religious outlook come so close to defining what it meant to be an insider in U.S. culture.

The Great Awakening and the Second Great Awakening bore important similarities, and one major difference. Both emphasized the authority of the Bible, a definable conversion experience based upon faith in Jesus Christ, and the importance of spreading the good news to others. But in the first Great Awakening men and women seemed to think and speak in the passive mood, as if to underscore God's action upon them. They saw themselves so hopelessly mired in sin that they could not even reach out to accept God's offer of grace. In dramatic contrast, the preachers of the Second Great Awakening routinely suggested that God had already given sinners the ability to accept grace when he offered it. It was up to them to take it or not. In the rough-and-tumble setting of nineteenth-century America, this message of human ability proved to be a spark in a powder keg.

The new revival began at roughly the same time, but in two different places. The first was in the Old Southwest, defined in those days as what is now Kentucky and Tennessee. Presbyterian pastor James McGready kindled the excitement. In 1797,

McGready started praying fervently for the conversion of sinners in south-central Kentucky, where he lived. In the summer of 1800, scores of anxious men and women gathered outdoors to hear him speak. After four days of white-hot preaching, some of McGready's hearers nearly collapsed as they felt the weight of their sins. This pattern of coming together for days or even weeks for outdoor revivals—called camp meetings—resembled similar events that took place each fall in Scotland, but in the United States they proved to be more intense. One of the largest camp meetings in U.S. history soon followed. In August 1801, throngs of seekers gathered on a bluff called Cane Ridge, several miles northeast of Lexington. Estimates ranged from 10,000 to 25,000 souls. At the time Lexington itself numbered only 2,000 residents.

The Cane Ridge Revival, as it came to be known, is probably the most famous religious meeting in American history. Stirred by days of intense preaching, people responded with deep emotion. Observes noted that some worshippers wept uncontrollably while others appeared to laugh, twitch, and run in circles. Some even fell to their knees and barked like dogs. (At the time, outsiders called these actions "exercises." Today scholars call them trances, or involuntary motor behavior, a situation in which the brain loses control of the muscles under extreme stress.)

One observer described another outdoor meeting, also near Cane Ridge:

Some [said] they feel the approaching symptoms by being under deep conviction; their heart swells, their nerves relax, and in an instant they become motionless and speechless.... It comes upon others like an electric shock, as if felt in the great arteries of the arms or thighs.... The body relaxes and falls motionless; the hands and feet become cold, and yet the pulse is as formerly.... They are all opposed to any medical application.... They will continue in that state from one hour to 24.

Soon hundreds of camp meetings of varying length and intensity erupted in the thinly settled territory beyond the Appalachians. Initially, well-schooled Presbyterians like McGready, as well as Baptist farmer-preachers and Methodist circuit riders, worked side by side to keep them going, but after a few years only Methodists participated. And by the 1820s even the Methodist camp meetings had toned down. After the Civil War, the Methodists set aside permanent sites—such as Round Lake in upstate New York, Martha's Vineyard in Massachusetts, and Ocean Grove in New Jersey—for annual religious encampments in pleasantly rustic settings. Although most people attended camp meetings primarily for religious reasons, many came for friendship and recreation as well.

The fires of the Second Great Awakening also burned brightly in the East, especially in the Congregational churches of southern New England. Yale College president Timothy Dwight took the lead. Dwight was no stranger to the revival tradition, for his grandfather, Jonathan Edwards, had led the first Great Awakening in Massachusetts. Dwight grieved deeply over the lack of faith among Yale's students. He was determined to stamp out infidelity through heartfelt preaching about the perils of unbelief, and about Christ's love for wayward humans. The college president's fervor soon sparked revivals in local churches up and down the East Coast.

Others who promoted the revival in the churches of the East included two of Dwight's students, Lyman Beecher, the father of Harriet Beecher Stowe, author of *Uncle Tom's Cabin*, and Yale theologian Nathaniel W. Taylor. Bucking centuries of tradition, Beecher and Taylor suggested that human beings, though deeply sinful, nonetheless possessed the ability to accept God's grace, if they would only do so.

Then came two of the most energetic and gifted figures in the history of American religion: Francis Asbury and Charles Grandison Finney. The former labored almost everywhere except New England, the latter mostly in the urban centers of the Northeast. Though Asbury was a Methodist and Finney a Presbyterian (later a Congregationalist), together they effectively defined the evangelical tradition in antebellum America.

The new land to the west offered Asbury a majestic stage for displaying his envangelical talents. Born in England in 1745, Asbury, like his parents, cast his lot with John and Charles Wesley, the founders of Methodism. He volunteered for service in the American colonies in 1771. In sharp contrast to virtually all Protestant clergy of the time, who married and settled down in a particular place, Asbury insisted that Methodist ministers must not marry. Instead he expected them to travel from meeting to meeting along a prescribed route as long as the Lord gave them strength to do so. (The Methodists developed their own vocabulary. They called this pattern *itinerating* to *charges* along a *circuit* by a *circuit rider*.)

Asbury himself set the example that would be emulated by thousands of nineteenth-century circuit riders. The Bishop, as many called him, traveled by horseback, incessantly—in heat and cold, rain and snow—disregarding illness and pain. By the end of his life, he had ridden nearly 300,000 miles, crossing the Appalachians more than sixty times and even penetrating into Canada. Some said that Asbury had seen more of the North American continent than any other person of his generation.

Besides carrying the gospel to thousands in backwoods areas of the young republic, Asbury became the prime spokesman for the developing theology of Methodism in the United States.

Like most nineteenth-century revivalists, he insisted that God gave all people the ability to accept God's grace. But he especially emphasized what he saw as the tender, almost mystical, relation between the believer and Christ. Following the model established by John Wesley, Asbury imposed high standards upon converts, prohibiting them from indulging in alcohol and tobacco, and he challenged their growing acceptance of slavery. Most importantly, Asbury, again like Wesley, displayed a clear sense of the importance of good organization. He insisted that power in the church should flow from the top down, not the reverse, as the Baptists and others affected by democratic ideals imagined. Thus Asbury, always the Bishop, sent circuit riders where he thought they were needed, when he thought they were needed, when he needed, with no questions asked. These riders gathered converts into small groups known as classes, defined by age and sex, for worship and mutual support. Classes in turn formed societies, or what other evangelical Protestants called congregations. Even on the frontier, strong organization counted.

The disciplined army of circuit-riding preachers Asbury recruited and dispatched into the seeming wilderness earned a permanent place in the mythology of the American West. Peter Cartwright, for example, stamped his mark on an Illinois circuit with his rough-tongued sermons and willingness physically to pick up and toss out hecklers. When a Presbyterian pastor complained that Cartwright had no right to invade his territory, Cartwright shot back: "I told him the people were a free people and lived in a free country, and must be allowed to do as they pleased." Methodists believed in order, but they also believed that people had a right to choose.

With typical brashness Cartwright ran for Congress in 1846 against an obscure politician named Abraham Lincoln.

The preacher lost, but the Methodists won. By the end of the Civil War the once-tiny sect of Methodists had swollen into the largest Protestant denomination in the United States, more than one million strong. The Methodists would proudly hold that place until they finally dropped behind the Baptists at the turn of the twentieth century.

Asbury's near-contemporary, Charles Grandison Finney, led the Second Great Awakening in the Northeast through the 1820s and 1830s. He shouldered the burden of keeping the revival going in the 1820s after Timothy Dwight had passed from the scene. Finney's parents, like thousands of other New England Yankees, had migrated to upstate New York at the beginning of the nineteenth century. There they reared Finney in a Presbyterian church. In keeping with that denomination's literate tradition, the young Finney studied to practice law. However, he underwent a life-transforming conversion experience in 1821 while reading the Bible in a wooded meadow. Finney later said that he gave up the law because he had received "a retainer from the Lord Jesus Christ to plead his cause." With the help of a local pastor the young preacher taught himself the basics of Puritan theology, though by his own admission he never worried too much about the fine points of it. He soon started preaching in the small towns dotting the Mohawk Valley and then in the larger cities of the region, including Rochester, Rome, and Utica. Eventually Finney settled in Oberlin, Ohio (near Cleveland), where he taught theology and later served as president of the new Oberlin College.

Finney proved to be notable for several reasons. Like the Wesleys and Asbury, he emphasized the sinner's ability simply to accept God's offer of grace. But more than the others he also stressed the innate ability of men and women to choose good over evil. If they did not, he argued that they should be held responsible. Beyond this insistence, Finney underscored Christians' obligation to consecrate their lives to Christ so fully that they no longer consciously desired to sin. He and others (especially at Oberlin) called this state Christian perfection. They did not mean by it that people would actually be sinless, let alone free of mistakes, but they did mean that perfected Christians would desire to please God over themselves. Finney also earned lasting fame for introducing "New Measures" into revivalism. These New Measures included allowing women to testify (though not to preach) in church, nightly meetings for praise and preaching, and the "anxious bench," a place set aside near the front of the meeting house where sinners could give their lives to Christ.

Like Asbury, Finney stressed the importance of an upright life and of avoiding tobacco, alcohol, dancing, and other recreational activities that might lead to trouble. And Finney, like Asbury, also harbored deep concerns about slavery. Although he did not endorse the views of abolitionists, who seemed extreme at the time, he urged white Christians to find every way possible within the law to restrict the growth of slavery and bring it to an end. Under his administration, Oberlin stood out as the first U.S. college to admit women and blacks. This evangelist did not endorse the formal ordination of women, but he supported women's right to speak in public settings. Each of his three wives (the first two died during his lifetime) distinguished themselves as eloquent proponents of evangelical Christianity, both writing and speaking for the cause. Finney was also an innovator in education. He led the move to drop lectures in favor of class discussion, and urged students to break up the tedium of homework assignments by chopping wood and planting crops.

Unlike the fiery and often unlettered pulpit thumpers of the western camp meetings, as a preacher Finney did not raise his voice or gesture wildly. Tall and physically imposing, he spoke directly, using metaphors drawn from everyday events, especially farm life. He never aimed primarily to arouse his hearers' emotions (although that happened sometimes). His goal rather was to persuade people rationally to confess their sins and embrace Christ's forgiveness. More importantly, he remained convinced that revivals could be cultivated by careful planning. There was nothing miraculous about them, if by miracle one meant "suspending the laws of nature." On the contrary, said Finney in a famous lecture titled "What a Revival of Religion Is," revivals "consist entirely in the *right exercise* of the powers of nature." They resulted from "the right use of the constituted means—as much so as any other effect produced by the application of means."

In later years, Finney tempered this view, allowing more leeway for divine influence. But his earlier insistence upon human preparation for revivals stuck in the public mind. By the end of his life, Finney had influenced the shape of American religion more than any person since the mid-eighteenth-century leaders John Wesley and Jonathan Edwards.

At this point it may be helpful to pause and think about the major denominational families of the age. Recall that McGready was a Presbyterian, Dwight a Congregationalist, Asbury a Methodist, and Finney a Presbyterian turned Congregationalist. Fortunately, this sequence is not as confusing as it may seem. By the beginning of the nineteenth century the Presbyterians and Congregationalists had grown virtually identical and, in many places, they simply merged. The Methodists (commonly nicknamed Wesleyans after their founders, the brothers John and Charles Wesley) shared many of the Presbyterian-Congregationalists' basic assumptions. Even so, the Methodists placed more emphasis upon human freedom and on the authority of their bishops. And on the whole, Methodists proved to be more sympathetic to emotional worship and were perhaps less well educated than their Presbyterian-Congregational rivals. At the turn of the century all three groups spearheaded the evangelical revivals. But as the nineteenth century progressed, a new group of enthusiasts, who had originated in England in the early seventeenth century, elbowed their way into the picture. They called themselves Baptists.

No one figure led the Baptists' expansion the way that Asbury prompted the Methodists' growth, but the Baptists flourished nonetheless. By the Civil War, they ranked as the second-largest Protestant denomination, and they finally overtook the Methodists at the end of the century. The Baptists gained their name because they believed that only adults should be baptized, and baptized by complete immersion, preferably in lakes or rivers. (Children were not to be baptized because they were too young to know what it meant.) In practice, however, the Baptists proved to be more concerned about other matters. They believed that each local church should elect its own pastor and make its own decisions about who should be admitted to membership in their congregations (unlike the Methodists, who received detailed instruction on such matters from their bishops and circuit riders). They also insisted that churches should not take tax money from the state. Above all, Baptists yearned to bring sinners to Christ through earnest preaching about the joys of heaven.

The growth of missions represented a natural extension of Baptists' desire to spread the gospel. Yet the missionary impulse, always paramount in the Baptist heart—and wallet— eventually collided with another desire: a determination to protect the institution of slavery. In the 1840s, Baptist mission-sponsoring agencies, which were centered in the North, proved to be increasingly reluctant to certify for mission service slave-owning missionaries. As a result, the southern Baptists banded together and in 1845, formed the Southern Baptist Convention. They did so primarily to protect slaveholders' rights in the church. (The Northern Baptists would not organize in a comparable way until 1907.) This rupture prefigured deep trouble to come. If the bonds of Christian fellowship could not hold a denomination together, what could?

The evangelical revival left important legacies in U.S. religious life. One was a new role for women. Although females had always composed a majority of church members, in the years of the awakening they seized the opportunity to speak out as well as up. Dorothy Ripley, an evangelical firebrand from England, earned the distinction of being the first woman to preach in the House of Representatives in 1806 and was probably the first woman to speak in Congress at all. Another evangelical exhorter, Harriet Livermore, the daughter and granddaughter of congressmen, preached in the House on at least four occasions. President John Quincy Adams, who once came to hear her, ended up sitting on the steps to the podium because all the available chairs had been taken.

And then there was Phoebe Palmer, whose life neatly spanned most of the nineteenth century. By the end of the century, it was clear that Palmer stood only slightly behind Asbury and Finney in terms of her long-range influence. Married to a wealthy New York physician, this largely self-taught woman used her considerable financial and intellectual resources to preach the gospel on both sides of the Atlantic. Though Palmer never openly advocated the formal ordination of women, she did strenuously argue, on the basis of Galatians 3:28 ("There is neither...male nor female; for you are all one in Christ Jesus") and Joel 2:28 ("Your sons and daughters will prophesy"), that women should enjoy full rights to speak in church and elsewhere of their Christian experience.

The evangelicals left additional legacies. They founded scores of colleges in all parts of the United States. Some of the better known ones include Denison, Kenyon, Knox, Mt. Holyoke, Oberlin, Trinity (now Duke), Tuskegee, and Wheaton (Ill.). By the Civil War, the Baptists and Methodists alone had sponsored one-third of these schools, and other evangelical groups sponsored and staffed most of the rest.

Many of these schools distinguished themselves for their teaching of what was known as Common Sense morality. This view, drawn from the Scottish universities of the previous century, stressed humans' innate capacity to see the difference between good and bad and then act accordingly. Later philosophers and moralists placed more emphasis upon the ways that culture, always changing, shaped humans' view of the world. In contrast, Common Sense morality focused upon the light of reason, standing above the shifting sands of culture to provide a great beacon to direct the moral life.

Finally, the tradition of evangelical singing and hymns enriched the lives of millions. The Puritans had sung only psalms. Although the Wesleys and other eighteenth-century hymn-writers penned countless lyrics, these remained stately works emphasizing the community's faith. In contrast, the lively tempos and sentimental lines of typical evangelical songs moved the toes while they stirred the heart. The blind composer Fanny Crosby, who lived for nearly a century, turned out hundreds of songs, many of which are still sung in evangelical churches today. "Rescue the Perishing," "Jesus, Keep Me Near the Cross," and "Blessed Assurance" rank among the well-worn favorites by Crosby.

By 1850, some 70 percent of Protestants belonged to one of the two main evangelical denominations, Baptist or Methodist. Millions more were members of the Presbyterian-

Congregationalists, as well as another group called Christians or Disciples of Christ. In a few decades the evangelicals would be sharply challenged by Jews, Roman Catholics, and non-evangelical Protestants like the Lutherans and Episcopalians. But for the better part of the century they dominated American religion and played a large role in public life.

The extraordinary growth in the number of evangelicals in the pre–Civil War years can be explained in a number of ways. One is to see the evangelical message as a response to a deeply felt need for order, following the disorder of the Revolutionary War and the rough-and-tumble whirl of frontier society. Evangelicals' preaching brought regularity to individuals' lives and provided ties of friendship and love among brothers and sisters in the faith. Another explanation for the growth of the movement involves the tie between evangelicalism and rising tides of democratic feeling. In both, individuals held themselves responsible for their behavior and thus their destiny. And finally one can explain the success of evangelicalism in terms of the exceptionally gifted men and women like Asbury, Finney, Palmer, and Crosby who led the movement. Such individuals asked no one's permission. They simply marched out and took upon themselves the hard work of converting, educating, and morally disciplining the tumultuous world around them. The young republic teemed with hardy religious pioneers, and the evangelicals provided more than their share.

Evangelist and college president Charles G. Finney preached that a purely intellectual grasp of the doctrines of Christianity was not enough. In his Memoirs *(1876), Finney described his own memorable conversion experience and subsequent call to ministry.*

[The] Holy Spirit descended upon me in a manner that seemed to go through me, body and soul. I could feel the impression, like a wave of electricity, going through and through me. Indeed it seemed to come in waves and waves of liquid love; for I could not express it in any other way. It seemed like the very breath of God. I can recollect distinctly that it seemed to fan me, like immense wings.

No words can express the wonderful love that was shed abroad in my heart. I wept aloud with joy and love; and I do not know but I should say, I literally bellowed out the unutterable gushings of my heart. These waves came over me, and over me, one after the other, until I recollect I cried out, "I shall die if these waves continue to pass over me." I said, "Lord, I cannot bear any more;" yet I had no fear of death.

CHAPTER TEN

Reformers and Visionaries

Stand up, stand up for Jesus, ye soldiers of the cross;
Lift high his royal banner, it must not suffer loss.
From victory unto victory his army shall he lead,
till every foe is vanquished, and Christ is Lord indeed.

—*George Duffield, Fr., "Stand Up, Stand Up for Jesus" (1858)*

W e are all a little wild here with numberless projects of social reform" was the way essayist Ralph Waldo Emerson described American religion to an English friend in 1840. Every reading person, Emerson continued, seemed to hold "a draft of a new community in his waistcoat pocket." In one sense Emerson was simply stating the obvious. For the better part of two thousand years Christians had tried to help the needy, and the same held true for Christians in colonial America. In the sixteenth century Roman Catholic friars had come to New Spain—now the Gulf Coast states and New Mexico—partly to spread the benefits of Christian civilization.

The Puritans journeyed to New England a century later, for some of the same reasons. They hoped to establish a justly ordered society in which the widow, the orphan, and the pauper would receive proper care. The Quakers, who started migrating to the middle colonies of Delaware, New Jersey, and Pennsylvania in the late seventeenth century, went further. They called for pacifism, humane treatment of the Indians, the temperate use of alcohol, and sanctions against slaveholders and slave traders. Nonetheless, these Christians thought in terms of relief, not reform. They assumed that poverty and pain were here to stay. For the most part, the best one could do was to ease the suffering. The idea of making fundamental changes in society lay beyond their ken.

In the early nineteenth century a new approach to poverty and human suffering began to emerge. By that point in the Industrial Revolution it was clear that capitalism had created great inequalities. But it also opened up people's mental horizons, persuading many that the world really could be fundamentally improved. Rationalists like Thomas Jefferson had taught that society, no less than nature, was subject to its own laws. By mastering those laws individuals could make life more just, more humane, indeed, more enjoyable. Above all, thoughtful men and women began to believe that human beings were not always and everywhere shackled by the chains of selfishness. Increasingly, a grandly biblical vision of self-sacrifice in the interests of others seemed truly possible. All these trends flowed together at the beginning of the nineteenth century. Little wonder that thousands of people, religious and otherwise, would begin to come up with fresh ideas for making this new American world a better place to live.

The decades between the turn of the nineteenth century and the opening of the Civil War witnessed an explosion of reform efforts. The largest and most systematic projects—centering in the 1820s and 1830s—stemmed from broadly evangelical groups, first the Congregationalists and Presbyterians, then the Baptists and Methodists. They took their cues from similar endeavors in Britain. The British groups sought to combat evils like slavery, prostitution, alcoholism, and poverty. They won the support of the most powerful and prestigious citizens, including Parliament member William Wilberforce, who belonged to sixty-nine reform societies and helped to end the British slave trade in 1807.

The U.S. crusade first concentrated on spreading Christianity and civilization to the West, to the backwoods regions of the South, and to non-Christian lands overseas. In 1810, for example, Samuel J. Mills Jr., a student at Williams College and later at Andover Seminary (both in Massachusetts), helped organize a voluntary agency called the American Board of Commissioners for Foreign Missions. Many, including Mills himself, whose health prevented him from going overseas, concentrated on evangelizing the American West. For example, in the 1830s Methodist missionary Jason Lee carried the gospel message to the Flathead Indians of the Pacific Northwest. The Presbyterian missionaries Marcus and Narcissa Whitman soon followed. Their deaths at the hands of Indians in 1847 increased public concern about the West. Hundreds of missionaries and then pastors, including many women, followed.

Evangelicals regarded the South too as a mission field, one desperately needing reform. And with good reason. Until the middle of the century probably the majority of southerners remained unchurched. The Episcopal church, dominant during the colonial era, had come to be identified with the privileges of the planter aristocracy. Moreover, a "culture of honour," which placed a premium upon drinking, gambling, dueling, aggressive sports, and male sexual conquests, pervaded the Old South. Evangelical religion, espoused especially by lower-class and lower-middle-class whites and slaves, challenged the culture of honor. Evangelicals esteemed humility, frugality, sexual chastity, humane treatment of slaves, mutual accountability, and "sweet fellowship" in Christ.

Besides missions, evangelical reformers spearheaded the growth of literacy in general and Bible knowledge in particular. For example, they formed the American Sunday School Union in 1824. It supplied libraries with spelling books, alphabetical cards, and tens of thousands of books. Voluntary societies launched more than 700,000 new Sunday schools in the nineteenth century, many of which provided general and religious instruction for frontier children. After the Civil War, Sunday schools all over the land adopted a standardized Uniform Lesson Plan, so that children would study the same Bible passages nationwide each week. Other agencies distributed Bibles and tracts. By 1815, 100 such agencies existed, then merged the following year into the American Bible Society.

Tract societies followed the same pattern, first organizing locally, then combining into the nationwide American Tract Society in 1825. The sheer number of pages that its partisans distributed without charge was startling by any standards. Between 1829 and 1831, for example, the American Tract Society turned out sixty-five million pages of tracts, five pages for every person in America. Successive editions of *Eclectic Readers*, edited by the Presbyterian minister William Holmes McGuffey, dominated public school classrooms in the Midwest and elsewhere for the better part of a century, eventually selling 122 million copies. Although these readers purported to be nondenominational, they presented stories saturated with evangelical values of sobriety, hard work, punctuallity, and respectfulness toward elders and persons in authority. Evangelical values also passed into the general culture through popular magazines such as *Godey's Lady's Book*.

The abuse of alcohol captured reformers' attention too. From the beginning Quakers had targeted alcohol's evils, but to little avail. Drinking increased steadily in the young republic, reaching an all-time high by 1830. Critics of drink organized the Society for the Promotion of Temperance in 1826. As growing industrialization and urbanization raised the risks of intoxication, the older call for moderation gave way to a demand for total abstinence. In the 1830s, certain localities started banning liquor. (Some of these so-called dry towns maintain similar bans even today.) In 1836, reformers formed the American Temperance Union. Ten years later Maine became the first state to pass statewide prohibition. The temperance crusade sputtered in the Civil War decade, but arose again with force in the last third of the century, leading to nationwide Prohibition in the 1920s. The later crusade captured the enthusiasm of reformers across the political and religious spectrum, enlisting conservative and liberal alike.

The growing determination to effect more equal treatment for women proved to be a great deal more controversial than the temperance issue. Evangelical and nonevangelical women alike first organized themselves into female antislavery societies in the early 1830s. Soon some women, including the Quaker sisters Sarah and Angelina Grimké, started speaking publicly against slavery. This practice provoked a bitter confrontation within the antislavery ranks. Should women be allowed to mount a platform and address men publicly, as equals? The majority of abolitionists said no, opposing the notion as untimely at best and fundamentally wrong at worst. But a few said yes. For example, in 1848 Elizabeth Cady Stanton and Lucretia Mott organized a Women's Rights Convention. Although Stanton had been reared in a strict Presbyterian home, by then she had grown deeply skeptical of traditional Christianity. And Mott regarded herself as a liberal Quaker. These and other advocates chose to meet in an evangelical Wesleyan Methodist Church in Seneca Falls, New York, where they would continue to meet throughout the 1850s.

Activist Christians formed many more voluntary groups for the reform of society. Some called for pacifism, others for the humane treatment of prisoners, some for asylums for the blind, still others for the abolition of cruel practices like dueling, which had taken the life of Alexander Hamilton and nearly that of Abraham Lincoln too. Other well-known societies of the time included the American Colonization Society (for resettling freed slaves in Liberia), the American Home Missionary Society, the American Education Society, and the American Antislavery Society. Friends dubbed the growing network of reform societies the Benevolent Empire. They had good reason, for at one point the Benevolent Empire boasted a budget larger than that of the federal government!

A small number of farsighted men and women, often wealthy and well educated, basically ran the operations of the Benevolent Empire out of offices in New York City. Two of the most prominent were the Tappan brothers, Arthur and Lewis. As prosperous New York silk merchants the Tappans financed a variety of antebellum reform projects. For instance, when the new Oberlin College came under heavy attack for admitting students with antislavery views, they kept the school going. They also supported Sabbath observance, temperance, and the abolition of slavery. Lewis Tappan in particular represented the changing outlook of evangelical Protestants. As a young man,

Puritanlike notions of divine sovereignty and human sinfulness had occupied his attention. As a mature man, however, Lewis showed increasing interest in the happiness of humankind and moral order in society.

Some of the major reform efforts of the antebellum years stemmed from liberal rather than evangelical Christian traditions. The Unitarians in particular offered a nonevangelical route to social reform. Formally organized in 1825, the Unitarians took their name from their insistence on God's essential unity (versus God as trinity). In practice, however, they proved to be primarily interested in individuals' ability to change themselves and the world for the better. For example, Horace Mann, a Unitarian educator in Massachusetts, helped to establish free schools for children in his home state and throughout the United States. He vigorously combated slavery, liquor, tobacco, lotteries, profanity, and dancing, all on the ground that these activities did people more harm than good. Like many other liberal reformers, Mann retained the moral energy of the old New England Puritan tradition even as he let the formal theology slip away.

Dorothea Dix, another Unitarian reformer, proved to be even more influential than Mann. Reared in the home of a strict Methodist minister just after the turn of the century, Dix gravitated toward the religious liberalism of a Harvard-educated uncle. Though Dix never doubted the truth of the Bible or the divinity of Jesus, she came to believe that Christianity's essence lay in Jesus' command to feed the poor and comfort the sick. For several decades Dix, who never married, wandered from one genteel vocation to another. She taught school and wrote children's books and uplifting adult fiction. But in 1843 things changed dramatically for her. A stint teaching Sunday school in a Boston-area jail left her appalled at the shocking conditions there, especially the mixing of ordinary criminals with the insane. Dix had found her life's work. In the next thirty years she would visit all of the jails, almshouses (poorhouses), and private homes for the mad in New England, documenting their squalid surroundings and forcing legislatures to make major reforms. In all, Dix spearheaded the founding or expansion of thirty-two mental hospitals in fifteen states, Canada, Britain, continental Europe, and Japan. In addition, after the outbreak of the Civil War, Dix became superintendent of women nurses, the highest office held by a woman in the Union army.

Dix's career proved to be instructive in another respect. Though she awakened the nation to the plight of the mad, she held conservative views about the place of women in society and remained aloof from the antislavery crusade. By any reasonable measure of such things, this New England reformer was a great woman. But her vision, like that of all reformers, was structured by the limitations of her time and place.

The reform impulses growing out of the dominant forms of Christianity, both evangelical and liberal, shared the landscape with alternate visions that emerged outside the boundaries of mainline Christianity. Some, such as the Millerites, straddled the border, drawing upon historically Christian concerns but taking them further than most Americans wanted to go. Others, such as the Shakers and the Oneida Perfectionists, moved far beyond Christianity's boundaries. Most such groups hoped to reconstruct society in more humane ways. Though scores of such groups emerged in the antebellum years, the three just named deserve a closer look, for they represented distinctive tiles in the larger mosaic.

The nineteenth century knew many self-educated Bible scholars and home-grown philosophers. One of the most imaginative and influential such figures was the New York farmer

Local organizers often had to construct special buildings such as the Scoville Tabernacle in Aurora, Missouri, in 1915, to hold the crowds attracted by early-twentieth-century itinerant preachers. Such gatherings often blended entertainment with religion.

Swami Vivekananda (wearing a turban) is surrounded by supporters at the Greenacre Religious Conference in Maine in 1894. After the World's Parliament of Religions, held in Chicago in 1893, Vivekananda traveled the country and organized Vedanta societies, dedicated to the advancement of Hinduism.

A nun teaches a class at St. Michael's School on the Navajo reservation in Arizona around 1910. Although Rome once considered the United States a target for missionary activity, American Catholics themselves became increasingly active in missions after the turn of the twentieth century.

The 1915 lynching of Leo Frank by an anti-Semitic vigilante mob in Georgia sent shock waves through the American Jewish community, especially in the South. Frank had been elected president of the local chapter of the Anti-Defamation League of B'nai B'rith in 1912.

ı Ohio chapter of the Knights of Columbus, around 1914. Especially during the World Wars, the ıights emphasized their allegiance to both the Catholic church and their country.

Two white Baptists at a church in Little Rock, Arkansas, turn away black worshipers on October 5, 1958. Some African Americans, emboldened by 1950s court rulings that challenged segregation policies and responding to Martin Luther King, Jr.'s, observation that eleven o'clock Sunday morning was "the most segregated hour in America," tried to worship in white congregations.

A huge tent, dubbed the "canvas cathedral," went up at the corner of Washington and Hill streets in Los Angeles in 1949 for Billy Graham's eight-week-long revival "crusade." His dynamic preaching and boyish good looks attracted thousands of people.

Celebrity panelists (from left) Ethel Waters, Herman Wouk, Grace Kelly, and Charles E. Wilson appeared on the 1950s television program Religion in American Life. *Many Americans believed that church and synagogue attendance was a crucial weapon in the cold war, and President Dwight Eisenhower encouraged it in this 1953 telecast.*

An organization calling itself Volunteers for the Preservation of Religious Freedom distributed this pamphlet opposing Senator John F. Kennedy's campaign for the presidency in 1960. Many Protestants warned that a Roman Catholic should not occupy that office because he would be subject to a "foreign power": the pope.

In the office of the Catholic Worker, *Dorothy Day (seated at right) and her colleagues work on a 1934 issue of the newspaper, which sold for a penny.*

Rabbi Abraham Joshua Heschel, a professor at the Jewish Theological Seminary in New York and considered by some to be the greatest Jewish theologian of the twentieth century, marched with the Reverend Martin Luther King, Jr., in Selma, Alabama, in 1965 to secure voting rights for African Americans.

Hundreds of corpses lay in row after horrifying row in fields at the Jonestown compound in Guyana after the 1978 mass murder/suicide.

A Black Muslim woman listens intently to an address by Elijah Muhammad, leader the Nation of Islam, in Chicago in 1974. Many African Americans, especially in the South, joined the civil rights campaign of Martin Luther King, Jr., in the 1950s and 1960s: others responded to Muhammad's separatist teachings.

At Hill Cumorah in New York, advocates for the equal rights amendment to the Constitution demonstrate against the Mormon church's opposition to their cause. Sonia Johns a Mormon housewife, created a stir within the Church of Jesus Christ of Latter-Day Saints by supporting the amendment.

William Miller. In the 1830s, Miller dropped his plow to take up exhorting in Baptist churches. But he was no ordinary preacher. Intensive study of Scripture, especially the numerical codes in the book of Daniel, led him to conclude that the Lord would probably return on March 21, 1843, and March 21, 1844. This prophet's interest in numbers may have reflected American's growing interest in technology, which depended upon making precise mathematical calculations. It also showed a growing conviction that the Bible held all the answers, which humans could decipher if they only studied it hard enough. Miller's message spread rapidly through his periodicals—significantly titled *The Midnight Cry* and *Signs of the Times*—as well as five million copies of tracts and booklets. His views reached a broad audience on the front page of a special edition of Horace Greeley's *New York Tribune*, complete with illustrations. Comets and meteor showers at the time added to the excitement. Some said that Miller attracted 30,000 to 100,000 followers. When the longed-for return of the Lord did not materialize in 1843, Miller changed the date to October 22, 1844. When that uneventful night also passed, most of his followers drifted away, brokenhearted. Miller himself and a handful of faithful disciples remained certain that they had only made a calculation error and that Christ would return shortly. Others reorganized themselves as an enduring sect called the Seventh-Day Adventists.

How did the Millerites advance social reform? In one sense not at all, for they expected the Lord suddenly to bring history to a crashing end. But in another sense they did, for they opposed slavery and all other activities they saw as harmful that prevented men and women from being ready for Christ's return. After his death, Miller's followers embraced a broad range of health reforms as well, involving strict notions of proper diet, rest, exercise, dress, and sexual discipline. Beyond that, the Millerites displayed a fierce optimism about the course of history. Most evangelicals felt responsibility for creating the kingdom of God on the North Amercian continent in their lifetimes. Miller's vision was even grander. For him the Lord was coming back any day. He would enlist believers in the exhilarating work of creating the New Heavens and the New Earth, making all things right.

A second visionary movement with an end-times message took the ponderous name of the United Society of Believers in Christ's Second Appearance. Mother Ann Lee, as her followers called her, started the sect among plain folk in England in the mid-1700s. A cook and washerwoman, Lee remained illiterate all her life. After her four children died in infancy, she came to the conclusion that all sexual activity, whether in or out of marriage, equaled sin. She argued that the path to salvation therefore started with celibacy (abstaining from sex). Eventually, Lee joined a band of Quakers whose chosen mode of worship involved whirling and trembling, or "shaking off their sins." And so it was that they came to be known as Shakers. Lee's band migrated to upstate New York in 1774. Within a decade Lee died from injuries inflicted by hostile neighbors, but her followers proclaimed the message of salvation through celibacy northward into New England and southward into Ohio and Kentucky.

The movement grew luxuriantly in the experimental atmosphere of pre–Civil War America. At their peak the Shaker communities or colonies numbered 5,000 adherents altogether. The Shakers regarded Lee herself as the incarnation of the Second Coming of Christ, the Holy Mother Wisdom. Shaker men and women maintained strict equality, with two male and two female leaders in charge of each group. The adherents worked side by side, sharing all things except minor personal items in common.

They reproduced themselves by adopting orphans, many of whom stayed in the community upon reaching adulthood. They opposed slavery, dressed plainly, and refused to fight. Shaker worship centered in ritualized or highly structured dancing that could go on for hours as a form of worship before the Lord.

Perhaps the most noted feature of the Shaker community was a scrupulous attention to simplicity, cleanliness, and usefulness. These traits found expression in the Shakers' furniture and in the simple lines of their buildings. In the mid–nineteenth century the Shakers embodied a powerful vision of what a carefully ordered society, free of sexual desire, greed, or waste, might look like. At the end of the twentieth century only a handful of Shakers remained, all at Sabbathday Lake, Maine.

The Oneida Perfectionists, located in the small upstate New York village of Oneida, embodied a third visionary movement. The Perfectionists grew out of the labors of John Humphrey Noyes. Born in Vermont in 1811, Noyes attended Dartmouth College, where he underwent a memorable evangelical conversion experience. He then went on to Andover Seminary and Yale Divinity School. At Yale, however, he found himself in considerable trouble for claiming—contrary to 2,000 years of Christian teaching—that he had achieved a state of Christian perfection, untainted by any residue of sin. This state was possible, he argued, because Christ had returned in A.D. 70 and given the church the power of his spirit. In 1841, Noyes established a community of followers in Putney, Vermont. They too pursued earthly perfection, expressed through economic sharing, divine healing, the mutual confession of sins (except by Noyes himself), and "complex marriage." The last involved the systematic rotation of husbands and wives among members of the community, based on the assumption that perfected people should share all things, including spouses.

Opposition from neighbors forced the community to relocate to Oneida, New York, in 1848. Undeterred, Noyes eventually instituted a still more radical plan of selecting a small number of men and women deemed worthy for breeding. In New York the business-savvy Perfectionists grew prosperous through the manufacture of steel animal traps, travel bags, and silver-plated flatware. Although by the late 1870s the settlement had dwindled to only 250 residents, neighbors had seen enough. Noyes escaped to Canada in 1879 and the community formally dissolved two years later. But the Perfectionists' notoriety long outlived them. Oneida silverware, now produced by a secular corporation, persists as a tangible reminder of one of the longest lived and most radical of all U.S. reform experiments.

All three of these groups emerged about the same time and in roughly the same area: western New York state, sometimes called the Burned Over District because of the succession of revival preachers and radical groups that blazed across the region. All of them tinkered with conventional notions of time by reconceiving the date of Christ's return. And all challenged conventional ideas of ownership: the Millerites regarding slaves, the Perfectionists and Shakers concerning private property. The latter two groups also reworked time-honored notions of family relations, but in opposite ways. All three represented a new vision, fired by the religious imagination, of better social arrangements.

Many, though not all, of these reform impulses flowed together in the life of one singularly influential woman. Her real name was Isabella Baumfree, but by the time of her death most Americans knew her as Sojourner Truth. By whatever name, she showed how fairly conventional ideas about reform could merge with some very radical ones.

Born a slave in upstate New York about 1797, Baumfree was torn from her birth family and sold twice while yet a child. She reached adulthood in a Dutch-speaking family, and thus spoke English with a Dutch accent the rest of her life. During that time she embraced a strict Methodist faith. Freed by her owner at the age of thirty, Baumfree moved to New York City, where she allied herself with a religious prophet named Elijah Pierson. He had established a commune calling for equality between men and women, between blacks and whites, and between wealthy and poor. This commune, known as the Kingdom of Matthias, did not last long, partly because Pierson was unable to live up to his own ideals. In the meantime, Baumfree received a vision from the Lord directing her to travel the land preaching a message of personal salvation, abolition of slavery, equal rights for women, and justice for the poor.

Because she believed herself a traveling messenger for the Lord, the name Sojourner Truth came to Baumfree naturally. Tall, bony, and articulate, she cut a dramatic figure on the lecture circuit. Hecklers, amused to see a black woman speaking publicly, got more than they bargained for with her quickwitted retorts. Truth lobbied President Abraham Lincoln on behalf of the slaves. After the war, she worked tirelessly for government policies to protect, educate, and resettle newly freed black men and women. She lobbied for hospitals and orphanages for former bondsmen. At the same time, she pressed former slaves to take responsibility for their own welfare. It was almost inevitable that Truth would finally end up in Battle Creek, Michigan, a center of late-nineteenth-century efforts to improve health by reforming diet, dress, and hygiene.

Why did the reform impulse emerge most often among groups that traced their roots back to the Protestant Reformation in England—the Congregationalists, Presbyterians,

Quakers, Baptists, Methodists, and Unitarians? (The same pattern proved true of radical groups too. The Millerites stemmed from the Baptists, the Shakers from the Quakers, and the Oneida Perfectionists from the Methodists.) Several answers are possible. Traditionally, English Protestant groups emphasized the parts of the Bible that spoke of responsibility to the whole of society. Also, members of those groups tended to be well educated and economically secure, which gave them both the vision and the means to help others. In contrast, a large minority of Christians, including Roman Catholics, Lutherans, and Mennonites, as well as Jews, rarely attempted to reform society as a whole. This was not because they were selfish but because they were confronted by the more pressing problems of taking care of their own families in a forbidding land.

This point raises a final question. How did the subjects—or rather the objects, we might better say—of the reformers' efforts feel about all the attention on their behalf? Some clearly appreciated the extended hand, but others resented the real or perceived interference in their lives. They saw the visionaries not as heroes but as do-gooders and busybodies. Echoes of that conversation persist today in debates about abortion and drug use. One side seeks to change the world for the better while the other side asks, who is to define what is "better"?

Shortly we shall look at the greatest reform crusade of all, the war to end slavery. That effort would take more than words, money, and sweat, however. It would cost lives—more than a half million of them. But before turning to the antislavery crusade, we need to look at two other major groups that also emerged in the mid-nineteenth century. Each manifested its own distinctive set of concerns; each made its own distinctive mark upon the American religious landscape.

FATHER PIERRE JEAN DE SMET'S
WORK WITH THE SIOUX

Christian missionaries, both at home and abroad, often experienced hardship in the pursuit of their ideals. In this 1864 letter to the archbishop of Cincinnati, U.S. army major general David S. Stanley described the work of Father Pierre Jean De Smet, a Jesuit missionary to the Sioux.

The Reverend Father is known among the Indians by the name of "Blackrobe" and "Big Medicine Man."...He is the only man for whom I have ever seen Indians evince a real affection. They say, in their simple and open language, that he is the only white man who has not a forked tongue; that is, who never lies to them....

[We] can never forget nor shall we ever cease to admire, the disinterested devotion of the Reverend Father De Smet, who, at the age of sixty-eight years, did not hesitate, in the midst of the heat of summer, to undertake a long and perilous journey, across the burning plains, destitute of trees and even of grass; having none but corrupted and unwholesome water, constantly exposed to scalping by Indians, and this without seeking either honors or remuneration of any sort; but solely to arrest the shedding of blood and save, if it might be, some lives, and preserve some habitations to these savage children of the desert, to whose spiritual and temporal welfare he has consecrated a long life of labor and solicitude.

CHAPTER ELEVEN

Restorers of Ancient Ways

The Spirit of God like a fire is burning;
The latter-day glory begins to come forth;
The visions and blessings of old are returning;
The angels are coming to visit the earth.
We'll sing and we'll shout with the armies of heaven,
"Hosannah, hosannah to God and the Lamb!"

— *W. W. Phelps, "The Spirit of God Like a Fire Is Burning" (c. 1830)*

In the second quarter of the nineteenth century thousands of Americans sought progress not by looking forward to the end of history but by looking backward to its beginning. Some wanted to restore the perfect order they saw in the New Testament. They called themselves simply Christians, or occasionally Disciples of Christ. Others, more radical, wanted to restore the perfect order they read about in both the Old and the New Testaments. The Church of Jesus Christ of Latter-day Saints, better known as the Mormons, formed the largest and most influential example.

The Christian movement began in two places. The first stirrings occurred in northern Kentucky, the second in western Pennsylvania. In Kentucky, just after the turn of the century, Presbyterian preacher Barton W. Stone cast his lot with the revivals taking place near Cane Ridge, discussed in chapter 9. Although Cane Ridge had gained a reputation for unrestrained expression of religious emotion, Stone supported its revivals for a different reason. He believed they freed people from oppressive control by denominational officials, giving them the right to worship when, where, and how they liked. He felt strongly about the right of individuals to choose or reject salvation for themselves. Thus, in 1803 Stone and other like-minded ministers withdrew from the Presbyterian Synod (a regional association of ministers) and soon established their own group. They decided to call themselves Christians—just Christians. They wanted to return to the plain words of the King James Authorized Version of the Bible for all instruction in the faith. They felt they did not need highly educated scholars to interpret scripture. In their minds the Bible was a simply written book that said what it meant and meant what it said.

About this same time, a Scottish immigrant in western Pennsylvania named Alexander Campbell also abandoned the Presbyterian church. Campbell was a brilliant though argumentative young man. Like Stone, Campbell felt that all people should be able to choose their own church, select their own pastor, and read the Bible in their own way. Campbell believed that the New Testament, and the New Testament alone, should serve as a blueprint for all things that Christians believed and did in the present—not the traditions of the church and not the speculations of school-taught theologians. His motto was "Where the Scriptures speak, we speak; where the Scriptures are silent, we are silent." Read the Bible, he said, as if mortal eyes had never seen it before. In addition, Campbell felt that by using the New Testament alone as a guide, believers could avoid all the squabbling about which church was right. If they would only look to the Scripture, and not at human interpretations of it, there would be no more divisions or fighting. Campbell's followers sometimes called themselves Christians and at others Disciples of Christ, in order to emphasize the simplicity and unifying power of their message.

Various ideas circulating within the antebellum culture of the United States influenced both of these groups, the Stoneites in Kentucky and the Campbellites in Pennsylvania. Specifically, their emphasis upon the right of ordinary persons to make decisions for themselves in matters of religious belief and church government found an echo in the ideals of President Andrew Jackson, which emphasized the right of ordinary people to make crucial decisions for themselves in matters of political belief and civil government. Both the Stoneites and Campbellites evinced a strong dislike of intellectual elites. They particularly scorned the pretense of well-born and well-educated people (especially those from the East) to make decisions on behalf of plain folk (especially those from the West).

In one important respect, however, the growing Christian movement departed from broad trends in the culture and from other evangelical denominations. The Christians avoided the open display of religious emotion. Their converts did not need to go through an intense conversion experience, marked by weeping or groaning or uncontrolled behavior. All they needed was to read the Bible, believe what it said, repent of their sins, and be baptized by immersion as a mark of obedience.

By the early 1830s the Stoneites and the Campbellites realized that they shared many ideas and practices. Consequently, they informally united in Lexington, Kentucky, in 1832, bringing together some 13,000 supporters. They went by various names: Christians, Disciples of Christ, or Restorationists. (The last term emerged because they aimed to restore the patterns of the New Testament church.) These three labels were interchangeable.

Toward the end of the century things grew even more confusing when the Christians split into a definably northern branch, by then usually called the Christian Church/Disciples of Christ, and an identifiably southern branch, by that time usually known as the Churches of Christ. Together they claimed about 650,000 adherents. Although the Christian movement never grew as large as the closely related evangelical one, it nevertheless represented one of the more impressive traditions to be born on American soil in the nineteenth century. Its hallmarks included restorationist fervor, radical democracy, and an enduring confidence in the power of individuals to think clearly and choose truth for themselves.

The Mormons, a second major group of "restorers" who arose in the nineteenth century, grew much larger and proved to be considerably more radical than the Christians. The story of the Mormons was, and remains, tied to the life of their founder, Joseph Smith, Jr. Born in 1805, young Joseph matured in difficult circumstances. His father's farming efforts in Vermont met with little success because of bad weather and rocky soil. Thus, in 1816 the Smith family, along with thousands of other struggling New Englanders, pulled up stakes and migrated westward. They settled in the small town of Palmyra, New York, in the north-central region of the state. Economic ups and downs, coupled with intense religious unrest, marked the area. In New York both father and son worked at a variety of jobs, possibly including efforts to find buried treasure with a magical seer stone. Over time the Smiths' fortunes improved, but they never knew real economic security.

Joseph's adolescent life proved to be troubled in other respects too. Neither of his parents was securely tied to any of the main Christian groups of the region. The senior Smith considered himself something of a freethinker, but he was never too sure about his unbelief. Joseph's mother, Lucy Mack Smith, regarded herself a Presbyterian, but she also seemed unclear of her commitments. For Lucy, too many different groups claimed to know the truth. Joseph inherited his parents' uncertainty about the current religious choices. But more than either of them he determined to settle the truth for himself.

Many years later Joseph told his own story. He said that one day in 1820, just before his fifteenth birthday, he was praying by himself in the woods. He asked God to show him which church was right. One day God the Father and Jesus Christ the Son appeared to him in a vision. They told him that none was right. The early Christians had lost the truth through sinful behavior and, once it was lost, there was no hope for finding it again until God restored it. Over the next seven years (between the ages of fourteen and twenty-one) young Smith experienced additional visions. The most important came in the fall of 1823 when the angel Moroni (an angel unique to Smith, and not existing in other Christian traditions) visited him. Moroni told Joseph about a set of golden tablets hidden beneath a stone on a nearby hillside, which held the wisdom he was seeking. In 1827, Moroni instructed Joseph to retrieve the tablets and translate what was written on them (in a lost language called Reformed Egyptian). Joseph recalled that he sat on one side of a curtain and deciphered each word, while Emma, his young bride, and two or three others sat on the other side writing down his remarks. He was only allowed to show the tablets to eleven other people named by Moroni.

By March 1830, the translation was complete. Smith found a printer and published the work as the *Book of Mormon*. Although

Mark Twain would call it "chloroform in print," the volume bore many resemblances in theme and style to the beloved King James Authorized Version of the Bible. About 500 pages long, it featured an epic story much like the sagas recounted in the Old Testament.

According to the *Book of Mormon*, ancient peoples of Hebrew extraction came to the New World on barges about 600 B.C., settling in Central America. The leader was Lehi, a patriarch very much like the biblical Abraham. Lehi's sons divided into two clans, the Nephites and the Lamanites. Though both groups had their failings, on the whole the Nephites proved to be righteous, while the Lamanites did not. The tribes struggled against each other for centuries. Jesus Christ visited these New World Hebrews after his resurrection, offering them the message of salvation, but the conflicts persisted into the fourth century. Finally, in a terrible battle very much like the battle of Armageddon described in the New Testament book of Revelation, the Lamanites slew all but two of the Nephites: the great warrior Mormon, and his son Moroni. Mormon then wrote the story of these New World argonauts on the golden plates. In A.D. 384 Moroni hid them on the hillside near Palmyra, New York, where Smith ultimately found them. In the meantime the victorious Lamanites became increasingly dark skinned and ignorant. Their descendants formed the Indians whom the Europeans encountered a thousand years later.

It is hard to know how to account for the *Book of Mormon*'s origin or its success. Smith had received little formal education. How then could he write so much in such a short time? For those who became Mormons, the book contained a direct revelation from God proclaimed by God's specially selected prophet. For those who did not, the book represented great religious imagination at best, or outright fraud at worst. Whatever one believed about the authorship of the book, the volume clearly offered answers to questions people of the 1830s were asking about their new continent. It explained signs of advanced civilization in Central America, such as pyramids and elaborate stone calendars. It accounted for the origins of the Indians. It gave citizens of the United States, anxious about their lack of deep historical roots, a secure place in the grand scheme of things. Above all, it helped believers see America itself as a uniquely chosen place, for God had selected Americans to serve as the carriers of a restored gospel.

Scores of hardworking plain folk soon flocked to Smith. He organized them into the Church of Jesus Christ (later adding "of Latter-day Saints" to the title). But opposition arose, partly because other Christians, whom the Mormons called Gentiles, strongly resisted the idea that any collection of writings outside the Bible should be considered equal to the Bible. They also doubted that God would single out an ordinary person like the roughly hewn Smith to receive new revelation. To escape harassment, Joseph and Emma Smith and a small band of followers moved to Kirtland, Ohio, near Cleveland, in 1831. There they built a temple, and Smith began to receive additional direct revelations about doctrinal matters. Some of these had to do with the nature of God (who was material), humans (who were gods in the making), and marriage (to be patterned after the Old Testament model of multiple wives). For a short time the Mormons also tried to abolish private ownership of property, calling for the sharing of material and economic resources.

Opposition continued to dog the Mormons even in Ohio. Once a group of ruffians dragged Smith from his home and tarred and feathered him. So in 1838, many members of the sect moved on to Missouri, where they occupied a number of different locations in the northwestern part of the state near

present-day Kansas City. Constant friction and occasional violence with their neighbors followed. The Missourians proved
to be intolerant, but the Mormons also seemed to go out of
their way to provoke them. The Mormons, like most religious
sects, instinctively sensed that opposition toughened the spiritual muscles. And opposition also helped them distinguish
loyal partisans from fair-weather friends. But enough was
enough. Ten months later Smith and most of his followers
moved back eastward to Nauvoo, Illinois, a dusty village on the
Mississippi.

Nauvoo thrived—for a while, at least. Thousands of converts, including many won by Mormon missionaries in England,
flocked to the settlement, boosting the population to 10,000 by
1840. The Mormons' businesses prospered. Smith received
additional revelations, which took the Mormons farther and
farther from evangelical Protestantism. For example, Smith
received instructions that the Mormons should secure their
dead ancestors' places in heaven by baptizing them by name,
going back at least four generations (thus accounting for the
Mormons' impressive efforts to recover the genealogical history of thousands of U.S. families). In Nauvoo, Smith gradually
put into practice his earlier revelation about plural marriage.
Whether these were actual or symbolic marriages remains dis-
puted, although solid evidence supports the former. Before long,
Smith also established a Mormon militia, declared himself king
of the kingdom of God, and announced his intention to run for
president of the United States. When an opposition newspaper
questioned these moves, the Prophet closed it in the spring of
1844. Then, finding himself in grave trouble, he gave himself up
to the law. The authorities jailed him and his brother Hyrum in
nearby Carthage. On June 27, 1844, a mob broke into the jail
and murdered the two brothers in cold blood.

A power struggle ensued. Soon the Mormons chose Brigham Young as president of the church. Like the Smith family, the Young family had migrated in the early nineteenth century from Vermont to upstate New York to find work. Although Young had been baptized as a Methodist, he remained dissatisfied with the exclusiveness of evangelical Protestantism. In 1832, he embraced the Mormon message. Young was not as charismatic as Smith, but he proved to be a strong leader and a superb organizer. Recognizing that the Gentile culture in Illinois would never tolerate the increasingly distinctive sect in their midst, Young led a contingent westward. Heading out along the Missouri River in the bitter winter of 1846, the first Mormons arrived in Utah's Great Salt Lake Basin seventeen months later. When Young initially eyed the awesome valley from the surrounding Wasatch Range, he reportedly declared, with characteristic finality: "This is the place." The Mormons called their newfound home Deseret, a word they coined meaning honeybee. In 1850 Utah organized itself as a territory. In 1852, the practice of plural marriage (which had grown quietly since the Prophet's death in 1844) was openly acknowledged. By the time of Young's death a quarter century later, Mormons had established 350 settlements, numbering 100,000 residents, stretching from Idaho to southern California.

A minority of Mormons, led by Joseph Smith's wife, Emma Hale Smith, and his son Joseph Smith III, never joined the main body in Utah. In 1852, they structured themselves as the Reorganized Church of Jesus Christ of Latter Day Saints (differently punctuated). The Reorganized Mormons, as they called themselves, remained strongest in northern Missouri and southern Iowa, where they established Graceland College. Theologically they came to resemble the restoration-minded Christians/Disciples of Christ. In 2001 this body changed its name to the Community of Christ.

Gentile visitors to Utah in the latter years of the nineteenth century encountered a well-ordered, economically prosperous society. An elaborate communal irrigation system helped the Mormons create a garden in the wilderness. Nonetheless, their insistence upon plural marriage sparked repeated confrontations with neighboring Gentiles and the U.S. government. Federal legislation in 1862 prohibiting bigamy was affirmed in a landmark 1879 Supreme Court case, *United States v. Reynolds*. In the face of ever-tightening sanctions by the federal government, not to mention continued outcries among the public back east, the Mormons finally suspended their practice of plural marriage in 1890. This move allowed the Utah Territory to enter the union as a state in 1896. (Mormons today no longer practice plural marriage; those groups who do are not officially recognized by the church.) Although Gentiles commonly assumed that Mormon plural marriage degraded women, Utah guaranteed women the right to vote in 1896, making it only the second state to do so, following Wyoming in 1890. In the late 1990s, the Latter-day Saints claimed nearly 10 million adherents worldwide, with half of them living in the United States.

How should we interpret the relationship between the Mormons and the rest of U.S. culture in the nineteenth century? To some extent the Mormons represented a new religion, one as different from historic Christianity as Christianity was from Judaism. Their tenets of plural marriage, a material God (made of matter, rather than just an idea), and continuing revelation set them apart. So did their insistence upon a centrally planned economy (especially in the 1850s, when they were forced to grapple with the harshness of the Utah desert). At the same time, however, the Mormons' strong sense of personal morality, their optimistic view of human nature, and their conviction that the United States provided the main stage for God's plan for all of human history drew them squarely into the American mainstream. By the end of the twentieth century the Mormons had become less recognizable as a distinct culture. Some of their theological beliefs still aroused suspicion among evangelical Christians. Socially, however, the Mormons were patriotic, hardworking, middle-class Americans.

One of the most important things to remember about the Mormons is that they were restorers. They believed that true Christianity had been lost, but God himself had reinstated it in nineteenth-century America. They saw themselves not simply copying the ancient Israelites and Christians, but *re-creating* both the Old Testament Israelites and the New Testament Christians in the modern world. It was an exhilarating vision. Little wonder that tens of thousands of Americans, as well as equal numbers in other countries, found Mormonism compelling enough to warrant the long trek to Utah.

GOD'S MESSENGER MORONI
VISITS JOSEPH SMITH

In September of 1823, at the age of seventeen, Joseph Smith experienced one of several visions that led him to abandon all the prevailing forms of Christianity in favor of a new one. In an autobiographical reminiscence written fifteen years later, History of Joseph Smith, by Himself, *the Prophet described the events that led to the discovery, translation, and publication of the* Book of Mormon.

I discovered a light appearing in the room, which continued to increase until the room was lighter than at noonday, when immediately a personage appeared at my bedside, standing in the air, for his feet did not touch the floor. He had on a loose robe of most exquisite whiteness. It was a whiteness beyond anything earthly I had ever seen; nor do I believe that any earthly thing could be made to appear so exceedingly white and brilliant....

When I first looked upon him I was afraid, but the fear soon left me. He called me by name and said unto me that he was a messenger sent from the presence of God to me, and that his name was Moroni. That God had a work for me to do, and that my name should be had for good and evil among all nations, kindreds, and tongues.... He said that there was a book deposited, written upon gold plates, giving an account of the former inhabitants of this continent, and the source from whence they sprang. He also said that the fullness of the everlasting Gospel was contained in it, as delivered by the Savior to the ancient inhabitants. Also, that there were two stones in silver bows...deposited with the plates, and the possession and use of these stones was what constituted seers in ancient or former times, and that God had prepared them for the purpose of translating the book.

CHAPTER TWELVE

Sojourners at Home

Swing low, sweet chariot,
Coming for to carry me home;
Swing low, sweet chariot,
Coming for to carry me home.
I looked over Jordan,
And what did I see,
Coming for to carry me home?
A band of angels coming after me,
Coming for to carry me home.

—*"Swing Low," African-American spiritual*

Who is an outsider? Sooner or later most people consider themselves outsiders: left out, unappreciated, maybe even despised. For most people these feelings can be written off as the gloomy sentiments that come and go like a rainy day. But not always—sometimes exclusion is very real. In the nineteenth century millions of Americans found themselves perennial outsiders. Some acquired that status because they held religious beliefs that the rest of the society judged unacceptable. Others experienced exclusion because they belonged to the wrong racial or ethnic group. We should not assume that the groups we shall study were always unhappy. Far from it. Much of the time, and perhaps most of the time, they built meaningful lives despite their forced separation from the rest of American life. Nonetheless, insiders could choose to recognize or not recognize outsiders as they wished. Outsiders never had that option.

The Native Americans were outsiders because of their faith. Their religious traditions stretched back at least 10,000 years, long before the oldest parts of the Hebrew Bible were written. Their traditions varied greatly. Those of the Iroquois in the Northeast, the Cherokees in the Southeast, the Sioux in the northern plains, and the Hopis in the Southwest (to name a few of the most prominent) differed as much from each other as those of the Protestants differed from the Roman Catholics. Native Americans spoke hundreds of languages with thousands of dialects. Like all other nations and peoples, they disagreed sharply among themselves.

Nonetheless, the Indian religions of the nineteenth century shared a number of features. Most notable, perhaps, was the firm link to tribe. It was no more possible to choose one's religion than to choose one's tribe. Granted, neither religion nor tribe remained timelessly stable. They changed like everything else. But the main point is that a person's religion, like a person's tribe, was simply inherited, like the color of one's skin. And just as religion was tied to tribe, it was also tied to place. Christianity and to some extent Judaism were portable. They could be disconnected from the sites where they began, and carried by migrants, travelers, or missionaries to other locations. Not so with the Native American religions. The land itself carried religious meanings—meanings peculiar to that place and to none other.

Indians commonly presupposed the continuity of time. Whereas modern Westerners subdivided time into religious and nonreligious units so that one did sacred things on Saturday or Sunday and secular things the rest of the week, the Native Americans knew no such distinctions. To them all time seemed the same. To be sure, they set aside certain seasons of the year for hunting or gathering, and periods within the seasons for festivities. They celebrated the fish run in the spring, the Green Corn ceremony in the summer, and marked the passage of time with stories and dances appropriate to the occasion. But they did not follow a specified calendar of six days for work and one day for worship, or a cycle of holy days (holidays) as Europeans did. The continuity of time manifested itself in the various Indian languages, which generally made no clear distinctions between the past, present, and future. This outlook dismayed Christian missionaries who wanted to teach the Indians about the future life.

Sacred threads wove all aspects of life into a single tapestry. As a result, Native Americans' notion of God or gods differed from Western ideas in quite striking ways. Most supposed a wide range of supernatural beings that had helped to create the human race. The creation process was regularly reenacted through rituals and the telling and retelling of sacred stories. Through the reenactment, the original life-giving power of creation itself could be tapped and used for beneficial purposes.

The Indians' cosmos brimmed with supernatural power everywhere. Anything—sky, dreams, mountains, lakes, crops, trees, animals, humans—could be sites of the holy. This supernatural power was neither good nor bad in itself. It all depended on how it was used. The shaman, or holy man (or occasionally holy woman), played a special role, too. Either through natural talents or through training, shamans traveled into the supernatural realm, where they received extraordinary powers. These energies enabled them to cure illnesses, interpret dreams, predict the weather, influence nature, and chart the movement of animals for hunting.

All of life involved exchanges—exchanges between humans and nature, between humans and animals, and between humans and other humans. Killing an animal for food meant, for example, that one creature's life would be taken so that another creature's life might survive. Religious rituals and sacred stories aimed to explain those transactions and restore the balances.

Women and elderly men bore a special responsibility for teaching these traditions to children. Their job was to pass along the culture from generation to generation. Given the absence of written traditions, oral traditions loomed large.

There is no reason to think that Indians proved more spiritual than anyone else—then or now—but those who were spiritual saw sacred dimensions in the mundane rhythms of life. Cooking, eating, dancing, painting, dressing, loving, marrying, and burying carried a sacred dimension. The wise among them discerned that dimension, and pondered how to live accordingly.

Though the core beliefs and practices of the Indian traditions remained firmly outside the U.S. religious mainstream, a lot of mixing took place at the edges. This mingling seemed most obvious in material things like clothing and foods. Many staples such as potatoes, tomatoes, corn, squash, beans, pumpkins, and hot peppers came from the Indians. Native Americans also influenced the encroaching European and African religious cultures, sometimes in quite dramatic ways. A few whites, sometimes known as "white Indians," boldly left their Christian exclusivism behind and accepted an Indian religion, wholly or in part.

More often, however, both whites and blacks quietly absorbed aspects of Native myths. Perhaps not thinking too much about what they were doing, they blended their own semi-Christian beliefs in ghosts, witches, demons, and sprites with Native accounts of similar experiences. For example, Joel Chandler Harris's Uncle Remus tales, published in various forms in the 1880s and 1890s, featured a wise old black man telling stories about Brer Rabbit. As in the Cherokee and Creek legends, Brer Rabbit emerged as a trickster character who could change form at will, confusing his supposedly smart and powerful antagonists.

Finally, over the course of the nineteenth century, many Indians embraced Christianity. Indeed, by 1900, Christianity ranked as one of the main forms of Native religious expression. One could speak of Anishinaabeg Catholics, Lakota Episcopalians, Muskogee Baptists, Iroquois Quakers, Cherokee Presbyterians, Munsee Moravians, Shawnee Shakers, Hopi Mennonites, Navajo Methodists, Osage Lutherans, Paiute Pentecostals, Apache Mormons, and Aleut Orthodox. How did this astonishing transformation take place?

Not easily, is the short answer. From the beginning Christian missions to Indians were tainted with the rapacity of white traders and the brutality of white soldiers. As a result, many Native Americans resisted Christianity, either by passively ignoring it, vigorously opposing it, or violently fighting it. In 1813 and 1814, for example, thousands of Creek Indians in the Southeast battled U.S. government forces in a series of bloody conflicts, fueled by their resentment of whites who attacked the Indian ways. They also fought other Indians whom they deemed too friendly to whites. Boarding schools, such as the Indian School established in Carlisle, Pennsylvania, in 1879, aimed to teach Indian children literacy and the gospel. But they also removed children from the comforts of their own culture and imposed an alien way of life. Though the missionaries typically labored with the best of intentions, and often suffered great hardships, they rarely proved free of racial condescension.

Still, Indians converted, and they did so in great numbers. Their reasons varied. Some sought respectability, others desired education, and still others hoped for better job possibilities. It is impossible to know how many embraced Christian teachings because they believed that the gospel offered better answers to life's spiritual problems. But the steady growth of Christianity among Indian peoples, despite its connection with imperialism, suggests that many Indians found the gospel message persuasive in its own terms.

Some Indians even became missionaries to their own people. Catharine Brown, a Cherokee convert to evangelical Congregationalism, helped to found a school for Indian women in Alabama in 1820. Though Brown died of tuberculosis at the young age of twenty-three, she would be fondly remembered by generations of Christian Cherokees. The Oglala Lakota Black Elk, a veteran of the terrible Wounded Knee battle in South Dakota in 1890, converted to the Roman Catholic Church fourteen years later. Though Black Elk retained aspects of the Lakota religious outlook to the end of his life, he was renamed Nicholas Black Elk after Saint Nicholas, joined the Catholic Church's St. Joseph's Society, and for many years served as a teacher and missionary to other Indians in the Great Plains states.

The Ojibwa hymn-singers show how Native and Christian traditions often blended in a seamless whole. In the 1830s, missionaries to the western Great Lakes region started translating favorite gospel songs into the vernacular languages of the Indians. Lovers of singing, the Ojibwa readily incorporated the new songs into their traditional musical repertoire. By the

1870s, hymn singing and traveling hymn-singing bands had become a conspicuous feature of the people's life. If the missionaries saw these songs as a way of teaching Anglo-American as well as Christian values, the Indians saw them as a means for integrating the old with the new. The songs provided spiritual sustenance in the face of poverty, hunger, and enforced accommodation to American ways.

Some Shakers felt that Indian spirits regularly visited them and took possession of their bodies. The list of such cultural exchanges could be extended at length. In the give and take of ordinary life the lines between historic Christianity and non-Christian traditions blurred more than the purists on either side wanted to admit.

Asians also represented outsiders because of their faith. The Chinese started emigrating to the United States during the California gold rush of the 1850s, their numbers soon swelling into the tens of thousands. They brought their religions with them: Buddhism, Taoism, Confucianism, and an array of local beliefs. The Japanese laborers who joined the Chinese in the 1870s also brought their religious traditions with them, including distinctively Japanese forms of Buddhism and Taoism.

Other Asians followed. Just as Christian missionaries sailed westward to Asia in the later decades of the nineteenth century, so too Buddhist missionaries sailed eastward. They first journeyed to the Hawaiian Islands in the late 1880s, then to the West Coast of the continental United States the following decade. The Buddhist missionaries hoped to convert Christians to Buddhism, especially to the form of it known as Jodo Shinshu Pure Land Buddhism, which taught that a Pure Land awaited the faithful upon death. The missionaries also hoped to provide material and spiritual support for Japanese workers, most of whom were male, far from home, desperately lonely, and often seeking moral roots.

By the end of the century, sites for the practice of non-Western religions (including centers for Hindus from India and Baha'is from Persia) started popping up on the West Coast and in major cities elsewhere. The Pure Land Buddhists organized themselves in 1899 as the Buddhist Churches of America. Buddhism proved particularly appealing to American intellectuals because of its high ethical ideals. At the World's Parliament of Religions in Chicago in 1893 (part of the World's Columbian Exposition) some adventurous thinkers even tried to blend Buddhist and Christian teachings. Traditionalists on both sides of the religious fence worried about this mixing and matching of ancient faiths, but there was no going back—as the freewheeling religious marketplace of the late twentieth century has amply shown.

Jews too became outsiders of faith. To say that the Jews were marginalized because of their faith is perhaps only partly true, since Judaism formed the basis of Christianity. And in the course of the nineteenth century Jews moved from being a rarely seen minority to a conspicuous presence on the U.S. cultural landscape, especially in the urban Northeast. Yet the Jews remained distinct from the Christian majority. They did not eat some common foods such as ham or shrimp, they circumcised their male children, and they worshiped on Saturday, which they regarded as the true Sabbath. Unlike their Christian neighbors, who based their faith upon both the Old and New Testaments, Jews based their upon the Hebrew Scriptures (the Old Testament) alone. Jews also esteemed the Talmud, a set of ancient books that interpreted the Hebrew Scriptures. Most importantly, the Jews saw themselves as a people specially chosen by God to serve as the bearers of God's laws, including the Ten Commandments, to the rest of the world. The Jews represented the oldest recorded, continuously practiced religious tradition on the North American continent.

The Jewish story in America started long before the Revolutionary War. A handful of Spanish-speaking believers emigrated from Brazil to Rhode Island; Savannah, Georgia; and Charleston, South Carolina, in the seventeenth century. In the 1820s, German-speaking Jews started coming over in large numbers. They soon overwhelmed their Spanish forerunners. The German Jews found work as peddlers, artisans, and shopkeepers in many parts of the country, ranging from Charleston to New York to San Francisco. Many became prosperous and some, such as Judah P. Benjamin, a Confederate cabinet member, quite prominent.

The 1850s marked a watershed in the story of U.S. Judaism. A new and in some ways distinctively American form of the faith then started to crystallize. Its partisans called it Reform Judaism, because they hoped to reform ancient ways and make them more compatible with modern life. Isaac Mayer Wise's long career represented those forces of change well. This eloquent, dynamic Cincinnati rabbi embraced the European Enlightenment of the previous century. Enlightened thinkers had underscored the power of reason to unlock nature's secrets and guide history in the direction of progress. Wise thus called for the orderly worship of an orderly God, preaching and singing in English rather than Hebrew, and mixed seating, with men and women sitting together. More importantly, Wise departed from the ancient, nearly universal, Jewish conviction that the Messiah would be an actual person. Rather, the Messiah equaled the Jewish religion itself, especially when that religion embodied high ideals like justice, democracy, service to humankind, and the thoughtful worship of God. Wise cemented his ideas in brick. In 1875 he founded Hebrew Union College in Cincinnati, which grew into a leading university in the twentieth century.

Predictably, Reform Judaism provoked a reaction. The kind of faith that Wise promoted—urbane, reasonable, and comfortable with middle-class American values—was sharply challenged in the 1880s and 1890s. In those years wave after wave of Jews emigrated from eastern European countries, especially Russia, Poland, Hungary, and Austria. These newcomers proved to be different from the German Jews in several respects. They were poorer and unskilled and spoke languages few Americans understood (or wanted to make the effort to understand). Unlike the urbane Germans, these newcomers came from farms and isolated villages in the Old World. In the United States simple survival demanded struggle. As a result, they clustered together for protection in the cities of the urban Northeast, especially in New York. Most found their lot in the New World extremely hard, even when they were fortunate enough to land a job working for their German brethren. They probably did not possess much sense of ethnic identity before they came, but once here and being reminded daily how different they were, this sense mushroomed.

The newer eastern European Jews proved different from the older German ones in another respect. Simply stated, in matters of religion they often moved to one of two extremes. A minority gave up religion altogether and dubbed themselves freethinkers—free, that is, from the shackles of belief. The majority, in contrast, clung tenaciously to the worship patterns they had nurtured for centuries in the Old World. This meant worshiping and singing in Hebrew, with the men and women sitting apart. It meant that the father exercised control over most aspects of the family's life. And it meant following, as far as possible, all 613 laws prescribed in the Torah, the first five books of Hebrew scripture. By the end of the century these eastern European Jews realized that they needed to organize, partly to distinguish themselves from the Reform Jews, but partly also to protect their beliefs and customs from evaporating in the religious gales of the New World. So they started calling themselves Orthodox Jews. Like numerous Christian bodies, the Orthodox founded schools (notably Yeshiva University in New York City) to preserve their faith among their children and grandchildren.

Not everyone liked these choices, however. For many, Reform Judaism was too liberal, Orthodox Judaism too traditional. Thus, a third major group emerged near the end of the nineteenth century. They called themselves Conservatives, because they hoped to conserve the best of the past without being enslaved by it. The Conservative Jews believed, for example, that the larger principles encoded in the laws of the Hebrew Scriptures remained binding upon modern Jews, but felt that those laws did not have to be followed literally in every respect. The Conservatives also strongly valued the nonreligious aspects of the Jewish heritage, including Jewish literature, drama, music, and cuisine. They too founded schools, most notably Jewish Theological Seminary in New York.

By the beginning of the twentieth century, then, Jews in America had arrayed themselves in three definable groups that looked very much like those of the Protestant denominations: Reform on the left, Orthodox on the right, and Conservative in the middle. To be sure, the Jews suffered discrimination at the hands of the Protestant majority, especially in clubs and private colleges, but less so than did the Catholics. Unlike the Catholics, the Jews remained too scarce to be perceived as a serious threat. Christians admired Jews' industriousness and their disinclination to seek government help. Besides, millions of Americans fancied themselves a biblical people, extended from the Old Testament Israelites as much as from the New Testament Christians. No wonder that Jews found the United States a congenial home, despite its hardships. For most, Emma Lazarus's timeless words chiseled on the Statue of Liberty rang true: "Give me your tired, your poor, your huddled masses yearning to breathe free."

Yet Lazarus spoke for some more than others. Throughout the nineteenth century, Africans Americans remained outsiders in the harshest sense of the term, chained to that status by centuries of custom and statutory law. More blacks embraced Christianity than any other single religious tradition, yet commonalities of faith proved to be less important than differences of skin color. At the beginning of the century one million blacks lived in the United States. Some 90 percent were enslaved, and many lived in the South. By 1860 the black population had swollen to four million. Again 90 percent were enslaved, but by then almost all lived in the South. That much is clear. Tracking the slaves' religious progress is considerably more complicated, however.

Bondsmen (as slaves were commonly called) adopted Christianity only slowly. In the eighteenth century their masters frequently prevented missionaries from contacting the black laborers under their charge lest the Christian message of equality before God make them rebellious. And when missionaries did make contact, they usually met little success. They expected slaves to master lengthy creeds by rote memorization, since slaves could not read and in most places were forbidden by law or custom from learning to do so. Moreover, the church's formal liturgy, or its prescribed pattern of worship, seemed stiff and unnatural to souls accustomed to worshiping in more informal ways. Most damaging of all was that the Church of England's missionaries not only identified themselves with the masters but went out of their way to stress that the Bible taught slaves to be obedient.

The Revolutionary years of the 1770s and 1780s introduced dramatic change as upstart Baptist and Methodist preachers elbowed aside the established Church of England missionaries. The evangelical spokesmen asked no one's permission to preach to the slaves, and success followed. For one thing, they emphasized emotional, heartfelt conversion over the memorization of creeds. They talked about moral accountability—for masters and slaves alike. And they taught that slavery itself was wrong, a sin in God's eyes. This last claim, that slavery was a sin, was one they could not continue to make. By the 1830s, evangelical preachers, especially in the South, had lost the will to denounce the "peculiar institution," as southerners called it, for a variety of reasons. One of the most important was the swelling desire for respectability in the eyes of the vaguely Christian majority that endorsed slaveholding. Another involved the growing conviction that all workable societies needed a permanent class of menial laborers in order to survive. Yet the basic principles of evangelical Christianity had already taken firm root and would flourish in the slave community, especially the sense of the equality of all before God. The number of slaves who embraced Christianity is impossible to know, but that they were a large minority seems likely.

Between the Revolution and the Civil War, Christianity took a number of different forms among bondsmen. Most often, perhaps, African Americans worshiped with whites in white-run Baptist and Methodist churches. To say that all worshiped together is not to say that all distinctions faded away, however. Blacks normally sat apart or even in the balcony. And white preachers normally directed words about obedience specifically at them. Even so, whites and blacks heard the same sermon together. They sang and took Holy Communion together. They participated in church disciplinary meetings, not always as equals, but together. And at life's end they were buried in the church cemetery together. Flawed though the system was, Christian worship melded the races as they were nowhere else in southern society.

From time to time, African Americans worshiped independently of whites, a pattern that defined a second distinct form of black Christianity. Despite great odds, slaves managed to put up meeting houses of their own. The Silver Bluff Baptist Church in South Carolina offers a prominent example. There, numerous black preachers gained fame for their ability to move whites as well as their own people to tearful conversions. By the 1840s, however, independent black worship of this sort had fallen into decline. On at least three occasions Christian teachings had been used by fiery black prophets to justify slave insurrections: Gabriel Prosser's uprising in Richmond, Virginia, in 1800; Denmark Vesey's in Charleston, South Carolina, in 1822; and Nat Turner's in Southampton County, Virginia, in 1831. For these and other reasons, white authorities increasingly cracked down on any signs of black independence, including unsupervised worship.

And then there was the Invisible Institution, called invisible because it took place outside whites' vision. As the planters' oversight of slave life grew more oppressive, African Americans responded by praising God in their huts, in forested meadows, or simply in the dark of night—any place, in short, where whites could not see. In those settings black preachers delivered God's word freely, often in memorized phrases that evoked powerful images of past bondage and future liberation, both physical and spiritual. They spoke especially of Moses leading his people across the Red Sea to freedom, and of the lowly Jesus suffering for the sins of others.

In those unseen meetings the slaves experienced assurance of their worth in God's eyes, as well as the resources for bringing moral discipline to their lives and, by force of example, to their masters' lives. Those settings also moved the slaves to create a distinctive form of song, the spiritual. This type of music combined lyrics and tunes common in white evangelical circles with ones of their own creation. "Swing Low, Sweet Chariot" and "Joshua Fit de Battle of Jericho," at once powerfully rhythmic and melancholy, ranked among the timeless favorites.

Evangelical Protestantism by no means commanded the loyalty of all slaves, however. For one thing, probably a majority of African Americans, like a majority of whites, remained outside the reach of the church. Also, Roman Catholic missionaries won a small minority of followers, especially in Louisiana and Maryland. And finally, some blacks retained the religious traditions of their native West Africa. One of the most visible examples was voodoo, or Vodun, an import from Africa and Haiti that focused upon the healing powers in certain herbs and plant roots.

Before the Civil War most African Americans lived in the South as slaves, but about 10 percent resided in the North, sometimes enslaved but sometimes free, as slavery slowly died out in the North between the Revolution and the Civil War. Northern blacks scattered themselves along the whole spectrum of Protestant denominations. Shortly after the Revolution, however, the seeds of two independent black denominations were sown: the African Methodist Episcopal Church (commonly called the A.M.E. Church), and the similar African Methodist Episcopal Zion Church (commonly called the A.M.E.Z. Church).

Both groups claimed urban origins. The story of the A.M.E. began with Richard Allen. Born a slave in Philadelphia in 1760, Allen converted to Methodism as a teenager and entered the ministry. Clearly he had found his calling, for soon afterward Allen's master also converted and allowed him to purchase his freedom. The young evangelist preached in the Philadelphia area, eventually making that city's St. George's Methodist Church his church home. For a while things went well, but the growing presence of African Americans at St. George's eventually aroused whites' fears. One Sunday morning (probably in 1787) some white trustees yanked a prominent black man to his feet because he was kneeling in an area reserved for whites. Outraged, Allen determined never to return. In 1794 he opened Bethel Church for Negro Methodists, probably the first regular black church meeting in the United States. Bethel evolved into the A.M.E. in 1816. A similar train of events, augmented by rivalry for scarce resources within the black community, prompted the formation of the A.M.E.Z. in New York in 1821. Although both groups prospered after the Civil War by attending to both the material and spiritual needs of their people, the A.M.E. in particular gravitated toward structured worship and middle-class respectability.

Following the Civil War, African Americans established additional groups. After several false starts they organized the National Baptist Convention in Atlanta in 1895. This body soon became the largest black denomination in the United States. Regional pride played a powerful role for blacks, just as it did for whites. The Colored (now Christian) Methodist Episcopal Church established itself in 1870 to provide a home for southern black Methodists who did not feel at home in either of the northern A.M.E. churches, because of the churches' growing respectability and Yankee flavor, or in the mostly white Methodist Episcopal Church, South. At the very end of the century a group of fervent evangelicals in Mississippi and Tennessee coalesced in a loose fellowship called the Church of God in Christ. This body endorsed divine healing and, by 1907, speaking in tongues (a kind of rapid, involuntary speech that always sounded like a foreign language). Both healing and tongues formed hallmarks of the emerging Pentecostal movement.

By the end of the century probably about half of the African Americans in the United States considered themselves Christians in a self-conscious way, and nearly all in a broadly cultural way. The great majority, in any event, were affiliated with Baptist or Methodist bodies. Most of the rest were Catholics living in Louisiana. Nineteenth-century blacks also fashioned hundreds of quasi-religious brotherhoods and sisterhoods for recreation, fellowship, and mutual help. Well-known examples included the Prince Hall Masons and the Colored Oddfellows.

The African-American church served as a center for many aspects of life. Excluded from white-run schools, businesses, and churches, blacks created a separate world of their own inside the limits of their churches. Those settings offered ambitious and talented young men a place to display their abilities. Black groups rarely ordained women, but females—affectionately dubbed "Mothers of the Church"—routinely shouldered the hard, day-to-day work of visiting the sick and teaching the young. Women also exercised powerful leadership roles in informal ways. Male ministers ignored them at their peril. Beyond all this, many (although certainly not all) black churches retained the worship patterns of the antebellum years, emphasizing clapping, enthusiastic singing, and a call-and-response style of preaching.

In the latter part of the nineteenth century many of these currents flowed together in the life of Amanda Berry Smith. Born a slave in 1837, Smith knew that God had called her to the ministry. Unable to receive ordination because of her sex, Smith nonetheless launched out on her own as an independent evangelist in the Wesleyan tradition. Thousands professed conversion under her ministry. Smith gave the word *energetic* new dimensions of meaning. She traveled to England in 1878, to

India in 1879, to Liberia in 1881, and back to England in 1889, and finally settled in Chicago in 1892. She started a home for orphans near there in 1899. Outsiders smirked, saying that leaders like Smith offered pie-in-the-sky rewards in heaven rather than real-life ones in the here and now. But she knew they were wrong—as did millions of others—for the old-time religion met enduring needs of the human spirit in the trials and tribulations of the present.

RABBI WISE SPEAKS OF
THE NECESSITY OF CHANGE

Isaac Mayer Wise, one of the most prominent and controversial rabbis of the nineteenth century, urged Jews to accommodate themselves both to American ways and to the most advanced thinking of the age. In this 1871 speech Wise argued that the willingness to embrace change constituted the essence of Reform Judaism in America.

Change, universal and perpetual, is the law of laws in this universe. Still there is an element of stability, the fact of mutation itself; the law of change changes not.... Wisdom, boundless and ineffable, and the revelations of Deity lie in this law of laws....

As an illustration of this, it is to be remembered that the Israelite of the reformed school does not believe in the restoration of the ancient mode of worship by the sacrifice of animal victims by a hereditary priesthood. He considers that phase was necessary and beneficial, in its time and locality, but that it would be void of all significance in our age when entirely different conceptions of divine worship prevail, and it would appear much more meaningless to coming generations. The divine institutions of the past are not obligatory on the present generation or on coming ages, because the conditions that rendered them necessary, desirable and beneficial have been radically changed. Therefore, Progressive Judaism [might] be a better designation than Reformed Judaism.

Warriors for God
and Region

Mine eyes have seen the glory
of the coming of the Lord;
He is trampling out the vintage
where the grapes of wrath are stored;
He hath loosed the fateful lightning
of his terrible swift sword;
His truth is marching on.

   —Julia Ward Howe, "Battle Hymn of the Republic" (1861)

I t proved to be the costliest war in American history. Six
hundred thousand died, and another million fell as casualties. All the wars that the United States fought combined—
from the Revolution through Vietnam—totaled fewer deaths
than the Civil War. Besides unprecedented destruction, the
Civil War (or the War between the States, as it was, and still is,
commonly called in the South) harbored many ironies. More
died of disease than of gunshot wounds. Early in the conflict

President Abraham Lincoln asked Colonel Robert E. Lee of Virginia to lead the Union army (Lee would ultimately lead the *Confederate* forces). Three of Lincoln's brothers-in-law would fight for the South, and one would die in the Rebel cause.

Religion accounted for many of the deepest ironies. Some of the bloodiest battles ever fought on the North American continent, including Shiloh and Antietam, were waged in the front yards of country churches. The Battle of Gettysburg, by some accounts the grisliest of all, unfolded on the outskirts of a Lutheran seminary campus. Christian pastors on both sides of the Mason-Dixon line incited conflict by their unwillingness to compromise. And once the fighting started, they intensified its ferocity by invoking the fires of divine sanction (the idea that God supported one or the other side in the conflict). When the bloodshed stopped, they perpetuated ill feelings for years by their unapologetic defense of their own side's cause.

Religious beliefs fed the ideologies that fed the war. Elijah P. Lovejoy, a Presbyterian minister turned newspaper editor, offers a case in point. When this Maine-born, Princeton-educated pastor first opened his printing press in St. Louis, he seemed mostly concerned to attack Catholics, Baptists, and members of the Disciples of Christ. But the sin of human bondage gnawed at his conscience. By the 1830s, Lovejoy had moved across the river to Alton, Illinois, and pitted himself unalterably against slavery. Convinced that slaveowners routinely raped their female slaves, among other evils, Lovejoy devoted himself to the cause of immediate abolition. Mobs destroyed his press three times and, in 1837, they took his life as well.

For Southerners too, religion and politics merged. Exactly twenty-five years after Lovejoy's death Leonidas Polk, Episcopal bishop of Louisiana, heard his region's call. Polk promptly exchanged his bishop's robes for the uniform of a Confederate major general. In years past he had devoted his efforts to the conversion and religious instruction of slaves, winning respect for humane treatment of the hundreds of bondsmen he himself had owned. But now it was time to fight, and fight he did, with brilliance and valor, until the summer of 1864, when a cannon-ball claimed his life in the Battle of Atlanta.

Where religious conviction ended and outright fanaticism began was sometimes hard to say. Two of the men who did the most to stir up undying hatred, Northerner John Brown and Southerner John Wilkes Booth, both felt that they had been called by God to carry out their bloody tasks. Brown, a radical Presbyterian, believed not only that slavery was wrong but also that God had called him to start a war that would smash the slaveholding system. In the 1850s, this avenger journeyed to Kansas, where he murdered five proslavery sympathizers in cold blood. He then moved on to Harpers Ferry, Virginia (now West Virginia), where he tried to spark a nationwide slave insurrection by taking over a federal arsenal. Brown went to the gallows on December 2, 1859, convinced that he had served his nation and his God well.

The same pattern held true for stage actor John Wilkes Booth, who had hurried from Richmond to Harpers Ferry to witness Brown's execution. Though Booth never possessed the courage actually to enlist in the Confederate army, he felt that God had called him to execute the president who had plunged his beloved South into smoking ruins. Thus, on April 14, 1865, he slipped into Ford's Theater in Washington, D.C., and shot Lincoln point blank in the back of the head. Booth too met violent death—his turn came twelve days later—convinced that he had obeyed the plain instructions of his conscience and his Lord.

The Civil War stemmed from many causes. Dramatically different notions about what a United States of America really meant played a large role. Indeed, until the mid–nineteenth century many Americans, especially Southerners, customarily used a plural verb when speaking of the nation ("the United States are…"). After all, what came first, the federal Constitution or the rights of the individual states? Growing sectional rivalry contributed to the bitterness as well. Nonetheless, most historians believe that the question of black servitude remained the primary cause of the war. The problem of course was that the Constitution guaranteed the states' right to practice slavery if they wished. The slave trade ended in 1808, but not the practice. The number of bondsmen had grown from 400,000 at the time the Constitution was ratified in 1791 to 3.5 million on the eve of the Civil War. Although Northerners had long profited from the goods that Southerners produced with slave labor, the Northern states had gradually abolished the system. Slavery remained the South's peculiar problem.

White Christian opposition to slavery began nearly a century before the Civil War. Although a few Puritans and many Quakers had spoken out against the practice since the early eighteenth century, serious opposition to it began in 1784 when the Methodist church prohibited both clergy and lay persons from holding slaves. The Baptists and Quakers instituted similar measures in the same period, both in the North and the South. As late as 1818, the General Assembly of the Presbyterian church declared slavery a "gross violation of human nature" and called Christians to erase it as speedily as possible. Although all these admonitions received mixed enforcement, the principle remained clear.

Gradually, however, opposition to slavery localized in the states north of the Mason-Dixon line. Much, and perhaps most, of the antislavery sentiment stemmed from religious impulses. The year 1819 saw the formation of the American Colonization

Society, which sought to buy slaves and send them back to Africa. Several thousand went, forming the nation of Liberia. Although later generations viewed this recolonization scheme as impractical at best and racist at worst, at the time many thousands of Christians, both white and black, deemed it a reasonable solution to an unreasonable problem.

By the 1830s, millions of Christians, mostly in the North, were pressing for the abolition of the "peculiar institution." Some wanted all the slaves freed immediately, with little regard for the economic consequences for owners or to the slaves themselves. William Lloyd Garrison, a Boston journalist, emerged as one of the most outspoken representatives of this approach, commonly called immediatism. Once influenced by the Quakers, this fiery New Englander found himself increasingly alienated from all forms of orthodox Christianity. Nonetheless, his conscience burned brightly. In 1831 Garrison launched a radical paper called the *Liberator*. His speeches and articles stirred evangelicals and nonevangelicals alike to form antislavery societies. Garrison's constant agitation not only raised Northerners' awareness of the cruelties of slavery but also helped characterize the system as sinful. The evil of slavery so incensed Garrison that he soon urged the *North* to secede from the Union lest it soil itself by association with the South.

For most Northerners, immediate abolition seemed impractical. They opted instead for step-by-step elimination of the slave system—an approach commonly called gradualism— either by halting its spread into the territories of the West or by compensating slaveowners for loss of their "property." Many of these reformers had been converted to evangelical Christianity during the revivals of the Second Great Awakening. For example, the revivalist Charles G. Finney forthrightly defined slavery as sinful. Because the Constitution guaranteed the legality of slavery, Finney urged Christians to do the next best thing: mount moral pressure against the system in every way possible. Although he saw no way to make slavery illegal, he wanted to make it unthinkable.

Many evangelicals fell somewhere between Garrison's desire for immediate abolition and Finney's willingness to accept gradual abolition. Consider, for instance, the career of Theodore Dwight Weld, one of Finney's most energetic converts. This young firebrand was expelled from the Presbyterians' Lane Theological Seminary in Cincinnati, where he was a student, for preaching against slavery and for associating with blacks as friends. Weld and a group of supporters, known as the Lane Rebels, then moved to the infant Oberlin College, near Cleveland. In time they formed influential networks of friendship and communication, and Weld himself later married the prominent abolitionist and women's rights advocate Angelina Grimké. Many secular abolitionists were driven by principles of universal brotherhood and sisterhood, derived from the mid-century democratic and humanitarian revolutions going on in Europe. In contrast, evangelicals like the Lane Rebels acted from a biblical notion of humans' equality before God, as well as a conviction that the United States could never become God's land until Christians purged the sin of slavery from their midst.

Orator Frederick Douglass exposed the hypocrisy of white Christianity as incisively as any. Born a slave in Maryland about 1817, Douglass taught himself to read by poring over the Bible. He escaped to Massachusetts in 1838. Once free, he championed the causes of temperance, women's rights, and, above all, antislavery. In his autobiography (published in 1845 as *Narrative of the Life of Frederick Douglass*), the former slave argued that a canyon separated the false religion of the slaveholder from the true religion of Christ. In the former, Douglass declared, the man who wielded the "blood clotted" whip during the week stood behind the sacred pulpit on Sunday. The man who robbed the slave of his earnings presumed to teach him the Bible. The man who stole the slave's sister and sold her into prostitution presented himself as an "advocate of purity." The man who tore wives from husbands and children from their parents in order to turn a profit preached about the wholesomeness of families. In sum, Douglass proclaimed with righteous indignation, "[We] have men-stealers for ministers, women-whippers for missionaries, and cradle-plunderers for church members."

One religiously inspired woman, Harriet Beecher Stowe, may have done more to undermine slavery than any other single person. Stowe's Christian credentials ran deep. Her father, Lyman Beecher, was a well-known Presbyterian theologian and seminary president in Ohio. He strongly disliked slavery and said so. Stowe herself won lasting fame for her novel *Uncle Tom's Cabin*, which was published in 1852 and frequently republished and, more importantly perhaps, turned into a long-running New York play. The novel told the story of a God-fearing slave family, ruthlessly broken up by traders who bought and sold the laborers as if they were nothing but horses. Although the novel bordered upon allegory, with most of the characters overdrawn as either entirely evil or entirely good, it powerfully stirred the Northern conscience against the brutality and un-Christian character of the slave system.

Southern Christians took none of this agitation lying down. They mounted a fierce defense of their way of life. As far back as the 1640s, the Church of England (later the Episcopal Church) in Virginia had stated unequivocally that slavery remained compatible with Christianity. For the sixty years or so from the 1760s through the 1820s the Methodists and Baptists in the South had opposed slavery. They considered it sinful and associated it with elite plantation owners, whom they strongly disliked anyway. But by the second third of the nineteenth century most Southern Christians, including the Methodists and Baptists, had changed their minds: maybe slavery was not so sinful after all.

Slavery's advocates offered several reasons. They typically began by noting that the Old Testament patriarchs owned slaves and the New Testament did not condemn them for it. Indeed, the New Testament urged slaves to be obedient to their masters. In the book of Philemon, for example, Saint Paul himself urges a runaway slave to return to his owner. (Southern and Northern Protestants looked to the same Bible, but the former tended to interpret it literally, the latter figuratively.) Southerners added that most slaves would have remained ignorant of Christianity if they had been left in Africa, where their immortal souls would have perished in hell. Southern Christians also argued that the slavery system compared favorably with the inhuman working conditions in the mines and factories of the North. Above all, they believed that the slave system embodied a reasonable way to organize a society, especially if the slaves were Christianized and treated as fully human children rather than as less-than-human brutes.

Given such enormous differences in outlook between the regions, by the mid-1840s millions of men and women on both sides of the Mason-Dixon line had come to believe that the separation of the North and South was inevitable. And so it was that the churches embarked upon the road to war.

The largest Protestant sects led the way. First came the Presbyterians, who split into "new school" and "old school" factions in 1837. This rupture primarily involved other issues, such as whether humans had any ability to embrace Christ on their own (the new schoolers said yes, the old schoolers no). The new school split along sectional lines in 1857, the old school in 1861.

Next came the Methodists, the largest Protestant denomination and one of the largest organizations of any kind in the nation. In 1843, a sizable bloc in New York state broke from the Methodist Church, because they felt the church was too timid about condemning slavery. This faction called themselves Wesleyan Methodists, partly to underscore John Wesley's own opposition to slavery. In 1844, things came to a head among the main body of Methodists when a Georgia bishop acquired slaves through marriage. When the General Conference of the Methodist Church demanded his resignation, the Southern Methodists walked out. They formed their own body the following year, labeling it the Methodists Episcopal Church, South. Similar resentments triggered the separation of Northern and Southern Baptists in 1845. For the Baptists the question was whether missionaries could own slaves. When it became clear that Northerners, who controlled the Baptist missionary agencies, would no longer endorse having slaveowning missionaries, the Southerners set up their own group, the Southern Baptist Convention.

All these animosities ran deep. The Northern and Southern Methodists did not reunite until 1939 (and the black Methodists were effectively kept out until 1958), the Presbyterians did not come together again until 1983, and the Northern and Southern Baptists have never reunited.

Among the other main religious groups, the northern and southern Roman Catholic churches broke apart when the nation did in 1861, but readily reunited at war's end, partly because they owed final religious allegiance to the church in Rome, not to any one region of a nation. The Episcopalians followed a similar pattern of splitting and reuniting as the nation did. Most of the remaining Christian bodies did not officially separate, but that was not because of tender feelings for one another. Some, such as the Unitarians and Congregationalists, were already concentrated in the northern section of the country. Others, like the Disciples of Christ, proved too locally based to break apart. The Lutherans were too preoccupied with their own ethnic and doctrinal concerns to focus on separating. The same held true for the Jews.

But the largest denominations had fractured, one by one. And when they did, Americans of all persuasions resigned themselves to the inevitability of war. A Presbyterian preacher said in 1837 that the Potomac River would be "dyed with blood." Seven years later a Methodist clergyman predicted that the "fiercest passions" of human nature would soon be arrayed against each other. If Christians who shared so much could not work things out, how could others expect to be successful?

When the fighting actually erupted in the green fields of Virginia in the spring of 1861, religious men—and not a few women—rushed to do their share, and perhaps a bit more than their share. Ministers on both sides rallied partisans to fight for their cause and their region. Northern clergy argued that the sin of slavery would have to be purged before the millennium (the thousand years of peace and prosperity the Bible promised) could dawn. Southern clergy countered that the North was the land of infidelity, the South the land of faithfulness to biblical ideals. God had, they said, specially chosen the South to show the world what a truly Christian society looked like. Indeed, the Constitution of the Confederate States of America (unlike that of the United States) explicity identified the Confederacy as a Christian nation.

As the fighting dragged on, Christian organizations on both sides supplied spiritual and material comfort. Northern churches provided hundreds of chaplains and relief workers to the war effort. Scores of women served as nurses. The American Red Cross had its beginnings in the Sanitary Commission, a

Unitarian effort to care for the wounded and dying. By the same token, Southern armies saw wave after wave of revival fervor. Some Southern chaplains even promised young Rebels that they would go directly to heaven if they were slain on the battlefield.

When Confederate general Robert E. Lee surrendered to Union general Ulysses S. Grant at Appomattox Court House, Viriginia, on April 9, 1865, the military war effectively ended, but the religious war only moved into an even higher intensity. The Northern clergy interpreted the Union victory as a sign of God's pleasure with the North. "I charge the whole guilt of this war upon the ambitious, educated, plotting political leaders of the South," thundered the Brooklyn, New York, preacher Henry Ward Beecher, brother to Harrier Beecher Stowe, in 1865. Someday, he continued, "These guiltiest and most remorseless traitors, these high and cultured men with might and wisdom... shall be whirled aloft and plunged downward forever and ever in an endless retribution."

The Southern clergy proved themselves equally unrepentant. Although none could deny that the South had been vanquished, few Southern Christians saw the defeat as a sign of divine displeasure. Rather, they interpreted their situation as a trial. God chastised the children he truly loved, did he not? Americans had always been prone to say that God's purposes echoed the nation's. But nowhere did civil religion flourish so grandly as in the Old South during and after the War between the States. By the 1870s former Confederates talked reverently about the Lost Cause, or the Southern way of life, almost as if it were a religion itself.

But even if most Northern and Southern Christians saw God's blessing upon their respective regions, not all did. One of America's greatest presidents, who would be assassinated on

Good Friday of 1865, rose above regional passions to reflect on the religious meaning of the war.

What was Lincoln's own religion? This question has provoked heated debate. On the one hand, we know that as a young lawyer in Illinois Lincoln rebelled against the rigidity of his parents' Baptist faith and the unseemliness of Christian churches fighting each other as ardently as they had fought the Devil. One of Lincoln's political foes in Illinois, the Methodist circuit rider Peter Cartwright, went so far as to say that Lincoln held no religion at all. After the president's death even some of his closest friends said the same. They had a case. Lincoln was the only president who never joined a church, and he never publicly affirmed any of the main doctrines of Christianity.

On the other hand, in his childhood home the inquisitive Abe heard the Bible quoted often. He may have memorized the Psalms and most of the New Testament. As an adult, Lincoln regularly attended a Presbyterian church, both at home in Springfield and in Washington, D.C. He quoted the Bible often, which suggests that he read it regularly. Most importantly, however, his maturity and tragedy prompted Lincoln to think about the larger meaning of life. The legacy of his parents' stern beliefs that all people were predestined by God to go to heaven or to hell, the untimely deaths of two of his four young sons, and the mounting suffering of the war taught Lincoln to see God as a deity who loomed above the wishes of factions and regions no less than those of individuals.

Consider the religious themes in Lincoln's second inaugural address, given less than a month before his death. Each side had looked for an easy triumph, he began, but it was not to be. Both sides read the same Bible and prayed to the same God, invoking his aid against the enemy. Lincoln expressed dismay that anyone would seek God's help in perpetuating slavery, yet he immediately added (following Jesus' words in the New Testament) that no one should judge another's motives. "The prayers of both could not be answered; that of neither has been answered fully."

Then Lincoln rose to one of the most profound religious reflections in American history. God, he judged, had allowed this "terrible war" to come in order to punish both sides for allowing slavery. No one could know how long the Almighty would permit the killing to continue, for "every drop of blood" drawn by the slave master's lash would have to be paid for with the sword. And who could question God's purposes? "[As] was said three thousand years ago, so still it must be said: 'The judgments of the Lord are true and righteous altogether.'"

Did Christianity cause the Civil War? No. But Christians contributed to making a peaceful solution to the scandal of slavery impossible. Did Christians acknowledge their guilt in the matter? Rarely. Still, a few, including the president, sensed the mystery of God's ways with defiant humans. That sense did not atone for all the killing, let alone for slavery, but it may have made Americans more humble about their complicity in the two great tragedies of the age.

In the Narrative of the Life of Frederick Douglass *(1845), this eloquent former slave distinguished authentic Christianity from the vicious, corrupted form of that religion that pervaded the South and legitimized the slave system. Douglass's anger about the hypocrisy of slave Christianity was shared by many whites as well as blacks and helped to spark the Civil War.*

What I have said respecting and against religion, I mean strictly to apply to the *slaveholding religion* of this land, and with no possible reference to Christianity proper; for, between the Christianity of this land, and the Christianity of Christ, I recognize the widest possible difference—so wide, that to receive the one as good, pure, and holy, is of necessity to reject the other as bad, corrupt, and wicked. To be the friend of the one, is of necessity to be the enemy of the other. I love the pure, peaceable, and impartial Christianity of Christ: I therefore hate the corrupt, slaveholding, women-whipping, cradle-plundering, partial and hypocritical Christianity of this land.... [R]evivals of religion and revivals in the slave-trade go hand in hand together. The slave prison and the church stand near each other. The clanking of fetters and the rattling of chains in the prison, and the pious psalm and solemn prayer in the church, may be heard at the same time. Dealers in the bodies and souls of men erect their stand in the presence of the pulpit, and they mutually help each other. The dealer gives his blood-stained gold to support the pulpit, and the pulpit, in return, covers his infernal business with the garb of Christianity. Here we have religion and robbery the allies of each other—devils dressed in angels' robes, and hell presenting the semblance of paradise.

CHAPTER FOURTEEN

Fashioners of Immigrant Faiths

Faith of our fathers! living still
In spite of dungeon, fire and sword:
O how our hearts beat high with joy,
Whene'er we hear that glorious word: holy faith!
We will be true to thee till death.

—*Frederick W. Faber, "Faith of Our Fathers" (1849)*

Oscar Handlin, a distinguished U.S. historian, once said that he set out to write the story of immigration to America and ended up writing the story of America itself. He spoke well. Statistics never give the whole account of anything, but in this case they provide at least a hint of the vastness of the changes that overtook the nation between 1820 and 1920. In the 1820s, some 140,000 immigrants, almost all European, streamed into the young republic. In the 1830s that number rose to 600,000; in the 1840s, 1.7 million; and in the 1850s, 2.6 million. The 1860s, a decade torn by the Civil War, saw a slight drop, but in the 1870s the rate shot up again, to 2.8 million. Between 1881 and the outbreak of World War I some thirty-five years later, 23 million more arrived. This seemingly ceaseless river of humanity finally shrank to a trickle only when Congress imposed severe restrictions upon immigration in the early 1920s.

The overwhelming majority of the late-nineteenth-century immigrants were Roman Catholics. Many, probably most, were fairly inactive yet loyal members of the church. The growth of Catholics as a percentage of the larger population is startling. The first U.S. census, taken in 1790, showed that 85 percent of white Americans came from British Protestant traditions. At that time less than 2 percent of the white population claimed to be Catholic. But things changed dramatically over the next seventy years. By the opening of the Civil War in 1861, 10 percent of the population identified itself as Catholic, making it one of the largest religious groups in the United States. (Different accounts rendered different figures, but all placed Roman Catholics among the six largest groups.) The surge of Catholic immigration continued apace after the War between the States. By 1906 fully 17 percent of the population said they were Catholic.

U.S. history did not, of course, begin in the nineteenth century, and neither did Catholic history. Spanish Franciscans reached Florida in the 1560s and northern New Mexico in the 1590s. Indeed, the oldest continually used church in the United States, the San Miguel Mission in Santa Fe, New Mexico, dates from 1609, more than a decade before the Pilgrims touched Plymouth Rock. But the Spanish, Mexican, and Indian Catholics of the Southwest did not figure promently in the development of U.S. religion until after World War II. That honor fell to the English Catholics who settled in Maryland in the 1630s and then, especially, to the successive waves of Catholic immigrants who came from Ireland, Germany,

Poland, Italy, and eastern Europe in the latter two-thirds of the nineteenth century.

John Carroll, the first Catholic bishop in the United States, exemplified the high social status of English Catholics at the beginning of the nineteenth century. His younger cousin Charles Carroll signed the Declaration of Independence, and his older brother Daniel Carroll won a footnote in the history books as a signer of the Constitution. Carroll himself, born the son of a wealthy Maryland merchant in 1735, was educated by Jesuits in France. He returned to Maryland two years before the Revolution to serve as a parish pastor. Both laypeople and the pope soon recognized Carroll's exceptional abilities. He rose through the ranks, becoming vicar apostolic (leader) of the Mission in the United States in 1784, bishop five years later, and archbishop in 1808. Carroll's non-Christian friend Ben Franklin once urged the pope to appoint Carroll bishop! Carroll strongly supported the separation of church and state. His many accomplishments included founding Georgetown Academy for boys near Washington, D.C., in 1789, which evolved into one of the nation's most distinguished universities.

The ethnic makeup of the Catholic Church in the United States started to change noticeably in the 1820s. The long-range source of that change stemmed from the modernization of farming techniques in Europe, which drove millions of peasants off their land in search of jobs. The immediate source stemmed from farming depressions that struck Ireland in the 1820s, followed by a decade of crop failures in the 1840s. During those desperate years some 1.5 million souls starved to death. Another 2.5 million—20 percent of the total population—emigrated from the Emerald Isle in search of food and work. Nearly two million of those came to the United States, almost all of them Catholic.

The successive waves of Irish immigrants quickly overwhelmed and eventually displaced the comfortable reign of the English (and some French) Catholics on U.S. soil. The Irish dominated the church's membership rolls through the middle third of the century and controlled the church's hierarchy until the late twentieth century. In the process they set the church's tone for the better part of two centuries.

Rank-and-file Irish Catholics had a distinctive approach to their faith. For one thing, they held the church and the clergy in high esteem. Back in Ireland the church had helped resist the English Protestants who had oppressed them for centuries. Because Irish Catholics had been accustomed to looking to the church for protection against the English, in the United States they looked to the church for protection against unscrupulous bosses. Church officials in turn readily supported political figures who assisted their people—one thinks especially of the Irish Catholic political dynasties in Boston and New York. Moreover, traditions brought from the homeland encouraged Irish Catholics to raise large families, to insist upon strict sexual morality, and to uphold traditional beliefs in matters of doctrine.

In the middle years of the century the Irish found themselves competing with a new wave of migrants, this time from the German-speaking provinces of central Europe. Some 400,000 Germans arrived in the 1840s, and nearly a million more in the 1850s. Again, many were Catholic—but with a difference. Where the Irish had settled mostly in the towns and cities of the Northeast, the Germans now established themselves mostly in the upper Midwest, in a triangle defined by Milwaukee, St. Louis, and Cincinnati. Occupational and class differences emerged too. The Irish worked mainly in mines and factories, while Germans labored mostly on farms and in towns as craftsmen and shopkeepers. And where the Irish remained poor, often bordering upon destitution, the Germans were generally self-sufficient and often quite prosperous.

Beyond these social differences, the Irish and the Germans represented quite different ways of relating to the largely Protestant environment. The Irish found it easier to engage outsiders, partly because they spoke English. The German Catholics, on the other hand, resisted assimilation. They felt that they could best preserve their faith by worshiping in German, sending their children to German parochial schools, and associating only with other Germans. At one point the antagonism between Irish and German Catholics grew so intense that Germans in New York City tried to establish their own cemetery so that they could still shun the Irish after death.

After the Civil War new waves of Catholic immigrants from other parts of Europe started to wash across U.S. shores. The most conspicuous of the postwar migrations included Poles and Italians. More than two million Polish Catholics arrived between 1850 and 1924. Like the Irish, they proved intensely loyal to their church. Indeed, for many daily life revolved around church activities. At the Sacred Heart parish in New Britain, Connecticut, for example, the church established a school, an orphanage, an old-age home, a newspaper, and a cemetery, all run by sisters (women religious persons) of the parish. Also like the Germans, the Polish Catholics wanted to worship in their native language and avoid needless association with Protestants. Another trait the Poles shared with the Germans was resentment of the Irish. As far as the Poles could see, the Irish bishops and archbishops ran the Catholic Church in the United States mostly for the benefit of the Irish.

Italian Catholics, who also started arriving in large numbers in the latter half of the century, left their distinctive mark on the religious landscape as well. Until 1870 northern Italy remained divided politically from southern Italy and Sicily. Northern Italian Catholics gained a reputation for learning, artistic achievement, and religious restraint. Southern Italian Catholics, in contrast, gained a reputation for intense piety, marked by fervent emotionalism and (in the view of outsiders) irregular beliefs and practices. The latter included carnival-like street festivals, or *festas*, involving days of celebration and parading in honor of the patron saints of local towns or regions.

Another big difference separated the two regions and two forms of Catholicism. The north of Italy enjoyed good relations with the papacy, the south did not. Hence, when southern Italian Catholics came to the United States they resisted the church and the clergy, preferring to carry out their devotional practices in the home, if at all. And they too resented the Irish, who dominated the church and seemed determined to keep the best appointments for themselves.

By now it should be evident that the Catholic Church in America in the nineteenth century faced enormous challenges. It had to cope with internal diversity almost as bewildering as the diversity of the Protestant denominations. But the church enjoyed one advantage the Protestants did not. It was the oldest continuous institution in the Western world. The sense of tradition and the ever-present resource (or threat) of theological direction from Rome enabled the church to stand as a rock of stability in a rapidly changing environment.

Putting aside their ethnic differences, bishops, priests, and nuns rolled up their sleeves and went to work. They built churches, of course, but also schools, colleges, hospitals, orphanages, and lodges. They provided emergency funds for the destitute and medical treatment for the sick. They helped frightened immigrants who knew no English to find housing and jobs. They shielded laborers from shifty bosses. They served as intermediaries between the immigrants and city officials. They established the largest private school system in the world, mostly staffed by nuns. Scores of nuns served heroically as nurses and cooks in the Civil War and the Spanish-American War of 1898. One prominent order, the Sisters of Mercy, established and ran one of the larger hospital systems in the United States.

Catholic clergy and sisters distinguished themselves for their ability simultaneously to tend both the physical and the spiritual needs of immigrants. Elizabeth Bayley Seton, for example, won distinction doing both. Reared as an Episcopalian in New York City after the Revolution, Seton and her husband journeyed to Italy in 1803 in the hope that the warm Mediterranean sun might reverse his deteriorating health. He met an untimely death, but Seton found comfort in the concern and piety of the local Catholics who cared for her. She also found her life's calling.

Returning to the United States, Seton converted to the Catholic Church. She soon moved to Baltimore to escape the harsh criticism of relatives and friends who were appalled that a Protestant would stoop to become a Catholic. In Baltimore, Seton established the Sisters of Charity in 1809. She soon moved to a beautiful valley near Emmitsburg, Maryland, where the Sisters opened St. Joseph's Academy as well as a free school. They nursed the sick and needy in that area. The Sisters then fanned out to other cities in the East and on to the West. In St. Louis they built the first hospital west of the Mississippi River. Seton died in her fourty-sixth year, but in 1975 the church canonized her, making her the first American saint.

As the nation sprawled westward across the Appalachians and into the desert Southwest and California, the church followed. Bishop Jean-Baptiste Lamy, the midcentury cleric immortalized in Willa Cather's 1927 novel *Death Comes for the Archbishop*, typified the bravery of the Catholic clergy:

> During the first year after his arrival in Santa Fe, the Bishop was actually in his diocese only about four months. Six months of that first year were consumed in attending the Plenary Council at Baltimore....He went on horseback over the Santa Fe trail to St. Louis, nearly a thousand miles, then by steamboat to Pittsburgh, across the mountains to Cumberland, and on to Washington by the new railroad. The return journey was even slower, as he had with him the five nuns who came to found the school of Our Lady of Light.

Dispatched from France (where he was born) to serve as a missionary in Ohio, Lamy had been appointed vicar apostolic of New Mexico in 1850. Traveling mostly on horseback, fighting thirst, heat, and sun, Lamy brought the vast, largely uncharted territories of Arizona, New Mexico, and much of Colorado under his jurisdiction. With the aid of many now-nameless sisters, Lamy attended to the spiritual needs of the 100,000 Catholic Indians living in those regions.

Success proved to be costly, however, for the church's growing visibility invited growing persecution. In the United States Catholics had rarely enjoyed the same liberties as Protestants. In colonial times even Pennsylvania, which prided itself on its high degree of religious toleration, restricted Catholics from voting, holding public office, or celebrating mass in public. But on the whole Catholics managed reasonably well in early English-speaking America, especially after the Revolutionary War, when they basked in Catholic France's support of the patriot cause. But things changed dramatically, and for the worse, in the 1830s.

Many factors accounted for Protestants' fears of the Catholics. Most fundamentally, the Catholic religion was different.

Though Catholics and Protestants shared many assumptions, important distinctions separated them. Most Protestants believed in the right of congregations to choose their own pastors, in the final authority of the Bible, and in salvation through faith in Jesus Christ. Most Catholics, on the other hand, believed that churches should be run by bishops and priests, that final authority should rest in the church's interpretation of the Bible, and that material sacraments like bread and wine, assisted by saints, mediated salvation. Many Protestants felt that Catholics were mired in the mud of superstition. President Thomas Jefferson, for example, despised the Roman Catholic Church for resisting modern science and rationality.

Other suspicions aggravated religious differences. For the better part of 400 years Protestants had believed that the pope in Rome embodied the Antichrist (the evil world ruler described in the New Testament book of Revelation). Prejudices so deeply rooted were not easy to shake, even in the sunlit optimism of the New World. Class and cultural antagonisms further darkened the picture. The Irish, desperate for work, were willing to toil at rock-bottom pay, thus undercutting the wages of the laborers already present. (In time the Irish and German Catholics would despise Polish, Italian, and other newcomers for precisely the same reason.) And Catholics often displayed cultural habits that seemed alien if not downright dangerous to the Protestant majority. They gambled. They played sports on Sunday. And just when the Protestants felt that they were beginning to win the battle against alcohol, the Catholics arrived with strong attachments to their pubs and beer gardens. Beyond that, Catholics got their news from foreign-language newspapers, sent their children to their own schools, and even buried their dead in their own cemeteries. Protestants wondered, why so much secrecy?

And then there was the problem of democracy. Protestants believed that the long history of the Catholic Church in Europe proved that the church would tyrannize the state if it got the chance (Archbishop Carroll's efforts to assert Catholic patriotism notwithstanding). These Protestant suspicions were indeed grounded upon some fact. For centuries the papacy had insisted that the church ultimately should control the state. When democratic revolutions swept Europe in the late 1840s, the pope condemned them. In 1864 the pope issued a letter (called an encyclical) attacking modern errors, including the notion of church-state separation. And then there was slavery, which the church had failed to condemn, for complex theological reasons. Moreover, rank-and-file Irish laborers in the North, who rioted in New York City in 1863, feared that free blacks would rob them of jobs. Whatever the explanation, the church appeared to favor Old World traditions of repression and privilege.

One more factor loomed large in Protestants' suspicions. They suspected that Catholics might succeed all too well in the free air of the New World, even winning converts from Protestant churches. There is no evidence that large numbers of Protestants actually converted, but a number of prominent intellectuals did. Isaac Hecker showed what could happen. Born to a prosperous German family in New York in 1819, Hecker first attended a Methodist church, then joined a Transcendentalist community near Boston. (Among other things, Transcendentalist believed in radical economic and social equality.) But Hecker found himself drawn to the lush rituals of the Catholic Church. More importantly, he grew persuaded that the Christian tree, with its hundreds of branches, all stemmed from a single trunk; the Roman Catholic Church.

Thus, at the age of twenty-five Hecker converted. Fourteen years later he founded one of the most famous of Catholic orders for men, the Paulist Fathers. Hecker spent the rest of his busy life seeking to bring lax Catholics back to the faith through vibrant preaching and impassioned writing. He targeted Protestants, trying to persuade them that the Catholic Church not only offered the truth but also offered hope and strength for America. A democratic land needed the unity and stability of an ancient faith.

The Protestants reacted, sometimes vigorously, sometimes viciously, and even at times violently. Lyman Beecher, then president of Lane Theological Seminary in Ohio, unleashed his fears in an 1832 book called *A Plea for the West*. In this influential volume Beecher warned that America would lose its democratic freedoms if the Protestant majority allowed Catholics to overrun the newly opening territories of the West. After all, he grumbled, Catholics were accustomed to slavish obedience to the pope.

Other Protestants established newspapers to combat the perceived Catholic peril. One carried the revealing title *Protestant Vindicator*. Others turned out propaganda tracts about cruelty, enslavement of women, sexual immorality, and even infant murder in convents. Two of the most notorious were called "Six Months in a Convent" (1835) and "Awful Disclosures of the Hotel Dieu Nunnery of Montreal" (1836). The 1850s saw the brief rise of a new political party devoted to curbing the imagined Catholic threat. The Know-Nothings, as they were popularly called, nominated former president Millard Fillmore as a presidential candidate in 1852 and actually sent seventy-five men to Congress two years later.

After the Civil War, relations between Protestants and Catholics slowly improved. Several factors helped. For one thing, thousands of Irish served in the Union army with valor. Also, many Catholics, especially Germans, had risen in economic, social, and educational status and thus posed less of a threat to Protestant workers. By the final third of the century many Catholic leaders, particularly Irish ones, began to think that they had more to gain than to lose by cooperating with the Protestant majority.

Those who advocated cooperation came to be known as Americanists. Irish bishops and priests dominated the Americanist faction in the Catholic Church (although a few, such as Hecker, were German). The Americanists loved their church and, precisely for that reason, felt that Catholics should embrace America. In their view Catholics needed to play a more prominent role in public affairs. With that end in mind, the first U.S. cardinal, James Gibbons of Baltimore, went so far as to speak at the World's Parliament of Religions in Chicago in 1893. Gibbons did not think Catholic Christianity could be reduced to other forms of Christianity, let alone other religions, but he thought that talking with religious outsiders was better than ignoring or scorning them.

John Ireland, the archbishop of St. Paul, Minnesota, also effectively represented the Americanists' outlook. "We should live in our age, know it, be in touch with it," Ireland insisted in 1889. "Let no one dare to paint her brow with a foreign taint or pin to her mantle foreign linings." Ireland put teeth into his admonition. He doubted that Catholics should isolate their children by sending them to parochial schools. To be sure, this was a tough question. Most public schools taught history through a Protestant lens, extolled Protestant heroes, and read from the thoroughly Protestant King James Authorized Version of the Bible. Yet Ireland felt that Catholic children could thrive in a pluralistic environment.

Others were not so sure. The traditionalists, typically German, coveted the value of preaching in their own language and maintaining the rich musical and liturgical heritage of German Catholic worship. The traditionalists urged Catholics to reap the economic and political benefits of living in the United States, but harbored dark suspicions about whether any good could come from needless interaction in matters of culture. In some ways the traditionalists seemed out of step with the times, but they understood, more clearly than the Americanists, how easily love for the land could displace love of the church.

In the end, Pope Leo XIII largely agreed with the traditionalists. Official letters he issued in 1895 and 1899 urged U.S. Catholics to remember that separation of church and state was not the ideal. Loyal Catholics should not be swept away, he wrote, by the popular but erroneous idea that democracy was king—an idea he indirectly, and somewhat unfairly, attributed to the Catholic Americanists. Christ was king, and the church, though flawed, represented Christ's will on earth.

At the end of the century Catholics could take pride in vast achievements. They had become the largest Christian denomination in the United States. They had established an impressive system of schools, hospitals, and mutual benefit societies. They had helped millions of immigrants adjust to American life. And they had kept the faith. They emerged from the intellectual storms of the late nineteenth century with their theological foundations still firmly intact (some said too much so). By any reasonable measure of such things the church had reached maturity. Just after the turn of the century, in 1908, the pope acknowledged that fact by officially declaring the church no longer a mission (a dependent outpost). Henceforth it would stand on its own as the Roman Catholic Church in the United States of America.

Although Roman Catholics remained much larger in numbers and cultural influence, Orthodox Catholics maintained their own quiet presence in American life. The latter resembled Roman Catholics in several respects. They both worshiped with rich liturgies, decorated their churches elaborately, and preserved a strong sense of tradition. Orthodox Catholics resembled Protestants, however, in that they placed final authority in the ancient creeds of Christianity, not the pope in Rome. And more than either Roman Catholics or Protestants, the Orthodox pursued a mystical union with God as the highest aim of the religious life. Architectural splendor aided that aim. Their churches, often exceptionally beautiful, were (and remain) recognizable by an onion-shaped dome or domes at the top, often brightly painted.

The Orthodox originated in the countries hugging the eastern rim of the Mediterranean, primarily Greece, Albania, and Syria, as well as Russia. In the middle of the eighteenth century Russian traders, explorers, and fur trappers started streaming into the vast wilderness of Alaska. Monks followed in the 1790s. The Orthodox stamped their faith upon the landscape, giving their outposts luminous names like Three Saints Harbor and New Archangel. When the United States bought Alaska from Russia in 1867, the Orthodox were already well rooted there—so well rooted, in fact, that they soon spread down the Pacific Coast into northern California. This made the Russian Orthodox Church the only major religious group (until the late twentieth century) that had moved from the west to the east. At the end of the nineteenth century the Orthodox reported only 90,000 members, but in the next hundred years that figure would swell to 3.5 million. Many said that Orthodox believers constituted the fourth major religious tradition in America, alongside the Catholics, Protestants, and Jews. However defined, they added another richly colored tile to the American religious mosaic.

Nuns shouldered more than their share of the hard, day-to-day work of planting and nurturing the Catholic faith on American shores. Their lack of familiarity with American ways compounded the difficulty of dealing with an overwhelming Protestant majority. In this 1847 letter to Father Mathias Siegert back home in Munich, Germany, Mother Theresa Gerhardinger vented her frustrations.

[In America, schools] will not become large, for there are too many of them, and attendance is voluntary, which is bad. Children attend one school today, another tomorrow, just as they please. If they are corrected they do not come back; learning they often consider recreation. All they want to do is eat cookies, taffy and molasses candy, a cheap sweet. This causes us much trouble. If we forbid it they threaten not to come to school any more. At the slightest punishment the parents say, "In this country one many not treat children so severely; they, too, must be given freedom." They do not listen to any one, and even strike their parents if they do not give in to them. They laugh and jeer at priests.... They will not write one letter of the alphabet at home. "I go to school for that," is their answer. Homework cannot be introduced here; the parents do not want it either.... They do not manifest the slightest eagerness to learn German.... All one hears is English. If they want to insult each other they say, "You German!"

CHAPTER FIFTEEN

Innovators in a World of New Ideas

Thou art giving and forgiving, ever blessing, ever blest,
wellspring of the joy of living, ocean depth of happy rest!
Thou our Father, Christ our Brother—all who live in love are thine;
Teach us how to love each other, lift us to the joy divine.

—*Henry Van Dyke, "Joyful, Joyful, We Adore Thee" (1907)*

Just after the turn of the twentieth century Henry Adams sat down to write his autobiography, *The Education of Henry Adams*. Looking back over a distinguished career as a teacher at Harvard, he wondered whether the outlook of a child born in 1854 was closer to 1904 or to the beginning of Christianity. Adams had good reason to wonder. In the fifty years from the Civil War to World War I, thoughtful men and women everywhere formed powerful new ideas about the immanent (intimately close) nature of God, the human authorship of the Bible, the evolutionary origin of human beings, and the similarities between the Hebrew-Christian tradition and other major religions of the world. New notions won acceptance because they seemed more credible in the modern world. The people who refined and spread these new ideas gave themselves various labels but, for the sake of simplicity, we shall call them all innovators.

If we think of innovators as people who were prepared to challenge old ideas in the light of science and the expanding horizons of world discovery, then innovators had been around for a long time. Decades before the Revolutionary War, for example, many Puritans had doubted their parents' view of God as a stern, judgmental deity. They insisted instead that God was both too rational and too kindhearted to cast anyone into hell. During the Revolutionary era a small but influential group of men and women, including founders such as Benjamin Franklin and Thomas Jefferson, came to more startling conclusions. They believed that God had created the world as a finely tuned machine, much like a jeweler fashioning an exquisite clock. Once the world was made, God would not disturb it with miracles any more than a jeweler would disturb a perfectly running clock. By the same token, stories in the Bible that seemed inconsistent with God's rational, moral nature had to go. One example was the Genesis legend about Abraham and Isaac. In that ancient account, the Lord instructed Abraham to take his son Isaac to a distant mountaintop, build an altar, lay Isaac upon the altar, then slay him and burn his body as a holy sacrifice. Abraham dutifully obeyed each step, until the Lord sent an angel to stay his hand just before he was to plunge the knife. Stories of that sort now seemed immoral.

In the mid-nineteenth century innovators found an eloquent new voice in the ideas of Ralph Waldo Emerson. Born into an elite Unitarian family in Boston in 1803, Emerson served as a Unitarian pastor in that city until he concluded that he no longer believed even the stripped-down claims of that tradition. Emerson spent the rest of his life in the nearby town of Concord, writing essays and lecturing to almost anyone who would listen. He challenged traditionalists to test religious concepts for themselves. Everyone, Emerson insisted, must make their own decisions about what was true about God, humans, and the world. In the grand tradition of American individualism Emerson concluded that the only valid authority was the authority of each person's private judgment.

Emerson plunged ahead, boldly, without fear of others' views. The Concord sage argued that God was not a stern judge, not a kind grandfather, and not a distant clock-maker. Instead, God was best understood as a spirit, an ideal, a breath of life, everywhere and always filling the world with the inexhaustible power of the divine presence. God, he said, was as close as the atmosphere, as intimate as the "blowing clover and the falling rain." And if God was everywhere, then miracles were not necessary. Indeed, they were not even possible, because God could hardly impose a miracle—a violation of natural law—upon himself.

That insight led Emerson to ask a bigger question: If God really was everywhere, how did people know about him? By reading the Bible? By listening to the pronouncements of the bishops of the church? No. People knew God through intuition, especially when they applied their intuitive abilities to the wonders of nature. People sensed God's reality in the same way they sensed the reality of other human beings. God remained beneath the surface appearances of the natural world, just as a friend's personality remained beneath the surface appearances of his or her physical body. Because truth transcended the ordinary realm of daily sense perception, Emerson and an elite band of like-minded friends called themselves Transcendentalists.

Emerson's pioneering concepts opened the floodgates to other ideas. In the 1870s, 1880s, and 1890s a torrent of new religious notions surged across the landscape. Taken together they changed the way in which millions of people in all stations of life thought about things heavenly and earthly.

Fresh thoughts about the nature of the Bible came first. Close attention to the content of the Bible was nothing new. For many centuries preachers and rabbis had carefully studied the text of the Scriptures in order to know exactly what they said and meant as a guide for life. But the late nineteenth century witnessed special attention to questions of authorship. Who wrote the different parts of the Bible? How did those authors reflect the assumptions and prejudices of their times? How did the Bible acquire its present list of books of vastly differing length and literary style? The men and women who pressed such questions came to be known as higher critics (versus the so-called lower critics, who busied themselves primarily with the "lower" or less controversial task of finding accurate texts and creating precise translations). The answers the higher critics came up with proved exciting to some, profoundly disturbing to others.

Charles Augustus Briggs was one of those who wrestled with these matters. A Presbyterian Old Testament professor at Union Theological Seminary in New York City at the end of the century, Briggs gained a reputation for brilliant, outspoken advocacy. By the end of his career, tens of thousands had heard of him. Some responded with approval, many others with sharp disapproval, leading to his removal from the church for heresy in 1893. Briggs insisted that the Bible should be read as any other ancient text, without imposing supernatural explanations. For example, the Bible claimed that a great fish swallowed the prophet Jonah and then regurgitated him unharmed three days later. Should claims of that sort be accepted as factually true, no matter how much they strained credibility? Or should they be assessed as other ancient legends would be, as prescientific myths, or perhaps as poetry, carrying a moral meaning? To be sure, Briggs, like many innovators, was not entirely consistent. He felt that some miracles, such as the virgin birth of Christ, rested upon solid evidence, especially if one looked to the data contained in the ancient creeds. But on the whole he urged Christians and Jews to be more critical about what was demonstrably true and what was mere legend in the Bible.

The rise of modern science in general, and the evolutionary view of human origins in particular, posed a second major challenge to traditional ideas. At first glance there was nothing new about evolutionary theories. Believers on both sides of the Atlantic had long accepted the great antiquity of the earth. Many had early on doubted the literal truth of the Adam and Eve story. Many had recognized that animals had evolved within species, so that larger dogs had emerged from smaller dogs, or darker horses from lighter ones. Many too had acknowledged the terrible cruelty of nature, for creatures often survived by killing and eating others.

But these ideas became more startling with the publication in England in 1859 of Charles Darwin's massive book *Origin of Species by Means of Natural Selection*. In it this English scientist introduced Americans to the disturbing notion of natural selection. According to this principle, all plants and animals, including humans, changed over time in response to changes in the natural environment. Thus, if the climate in a particular region grew colder, animals that happened to be born there with thicker and warmer coats were more likely to survive than those with lighter coats. The obvious similarities between humans and primates, or the equally obvious fact that nature was a battleground drenched in red, could now be satisfactorily explained.

Many intellectuals found Darwin's theories liberating, for they enabled thoughtful men and women in all parts of the United States to make sense of the natural world. Lyman Abbott, editor of the influential religious periodical the *Outlook*, jauntily embraced evolution as "God's way of doing things."

Darwin did not intend to upset anyone's faith, but he did, perhaps more than any other thinker of the nineteenth century. The idea, inferred from Darwin's book, that all natural processes proceeded at random, like the roll of dice, upset many believers. But that was not the worst of it. If the principle of natural selection were true, then the only measure of good or bad actions was survival. The Hebrew prophets' and Christ's teachings about personal sacrifice in the interest of a higher cause seemed pointless. To suggest that the Adam and Eve story was mere legend seemed bad enough, but to argue that Jewish and Christian moral teachings equaled only warm sentiments— sentiments that could be discarded whenever they appeared to block progress—seemed immeasurably worse.

A growing awareness of religions in other parts of the world formed a third major challenge to older ideas. For thousands of years Jews and Christians had firmly believed that the biblical tradition remained different from all other faiths. Jews thought that God had called them alone to be the bearers of God's law. Christians believed that God had singled them out to be the bearers of the message of salvation. American Jews and Christians had long known, of course, that many other religions existed. As far back as 1784 Hannah Adams, possibly the first woman in America to make her living by writing, had published a *Dictionary of All Religions*. But until the late nineteenth century that knowledge remained mostly theoretical, mediated through rare travelers' reports and romantic tales about faraway places.

This narrow outlook changed dramatically in the 1880s and especially in the 1890s. In those decades the rest of the world arrived at America's doorstep and knocked—insistently. Many factors were involved. The rapid development of shipping and railroad technology helped the expansion of trade. Military muscle flexing took thousands of young men to distant lands. So did increasing wealth, which allowed vacation travel to places other than Europe for the upper-middle and upper classes. Above all, the rapid growth of Christian missions themselves fostered a new and worrisome fear that the Hebrew-Christian tradition was not unique. Young men and women from small towns in New England and the Midwest, who had never seen a real Hindu or Muslim, now found themselves face to face with living representatives of those faiths. Hundreds of missionaries, and thousands of their supporters back home, began to suspect that Islam, Hinduism, and especially Buddhism carried highly developed ethical systems of their own. From there it was only a short step to the conclusion that those religions offered equally valid paths to God.

The World's Parliament of Religions, held in conjunction with the Columbian Exposition in Chicago in the fall of 1893, marked a turning point. The parliament may not have been, as one reporter put it, the most important event of the century, but at the time it must have seemed so. For seventeen days running, thousands of spectators jammed the Hall of Columbus hoping to catch a glimpse of the colorfully garbed holy men who had traveled from all parts of the earth to describe the faiths of their homelands. For most of those visitors in Chicago, as well as countless men and women who read about the fanfare in home-town newspapers, the parliament offered their first real exposure to any religion besides Judaism or Christianity. Many came away wondering what some missionaries out in the field had suspected for a long time: did not other religions offer their own perfectly respectable paths to God?

In the late nineteenth century, then, religious innovators both received and contributed to new notions about the Bible, human nature, and the origins of Judaism and Christianity. But innovators did not all think alike. They fell along a spectrum, ranging from agnostics on the left to liberals on the right, with free religionists of various stripes scattered in between. We shall briefly look at each position through the eyes of one representative figure, concentrating on the Protestants, who formed the great majority.

Agnostics, who took their name from a Greek word meaning "no knowledge," believed that humans simply could not know whether a personal God existed or not. Although agnostics never represented more than a tiny minority of Americans in the nineteenth century, they seemed conspicuous because a disproportionate number of vocal and articulate spokespersons championed this point of view. Robert G. Ingersoll, for example, won enduring fame—and lasting contempt—as a skilled advocate of agnosticism on the lecture circuit. This Congregational pastor's son turned against Christianity when he reached adulthood in the 1850s. Ingersoll held that humans simply had no way of knowing whether God existed or what happened after death. Since one could never know the answer to big questions of this sort, it remained better not to guess, let alone to impose one's beliefs upon others. Ingersoll also scorned efforts to harmonize science and Christianity. In place of idle speculation, he called for a faith that concentrated on improving the human lot in the present world. Use science, he urged, to create a civilization that was more just, more humane, more democratic. Ingersoll's high personal moral standards disarmed critics who feared that his agnosticism would leave society in shambles.

Free religionists occupied something of a middle position on the spectrum. Only a few actually used the term "free religionist," but the label fit thousands of maverick spirits who sought to develop their ideas on their own, without the constraint of inherited creeds or communities of faith. Elizabeth Cady Stanton exemplified this outlook. We met her in an earlier chapter as an advocate of woman suffrage and employment rights, but she displayed additional interests too. Born in 1815, Stanton grew up in a sternly Presbyterian home in Johnstown, New York. As a child, however, she recoiled from the "church, the parsonage, the graveyard, and the solemn, tolling bell." She associated institutional Christianity with gloomy teachings about hell, an obsession with saving souls for the afterlife, and a determination to keep people from thinking for themselves. In time she embraced a more nourishing faith. Although this happily married mother of seven argued for a benevolent God, an orderly universe, and the immortality of the individual soul, she doubted that God would interfere in history or give special revelation to particular persons or groups. Late in life Stanton helped write a commentary on the Bible, published in 1895 as *The Woman's Bible*, which sought to expose the repressiveness of the Bible's teachings about women. This tough-minded reformer sought a religion worthy of a free mind.

And then there were the large number of liberals, men and women who positioned themselves closest to traditional ideas. Liberals assumed that faith began in direct experiences of the beauty of God's presence in daily life. Henry Ward Beecher, pastor of Plymouth Congregational Church in Brooklyn, New York, from 1847 until his death in 1887, represented this vein of thought. Beecher was almost as famous as his sister, Harriet Beecher Stowe (author of *Uncle Tom's Cabin*). In an age graced by distinguished preachers—often called princes of the pulpit—Beecher reigned as king. His sermons combined wit, learning, and soaring oratory. People loved him. Most never seemed to notice that his views of Christ, miracles, and future punishment remained hopelessly fuzzy.

Henry Ward Beecher taught a generation of liberal leaders that it was more important to sense God's presence in their hearts than to dream up abstract theories about God in their minds. In this view Jesus was best seen not as the unique Son of God but as an ethical example and a guide for navigating through life's troubled times. The Bible was best read, they argued, as the story of God's saving activities in history.

Liberals like Beecher enjoyed wide influence. They soon dominated the most prestigious divinity schools, including Harvard, Yale, and Chicago. Directly or indirectly they shaped the thinking of thousands of pastors and tens of thousands of Sunday school teachers. By the early twentieth century liberals' ideas could be heard from possibly half the Protestant pulpits in the land. Most mainline denominations, especially Baptists, Congregationalists, Disciples, Episcopalians, and Presbyterians in the North and West, were defined by liberals. Their concepts found echoes in other religious traditions too. Reform Jews, in particular, embraced the notions of divine nearness and the importance of social justice. Irish Catholic intellectuals distinguished themselves by their growing appreciation for the insights of modern biblical criticism and the intellectual freedom of America.

Of the three forms of innovative thinkers considered—agnostics, free religionists, and liberals—the last proved by far the most effective in spreading their ideas among millions of ordinary believers. Why did liberals' notions catch on so easily?

First, it helps to remember that liberals' ideas were part of a larger process of rapid change. Urbanization forced people of varying outlooks to live close to each other. Thoughtful persons could no longer assume that their own view of the world was the only one that existed. Moreover, for thousands of years people had lived close to the land, but now indoor labor and human-made time permitted people to suppose that their destiny lay within their control. The rise of research universities such as Cornell, Stanford, Chicago, and Johns Hopkins, and the emergence of scientists as the new elite, played an important role too. University-based researchers increasingly displaced the clergy as the final judges of what was true or not true.

Second, virtually all religious liberals saw themselves not as debunkers but as lonely prophets, helping humankind achieve intellectual freedom. They saw themselves saving, not harming, the core of traditional faith. In their minds the growth of critical methods in the study of history, science, and other cultures had rendered the older notions obsolete. The choice, then, was either to discard faith entirely or rethink and reclaim what was true in light of recent advances in knowledge. They took special pride in their ability to accommodate the old to the new and thus retain the best of both.

Finally, many liberals tried to apply the new ideas to the righting of social wrongs, which brought them in tune with the broader reform impulses of the age. They believed that the most ethically advanced portions of the Bible, as well as the best of modern thought, proved that God was not wrathful but essentially kindhearted. They also believed that the Bible demanded social justice. The older focus upon individual salvation was plainly inadequate. The Hebrew-Christian tradition required all decent, God-fearing men and women to address the terrible disparities of wealth and the inhumane working conditions that crippled American life. In a word, the Bible demanded social justice.

The intellectual challenges of the late nineteenth century forever changed the landscape of religion in America. The new ideas shaped the thinking of ordinary men and women as profoundly as Copernicus's discovery in the fifteenth century that the earth moved around the sun. To be sure, many thoughtful men and women resisted the most advanced trends of the age, but none could ignore them. A few of the innovators, like Ingersoll, gave up belief altogether. Others, like Stanton, focused on purging the Hebrew-Christian tradition of its morally and intellectually distasteful features. But most followed Beecher's constructive pattern of seeking creative ways to retain the essence of their faith while taking modern challenges seriously. If in their hands God became less a supernatural being and more an immanent divine presence, he also became a source of enduring comfort in times of breathtaking change.

CHAPTER SIXTEEN

Conservers of Tradition

O God, our help in ages past,
our hope for years to come,
be Thou our guide while life shall last,
and our eternal home.

—*Isaac Watts, "O God, Our Help in Ages Past" (1719)*

In the later decades of the nineteenth century millions of thoughtful Americans acquired a renewed appreciation for the religious wisdom of the past. We call these Americans conservatives because they felt that time-honored truths, tested and refined in the long experience of the human race, offered the most effective way to deal with the intellectual, social, and technological challenges of the modern world.

Religious conservatives came in a bewildering variety of species. Some proved primarily interested in defending the authority and accuracy of the Bible. Others concerned themselves above all with strict standards of personal conduct. Some found their greatest joy in the biblical promise that Jesus

Christ would soon return. Still others looked to the traditions of their own extended family or ethnic group for guidance. What they all held in common was a simple though powerful conviction that the past held the key to the future.

From the early seventeenth century through the late twentieth century the Bible formed the bedrock of religious tradition in America. Before the Revolution the Crown barred colonial printers from producing the King James Authorized Version (hoping to protect sales for the king's printers). But after independence Americans rushed to meet the demand for English-language Bibles. Voluntary groups joined them. The largest, the American Bible Society, founded in 1816, was soon producing 300,000 copies per year—for a population under 13 million. (In time the society would print nearly four billion Bibles or portions thereof.) Nineteenth-century travelers, encountering town after town bearing names like Eden, Salem, and Bethlehem (not to mention Zoar, Ohio, and Mount Tirzah, North Carolina) might well have imagined themselves wandering through biblical lands in biblical times.

In many familes children received intentionally biblical names such as Ezra, Elijah, and Naomi almost as frequently as John, Paul, and Mary (also biblical). All U.S. presidents took office by swearing an oath on an open Bible. Many presidents, including Abraham Lincoln, Woodrow Wilson, and Jimmy Carter, memorized large portions of the Scripture and quoted it often. Even Thomas Jefferson, a skeptic, took the trouble to translate and print his own version of the New Testament. The great biblical images of Moses freeing his people, or of the city on a hill, or of the New Heavens and the New Earth, stirred deep feelings and provided an orientation for life. Jews cherished their Hebrew Scriptures with equal fervor. Some of the bitterest battles fought in the U.S. court system revolved around the proper use of the Bible in public schools—showing, among other things, that the Bible was never inconsequential.

When the literal truthfulness of the Bible came under heavy fire from liberals in the late nineteenth century, believers everywhere rose to its defense. Charles Hodge, a theology professor at Princeton Theological Seminary for much of the nineteenth century, led the charge. Like many Bible scholars, Hodge had studied in Germany, where higher critical approaches to Scripture flourished in the universities. He determined to sink the new and, in his mind, destructive ideas before they reached U.S. shores. He believed that the Bible could be proved wholly accurate if its readers would 1) disregard trivial discrepancies in numbers and dates, 2) allow for minor errors of translation and copying over the centuries, 3) distinguish between what the Bible writers personally believed and what they formally taught, and 4) use reasonable or common-sense standards of what constituted accuracy. Thus, if the Bible spoke of the sun rising and setting, that statement should be read as "the language of common life," not as a scientific statement to be taken strictly literally. Hodge boasted that no new idea had ever penetrated Princeton Seminary. What he meant, of course, was that all significant truth had been revealed by God long ago in the Bible. Humans should try to see the full range of meanings the Holy Book contained, not add to or subtract from them.

At the turn of the century the battle between the Bible's critics and its defenders grew more heated, and both sides made extreme statements. After World War I the former came to be known as modernists because they wanted to apply modern standards of scientific credibility to the Bible. The latter, on the other hand, came to be known as fundamentalists because they insisted that the Bible's accuracy in matters of history and science was fundamental (or essential) to the truth of Christianity. The most strident voices won wide publicity, but a majority of Protestants undoubtedly remained closer to the moderately conservative position held by Hodge.

> Jesus loves me! This I know, for the Bible tells me so.
> Little ones to him belong, they are weak, but he is strong....
> Yes, Jesus loves me! The Bible tells me so.

These words, penned by Anna B. Warner in 1860, not only represented one of the best-loved hymns in American Christianity but also expressed the piety of millions of ordinary Christians as traditional as it was heartfelt. Such people worried little about scholars' proofs for the historical accuracy of the Bible. They simply assumed that it could be trusted, especially in matters of faith and morals. This meant seeking forgiveness for their sins and living purified lives—what thousands of Sunday school teachers across the land called conversion and sanctification.

Dwight L. Moody represented this concern. By the time of his death in 1899, this 300-pound evangelist had become the most famous preacher of the age, very much like Billy Graham in the late twentieth century. Born in the rural village of Northfield, Massachusetts, Moody moved to Chicago as a young man and soon mastered the shoe business. But a conversion experience turned his attention from business to religion. Although he never received ordination, he put his considerable organizational abilities to the Lord's use by starting a church, launching Sunday schools, and supporting the work of the newly formed Young Men's Christian Association (YMCA). By the 1870s Moody and his song leader, Ira Sankey, were preaching all across the northern and midwestern United States and even in Britain.

Moody won the affection of millions for a number of reasons. One was his preaching style. In it he avoided technical theological discussions. He focused upon what he called the three Rs: ruin by sin, redemption by Christ, and regeneration by the Holy Spirit. Rarely speaking of hell, Moody stressed instead God's love for all. He told homey, sentimental stories about sinners falling upon hard times until they gave their lives to Christ—unless of course they waited until it was too late and perished for their sins. All this took place against a backdrop of stirring revival tunes adroitly led by Sankey.

Critics sometimes groused that Moody possessed little formal education, but they failed to see that he was no bumpkin. His simple words carried profound messages. Keenly aware that a visible commitment would be hard to abandon, Moody urged his hearers to step forward and give their lives to Christ in public. He carefully secured the support of a broad spectrum of local pastors before entering a city, thus creating the impression that he spoke for the community at large. And he took care to institutionalize his message after he departed. Moody founded schools for young women and young men in his home town of Northfield and a Bible training school in Chicago for students too poor to go to college. After his death trustees renamed it Moody Bible Institute. (It was to thrive in the twenteeth century as one of the wealthiest, strongest, and most prestigious of the conservative Protestant colleges.)

If Moody focused upon winning men and women to Christ, other evangelists tried to help converts nurture a vigorous Christian life after conversion. Their aim was to have converts love Christ so completely that they would never desire to sin again. This emphasis on spiritual growth went by various names: sanctification, holiness, second blessing, consecration, higher Christian life, or Holy Spirit baptism. By whatever label, the movement washed across thousands of evangelical groups, white and black, north and south. It waxed strongest among the Methodists, from whose ranks emerged several small but influential sects, including the Salvation Army and the Church of the Nazarene.

No one did more to stir a desire for sanctification than Phoebe Palmer. The wife of a wealthy New York physician, Palmer pressed Christians to trust Christ's promise that all residues of sin could be removed and replaced with a single-hearted love for God and others. She expressed her ideas in best-selling books, in a steady stream of articles in her monthly magazine, *Guide to Holiness*, and in sermons preached on both sides of the Atlantic. Under her ministry, which spanned the middle third of the century, hundreds of thousands, perhaps millions, professed sanctification. Contrary to popular stereotypes about women preachers, Palmer was tough minded and clear eyed. Although she esteemed deep emotion as a desirable fruit of conversion and of Holy Spirit baptism (as she usually called it), she insisted that the initial commitment to Christ was a rational process of first believing the Bible's promises, then acting upon them.

Sanctification's advocates distinguished themselves in several ways. They championed missions, both at home and abroad, especially among the humbler classes. Although they rarely involved themselves in secular politics, they urged well-fed, middle-class Christians to take off their gloves and help the down and out, especially in the squalid cities. They spent considerable time establishing and working in urban rescue missions, such as Jerry McAuley's famed Water Street Mission in New York's Bowery district. They insisted that women be allowed to preach (though not necessarily ordained). And they called for strict standards of personal conduct, sharply condemning smoking, drinking, dancing, gambling, and sex outside of marriage.

These restrictions emerged from a conviction that such conduct undermined social stability and wrecked personal happiness.

The emphasis upon spiritual growth and personal uprightness that swept across evangelical Protestantism at the end of the nineteenth century challenged men more directly than women. Respectable middle-class men and women of the late nineteenth century quietly assumed that women most properly served God as wives and mothers. As such they were supposed to stay home and guard the moral purity of the household. Men, on the other hand, were expected to achieve success in the rough-and-tumble world of business, industry, and finance. Very few conservative Protestants openly endorsed the idea of men breaking the rules, let alone living immoral lives, but sometimes it seemed necessary to stretch the rules a bit in order to make a dollar. Sanctification's adherents tolerated none of that. Like fiery Old Testament prophets, they denounced all expressions of the double standard.

The desire to conserve the best of historic Christianity took still another form—one that persists with great force today. After the Civil War, millions of earnest Americans came to believe that the Bible taught that Christ would soon return to the earth in literal, physical form. Partisans of this view called themselves premillennialists. (This term meant that Christ would come back before the millennium, the thousand years of peace and righteousness that, according to the New Testament, would mark the end of history.) Though premillennialist beliefs had cropped up only rarely in the long history of Christianity, in North America in the late nineteenth century they gained broad appeal. The Seventh-Day Adventists, an offshoot of the midcentury Millerites discussed earlier, formed one prominent example. Like the Millerites, the Adventists eagerly anticipated Christ's visible Advent, or

Second Coming, but unlike the Millerites they did not set precise dates. We shall return to the Adventists' story later in the context of diet and health, which they linked to end-time preparations.

The waning years of the century saw the birth of another premillennialist group that became a household name after World War II. These believers, now called Jehovah's Witnesses, originally labeled themselves Russellites after their founder, Charles Taze Russell. Born in 1852, this thoughtful, energetic leader grew up in a Presbyterian household near Pittsburgh. Russell left school early to run his family's clothing business while studying the Bible intensively on his own. His Zion's Watch Tower Society, which he organized in 1884, heralded beliefs measurably different from those of most Christians. For one thing, hell did not exist. Neither did the Trinity (Father, Son, Holy Spirit). Instead, God, properly known by his Old Testament name, Jehovah, reigned alone. Christ existed as a divine though lesser being. Russell maintained that Christ had returned to earth in spirit in 1874. Soon Jehovah, along with Christ and the Holy Angels, would launch a terrible war upon Satan and his followers. Jehovah's victory over Satan would be followed by a thousand years free of poverty, suffering, and injustice, including racial injustice.

In the meantime, Russell taught, the Jehovah's Witnesses must keep themselves pure by not smoking, drinking, or associating with the government in any form. Russell believed that government, most businesses, and the traditional Christian churches oppressed the poor and needy even as they increased the wealth and power of the wicked. This meant of course that Witnesses should not fight in the country's wars. It also meant refusing to salute the flag, which aroused the ire of their neighbors. Nonetheless, Russell's controversial ideas proved to be appealing. One early book sold five million copies, and all of his writings together sold 15 million copies in thirty languages.

Fundamentalists represented by far the largest, most influential cluster of believers concerned about Christ's second coming. These believers did not acquire the name *fundamentalists* until the 1920s. But the label was a good one, even in the 1870s, because they fervently believed that the promise that Christ would soon return formed one of the fundamental teachings of the Bible. Fundamentalists did not possess a single dominant leader, but hundreds of forceful men and women took up the cause. They supposed that every word of the Bible, rightly translated and interpreted, was factually true. Working from that assumption, most fundamentalists divided history into distinct eras, usually seven. By their reckoning history was nearing the end of the sixth era. Soon, they taught, Christ would come back to earth, defeat Satan, then launch a thousand years of peace and righteousness. They called this seventh era of human history, when Christ alone would reign, the millennium. At the end of the millennium, God would judge all humans, living and dead, sending the righteous to everlasting heaven and the evil to eternal hell.

Why did these notions, supposedly so much out of step with the secular trends of the age, seem so persuasive to millions of Americans? Several answers come to mind. For one thing, the movement was blessed with gifted leaders who built a nationwide network of schools, colleges, and periodicals. These leaders pressed their ideas in summer Bible conferences, boosted by the spread of railroads and the growing popularity of summer vacations. Moreover, fundamentalists seemed to offer a credible explanation for the trend of world events. Look around, they urged. What do you see? War, greed, and sexual immorality. Surely God's patience must be wearing thin and he would bring history to an end very soon. Above all, millions found joy in the prospect that Christ, whom they loved, would soon come back to earth. Not surprisingly, they called that prospect the Blessed Hope.

Other Protestants found security in the traditions of their particular denominational traditions or ethnic groups. None proved as visible to the broader public as the groups we have been discussing, but they won thousands of adherents, and most continued to flourish in the late twentieth century. The Churches of Christ, best known perhaps for their refusal to allow pianos or musical instruments in their worship services, illustrated the trend. Their story goes back to the Christians/ Disciples of Christ who emerged before the Civil War. The Disciples aimed to restore the simplicity of New Testament patterns of belief and worship, discarding complex confessions and theologies. After the Civil War they increasingly accepted modern values, such as biblical higher criticism (indeed, many of the most prominent liberals were Disciples). Near the turn of the century a large minority of Disciples pulled away from the larger body, calling for a return to simple New Testament standards. They called their gatherings churches of Christ (*churches* was spelled with a lowercase *c* to make clear that they were individual churches, not a new sect).

Members of the churches of Christ were not really evangelicals, for they did not encourage emotional conversion experiences. But they insisted that the Bible must be read rationally and obeyed strictly, because it was true in all respects. Churches of Christ flourished everywhere, especially in the upper South states of Tennessee, Missouri, Arkansas, Oklahoma, and Texas.

Another large family of Christians, loosely called the Peace Churches, also marked American religious life at the end of the century. The Peace Churches consisted of two large branches, the Quakers and the Mennonites. The Quakers stemmed from the English Reformation in the seventeeth century, the Mennonites from the Reformation in continental Europe in the sixteenth century. Both had put down roots in the United States long before the American Revolution, clustering in eastern Pennsylvania, where they enjoyed freedom from persecution. By the late nineteenth century both could be found almost everywhere, although they remained strongest in Pennsylvania and later in the central Midwest.

In America, Quakers and Mennonites followed parallel theological paths. After the Civil War the majority of Quakers embraced liberal religious attitudes, but a large minority continued to emphasize traditional ideals of pacifism and a simple lifestyle. Most Mennonites, including the Mennonite offshoots of the Amish and the Brethren in Christ, did the same. All these groups suffered severe persecution for refusing to fight in World War I. Though never large in numbers, they loomed large in the popular imagination. Their stance provided other Americans with a compelling example of what it meant to take one's faith seriously, whatever the cost.

Another expression of tradition flowered on the Iowa prairie and the eastern shore of Lake Michigan in the latter half of the century. These earnest, hardworking believers were the Dutch Reformed, Calvinists who had emigrated to the United States from the Netherlands in the early nineteenth century. In the United States they split into the Reformed Church in America and the more conservative Christian Reformed Church. Members of the latter, especially, kept to themselves, carefully charting their lives by the creeds of the Protestant Reformation. Strict observers of the Sunday sabbath, they enjoyed their cigars no less than their tulip gardens. They made a lasting mark upon U.S. education by erecting a private school system second to none and by cultivating distinguished scholars in theology, philosophy, and history.

We do not have to look to the smaller groups on the margins of the culture to see tradition at work. Many believers in the large, well-established denominations also found their primary identity in the heritage of the past. One of the most conspicuous examples emerged among the Episcopalians. Calling themselves High Church Episcopalians, these Christians emphasized ancient creeds. They relished elaborate liturgies resembling the practices of the Church of England in the age of King James I. Some even adopted processions, incense, and the use of bells in worship. Inspired by the art and architecture of European Christianity, they built lovely Georgian, Romanesque, and Gothic churches and cathedrals. Many of those structures, such as Trinity Church in lower Manhattan and Trinity Church in the heart of Boston, continue to grace U.S. skylines.

Memories of the past strongly shaped the Lutheran experience in American too. The first Lutherans emigrated from Sweden in the early seventeenth century to settle in lower New York and upper Delaware. But they remained small in number until after the Civil War, when their ranks swelled rapidly with newcomers from Germany and Scandinavia. Claiming half a million followers in 1870, Lutheran rolls swelled to two million in 1910, making them the fourth-largest Christian denominational family.

The Lutherans had a hard time working with each other. They spoke multiple languages, including German, Danish, Norwegian, Swedish, Finnish, and Icelandic. Moreover, they often lived on farms or in tightknit rural communities very much like the fictional Lake Wobegon in Garrison Keillor's "Prairie Home Companion" books and radio shows. This settlement pattern reduced the need for interaction with other

Lutheran ethnic groups. Nonetheless, in the end Lutherans tried to embrace common historic traditions in the continental Reformation rather than modern America for a shared point of reference.

Looking to the Old World for spiritual guidance was, however, easier said than done. Again, Lutherans differed among themselves. The sharply contrasting outlooks of two leaders, Samuel Simon Schmucker and C. F. W. Walther, illustrate the problem. Their lives spanned the first three-quarters of the century. Both gained a wide reputation for piety, learning, and commitment to Lutheran success in America. Both founded important schools. And each felt that the historic confessions of the church, especially the Augsburg Confession of 1530, accurately summarized the Bible's main teachings. But there their paths separated. Schmucker wanted Lutheran worship to be less liturgical and spoken in English. Like most American Protestants he supported temperance (no alcohol) and strict Sabbath observance. He also urged cooperation with other Protestants in missions and Sunday schools.

Walther, on the other hand, opposed all these moves. Because the true faith had flourished in the Old World, he saw no reason to accommodate U.S. patterns. With great determination Walther insisted that Lutherans needed to uphold all the doctrines summarized in the historic confessions of the church. Nor was English an adequate substitute for the purity of the German tongue.

In the end Schmucker lost and Walther won. The majority of Lutherans felt that Schmucker gave away too much. Walther expected sacrifice, and ordinary people took pride in their ability to stand the test. Sometimes Americans clung to marginalized traditions precisely because it was the most difficult thing to do.

The effort to find spiritual resources for the present in the traditions of the past extended beyond Protestants, beyond Christians, beyond Jews. The Native Americans too looked back—but with a difference. If European Americans used religious traditions to make life better and more meaningful, Native Americans used them to make life possible.

The suffering that the European invaders inflicted on the Native American population in the Western Hemisphere staggers the imagination. Some of the pain stemmed from military conquest and cultural aggression—the relentless uprooting of Indian languages, religious practices, and daily folkways. But the greater part of the misery grew from the lethal diseases that Europeans inadvertently brought with them—diseases that whites found less deadly because they had built up a measure of immunity. Smallpox, diphtheria, typhoid, influenza, mumps, measles, cholera, malaria, whooping cough, bubonic plague, and scarlet fever ravaged the Indian population.

No one knows how many Indians were living in North America when Europeans started arriving in the fifteenth century. Estimates vary wildly, from two million to more than fifteen million. But there can be little doubt that a vast number—perhaps 90 percent in places like coastal New England—died from imported diseases. This demographic disaster, among the worst in human history, forms the backdrop against which we must view the Indians' efforts to establish a more secure way of life.

On several occasions in the eighteenth and nineteenth centuries, American Indian prophets had called their people to embrace the ways of the distant past in order to find the resources, both material and spiritual, to expel whites from their lands. In about 1800, for example, Handsome Lake led a revitalization movement, as outsiders later called it, among his Seneca people in upstate New York. The movement grew from instructions that Lake had received during a spiritual journey. These directions banned alcohol, witchcraft, and abortion. The Shawnee Indian, Tenskwatawa, and his brother, Tecumtha (or Tecumseh), led a similar revival in the middle years of the nineteenth century. They too banned alcohol and witchcraft, as well as marriage with whites. Tenskwatawa's influence centered in Ohio but spread widely from Florida to Saskatchewan.

The Ghost Dance, inspired by a Nevada Paiute Indian named Wovoka, produced one of the most widespread expressions of tradition-based Native American religion. In the winter of 1889, Wovoka, a twenty-eight-year-old weather doctor, dreamed that he was taken up into a realm of green grasses and abundant game. The Indian dead of ages past, now restored to robust strength, populated the realm. There, Wovoka received instructions for his people. They were to be honest and give up warfare with each other and with whites. He learned of a special dance that would hasten the day when whites would disappear from the land, the earth would be restored to its original beauty, and the Indians would be reunited with their ancestors. Wovoka's message quickly spread eastward across the Great Plains.

The Oglala Sioux, one of the most warlike plains tribes, adapted Wovoka's dance to their own needs. The Sioux had long practiced a Sun Dance, which involved circling a sacred tree and staring at the sun as a purifying rite. They blended the two traditions into a new ritual called the Ghost Dance. Members believed that the Ghost Dance would reunite them with their dead ancestors in peace. Some also believed that they would be protected if they performed the Ghost Dance wearing special long white shirts painted with red symbols of lightning, eagles, and stars.

A series of confrontations with federal soldiers followed. Some of the Sioux may have supposed that the white shirts would make them invincible in battle. In the end, 200 Sioux were slain at Wounded Knee, South Dakota, in the cold winter of 1890. The songs and rituals of the ceremony eventually faded into a variety of local practices. Other venerable practices of Indian traditional religion, along with Indian Christianity, would see a powerful rebirth in the twentieth century. But the soul of the Ghost Dance, like much of Native American culture, died in the collision of cultures.

The last decades of the nineteenth century saw the emergence of one of the most legally controversial forms of Native American religion. The founder was a Comanche, Quanah Parker, a prosperous Oklahoma businessman and visionary. Parker argued that Indians must accommodate to the surrounding Anglo civilization in order to prosper. But he also called for the adoption of a pre-Columbian ritual, centered in northern Mexico, that involved the eating of a bitter button from the peyote cactus. This button bore hallucinogenic properties. It first caused nausea and dizziness, but then contentment and euphoria.

Parker's message spread quickly and widely. The peyote ritual began on a Saturday evening and ran to the next morning. It involved all-night singing, praying for the sick, the ceremonial use of tobacco and, most conspicuously, the eating of peyote buttons. The custom sometimes used Christian prayers and, some said, offered a way to salvation. In 1918, Oklahoma Peyotists organized themselves into the Native American Church. In the twentieth century the church, though banned in some states, would win a measure of protection in the courts and in Congress. It proved especially strong among the Navajos in Arizona and New Mexico.

It has been said that traditionalism is the dead faith of living people, but tradition is the living faith of dead people. This truism rightly suggests that in the nineteenth century many Americans, of diverse religious heritages, looked steadily and creatively to the past to find resources for the present and hope for the future.

Phoebe Palmer, editor of Guide to Holiness *(1864–74), one of the most influential religious periodicals of the nineteenth century, did not think of herself as a crusading feminist. Yet she insisted that women should be encouraged to speak publicly about matters of faith and morals. In* The Promise of the Father *(1859) Palmer argued that the customs of the churches must give way to the plain teachings of the Bible and Christ's will.*

What is meant by preaching the gospel? Says the devoted Dr. Wayland [a well-known Baptist theologian]:... "The words translated [as] preach in our version are two. The one signifies, simply, to herald, to announce, to proclaim, to publish. The other, with this general idea, combines the notion of good tidings, and means to publish, or be the messenger of good news."...And if this be the scriptural meaning of the word preach, then where is the Christian, either of the clergy or laity, but would have every man, woman, or child, who had an experiential knowledge of the saving power of Christ, herald far and near the tidings of a Saviour willing and able to save?...

But the well-known fact, that earnestly-pious and intelligent women are ever withstood, and the testimony of their lips ruled out, with but few exceptions, in the presence of the men, in nearly all church communities, seems of itself more like a return to barbarism than a perpetuation of Christianity.

CHAPTER SEVENTEEN

Adventurers of the Spirit

Onward, Christian soldiers, marching as to war,
with the cross of Jesus going on before,
Christ, the royal Master, leads against the foe;
forward into battle see his banners go!

   —*Sabine Baring-Gould, "Onward, Christian Soldiers" (1864)*

A s the nineteenth century drew to a close, religious men
and women everywhere reached out to embrace the
world and transform it in positive ways: adventurers of the
spirit, we might call them. Just as religious ideals had energized
visionary reformers before the Civil War, so too did they ener-
gize farsighted souls two generations later. But this time there
was a difference. In the intervening fifty years the nation itself
had changed, in fundamental ways. The extremes of wealth
and poverty had widened. Class suspicions had sharpened.
Farmers' lives had grown more risky economically. Blacks'
new freedom had stirred whites' fears. Technology had opened
the non-Western world to Western involvement. Religious

citizens responded to these challenges in a wide variety of ways, some effective, others less so. But respond they did. Americans had many sins, but indifference was rarely one of them.

Four efforts to reach out and change the world for the better stand out above the others. These attempts included new ideas about the care of the human body, the easing of poverty in the nation's swelling cities, the reduction of the suffering caused by alcohol abuse, and the vast effort to Christianize and aid people in other lands. In the 1880s and 1890s reformers targeted many additional evils, including prostitution, the misuse of the Sabbath, and the repression of women. However, health, poverty, alcohol, and missions took precedence.

The concern for health was an old story. All Western religions, including Judaism and Christianity, had much to say about the care of the human body. But the terrible carnage of the Civil War, plus new ideas in the late nineteenth century about how to improve and even lengthen human life, prompted believers to think about the relation between religion and health in creative ways.

Three distinctly different health efforts marked the religious landscape. The first was divine healing. This trend proved to be especially strong among radical evangelicals—mostly individuals with Baptist or Methodist backgrounds notable for their fierce independence and stormy preaching. Radical evangelicals assumed that sin produced physical suffering. Thus, they argued that when Jesus promised to bear away the sins of the world, he also promised to bear away suffering. "Only Trust Him" said a popular hymn, only trust that Christ would do what he promised to do.

Divine healing prompted the formation of several sects specially committed to the practice. Best known perhaps was the Christian and Missionary Alliance, which emerged in the 1880s and soon spread around the world. The idea of healing through Christ also undergirded the Pentecostal revival, which arose just after the turn of the twentieth century. (Pentecostals took their name from the Day of Pentecost when, according to the New Testament, Christians miraculously spoke languages they had never learned.) Following World War II, television evangelists like Oral Roberts and Kathryn Kuhlman helped make Pentecostalism the largest new Christian movement of the twentieth century.

A second healing movement stemmed from the teachings of Ellen G. White. In the 1850s White joined the remnants of the Millerites, who had predicted Christ's return in 1844. She first led the crestfallen believers into Saturday worship (prompted by powerful dream visions), then into strong interest in the care of the physical body (also prompted by visions). White reminded her followers that the body remained the temple of the Lord. Declaring that people made "a god of their bellies," Adventists paid close attention to what people should and should not eat. They opposed eating any form of meat, especially red meat, swine's flesh (ham), and shellfish like shrimp. They urged people to avoid cooking vegetables with lard and salt in favor of steaming and eating them with scarcely any seasoning. Realizing that people would find such a diet unattractive, Adventists invented tasty substitutes, including cold breakfast cereals. Battle Creek, Michigan, their headquarters, became synonymous with cornflakes, created by Adventist leader John Harvey Kellogg.

Spurred by White, Adventists urged additional health reforms. These included hard beds, regular exercise, sunshine, fresh air, frequent bathing in warm mineral waters, avoidance of alcohol and tobacco, and safer, more comfortable clothing for women (thus doing away with corsets and high heels). Adventists denounced undue sex within marriage. They scorned physicians and the use of chemical drugs. Some of their health reforms received mixed support at the time but enjoyed wide approval—often for different reasons—later on. In time the Adventists established colleges, universities, orphanages, and state-of-the-art hospitals belting the globe. Loma Linda University Medical Center in California ranked among the finest medical research institutions anywhere.

A third health-focused movement, commonly called Christian Science, emerged from the genius of Mary Baker Eddy. This forceful though somewhat mysterious woman was born in New Hampshire in 1821. She suffered from depression, economic insecurity, an unhappy marriage, and constant ill health throughout her young adulthood. In desperation Eddy dabbled in hypnotism and water cures, which in those days were a common remedy entailing frequent "flushing" of the body's system. A New England folk healer named Phineas P. Quimby finally helped her find relief. Quimby taught Eddy that all reality was simply an idea in God's mind. Because God's pure and perfect mind could hold no error, let alone suffering or death, the unhappy facts of everyday life were in fact illusions. Eddy adopted and elaborated these notions. She argued that a truly modern or scientific understanding of Jesus Christ would see him not as a divine being but rather as a human who understood that material things as well as sin, error, and illness existed only in the dark recesses of the human imagination.

Eddy's teachings found particular favor in the Boston area. There, in the historic citadel of Puritans, Unitarians, and Transcendentalists, she founded the Massachusetts Metaphysical College in 1881. That institution eventually grew into one of the wealthiest and most influential sects in the United States: the Church of Christ, Scientist. Christian Scientists, as its partisans called themselves, did not endorse preachers. Instead, worship was led by "readers" or "practitioners" who read from the Bible and from Eddy's main writing, *Science and Health, with Key to the Scriptures* (1875). These men and women helped converts preserve their health by seeing the illusion of matter, error, and illness. Drugs—including tobacco, alcohol, and sometimes caffeine—clouded the mind's ability to see the truth. Perhaps more than any other religious tradition in America, Christian Science proved to be congenial to middle- and upper-middle-class women. Though the church was never large (by 1910, at Eddy's death, its membership had reached only 100,000), Eddy's teachings nonetheless strongly appealed to the wealthy and well educated.

Unfortunately, America's cities harbored millions who were neither wealthy nor well educated. While the population of the nation tripled between 1880 and 1910, the number in the cities grew thirtyfold. Millions abandoned farms, especially in the South, for better-paying jobs in the cities. And millions more swept through the port cities, in a vast migration from eastern and southern Europe and, to a lesser extent, from Asia as well. Though many found opportunities unknown in their previous lives, others (perhaps a majority) encountered twelve-hour days, six-day work weeks, and the constant danger of loss of limb in the fast-moving machinery of the factories. Newcomers found themselves jammed into tenement houses, entire families living in a single room without plumbing or adequate heat or ventilation.

Humane souls of all sorts rose to the challenge, Christian and Jew, Protestant and Catholic. In retrospect two of those many efforts to ease the squalor and suffering in the cities particularly stand out. One was called the Social Gospel, the other the Salvation Army.

Earlier efforts by British Protestants to ease the pain of the urban poor, especially in London, influenced the American Social Gospelers. The latter believed that most Christians spent too much time trying to save the soul and not enough saving the body. The Social Gospelers thus established a string of churches in the urban Northeast, often called institutional churches, that offered a variety of social services, including health care, help in finding jobs, and recreational facilities. Starting in the 1870s, Washington Gladden, a Congregational pastor in Columbus, Ohio, wrote thirty books and hundreds of articles challenging wealthy Christians to search their consciences. He especially urged business owners to give laborers a living wage. At a time when 10 percent of the nation's families had cornered 70 percent of the nation's wealth, it seemed high time for decent, God-fearing folk to ask themselves what was fair.

The answers were not long in coming. *In His Steps*, an 1897 novel written by a Topeka, Kansas, Congregational minister named Charles M. Sheldon responded to this question without flinching. This popular book, one of the best-selling American novels of the nineteenth century, portrayed the dilemmas that typical Americans would face if every time they faced an ethical decision they honestly asked themselves a single, disturbing question: "What would Jesus do?" Later on, especially after the turn of the century, the Social Gospelers promoted more concrete solutions to urban ills. They urged state and federal governments to step in and force employers to limit the working day to ten (and later eight) hours, to guarantee a day of rest each week, to keep children out of the mines and away from dangerous machinery, and to provide at least minimal health and sanitation facilities.

These solutions resembled proposals advanced by labor unions such as the Knights of Labor. But there was a difference.

The Social Gospelers armed themselves with the teachings of the Hebrew prophets and the example of Jesus. The Bible, they insisted, never presented the gospel as good news for individuals alone. True biblical faith aimed to redeem society too.

The Salvation Army spearheaded another major effort to meet the urban challenge. Founded in London in the 1860s by Methodists William and Catherine Booth, the Army arrived in the United States, horns blowing, in 1880. In the United States the Army found its main supporters among radical evangelicals, especially those with Methodist roots. After the turn of the century the Booths' flamboyant, strong-willed daughter, Evangeline, ran the U.S. operation with the efficiency of a well-oiled machine. Dressed in their distinctive uniforms, caps, and bonnets, the Army's corporals and captains—male and female alike—aided the urban poor in many ways. They provided low-cost coal in winter and ice in summer. They distributed free food and medicine to the destitute and hungry. They sheltered orphans and unwed mothers. They fashioned education and training programs to help the penniless break the cycle of poverty. They helped alcoholics kick the habit and find productive work.

The Social Gospelers and the Salvation Army's workers sought similar goals. They both wanted people, especially the poor, to be treated fairly, to receive a living wage, to enjoy the benefits of clean housing and good medical care. But their approaches differed. The Social Gospelers increasingly looked toward long-range solutions, involving labor unions, laws and regulations, and the enforcing power of the state. The Army, on the other hand, looked toward more immediate solutions, helping the unemployed laborer next door find a meal this morning and a job this afternoon. It was a perenial dilemma. Should Christians try to solve the underlying causes of poverty?

Or should they concentrate on the suffering at hand? Neither movement showed much interest in the main reform causes of the late twentieth century, equality for minorities and for women. But both proved that biblical faith carried within itself powerful forces for the social as well as spiritual redemption of the cities.

Reforming the cities meant reforming Americans' misuse of alcohol. For the better part of a century, from the 1820s through the 1920s, religious men and women increasingly turned their attention to the harmful effects of excessive drinking. Although many antebellum abolitionists had championed temperance—Jonathan Blanchard, the first president of Wheaton College in Illinois, comes to mind—the four decades flanking the turn of the twentieth century marked the high point of that crusade. In colonial America, Christians had never endorsed drunkenness, yet they seemed rather lax about enforcing sobriety. Weddings involved considerable drinking, especially in the Anglican South and sometimes in the Puritan North.

In the early nineteenth century the quantity of drinking grew, with the typical adult male consuming an average of a half-pint of hard liquor each day. But at the same time, with the coming of industrialization and its attendant need for punctuality and carefulness around machinery, the demand for sobriety also grew. Thus in the 1840s Maine and Massachusetts passed laws against the production of hard liquor. These prohibitions did not last long, old consumption habits being hard to break, but they prefigured bigger things to come.

The real push for temperance emerged in the 1880s. Before the Civil War, temperance meant exactly what the word suggested: moderation. But eventually it came to mean abstinence: drinking no alcohol at all, not even medicinally. Reformers assumed that one drink led to another. The cause united men and women across the religious and political spectrums. They commonly worried about the sinister effects of drunkenness upon the home and the workplace. They labored together to pass laws to stop the production and sale of alcohol. They also worked together to create the unspoken expectation that sobriety was good and drunkenness disgraceful. The point was less to make intoxication illegal than to make it unthinkable. But making it illegal helped. In 1919 a broad coalition of religious groups persuaded Congress to pass the Eighteenth Amendment to the Constitution, prohibiting the sale of alcoholic beverages anywhere in the United States. Fourteen years later, in the face of widespread flouting of the law, Congress reversed itself and passed the Twenty-first Amendment, abolishing the Eighteenth.

Who supported temperance and who opposed it? Its main adherents included English-speaking Protestants, especially Methodists and Baptists, north and south, and a number of Irish Catholic leaders concerned about the perils of drinking among workers. The opposers included Continental Protestants and Catholics, especially Germans, who clung to Old World folkways. They also included the lower and upper classes of all (and no) religious persuasions, who saw temperance as an effort by middle-class do-gooders to run other people's lives.

And then there were the women who saw drink as part of a larger complex of social ills. No one did more to curb alcohol abuse than Frances Willard. This earnest crusader grew up near Chicago in a Methodist home, an affiliation she retained to the end of her days. As an instructor in the women's college of Northwestern University, Willard advocated equal opportunities for women in higher education. But her concern about the harmful effects of alcohol upon the home drew her into the newly formed Woman's Christian Temperance Union, better known as the WCTU. Willard's business skills soon propelled her to the presidency of that organization. For the three decades from the 1880s to 1910 she tirelessly crisscrossed the United States, calling for self-discipline for the willing, temperance laws for the unwilling.

Willard's reforming instincts ranged widely. In her mind, drunkenness persisted as one of many closely linked social problems, including, most notably, the sorry status of women. After the Civil War, middle-class women found themselves increasingly restricted to the home or to the company of other women outside the home. They were supposed to protect the morals of the family but not enter the public workplace. Willard was no radical. She did not seek to overturn the basic gender roles. But she forcefully agitated for woman suffrage—the right to vote—and for a woman's right to enter into business or political life if she wished.

Frances Willard also attacked prostitution and the abusive treatment of children. Ironically, perhaps, her crusade for woman suffrage, social purity (antiprostitution), and child protection laws would see more success in constitutional amendments and federal and state legislation in the twentieth century than would her concern for alcohol abuse.

By any reasonable measure of such things, the most spectacular religious adventure of the late nineteenth century started in the United States but ended far away, on countless mission fields overseas. To be sure, some groups never caught the spirit. The Jews and Lutherans, for example, remained more interested in nurturing their faith among their own children, generation after generation, than in extending it to outsiders. And some caught it late. Although U.S. Catholics launched the Maryknoll Missioners in 1908, until the twentieth century they had to work hard just to survive in an unfriendly environment. All of this is to say that the older English-speaking denominations—Congregationalists, Presbyterians, Methodists, and Baptists—served as the main carriers of the missionary vision in nineteenth-century America.

Domestic missions to Native Americans came first. One of the most conspicuous efforts involved the mission to the Cherokees, historically clustered in the southern highlands. By the 1820s, when Andrew Jackson became president, the Cherokees had already moved far toward Christianity, unlike most Indian groups. Even so, their grim fate was settled when whites discovered gold in the Georgia hills. Despite treaties guaranteeing the natives' right to stay, in the 1830s Jackson forcibly marched them along the Trail of Tears to the Oklahoma Territory. In the meantime, though, numbers of missionaries had grown deeply to respect the Cherokees' integrity and way of life, Christian or not. Some, such as Evan Jones and his son John B. Jones, both Baptists, struggled alongside the Indians against the federal forces. In the end, everyone lost. The Cherokees lost their homes, the missionaries their credibility, and the federal government its honor.

After the Civil War the missionary spirit targeted another evil: white racism and its stepchild, black poverty. Concern about the treatment of blacks had preceded the Civil War. It stirred the conscience of reform-minded sects like the Quakers and Free Methodists, prompted the formation of abolitionist societies, and helped spark the war itself. But if the Thirteenth Amendment (passed in 1865) abolished slavery, white racism persisted in other forms. In the late 1870s, for example, the federal government withdrew troops from the South. This move allowed Southerners to pass regulations, called Jim Crow laws, that required blacks to go to separate schools and avoid informal contact with whites on trains, in restaurants, or in public parks. Also, blacks' inability to find fair-paying jobs drove many into sharecropping, making it virtually impossible for them to gain any measure of economic independence. At the same time, whites displayed growing fear of black males. Some accounts held that the South witnessed three lynchings per week through the 1890s.

Both white and black Christians responded to these abuses. After the war, Northern white denominations sent hundreds of missionaries southward to build schools and orphanages and to distribute food and medical supplies. Many of these volunteers were women. The American Missionary Association, formed in 1846, focused upon educating freed slaves. Leading black colleges and universities, including Fisk, Hampton, Morehouse, Talladega, and Tougaloo, grew from such efforts.

Black Christians shouldered the burden too. Despite daunting obstacles they established Lane, Livingstone, Paul Quinn, and Morris Brown colleges, among others. They published books and newspapers (the A.M.E.Z.'s twice-monthly *Star of Zion*, published in the South almost continually since 1877, ranks as one of the oldest religious papers in the United States). Under the leadership of activists like A.M.E. bishop Henry McNeal Turner, they launched sustained efforts for the colonization of blacks in Africa as an alternative to the brutality of white racism at home.

And then, finally, there is the story of the foreign mission enterprise itself. This venture remains one of the great tales of U.S. religious history, filled with the feats of saints and heroes and, sad to say, the misdeeds of one or two scoundrels as well. Numerical data have to be used carefully, but they at least give us some idea of the size of the missionary effort of those years. Though a steady stream of Americans had been going abroad as missionaries ever since 1812, as late as 1890 fewer than a thousand lived overseas. By the turn of the century, however, that number had swollen to 5,000, which constituted a quarter of all the Christian missionaries in the world. (Twenty-five years later U.S. missionaries would constitute nearly half of the global total.) In 1886 evangelist Dwight L. Moody founded the Student Volunteer Movement, soon better known as the SVM. In the next fifty years the SVM stirred the imagination and touched the hearts of tens of thousands of young men and women. At least 13,000 actually sailed for far-off lands. A solid majority, perhaps 60 percent, of all U.S. missionaries were women.

Sometimes missionaries received support from their parent denominations. Starting in the 1880s, however, many who called themselves "faith" missionaries left without any initial promise of support. Independent organizations with exotic-sounding names like the Africa Inland Mission and the Sudan Interior Mission sent them to the remotest parts of the globe.

In the course of the nineteenth century U.S. missionaries fanned out literally all over the world. They won the Sandwich Islands (Hawaii) to Christianity by midcentury. Missions to Africa started in the 1820s. Spurred primarily by free blacks in the United States, missions in Africa grew steadily as European powers partitioned the continent piece by piece. In the later years of the century the majority of Protestant emissaries focused their attention upon Southeast Asia, especially China. Most tried primarily to win nonbelievers to the Christian faith, but in the process they also built hundreds of schools, hospitals, and orphanages. They mapped the landscape, measured volcanic eruptions, studied native plants and animals, reduced unwritten languages to written form, and translated the Bible into the vernacular languages of the local peoples. Often they did the reverse too: translating obscure languages into English. Missionaries were in some cases the first to render remote languages into *any* written form. In the Belgian Congo in the 1890s the Protestant missionaries were the first to codify in written form the Longkundo dialect, for instance.

All these trends—determination, brains, courage—manifested themselves in the lives of one particularly gifted and particularly famous missionary family, Adoniram Judson and his three successive wives. Just out of seminary, Judson and his first bride, Ann Hasseltine, sailed for India in 1812 as Congregational missionaries. They soon moved on to Burma (now Myanmar) where he suffered smallpox, tropical fevers, and nearly two years of brutal imprisonment. Ann endured terrible deprivations of her own, resulting in her death at the age of thirty-six. Ann's own translation work and her heart-rending stories of the sufferings of Burmese women found an eager audience in missionary magazines back home.

After Ann's death Judson married Sarah Hall Boardman, who worked with him shoulder to shoulder, spreading the gospel in the dangerous interior of Burma. Sarah completed the first translation of the New Testament into the Burmese language. When ill health claimed her life at the age of forty-two, Judson returned home for the first time in three decades and engaged a young writer named Emily Chubbuck to write Sarah's biography. They soon married and returned to Burma, where Judson himself died shortly afterward. By then he had completed monumental translation work and established a Burmese church with 7,000 followers. Emily's own illnesses and deprivations abroad resulted in her death from tuberculosis at the age of thirty-six.

These tales became the stuff of legends. Were missionaries like the Judsons heroes? The answer is yes if measured by the popular acclaim they enjoyed at home. Many graduated from the best colleges, presidents spoke at their conventions, and their missionary exploits captured front-page coverage in secular and quasi-secular magazines like the *Christian Herald*.

At the same time, however, thoughtful men and women—including novelists Herman Melville and Mark Twain—argued that missionaries were more interested in spreading American civilization than Christianity. After all, Christian expansion often paralleled U.S. business and military development overseas. And some critics raised deeper, more troubling questions. Did missionaries have the right to displace other people's religions at all? Some missionaries lost their zeal in the face of such questions, but most carried on, convinced that they possessed a message to share. Though these determined evangelists hardly silenced their critics, most Americans ranked them among the most courageous of the religious adventurers of the nineteenth century.

In Rudimental Divine Science *(1891) and in* No *and* Yes *(1891), Christian Science founder Mary Baker Eddy struggled to make clear to uncomprehending Americans that God was an Idea and that the world—which came from God—also was an Idea. Therefore, matter was an illusion and disease and death were lies, albeit terrible ones.*

What is the Principle of Christian Science? It is God, the Supreme Being, infinite and immortal Mind, the Soul of man and the universe. It is our Father which is in heaven. It is substance, Spirit, Life, Truth, and Love,—these are the deific Principle....

Is there no matter? All is Mind.... The five material senses testify to the existence of matter. The spiritual senses afford no such evidence, but deny the testimony of the material senses....

Disease is more than imagination; it is a human error, a constituent part of what comprise[s] the whole of mortal existence,—material sensation and mental delusion.... [T]he Science of Mind-healing destroys the feasibility of disease; hence error of thought becomes fable instead of fact....

Is healing the sick the whole of Science? Healing physical sickness is the smallest part of Christian Science. It is only the bugle-call to thought and action.... The emphatic purpose of Christian Science is the healing of sin; and this task, sometimes, may be harder than the cure of disease; because, while mortals love to sin, they do not love to be sick.

RELIGION IN TWENTIETH-CENTURY AMERICA

CHAPTER EIGHTEEN

A New Century

A t the dawn of the twentieth century the editor of a small magazine called the *Christian Oracle* thought that the turn of the calendar was so important that he would rename his publication *Christian Century*. "We believe that the coming century is to witness greater triumphs in Christianity than any previous century has ever witnessed," George A. Campbell, Jr., the editor, wrote from his Chicago office, "and that it is to be more truly Christian than any of its predecessors." The "Christian Century" that Campbell envisioned would be a *Protestant* century and, more specifically, a century defined by traditional, or "mainline," Protestant denominations—Presbyterian, Lutheran, Episcopalian, Methodist, Congregational, and Campbell's own Disciples of Christ.

Roman Catholics, however, had other ideas as they sought to make a place for themselves in the American religious landscape. In 1908 Pope Pius X declared that the United States was no longer a missionary territory for Roman Catholicism, meaning that the church in America was sufficiently well established that it required no further help from foreign Catholics. Later that same year, on November 16, American Catholics convened a missionary conference in Chicago to mark their passage from a church that *received* missionary help from others to a church that *sent* missionaries elsewhere. William H. O'Connell, archbishop of Chicago, noted the rapid maturity of the Roman Catholic Church in America. "It has covered the whole land of its birth and growth with its network of provinces and dioceses and parishes," he said, adding that American Catholicism had "taken on a character of its own; become conscious of its own mission and destiny; and full of a strength and courage born of the air and free institutions of the name whence it derives its name, is prepared to go forth conquering and to conquer in the cause of Christ."

Indeed, Roman Catholics in America had withstood the nineteenth-century assaults of nativism, the organized attacks by Protestants and others who resented the arrival of Catholic and other non-Protestant immigrants. "The United States is Rome's favorite mission field," John L. Brandt had warned under the auspices of the American Protective Association as late as 1895, adding that "our country has been flooded with hordes of foreigners, many of whom are uneducated Roman Catholics, and who, from infancy, have yielded implicit obedience to the Pope." Within three years of the Chicago conference, however, the St. Mary's Mission House was established in Techny, Illinois, for the purpose of training and sending missionaries to other countries. In addition, two priests, Thomas F. Price and James A. Walsh, founded the Catholic Foreign Missionary Society of America in 1911. This society, located in Maryknoll, New York, dispatched missionaries throughout the world, especially to Latin America.

Other religious groups besides Catholics and more traditional Protestants staked their claim on the hearts and souls of Americans. On the first day of the new century, January 1, 1901, an event at Bethel Bible College in Topeka, Kansas, signaled a new era in American Protestantism. Agnes N. Ozman, a student at the school, began speaking in an unknown language, which some witnesses later identified as Chinese, despite the fact that Ozman had never studied the language. Students interpreted her ecstatic speech, which sounded like babbling, as a gift from the Holy Spirit, a phenomenon known as glossolalia, or "speaking in tongues." According to Christian doctrine, the first time that anyone had spoken in tongues had been recorded in the New Testament, in the second chapter of the Acts of the Apostles, when the Holy Spirit descended upon the early Christians on the feast of Pentecost (so named because it occurred fifty days after Passover, the Jewish observance of the deliverance of ancient Israel from Egypt). On this occasion, after Jesus had been taken back into heaven, the Holy Spirit came upon the early believers "like a mighty wind," and they began speaking in unknown languages.

Although other incidents of glossolalia had been reported throughout church history—even Brigham Young, leader of the Mormons in the nineteenth century, claimed to have spoken in tongues—the small band of students at Bethel Bible College attached a special significance to the sudden reappearance of glossolalia on the opening day of the twentieth century. The students believed that the spiritual gifts mentioned in the New Testament, which included divine healing of sickness or physical deformity as well as glossolalia, had been restored to the church in the last days before Jesus would return to Earth. This outpouring of the Holy Spirit would serve as the final wake-up call both for unbelievers and for those who claimed to be Christians but who had become spiritually indifferent. Through the actions of the Holy Spirit, this small band of students in Topeka believed, God was alive and well at the dawn of the twentieth century, and God was issuing one final appeal before the end of time, just as the New Testament book of Revelation had predicted. These apocalyptic events, all promised in the book of Revelation, would engulf those who did not heed their urgent call to repentance.

As the Pentecostal revival spread among the students at Bethel Bible College, they were seized with a missionary zeal for bringing Christianity to America and to the world. These Pentecostals, however, represented only one strain of evangelicalism in America, a movement characterized by a belief that the Bible should be interpreted literally and by its insistence on a conversion, or "born again," experience as the criterion for entering the kingdom of heaven. Pentecostals were distinct in that they added the Spiritual gifts, especially tongues and healing, to this definition of godliness. Agnes Ozman and other pentecostals craved religious emotions and feelings as a way to verify the presence of God in their lives.

From Topeka, Pentecostalism spread rapidly. The founder of Bethel Bible College, Charles Fox Parham, had also spoken in tongues, which he interpreted as the "baptism of the Holy Spirit," an indication that God had especially blessed him and chosen him to proclaim the gospel. Parham was an itinerant preacher, and, following the New Year's Day revival in Topeka, he spread the word during his travels in Kansas, Missouri, and Texas. In Houston, Parham's message of Spirit baptism caught on with an African-American hotel waiter named William J. Seymour. A member of a group called the Evening Light Saints, Seymour carried the Pentecostal message with him when he migrated west to Los Angeles in 1906. There, he conducted prayer meetings and soon began preaching to large audiences from the front porch of the house on Bonnie Brae

Avenue where he was staying. Soon the crowds, spilling onto the streets, became too unwieldy, and the gatherings moved to an abandoned warehouse at 312 Azusa Street.

The Azusa Street Revival, as the gathering came to be known, drew national and even worldwide attention to the new Pentecostal movement. Meetings took place several times a day, and each lasted several hours. Participants sang hymns, listened to sermons, and heard testimonies from those who had been baptized by the Spirit, a scene reminiscent of the frontier camp meetings a century earlier. They raised their arms toward heaven in a gesture of openness to the Holy Spirit, and they spoke in tongues. The San Francisco earthquake, which occurred just after five o'clock in the morning on April 18, 1906, added a new sense of urgency to the Azusa Street Revival. Did the catastrophe just a few hundred miles to the north portend the end of the world? Was Jesus coming right now?

Although the interpretations differed, participants were certain that God was at work on Azusa Street. Even more remarkable was that the revival was interracial—the "color line has been washed away by the blood" of Jesus, one participant exclaimed—and that women preached and spoke publicly about their faith in an age in which women were fighting even for the right to vote. The Azusa Street Revival spread its message through its own newspaper, the *Apostolic Faith*, and by means of itinerant preachers who fanned out across North America—to Chicago, Toronto, and other cities—bringing the Pentecostal message of salvation and spiritual blessing. "Los Angeles Being Visited by a Revival of Bible Salvation and pentecost as Recorded in the Book of Acts," the *Apostolic Faith* proclaimed in its first issue, published in September 1906. "All over this city, God has been setting homes on fire and coming down and melting and saving and sanctifying and baptizing with the Holy Spirit," the newspaper continued, adding accounts of physical healings—of asthma, tuberculosis, even nearsightedness.

The *Apostolic Faith* also included news about a related phenomenon, called *xenolalia*, the gift of speaking a recognized language that the speaker had never before studied. "The Lord has given languages to the unlearned," the newspaper reported. "Greek, Latin, Hebrew, French, German, Italian, Chinese, Japanese, Zulu and languages of Africa, Hindu and Bengali and dialects of India, Chippewa and other languages of the Indians." Thus equipped and empowered by the Holy Spirit, missionaries left Los Angeles and carried news of the Pentecostal revival across North America and throughout the world.

Even as missionaries from North America took their Christian message around the world, however, the world continued to come to the United States. Between 1900 and 1915, 15 million immigrants entered the country, most of them from southern or eastern Europe. In 1893, the World's Parliament of Religions, a gathering of representatives of the world's major religions, had convened in Chicago, meeting in the building that now houses the Art Institute of Chicago, on South Michigan Avenue. For the first time, Americans learned about traditions other than Christianity and Judaism. Swami Vivekananda, for example, made the case for Hinduism, Krishna, and Vedantic philosophy, which derives from the Vedas. These spiritual writings, he said, contained "the accumulated treasury of spiritual law discovered by different persons in different times." To a society still suffering the ravages of unbridled capitalism, the concentration of wealth in the hands of a very small number of people, Vivekananda declared: "It is good to love God for hope of reward in this or the next world, but it is better to love God for love's sake, and the prayer goes: 'Lord, I do not want wealth, nor children, nor learning.'" Following the World's Parliament,

Vedanta societies sprouted up in the wake of Vivekananda's speaking tour throughout North America.

Anagarika Dharmapala of Ceylon (known today as Sri Lanka) introduced Americans to the "Middle Path" of Buddhism, the path between what he characterized as "the life of sensualism, which is low, ignoble, vulgar, unworthy and unprofitable," on the one hand, and "the pessimistic life of extreme asceticism," or self-denial, on the other. Buddhist beliefs and practices, which had already been present in Hawai'i and California in the nineteenth century—a Young Men's Buddhist Association was founded in Hawai'i in 1900, for instance—spread across the rest of North America. Mohammed Webb had the task of presenting Islam at the World's Parliament, asserting that Islam means "simply and literally resignation to the will of God." Like many of the representatives from other non-Christian religions, Webb lamented that most Americans had little understanding of religious traditions other than their own. As the twentieth century unfolded, these religions—Hinduism, Buddhism, and Islam—along with many others, became increasingly common on the religious landscape of North America.

White Americans, however, had yet to make peace with those who had inhabited North America long before their arrival. Driven by the doctrine of "manifest destiny"—the notion that it was the destiny, even the responsibility, of the white man to seize control of the West from Native Americans—the United States government had engaged in an aggressive campaign of almost uninterrupted conquest throughout the latter half of the nineteenth century. (The only major setback occurred in 1876 when the Sioux defeated George Armstrong Custer and his troops at Little Big Horn, Montana, thereby embarrassing white Americans on the centennial of their Declaration of Independence.) Although attempts to Christianize Native Americans date back to the sixteenth century, the efforts had intensified during the nineteenth century as Methodists, Episcopalians, Baptists, Roman Catholics, Mennonites, and Presbyterians made a determined effort to convert the Sioux and Cherokees and Navajos and Pueblos to Christianity. Most resisted. "Christianity speaks of far-off lands and places," one observer noted, whereas Indian stories "tell of the four sacred mountains, at least one of which is visible almost everywhere in Navajo country."

In 1906 the United States government even sought to appropriate those mountains. When the U.S. Forest Service annexed vast tracts of Pueblo territory into the newly formed Kit Carson National Forest of northern New Mexico, the Pueblos objected to the inclusion of Taos Blue Lake, a sacred site, and they became especially alarmed when the Forest Service began to cut trails and to allow grazing in the area. Although the 1848 Treaty of Guadalupe Hidalgo, which concluded the war with Mexico, had stipulated that the United States respect Spanish and Mexican land grants, a band of corrupt judges, lawyers, and territorial governors, known as the Santa Fe Ring, manipulated the bewildering court system to wrest lands from their rightful owners. Faced with the loss of Blue Lake, the Pueblos mounted vigorous protests; they staged demonstrations and wrote petitions, which argued for their religious freedoms based on the First Amendment to the Constitution and on the conviction that "the trees and all life and the earth itself...must be protected." "We have no buildings there, no steeples," Pueblo governor John C. Reyna noted. "There is nothing the human hand has made. The lake is our church. The mountain is our tabernacle. The evergreen trees are our living saints....We pray to the water, the sun, the clouds, the sky, the deer. Without them we could not exist. They give us food, drink, physical power, knowledge."

Many Americans early in the twentieth century, however, especially white Protestants, resented challenges to their status as the dominant religious group. Although Roman Catholics had been present in North America since the Spanish settlement of Florida and the Southwest and the French colonization of Quebec, Catholic immigrants from Germany and Italy were only beginning to acclimate themselves to the United States at the turn of the twentieth century. Jews had been present in New Amsterdam (New York City) as early as 1654, but if they felt secure in a society that was still overwhelmingly Protestant, the execution of Leo Frank in 1915 jolted them out of their complacency.

Frank, a Jew born in Cuero, Texas, and reared in Brooklyn, New York, was plant superintendent of the National Pencil Company in Atlanta when Mary Phagan, a fourteen-year-old employee, was found murdered in the factory's basement on April 27, 1913. Frank was arrested the following day and charged with the crime. Even though the evidence was flimsy and the witnesses for the prosecution of dubious character, mobs inside and outside the courthouse demanded Frank's conviction. The jury obliged; he was convicted of the murder and sent to death row.

Simmering anti-Semitism, which had been implicit since Frank's arrest, boiled over during the appeals process. In the *Jeffersonian* magazine, Tom Watson, who later represented Georgia in the U.S. Senate, angrily demanded the execution of "the filthy, perverted Jew of New York." Watson also helped to form an anti-Semitic society, the Knights of Mary Phagan, which organized a boycott of Jewish stores and businesses throughout the state. After the U.S. Supreme Court turned down Frank's appeal, a last-minute reprieve from the governor of Georgia, John Slaton, commuted Frank's sentence to life in prison. Upon hearing the news, however, a mob stormed the state prison in Milledgeville, abducted the prisoner, transported him to Mary Phagan's hometown, and lynched him on August 16, 1915, while hurling anti-Semitic insults.

The Leo Frank case stunned and outraged Jews across the nation, prompting increased membership in such organizations as the Anti-Defamation League of B'nai B'rith (which means "sons of the covenant," a reference to ancient Israel) and sending southern Jews scurrying for refuge in northern cities. The cities remained a proving ground for ethnic, racial, and religious diversity at the turn of the twentieth century. Several centuries earlier America's Protestants had envisioned a "city on a hill" and dreamed openly of establishing the kingdom of God in North America. By the close of the nineteenth century, however, so many "foreigners" had encroached upon that vision—Roman Catholics, Jews, African Americans, and even some practitioners of Eastern religions—that the squalid tenements on the lower east side of Manhattan, for instance, no longer resembled the kingdom of God.

"Where God builds a church the devil builds next door a saloon, is an old saying that has lost its point in New York," the social reformer Jacob Riis wrote in *How the Other Half Lives* in 1890. "Either the devil was on the ground first, or he has been doing a good deal more in the way of building. I tried once to find out how the account stood, and counted to 111 Protestant churches, chapels and places of worship of every kind below Fourteenth Street, 4,065 saloons. The worst half of the tenement population lives down there, and it has to this day the worst half of the saloons. Uptown the account stands a little better, but there are easily ten saloons to every church to-day. I am afraid, too, that the congregations are larger by a good deal; certainly the attendance is steadier and the contributions more liberal the week round, Sunday included."

America's Protestants were divided on their approach to the cities and to the social problems they presented. Many of the more conservative Protestants, known as evangelicals, who had condemned Charles Darwin's theory of evolution and who, in response to attacks on the Bible, had formulated a doctrine insisting that the Bible contained absolutely no errors or contradictions, grew increasingly suspicious of the cities, seeing them as seedbeds of sin and dens of political corruption. In 1892, for example, Charles H. Parkhurst, pastor of the Madison Park Presbyterian Church in New York City, had criticized the corrupt politicians in City Hall as a "lying, perjured, rum-soaked" lot and decried "the official and administrative criminality that is filthifying our entire municipal life, making New York a very hotbed of knavery, debauchery and bestiality."

Massive changes in American society following the Civil War, especially the rise of industry and the growth of the cities, had prompted evangelicals to revise their expectations that Jesus would return to Earth after they had built the kingdom of God. Although such organizations as the Young Men's Christian Association (YMCA), the Young Women's Christian Association (YWCA), and the Salvation Army made valiant efforts to sanitize the squalor and to rein in the rowdiness of urban life, and Carry A. Nation, a vigorous opponent of alcohol, had wielded her hatchet against the "hell holes" and "murder mills" of saloons, most evangelicals had succumbed to despair about the mess they saw everywhere around them. They revised their theology, insisting, contrary to the beliefs animating evangelicals earlier in the nineteenth century, that the world would *not* improve before Jesus came back to Earth. "I view this world as a wrecked vessel," Dwight L. Moody, a Chicago preacher, declared. "The Lord has given me a lifeboat and said, 'Moody, save all you can.'" In this new formulation, known as dispensationalism because it divides all of human history into ages, or time periods (dispensations), Jesus would return at any moment. History would come screeching to a halt, and the predictions contained in the book of Revelation would then unfold.

Dispensationalism, this revised interpretation concerning the end of time, may look harmless enough at first glance. It represented a way for America's evangelicals, at one time the majority religious group in North America, to reassert their importance. They might no longer dominate American society in the way they did before the Civil War, but this new interpretation of Revelation provided them the assurance that they understood the mind of God. They had figured it out, they had cracked the code, and they knew exactly how history would end. More important, however, dispensationalism exempted them from the daunting task of social reform. What was the use of reforming society according to the standards of godliness? Jesus would return at any moment, summon the "true believers" (the evangelicals), and unleash judgment against those who had opposed them. Dispensationalism, this "theology of despair," allowed evangelicals to walk away from the problems of the cities and to concentrate on the conversion, or regeneration, of individuals rather than society as a whole.

Not all Protestants followed this model. A large number, who were generally regarded as more liberal, theologically and politically, insisted that the gospel of the New Testament was capable not only of saving sinful individuals but of transforming sinful social institutions as well. The Christian gospel "has its ministry of rescue and healing for sinning men and women," Henry Sloane Coffin, a Protestant theologian, acknowledged, but it also "has its plan of spiritual health for society." These liberal Protestants, led by such pastors as Walter Rauschenbusch, Washington Gladden, and others, preached the Social Gospel, which held that Christians had a responsibility to reform abuses in the workplace, in the marketplace, and in the political arena. "No plan can be devised which will give us good city government," Gladden wrote in 1909, "so long as the great majority of our citizens are unwilling to take any responsibility for the government of our cities."

Whereas evangelicals had retreated to dispensationalism, believing that the evils of society stemmed from sinful individuals in need of redemption, those who promoted the Social Gospel believed that human nature was essentially good and that goodness had been thwarted by corrupt institutions. By the middle of the 1910s, however, that assumption of innate human goodness would be severely tested by the winds of war already gusting in Europe.

THE AZUSA STREET REVIVAL
IN LOS ANGELES

The first issue of the Apostolic Faith, *newspaper of the Azusa Street Revival, was published in Los Angeles in September 1906, providing news about the extraordinary Pentecostal revival taking place at 312 Azusa Street and elsewhere in the city. Many of the participants in the gatherings on Azusa Street spoke in tongues and claimed divine healing of sickness and physical deformity. This article appeared on the front page.*

PENTECOST HAS COME: LOS ANGELES BEING VISITED BY A REVIVAL OF BIBLE SALVATION AND PENTECOST AS RECORDED IN THE BOOK OF ACTS

The power of God now has this city agitated as never before. Pentecost has surely come and with it the Bible evidences are following, many being converted and sanctified and filled with the Holy Ghost, speaking in tongues as they did on the day of Pentecost. The scenes that are daily enacted in the building on Azusa Street and at Missions and churches in other parts of the city are beyond description, and the real revival is only started, as God has been working with His children mostly, getting them through to pentecost, and laying the foundation for a mighty wave of salvation among the unconverted.

CHAPTER NINETEEN

The Age of Militancy

Many religious leaders opposed the entry of the United States into World War I (known then as the "Great War"). Peace advocates included Henry Sloane Coffin, a theologically liberal professor at Union Theological Seminary in New York City, and the three-time Democratic candidate for president William Jennings Bryan, who was theologically conservative and politically liberal. Bryan served as secretary of state under Woodrow Wilson until 1915, when he resigned rather than take steps toward war. By early 1917, however, popular sentiments had changed.

"It is a terrible thing to lead this great and peaceful people into war," Wilson acknowledged in his war message to Congress, but Americans responded to Wilson's summons to "make the world safe for democracy." By and large only such long-standing pacifists as the Quakers and the Mennonites opposed the war, and the language of Christianity became the religion of American patriotism. Billy Sunday, for example, a flamboyant revivalist and former baseball player, conducted "hang the kaiser" rallies. "Christianity and Patriotism are synonymous terms," he declared, "and hell and traitors are synonymous."

Divisions between liberal and conservative Protestants hardened in the early decades of the twentieth century. The two camps had differed over their approach to the cities—liberal advocates of the Social Gospel had urged the redemption of sinful social institutions, whereas conservatives focused increasingly on the salvation of individuals—but liberals, known also as "modernists," generally sought to reconcile the gospel with the modern world. Darwin's theory of evolution, they argued, was not inconsistent with Christian faith; believers simply must shed their antiquated insistence on interpreting the Genesis account of creation literally. Human nature, they said, was basically good and altruistic, a notion that seemed to be contradicted by the war in Europe.

Conservatives, also known as evangelicals, came increasingly to distrust the modernists and the theological liberalism that evangelicals believed was steadily infecting Protestant denominations. In an effort to stanch the spread of modernist ideas, Lyman and Milton Stewart, founders of Union Oil Company in California, established a fund of $250,000 to publish and distribute a series of booklets "to every pastor, evangelist, minister, theology professor, theological student, Sunday school superintendent, YMCA and YWCA secretary in the English-speaking world." These twelve booklets appeared between 1910 and 1915 and were known collectively as *The Fundamentals*.

Subtitled *A Testimony to the Truth*, the series of booklets contained conservative theological statements written by prominent evangelical theologians from Great Britain, Canada, and the United States. The articles defended such doctrines as biblical inerrancy (the idea that the Bible was completely free from error in the original manuscripts), the virgin birth of Christ (that Jesus was born of the Virgin Mary), the authenticity of miracles (that the miracles attributed to Jesus took place exactly as recorded in the New Testament), and the Genesis account of creation. Those who subscribed to these doctrines came to be known as "fundamentalists." *The Fundamentals* served as a rallying cry for conservatives in their battle against modernism.

On May 21, 1922, one of the most articulate and influential liberal preachers in America, Harry Emerson Fosdick, laid down the gauntlet in his historic sermon "Shall the Fundamentalists Win?" "Already all of us must have heard about the people who call themselves the Fundamentalists," Fosdick told his congregation at the First Presbyterian Church in New York City. "Their apparent intention is to drive out of the evangelical churches men and women of liberal opinions." The venerable preacher proceeded to characterize fundamentalists as opposed to modern learning and poised to overtake American Protestantism. "In such an hour, delicate and dangerous, when feelings are bound to run high," he intoned, "I plead this morning the cause of magnanimity and liberality and tolerance of spirit." Fosdick concluded that the fundamentalists would never succeed in their effort "to drive out from the Christian churches all the consecrated souls who do not agree with their theory of inspiration."

Indeed, by the mid-1920s it appeared that the modernists had gained the upper hand, at least in their struggle to control the denominations. Fundamentalist forces among Baptists in the North decried the liberalism at the University of Chicago Divinity School and formed their own school in Chicago, Northern Baptist Theological Seminary, in 1913. Among Presbyterians, J. Gresham Machen, a professor at the denomination's Princeton Theological Seminary, published *Christianity and Liberalism* in

1923, arguing that liberal theology was, in fact, a new religion. It was *not* Christianity, he insisted, and liberals should do the honorable thing and leave the denomination.

The liberals, or modernists, would do no such thing. In 1924, when the Presbyterian general assembly adopted a measure that allowed clergy to restate historic doctrines in their own words, conservatives bewailed the move as a slippery slope into theological error. By 1929 Machen left his post at Princeton Seminary to form, successively, Westminister Theological Seminary in Philadelphia, a foreign missions board independent of the denomination, and the Presbyterian Church of America, later known as the Orthodox Presbyterian Church—all dedicated to conservative theology.

Fundamentalists defected from other denominations as well, seeking to separate themselves from what they regarded as heresy, a departure from traditional Christian doctrines. They embarked on an ambitious program of forming their own congregations, denominations, mission societies, publishing houses, colleges, seminaries, and Bible institutes—all of them free from the taint of modernism. This sprawling network of institutions throughout the United States and Canada would comprise an evangelical subculture, which provided the foundation for the return of evangelicals to political activism in the 1970s.

The fundamentalist-modernist controversies of the 1920s, the fights between conservatives and liberals, were often highly pitched battles, but the most famous skirmish of all took place on the second story of the Rhea County courthouse in Dayton, Tennessee. The state of Tennessee had passed the Butler Act, which prohibited, in the law's words, "the teaching of the evolutionary theory in all the universities, normals, and all the public schools of Tennessee." Almost immediately, the American Civil Liberties Union (ACLU) advertised that it was looking for someone to challenge the law, and on May 4, 1925, a group of civic boosters gathered at Fred Robinson's drugstore in Dayton and plotted a court case that would put the town on the map. They summoned the local high school's general science instructor and part-time football coach, plied him with a fountain drink, and asked if he would be willing to test the Butler Act. The teacher, John T. Scopes, it turned out, could not recall whether or not he had actually taught evolution, but that detail seemed irrelevant to everyone concerned. Scopes agreed to challenge the case, whereupon the local law enforcement officer served him with a warrant, and Scopes left the drugstore to play a game of tennis.

A much larger drama was being played out, of course, and the twenty-four-year-old teacher was lost in the shuffle. The ACLU retained the services of renowned trial lawyer Clarence Darrow as head of Scopes's defense team, while William Jennings Bryan, a stem-winding orator, assisted the prosecution. "We have the purpose of preventing bigots and ignoramuses from controlling the education of the United States," Darrow declared, "and that is all." Bryan saw the trial differently, as a test of whether tax-payers could determine what their children were taught. Bryan also harbored serious misgivings about the social effects of evolutionary theory, fearing that the survival-of-the-fittest doctrine could be used to justify the ravages of military force, territorial conquest, and the unbridled pursuit of wealth. As early as 1904 he had denounced Darwinism "because it represents man as reaching his present perfection by the operation of the law of hate—the merciless law by which the strong crowd out and kill the weak."

For ten sweltering days in July 1925, the Scopes trial unfolded amid a carnival atmosphere. Partisans from both sides squared off on the courthouse lawn; vendors sold souvenirs emblazoned with the likenesses of monkeys, a reference to the theory that humans evolved from apes. The media contingent, headed by H. L. Mencken of the *Baltimore Sun*, had arrived in full force, and the proceedings were broadcast live over radio station WGN in Chicago.

Whereas Darrow appealed to the "intelligent, scholarly Christians, who by the millions in the United States find no inconsistency between evolution and religion," Bryan sought to cast the issue in different terms: "Can a minority in this State come in and compel a teacher to teach that the Bible is not true and make the parents of these childern pay the expenses of the teacher to tell their childern what these people believe is false and dangerous?" The turning point of the trial occurred when Darrow persuaded Bryan to take the witness stand. In so doing, they flip-flopped the roles of prosecutor and defendant because Darrow, counsel for the defense, thrust Bryan into the role of defending the truth of the Bible. Darrow succeeded in making Bryan look foolish, especially as the trail was reported by Mencken, who was Darrow's close friend. Mencken relegated Bryan and fundamentalists to the "mean streets" of America, "everywhere where learning is too heavy a burden for mortal minds to carry."

A point nearly lost amid the overheated rhetoric from the overheated courtroom in Dayton was that Scopes was in fact found guilty of violating the Butler Act and fined $100, although the conviction was later overturned by the Tennessee Supreme Court on a technicality. Bryan and the fudamentalists lost in the larger courtroom of public opinion, however, just five years after one of their biggest triumphs—the enactment of the Eighteenth Amendment to the U.S. Constitution, prohibiting the sale and consumption of alcohol.

Bryan died five days after the conclusion of the trial, and in the years following the "Scopes monkey trial" fundamentalists continued their wholesale retreat from the broader American society, which they regraded as both corrupt and corrupting. For half a century after the trial—from 1925 until about 1975, with the presidential campaign of Jimmy Carter, a Southern Baptist Sunday school teacher—fundamentalists rarely ventured outside of the private world of churches, denominations, schools, Bible camps, and mission societies. Many even refused to vote, so convinced were they of the corruptions of the world outside their subculture.

The modernists, by all appearances, had prevailed in the fundamentalist-modernist battles during the 1920s. By absenting themselves from the denominations in large numbers, the conservatives had ceded Protestant denominations to the liberals. The spoils of victory included everything from church buildings and denominational offices to pension funds and seminary scholarships. While the fundamentalists had to start from scratch, the modernists sought to consolidate their positions. In 1925 the Presbyterians, the Methodists, and the Congregationalists in Canada merged to form the United Church of Canada. To the south, the Federal Council of Churches, which had been organized in 1908, continued to pursue the agenda, in the words of Charles S. Macfarland, the council's general secretary, of "modern movements towards Christian unity."

American Catholics also recognized the virtues of consolidation and cooperation. The Knights of Columbus, an organization for Catholic laymen, had been formed in 1882 to provide insurance and to offer recreational and social opportunities in the days before mass entertainment. During World War I, the Knights successfully petitioned the government to allow Catholic soldiers to use the Knights of Columbus as their service organization rather than the Protestant YMCA. The National Catholic War Council, which had been formed in 1917 to recruit and train military chaplains, took the name National Catholic Welfare Conference after the war. The organization, which provided the opportunity for Catholic bishops to speak with a united voice, set up offices in Washington, where they sought to influence public policy on issues relating to Roman Catholicism.

Perhaps the most important organizational efforts of the Roman Catholic Church were directed toward youth. In 1884, at a national gathering in Baltimore known as the Third Plenary Council, Catholic leaders had sought to address the perils of rearing Catholic children in an overwhelmingly Protestant culture. The bishops' battles against Protestant biases in public schools had triggered "great school wars" in New York, Philadelphia, and others cities, but despite, for instance, Catholic objections to the use of the Protestant King James Version of the Bible, little had changed.

The Third Plenary Council directed that all Catholic parishes set up parochial (parish) schools or otherwise provide for Catholic children's upbringing in the faith. By the early decades of the twentieth century, parochial schools had been established throughout the country in an effort to ensure that Catholic schoolchildren remained Catholic. In addition, the church had other strategies for appealing to younger Catholics and keeping them within the fold. The Catholic Youth Organization (CYO) was founded by a Chicago priest, Bernard J. Shiel, in 1930 to provide recreational activities for Catholics and an alternative to the Protestant-dominated YMCA and YWCA. Chapters of the CYO, which sponsored basketball leagues, boxing tournaments, and other athletic events, flourished around the country.

American Jews also began to organize in the early decades of the twentieth century. On November 9, 1926, a gathering of Jewish leaders in New York City led to the formation of the

Synagogue Council of America, based on the assumption that "it is desirable that the representatives of the synagogues in America meet from time to time in order to take counsel together for the sacred purpose of preserving and fostering Judaism." Conservative Judaism saw itself as a middle ground between the Orthodox, or strictly observant, Jews who had recently arrived from eastern Europe, and Reform Judaism, which had so assimilated to America that many Reform Jewish congregations had replaced Hebrew with English in the prayer book and had given up both the segregation of men from women during worship and the observance of kosher dietary laws.

Just as the American context has given rise to a variety of religious expressions, so, too, Judaism in America has taken a number of different forms. In 1922 Mordecai M. Kaplan, a rabbi and a professor at the Jewish Theological Seminary, assumed leadership of the Society for the Advancement of Judaism in New York City and opened a "Jewish Center" on Manhattan's West Side, a combination of synagogue, assembly hall, gymnasium, and classrooms. The Jewish Center reflected Kaplan's vision of religion serving the social needs of a minority culture. Judaism, he insisted, was the folk religion of the Jewish people, and it was no longer necessary to believe in an other-worldly, personal God. Instead, as Kaplan argued in *Judaism as a Civilization*, published in 1934, Jews should "reconstruct" their lives around Jewish culture. The movement Kaplan inspired, called Reconstructionism, assured Jews that religious observances were important only insofar as they reminded them of their history and culture, and Kaplan called on Jews to unite behind their common ethnic and cultural identity.

Other Americans consolidated as well. "America for Americans," Hiram Wesley Evans, who billed himself as "Imperial Wizard and Emperor, Knights of the Ku Klux Klan," declared amid a resurgence of Klan activity in the 1920s. The Ku Klux Klan, or KKK, a secretive organization of white supremacists, had been founded in Nashville after the Civil War and then revived as a Protestant lodge by a former Methodist minister, William J. Simmons, in 1915. Evans and others were attracted to the Klan's intolerance for Jews, Catholics, and African Americans. "The white race must be supreme, not only in America but in the world," Evans declared. "Protestantism is an essential part of Americanism; without it America could never have been created and without it she cannot go forward." Prejudice against Roman Catholics persisted to the north as well. In late 1922 and early 1923, sixteen large Catholic churches in Quebec caught fire under mysterious circumstances, and the three oldest shrines in the province were destroyed by fire—the Trappist monastery at Oka; Sainte Anne de Beaupre, noted for its miraculous cures; and the Basilica in Quebec City, which had been built in 1647.

After the turn of the twentieth century, the lynching of African Americans became frightfully commonplace, especially in the South. Reconstruction, the plan to rebuild the South after the Civil War, had failed to provide equality of opportunity across racial lines. In addition, the emergence of the so-called Jim Crow laws, which segregated whites and blacks, and the spread of the boll weevil, which caused cotton crop failures, all prompted many African Americans to leave the South and migrate to northern cities, bringing with them a rich cultural heritage. The musical tradition of the blues, for example, can be traced from the Delta region in Mississippi, north to Beale Street in Memphis, to Kansas City and St. Louis, and finally to the South Side of Chicago.

African-American migrations tended to follow the train lines, which ran south and north, and so blacks from Georgia and the Carolinas ended up in Washington or Newark or New York City, whereas blacks from Alabama and Mississippi settled in Cleveland or Chicago. Their religious beliefs and practices found new expressions in an urban setting. Many African Americans, seeking to replicate the close-knit communities of the South, found a spiritual home in storefront churches, where worship was marked by enthusiasm and ecstasy. Others sought the middle-class respectability of the Baptists or the African Methodist Episcopal churches. Still others gravitated toward a new generation of religious leaders—Father Divine or Marcus Garvey or Daddy Grace or Timothy Drew.

Garvey, a native of Jamaica who came to the United States in 1916, preached that God was black, and taught the gospel of black superiority and unity. He rallied his followers under the banner of the Universal Negro Improvement Association. The slogan for Garvey's movement was "One God! One Aim! One Destiny!" and he formed a steamship company, the Black Star Line, in order to resettle African Americans in Africa. The venture soon attracted the scrutiny of federal authorities, however; Garvey was convicted of mail fraud in 1925 and thrown into prison. Calvin Coolidge commuted his sentence in 1927, and Garvey eventually died in London in 1940. Despite Garvey's demise, other African Americans found his message of black pride irresistible. Timothy Drew, who became known as the Noble Drew Ali, insisted that the true religion of blacks was Islam, and his Moorish Science Temple, begun in Newark, New Jersey, in 1913, told blacks of their "true heritage" as Moorish Americans. Although Ali disappeared under mysterious circumstances in 1929, his message of black identity and pride would be picked up later by the Nation of Islam.

Other African-American religious leaders echoed the message of racial pride and uplift, especially during the heady days of the Harlem Renaissance, a flowering of black culture and the arts during the 1920s. One of the more riveting figures of this era was Major Jealous Divine, known to his followers as Father Divine. He operated a boardinghouse and an employment bureau in Sayville, Long Island, New York. Divine's lavish, sometimes raucous, celebrations, which in the theology of his Peace Mission Movement held religious significance, offended some of the Sayville neighbors, especially those who objected to the interracial nature of the gatherings. In 1931 Divine was arrested for disturbing the peace. He stood trial in the courtroom of Judge Lewis J. Smith, whose comportment betrayed his prejudice against African Americans. The jury returned a verdict of guilty but urged leniency in sentencing. The judge, however, imposed the maximum sentence and sent Divine to jail. Three days later Smith, who had apparently been in good health, died suddenly.

When informed of the judge's demise, Father Divine, who had never discouraged speculation among his followers that he possessed supernatural powers, responded with one of the most unforgettable lines in all of American religious history: "I hated to do it." Divine was released from jail shortly thereafter.

Although American soldiers had returned triumphant from Europe at the conclusion of the "Great War," having made "the world safe for democracy," it was clear that the United States still had much work to do at home to ensure freedom and equality for its own citizens. The Presidential election of 1928 demonstrated the persistence of anti-Catholic bias among the nation's Protestants. Alfred E. Smith, governor of New York and the Democratic nominee for president, faced relentless attacks because he was Roman Catholic, a fact that led some Protestant groups to oppose him outright. More often, however, Smith's detractors shrouded their anti-Catholicism behind rhetoric about the candidate's opposition to Prohibition and his support for repeal of the Eighteenth Amendment.

"I do not wish any member of my faith in any part of the United States to vote for me on any religious grounds," Smith declared during the campaign. "I want them to vote for me only when in their hearts and consciences they become convinced that my election will promote the best interests of our country." In part because of his faith, however, Smith lost the general election to Herbert C. Hoover, a Republican from West Branch, Iowa, in Hoover's first bid for elective office. (According to popular lore at the time, when Smith lost the election he sent a one-word telegram to the pope: "Unpack.") The Eighteenth Amendment and the republic itself, in the eyes of many Protestants, had been rescued from the threats of "Rum and Romanism," a reference to the Roman Catholic Church.

Hoover's triumph was short-lived. On "Black Thursday," October 24, 1929, less than eight months after he took office, the stock market collapsed and plunged the nation into the depths of the Great Depression. The new president was temperamentally incapable of the dramatic action needed to pull the nation out of its economic crisis, so when he faced another governor of New York, Franklin Delano Roosevelt, in the 1932 election, the results were different. Although Roosevelt had campaigned against any extraordinary governmental interference in the workings of the economy, his attitude had changed by the time of his inauguration. Roosevelt's New Deal offered wildly experimental approaches to economic renewal, an "alphabet soup" of federal agencies that would attack the root causes of the collapse and put Americans back to work.

Arguing that the only thing Americans need fear was "fear itself," Roosevelt took to the radio to provide comfort and assurance in his "fireside chats." In so doing he was using for political ends a medium already used to considerable effect by religious leaders. In 1922 a Pentecostal preacher named Aimee Semple McPherson became the first woman ever to preach a sermon over the radio, and her station, KFSG ("Kalling Four Square Gospel") was the nation's first station owned and operated by a religious organization. "Sister Aimee," as she was known, built her spectacular Angelus Temple in the Echo Park neighborhood of Los Angeles in 1923. That same year Charles E. Fuller began broadcasting his *Old Fashioned Revival Hour*, a mix of music and evangelical preaching. By the 1940s Fuller's weekly broadcast from the Long Beach Auditorium would be the most popular radio program in the country, eclipsing Amos 'n' Andy, Bob Hope, and Charlie McCarthy.

Not all religious radio broadcasters were Protestants. Charles E. Coughlin, a Roman Catholic priest from Royal Oak, Michigan, took to the radio airwaves in 1926 with the idea of explaining Catholicism to America's Protestants after the Ku Klux Klan had burned a cross at his Shrine of the Little Flower. Coughlin, who counted the automobile manufacturer Henry Ford among his friends, quickly expanded his purview to politics, sounding themes calculated to appeal to the masses. He established his National Union for Social Justice in 1934 and argued that "the old economic system of ragged, rugged individualism was nurtured at the win breasts of successive Republican and Democratic Administrations—the right breast exuding the sour milk" of wealth and privilege and the left breast the "skimmed milk" of socialism. Although Coughlin had initially supported Roosevelt's New Deal, the "radio priest" eventually turned against it, railing against the president and engaging in anti-Semitic and pro-Nazi rhetoric until the Catholic bishops forced him off the air in 1940.

Despite Roosevelt's best efforts, however, economic recovery proved elusive throughout the 1930s, giving rise to demagogues, religious and otherwise. The resurgent Ku Klux Klan directed some of its hatred toward Jews, in addition to its more traditional targets, blacks and Roman Catholics. Gerald Burton Winrod, head of an organization called Defenders of the Christian Faith, based in Topeka, Kansas, railed against modernism in its various forms, including Darwinism, the New Deal, communism, and what he believed was a worldwide Jewish conspiracy. Winrod's conspiracy theories anticipated some of the white supremacist rhetoric of various so-called Christian Identity movements in the 1980s and 1990s.

Not all of the religious rhetoric during the depression, however, was hateful. On May 1, 1933, Dorothy Day and Peter Maurin began distributing the *Catholic Worker* in New York City's Union Square. The small newspaper, published out of a dwelling on the Lower East Side of Manhattan, sold for a penny a copy, and it provided Roman Catholic social teaching regarding the poor and the unemployed. The cure for the ills of society, the newspaper declared, lay in a return to such radical Christian values as pacifism and concern for the less fortunate, including workers. Following Day's example, those associated with the Catholic Worker Movement lived in "voluntary poverty" and directed their energies toward people on the margins of society. Catholic Worker houses expanded to other cities, and the movement retained its opposition to the military through World War II and the Korean and Vietnam wars.

The years surrounding World War I and the Great Depression called traditional religious beliefs into question. Modernists cast off the moorings of creeds and biblical literalism. Fundamentalists came to regard science, especially Darwinism, as a threat, rather than an ally. Americans' faith in unfettered capitalism was sorely tested by the stock market crash of 1929, and that same year a young newly appointed professor at Union Theological Seminary in New York City, Reinhold Niebuhr, called liberal theology into question. Ever since the nineteenth century, theological liberals had asserted the essential goodness of humanity and had sought to reconcile the gospel of the New Testament with the modern world. They played down the notion of human sinfulness, argued that human nature was basically good and altruistic, and identified the kingdom of God with social progress.

For Niebuhr and other advocates of a theology that became known as Neo-Orthodoxy in a reference to their attempt to recover some traditional elements of Protestant theology, the ravages of World War I and the devastation of the Great Depression had shattered the liberals' naive belief in the goodness of human nature. Drawing in part on the writings of Karl Barth, a Protestant theologian from Switzerland, Niebuhr reintroduced the Christian doctrine of original sin, which explained the presence of evil in the world. What Niebuhr called the "political realism of Christian orthodoxy" took full account of evil and endorsed "the coercive force of governments to restrain those who will not voluntarily abide by the rule of rational justice." Although Niebuhr's Neo-Orthodoxy, also known as the theology of crisis, drew criticism from both the liberals and the evangelicals, its assertion of human depravity and its justification of force to restrain evil became especially prophetic as the world drifted once again toward war.

The Protestant magazine Christian Century *was founded as the* Christian Oracle *in 1884 and renamed at the turn of the twentieth century. Although the editors of the* Christian Century, *like many Americans, had initially been opposed to the entry of the United States into World War I, the magazine came to recognize the perils of German aggression. In this editorial, "The War and the Social Gospel," which appeared in the December 27, 1917, issue, the magazine used the occasion of armed conflict to meditate on the theological problem of evil, both personal and corporate.*

Even in the war itself, in its inherent character, we have the illumination of a great social principle which has a vital bearing on our theology of sin. Too long have we thought of sin in its personal and individual embodiment alone. A great hindrance in the way of realizing Christ's social gospel of the Kingdom of God has been the fact that we have been unable to recognize sin in its collective or social embodiment.... The sin we are fighting is not that of the individual German soldier through whose breasts our boys have to run their bayonets, but the social sin of the German nation as a whole.... With the mind of the world grown accustomed to think of Germany as a "super-personal" force of evil, it will be incomparably easier to apply the principle of social sinning to groups and institutions within a single nation and to bring to bear upon them through the social gospel the super-personal forces of condemnation and destruction.

CHAPTER TWENTY

In God We Trust

O ur form of government makes no sense unless it is founded in a deeply felt religious faith," President Dwight Eisenhower declared in 1952, "and I don't care what it is." By the middle decades of the twentieth century Americans were growing increasingly confused and uneasy about the varieties of religion around them. The days when Protestants dominated American society, as they had in the nineteenth century, were fading fast. Protestants had to make room for others, especially Catholics and Jews, who had taken advantage of the Statue of Liberty's famous invitation: "Give me your tired, your poor, your huddled masses yearning to breathe free."

American Protestants not only had to deal with the presence of Jews, Catholics, and others within the United States, they also had to reconsider their attitudes toward those of different faiths throughout the world. Although the missionary impulse had been strong in the nineteenth century (and it continued throughout the twentieth), some Protestants began to assess the entire missionary enterprise. In 1930 an organization called the Laymen's Foreign Missions Inquiry, with the support of seven Protestant denominations and the financial backing of the oil tycoon John D. Rockefeller, Jr., undertook a study of Protestant foreign missions. The organization sent delegates to interview missionaries in several countries throughout the world and then entrusted the findings to a commission chaired by William Ernest Hocking, professor of philosophy at Harvard University.

The Hocking commission issued a seven-volume appraisal of Protestant missions, together with detailed recommendations. The commission's report, and especially its one-volume summary entitled *Re-thinking Missions*, heralded a new era in missionary work, calling for American Protestants to be more sensitive to other cultures and other religions. "There is a growing conviction that the mission enterprise is at a fork in the road," the report began, "and that momentous decisions are called for." *Re-thinking Missions* argued for greater respect for the integrity of other religions, questioned the quality of missionaries in the field, and urged that "a much more critical selection of candidates should be made, even at the risk of curtailing the number of missionaries sent out."

Pearl S. Buck, a Presbyterian and the wife of a missionary to China, reviewed *Re-thinking Missions* in the Protestant magazine *Christian Century*. Buck, whose novel *The Good Earth* won the Pulitzer Prize in 1932, the same year that the Hocking Report appeared, hailed *Re-thinking Missions* as "inspired" and "a masterpiece of constructive religious thought." Other, more conservative Protestants were not so impressed, seeing the Hocking Report as yet another example of how liberals were backing away from truth and certainty, allowing themselves to be swallowed into the quicksand of theological relativism, where any other religion might be just as valid as Christianity.

While evangelicals and fundamentalists tried to walk the straight and narrow path of theological conservatism, however, other Protestants recognized the need to enlarge the boundaries, especially as the atrocities of the Holocaust, in the course of which the Nazis killed six million Jews during World War II, came to light. It was an evil that was, in the words of one Jew, "overwhelming in its scope, shattering in its fury, inexplicable in its demonism." As early as the 1930s, religious leaders began talking about something they called the Judeo-Christian tradition, which was a response to America's growing pluralism. The Temple of Religion at the New York World's Fair in 1938–39 used this notion of the "Judeo-Christian tradition" to exclude other religious groups: Mormons, Buddhists, Jehovah's Witnesses, and a host of others, even Pentecostals, whom they regarded as beyond the bounds of American respectability. As the movement evolved in the succeeding decades it asserted a solidarity between Christians and Jews that had been tragically lacking during World War II, and the widespread support for the formation of the state of Israel in 1948 also pointed to a collaboration across the two religious traditions.

The common ground among Jews, Catholics, and Protestants expanded into the realm of popular theology in the post–World War II period. Within the space of just a few years three books appeared—one by a Jewish rabbi, Joshua Liebman; another by a Catholic priest, Fulton J. Sheen; and a third by a Protestant minister, Norman Vincent Peale—all of which offered a kind of feel-good theology for Americans who, in the wake of World War II, were just then settling into their role as world leaders. The most popular of the three, Peale's *The Power of Positive Thinking*, first published in 1952, promised readers that they could "feel better about themselves," and, by extension, Americans could meet the challenges of the postwar world, especially the standoff against communism, if only they adopted a sunny, "can do" disposition and invoked the help of the "Judeo-Christian" God.

Will Herberg, a theologian at Drew University, gave this Judeo-Christian notion another boost in 1955 with the publication of his book *Protestant, Catholic, Jew.* "American religion and American society would seem to be so closely interrelated as to make it virtually impossible to understand each without reference to the other," Herberg wrote. He enlarged the boundaries of "the American way of life" to include Jews and Roman Catholics, but in so doing he effectively bracketed out all others. "The three great religious communions—Protestantism, Catholicism, and Judaism—constitute the three great American religions," Herberg concluded, "the 'religions of democracy.'"

As Americans confronted what many believed were the perils of pluralism in the twentieth century, the notion of a "Judeo-Christian tradition" sounded compelling. It suggested a kind of moral consensus between Christians and Jews that has never really existed, and the use of the term, especially by neoconservatives and by leaders of the Religious Right in the 1980s and 1990s, functioned as a code for exclusion. It implied that Christians and Jews were the "true" Americans and that everyone else—Hindus, Buddhists, Muslims, Sikhs, Taoists, humanists—professed beliefs outside the mainstream.

At the same time that religious leaders tried to adapt to America's new pluralism by devising the "Judeo-Christian tradition" and expanding the boundaries of acceptable religious life beyond Protestants to Catholics and Jews, Protestant leaders wanted to consolidate in order to avoid duplication of efforts and to present a more united front. This consolidation took the form of the National Council of Churches, an interdenominational organization that was gaveled to order during a snowstorm in Cleveland in November 1949. Even as Protestant leaders had agreed to cooperate, however, they disagreed about the location for the new organization's offices. Powerful forces were pushing for Manhattan, but the magazine *Christian Century*, with offices in Chicago, warned against locating the National Council of Churches in what may have been the only place in America where Protestants came out on the short end of the Protestant-Catholic-Jew formula. The editors argued that the population of New York City included 2.2 million Roman Catholics and 2 million Jews, but fewer than half a million Protestants. "Is the city of New York the appropriate, natural and representative place for the over-all policies and projects of Protestantism to be formulated and administered?" the magazine asked.

If the mainstream was expanding during the middle decades of the twentieth century, no religious group took better advantage of the situation than Roman Catholics. American Catholicism went from an "immigrant church" in the nineteenth century to one that had made a place for itself in America by the latter half of the twentieth century. Catholics managed to forge a unified church out of culturally and ethnically diverse elements, so that an Irish parish would not compete with an Italian parish or a German parish or a Hispanic parish. This "Americanization" strategy paid off early in the twentieth century as the church became the center of secular activities and socialization for all Catholics; the Catholic Youth Organization, the Knights of Columbus, and a number of social service agencies were designed to help new immigrants find homes and jobs and adjust to life in America.

The conduct of Roman Catholics during the two world wars was also crucial. Because many Catholics had come only recently from countries engaged in the European conflicts, the loyalties of these German or Italian Catholics were suspect. Whereas World War I had rekindled some prejudices against Roman Catholics, Catholic men enlisted in the American armed forces in large numbers during World War II, thereby "proving" their patriotism by fighting alongside other Americans. The sons of Roman Catholic immigrants also took full advantage of the GI Bill of Rights, passed by Congress in 1944, which provided discharged soldiers the opportunity to attend college at government expense. With college degrees in hand, the Roman Catholic sons of immigrants then became upwardly mobile in the 1950s and 1960s.

Indeed, Catholic education played a critical role in allowing American Catholics to feel comfortable in American society, and nothing symbolizes their coming of age more than the rise to prominence of the University of Notre Dame, probably the best-known Catholic university in the world. Founded in northern Indiana in 1842 as the Université de Notre Dame du Lac by Edward F. Sorin, a French priest, Notre Dame rose steadily toward academic excellence in the twentieth century at the same time that it attracted attention on the athletic field.

Knute Rockne arrived in South Bend, Indiana, as a student and a football player in 1910, helped his team beat Army in 1913, and stayed on at Notre Dame as a chemistry instructor and football coach until his death in 1931. The success of the Fighting Irish on the football field was important because Catholics succeeded in beating the Protestants at their own game; football was first played by students at elite Protestant schools—Princeton, Rutgers, Yale, and Harvard. More important, American Catholics could derive vicarious satisfaction whenever Notre Dame (or Fordham or Holy Cross or Boston College) beat Rutgers or Northwestern or Southern Methodist University on the gridiron—which they did with growing regularity.

Not all Catholic successes took place on the athletic fields. On the morning of October 4, 1948, a Trappist monk at the Abbey of Our Lady of Gethsemani in Kentucky sent a manuscript off to his literary agent. Father Louis, better known to those in the outside world as Thomas Merton, had been a rowdy undergraduate—and an avowed atheist—at Columbia University before his conversion to Roman Catholicism in 1938. Three years later he became a Trappist, which required that he assume a vow of silence. Merton's manuscript, an autobiography published as *The Seven Storey Mountain*, cast a wary eye on the frenzy of American life, extolled the virtues of contemplation, and criticized the growing secularism of American intellectuals. In the wake of the horrors of the Holocaust and Hiroshima, Merton recommended the solace of the interior and spiritual life.

The Seven Storey Mountain became a best-selling book whose commercial success landed its author on the cover of *Time* magazine. Whereas Catholics until the postwar era had been eager to adapt to American culture, Merton's autobiography reflected a growing Catholic maturity, a confidence so great that a Roman Catholic could offer a trenchant critique of American values and the American way of life.

As Roman Catholics began to gain confidence about their place in American society, another religious group, evangelicals, began to enjoy a resurgence at midcentury. The impetus came from an unlikely source—a gangly young preacher just out of Wheaton College, located west of Chicago. William Franklin Graham, reared on a dairy farm near Charlotte, North Carolina, had attended revival meetings conducted by an itinerant evangelist, Mordecai Ham, in 1934 and experienced an evangelical conversion. Billy Graham, who once aspired to be a baseball player, decided instead to attend Bob Jones College (now Bob Jones University) but later transferred to Wheaton, an evangelical liberal-arts college. In 1946 a newly formed organization called Youth for Christ hired Graham, already an accomplished preacher, as its first full-time evangelist.

Graham toured the country (and later the world), preaching to church groups, youth rallies, and stadium gatherings. His charisma and charm, with just a touch of Carolina drawl, opened doors, and his message was beguilingly simple: Repent of your sins, ask Jesus into your heart, and you will be saved. Youth for Christ soon hired another evangelist, Charles B. Templeton, to join Graham on the revival circuit, and they sought to project an air of youthful excitement and enthusiasm. They preferred sport coats to suits and wore loud, colorful ties to emphasize that they were not the stodgy old evangelists of times past. They sought as well to move beyond the separatism and the narrow judgmentalism of the fundamentalists, although their theology remained similar to that of their fundamentalist forebears.

Templeton matched Graham in preaching ability—indeed, many thought that Graham was the lesser preacher of the two men—but Templeton also possessed a restless intellect. He decided to attend Princeton Theological Seminary, and before enrolling he challenged Graham, who also had no formal theological training, to accompany him. Templeton's proposal prompted something of a crisis in young Graham; he pondered the offer at some length but finally decided, while on a spiritual retreat in the San Bernardino Mountains of southern California, to set aside intellectual questions and simply to "preach the gospel."

Although they remained friends for the rest of their lives, the two men followed very different paths. After Templeton graduated from Princeton Seminary in 1951 he became an evangelist for the newly formed National Council of Churches, the federation of mainline—and generally liberal—Protestant denominations, but his doubts about the truth of Christianity festered and eventually overwhelmed him. "I came to a point finally where to go on would have meant preaching things I didn't believe," he recalled decades later. In 1957 he returned to his native Toronto and embarked on an illustrious career as a journalist, sports cartoonist, editor, television news director, author, novelist, playwright, and screenwriter.

Graham, on the other hand, having made his momentous decision to "preach the gospel," descended from the San Bernardino Mountains in 1949 and embarked on his Los Angeles crusade. Week after week the crowds flocked to his tent, dubbed the "canvas cathedral," in downtown Los Angeles. He claimed converts from the worlds of politics, music, Hollywood, and even organized crime—individuals who had led sinful, wretched lives but were suddenly made new when they, in Graham's words, "made a decision for Christ." One of Graham's converts, Stuart Hamblen, an actor and singer-songwriter, commemorated his conversion with a song, "It Is No Secret (What God Can Do)," which became popular at revival gatherings.

Aside from the crowds and the conversions in the City of Angels, Graham also caught the eye of newspaper publisher William Randolph Hearst, who was apparently attracted by Graham's strong denunciations of communism. With a mere two words, "puff Graham," Hearst instructed his newspapers to give the young evangelist lots of favorable publicity. Like a seasoned surfer who caught "the big one," Graham rode the wave of press attention to national prominence, appearing on the cover of *Time* magazine and, in the midst of the cold war, enjoying celebrity status as a clean-cut preacher who defended American middle-class sensibilities against the attacks of what he referred to as "godless Communism."

Graham came to prominence at a unique moment in history, when technological innovations in travel and communications made it possible for him to consider all of the United States (and many parts of the world) as his parish. Whereas the Methodist circuit rider of the previous century traveled by horseback and preached from a soapbox to anyone within earshot, Graham took full advantage of both air transportation and the airwaves. He hopscotched the country on airplanes and used radio and television to broadcast his sermons to the masses. During his crusade in Portland, Oregon, in 1950, Graham made the decision to form a not-for-profit corporation to handle finances and to organize his crusades. The Billy Graham Evangelistic Association, with its headquarters in Minneapolis, became a well-oiled corporate machine with advance work that would be the envy of any politician. One of Graham's most impressive legacies over a career that extended more than half a century was that no one ever seriously questioned the integrity of his financial dealings or his moral conduct.

As middle-class Americans—Protestants, Catholics, and Jews—basked in postwar prosperity they pushed out of the cities and toward the suburbs. Levittown, New York, a suburban housing development with cookie-cutter architecture and postage-stamp yards, became the prototype for the bedroom communities surrounding the cities. For many Americans in the 1950s belief in God and some kind of religious affiliation were essential ammunition in the cold war that the United States was waging against the Soviet Union and its satellite nations. "America should be grateful for the spiritual tide which flows unceasingly into our national life through its institutions of religion," the editors of *Christian Century* exuded in 1951. "This Christian heritage can survive even if our civilization falls." Congress added the words "under God" to the Pledge of Allegiance in 1954, so that thereafter the United States would be "one nation, *under God*, indivisible, with liberty and justice for all."

But America was divided, deeply divided along racial lines, and African Americans did not enjoy "liberty and justice for all." Although northern evangelicals had pressed for the abolition of slavery in the nineteenth century and had assisted freed blacks after the Civil War, they lost interest after Reconstruction. A cynical system of Jim Crow laws across the South conspired to keep African Americans in a subordinate status, and if blacks stepped out of line there was no shortage of vigilantes to remind them of their place. Lynchings became all too common. More than 1,200 African Americans fell victim to lynch mobs in the final decade of the nineteenth century, and a thousand more died by lynching between 1900 and 1915, some of them in public spectacles meant to intimidate the entire black community. More than 10,000 people witnessed a lynching in the public square of Waco, Texas, in 1916, for example.

"If it is necessary every Negro in the State will be lynched," James K. Vardaman, governor of Mississippi, declared in one of his more temperate comments about blacks, "it will be done to maintain white supremacy." After Booker T. Washington, African-American educator and head of the Tuskegee Institute in Alabama, dined with President Theodore Roosevelt at the White House, Ben Tillman, U.S. senator from South Carolina, remarked that it "will necessitate our killing a thousand [Negroes] before they will learn their place again." The Scottsboro case in Alabama, where nine black men were convicted in 1931 of raping two white women on the flimsiest of evidence, underscored that blacks had no guarantee of justice in white-dominated courtrooms.

Although African Americans who migrated to northern cities fared little better, facing poverty, hunger, and the lack of safe, adequate housing, they made steady, albeit slow, progress toward equality in the middle decades of the twentieth century.

On April 15, 1947, Jackie Robinson became the first black to play major league baseball, and a bit more than a year later President Harry Truman's executive order desegregated the armed forces. On May 17, 1954, the U.S. Supreme Court finally laid the legal groundwork for racial integration with its landmark *Brown v. Board of Education of Topeka, Kansas* ruling.

Reversing the infamous 1896 *Plessy v. Ferguson* decision, which had enshrined the notion of "separate but equal" accommodations for blacks and whites, the Court declared that separate facilities for whites and blacks were "inherently unequal," although the Court's implementation order the following year required only a gradual approach to desegregation and left details to local federal judges and school boards. The *Brown* decision nevertheless demonstrated that the strategy of litigation could undermine entrenched southern practices; full desegregation, however, would require the cooperation of blacks to demand the reforms mandated by the Supreme Court.

One African American willing to make demands on behalf of his people was Vernon Johns, pastor of the Dexter Avenue Baptist Church, a middle-class black congregation located near the statehouse in Montgomery, Alabama. Johns found small ways to annoy racists. After police beat a black man, Johns advertised his sermon title for the following Sunday: "It's Safe to Murder Negroes in Montgomery." One day he ordered a sandwich in a white restaurant and, contrary to custom, decided to eat it there rather than take it out, whereupon a gang of customers went to their cars for guns. "I pronounced the shortest blessing of my life over that sandwich," Johns recalled later. "I said, 'Goddam it.'"

Like other African Americans in Montgomery, Johns chafed at the Montgomery bus system, which required blacks to pay their fares to the driver at the front of the bus and then move to the rear or even exit the bus and reboard, behind the "whites only" section. Cynical drivers sometimes drove off after collecting the fare and before the black rider could reenter at the rear. Johns paid his fare one day and sat in the "whites only" section at the front. The driver refused to move, but Johns demanded— and received—his money back, thereby providing a minor victory for blacks against the Montgomery bus system.

The crippling blow against the segregation of Montgomery buses was delivered, however, by a diminutive woman, Rosa Parks. On December 1, 1955, while Parks was riding home on the Cleveland Avenue line and sitting in the first row of the "colored" section, the driver instructed her to move to the back of the bus to make room for a white patron (a "sliding divider" between whites and blacks would be moved farther back if more whites entered the bus). Parks refused to move and was arrested. The incident fanned the long-smoldering anger of the African-American community, which responded by launching a boycott against the bus system. The local black clergy gathered to form the Montgomery Improvement Association (MIA) to coordinate the boycott and, when it came time, to choose a twenty-six-year-old preacher who had succeeded Johns as pastor of the Dexter Avenue Baptist Church. Martin Luther King, Jr., who had been reluctant to get involved in the protest, nevertheless accepted the presidency of the association. "Well, if you think I can render some service," he said, "I will."

King later remarked that the summons to leadership "happened so quickly that I did not have time to think it through. It is probable that if I had I would have declined the nomination." King, the son of a black preacher in Atlanta, had studied at Morehouse College, Crozer Theological Seminary, and Boston University, where he received a Ph.D. in theology in 1955.

Even during his lifetime, George Washington was seen as an almost divine figure. Sitting on a cloud with an arm outstretched and an angel placing a halo-like wreath on his head, Washington is clearly an icon of Christian veneration in this early American painting.

John Hagerty, a Baltimore Methodist preacher, published this Tree of Life in 1791. The twelve fruits of salvation, esteemed by evangelicals everywhere, hung on the tree and suggested the condemnation of the smug sinners below.

Competition among religious groups vying for the souls, and money, of churchgoers in the nineteenth century was often a confusing experience. In this satirical 1879 cartoon from Puck *magazine, a cardinal (far right) collects money, Henry Ward Beecher (center) sells white souls, a Baptist offers hot-or cold-water baptisms, and a charlatan (on the roof) conducts a spirit show at a street fair.*

In the comparative freedom of the evangelical meeting, women felt comfortable testifying about their own religious experiences. However, very few sought—or received— ordination as clergy.

William Miller's followers used elaborate drawings, like this 1843 chart, to help Christians understand the complex predictions about the end of the world that the followers saw in the biblical books of Daniel, Ezekiel, and Revelation.

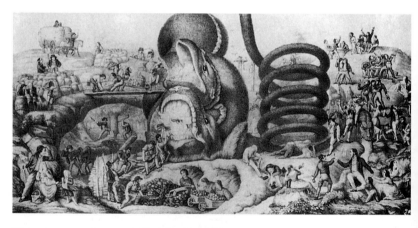

This temperance chart, probably from the middle nineteenth century, contrasts the benefits of remaining sober against the perils of drunkenness. The dragon of alcohol destroys those who are not careful.

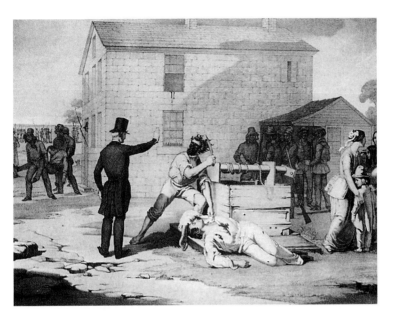

Mormons in Illinois antagonized their "Gentile" neighbors, and their neighbors responded with deadly violence. Although the details remain fuzzy, tradition holds that one of Joseph Smith's murderers tried (without success) to behead him.

A Shoshone Indian ritual, the traditional Sun Dance performed to ensure successful buffalo hunting, is painted on this nineteenth-century elk hide. The dancers' orientation to one another and to the Sun Dance center pole, topped with a buffalo head and tail, express the well-being of the society.

MISSIONARIES OF
THE BUDDHIST FAITH.

Two Representatives of the Ancient Creed
Are in San Francisco to
Proselyte.

DR. SHUYE SONODA   REV. KAHURYO NISHIJIMA

DR. SHUYE SONODA and Rev. Kahuryo Nishijima, two Buddhist priests, who are the sons of Buddhist priests of Japan, have come here to establish a Buddhist mission at 827 Polk street and to convert Japanese and later Americans to the ancient Buddhist faith. They will teach that God is not the creator, but the created; not a real existence, but a figment of the human imagination, and that pure Buddhism is a better moral guide than Christianity.

Their priestly robes are as interesting as the lessons that they would present. As they posed before the camera in a hallway near their rooms in the Occidental Hotel yesterday, they were the wonderment of all the Japanese employes who could assemble for a glimpse of the sacred garb.

*Dr. Shuye Sonoda and the Reverend Kahuryo Nishijima
were the first Buddhist missionaries to the United States. According to this 1899* San Francisco Chronicle *article, they
came to America to teach that God is "not a real existence,
but a figment of the human imagination."*

This photograph by Mathew Brady captured Catholic services in a Civil War camp. Religious gatherings, which structured both northern and southern army life, brought moments of hope in the midst of death and destruction.

is 1870 cartoon blames bitterness between the races and religions on the practice of having separate ools for different religious and ethnic groups. The solution, it suggests, is for all children to attend sectarian public schools.

infirmity. Accepting the view that man was prior in the creation. Some scriptural writers say that as the woman was of the man, therefore her position should be one of subjection. Grant it, then as the historical fact is reversed in our day; the man is now of the woman; shall his place be one of subjection?

The equal position declared in the first account. must prove more satisfactory to both sexes; created alike in the image of God.

In this handwritten draft of Elizabeth Cady Stanton's 1895 Woman's Bible, she addresses selected verses of Genesis and notes that some form of the creation story is found in "the different religions of all nations."

He had been influenced by the Social Gospel, especially by Walter Rauschenbusch, the Baptist minister who sought social reform in the name of Christianity, and by Mahatma Gandhi's nonviolent strategy for social change. As the Montgomery bus boycott continued into 1956, King attracted notice for his oratorical skills and his courage, although he harbored misgivings, seeking a way to "move out of the picture without appearing a coward."

The boycott was a masterpiece of logistical planning and dogged persistence. For nearly a year the blacks of Montgomery spurned the bus company that had so mistreated them and had taken their business for granted. Some traveled by carpool, but most went on foot, some of them over long distances. The African Americans of Montgomery, in King's words, "came to see that it was ultimately more honorable to walk the streets in dignity than to ride the buses in humiliation."

For King himself the Montgomery boycott shaped the remainder of his career as a theologian, an activist, and a pastor. King was not yet a convinced pacifist when the boycott began. When his house was bombed in late January 1956 he had been seeking a gun permit and had the protection of armed bodyguards; a friend described his house as "an arsenal." His views changed, however, as the boycott continued. "Living through the actual experience of the protest, nonviolence became more than a method to which I gave intellectual assent," King said. "It became a commitment to a way of life."

King and other leaders of the MIA were convicted of conspiracy to interfere with the bus company's operations, but in November 1956 they prevailed when the U.S. Supreme Court declared Alabama's segregation laws unconstitutional. Thus emboldened, King and others sought to build on their success. In 1957 they formed the Southern Christian Leadership

Conference (SCLC), an organization of black leaders, many of them ministers, who worked for desegregation and civil rights. That same year King, who was chosen president of the new group, articulated the goal of voting rights for blacks during the Prayer Pilgrimage for Freedom at the Lincoln Memorial. King's efforts on behalf of black Americans had now taken him far beyond Montgomery, and by the end of 1959 he resigned from the Dexter Avenue church and moved to Atlanta to devote his full energies to the civil rights movement.

The editors of *Christian Century* had argued that the headquarters for the National Council of Churches be located near what they called the "center of its constituency to insure the maximum response to its leadership," and readers chimed in with suggestions ranging from St. Louis and Chicago to Manhattan, Kansas, and "the southeastern part of Nebraska." Nevertheless, the National Council of Churches chose the Upper West Side of Manhattan for its offices, on a site adjacent to Columbia University overlooking the Hudson River. This neighborhood, known as Morningside Heights, had been a place of refuge for Protestants around the turn of the twentieth century. As Jewish and Catholic immigrants overwhelmed the precincts of lower Manhattan late in the nineteenth century, Protestants steadily constructed their own "city on a hill" in Morningside Heights, just as the Puritans had sought to carve their city on a hill out of the howling wilderness of Massachusetts in the seventeenth century.

A steady stream of Protestant institutions moved to the Upper West Side: Columbia (originally an Anglican—or Episcopal—school), Union Theological Seminary (Presbyterian), St. Luke's Hospital (Episcopal), Riverside Church (Baptist and Congregational), and the (Episcopal) Cathedral of St. John the Divine, which the architect Ralph Adams Cram intended as a kind of medieval walled city. By the late 1950s the National Council of Churches joined this Protestant pantheon in a hulking, modern building known formally as the Interchurch Center and informally as the "God Box" or the "Protestant Kremlin." All the warnings about isolation from the "psychological center" of American Protestantism went unheeded, and when it came time to lay the cornerstone for the Interchurch Center, which symbolized the fusion of Protestant respectability with the American way of life, the logical choice for the task was President Dwight Eisenhower, who offered a paean to religious liberty and toleration in an age increasingly marked by pluralism.

"In this land, our churches have always been sturdy defenders of the Constitutional and God-given rights of each citizen," Eisenhower declared at the cornerstone-laying ceremony on October 12, 1958. "We are politically free people because each of us is free to express his individual faith." Those maxims would again be tested in the decades ahead as even the Protestant-Catholic-Jew consensus and the Judeo-Christian formula proved inadequate to contain the rising tides of religious pluralism.

The conversion of Thomas Merton to Roman Catholicism provided American Catholics with an articulate, intelligent, and persuasive spokesman for the faith. In this passage from his autobiography, The Seven Storey Mountain, *Merton recounts his initial visit to the Trappist Gethsemani monastery, outside Louisville, Kentucky, which he would later join as a monk.*

There were still about three weeks left until Easter. Thinking more and more about the Trappist monastery where I was going to spend Holy Week, I went to the library one day and took down the *Catholic Encyclopedia* to read about the Trappists. I found out that the Trappists were Cistercians, and then, in looking up Cistercians, I also came across the Carthusians, and a great big picture of the hermitages of the Camaldolese.

What I saw on those pages pierced me to the heart like a knife.

What wonderful happiness there was, then, in the world! There were still men on this miserable, noisy, cruel earth, who tasted the marvelous joy of silence and solitude, who dwelt in forgotten mountain cells, in secluded monasteries, where the news and desires and appetites and conflicts of the world no longer reach them.

They were free from the burden of the flesh's tyranny, and their clear vision, clean of the world's smoke and of its bitter sting, was raised to heaven and penetrated into the deeps of heaven's infinite and healing light.

They were poor, they had nothing, and therefore they were free and possessed everything, and everything they touched struck off something of the fire of divinity. And they worked with their hands, silently ploughing and harrowing the earth, and sowing seed in obscurity, and reaping their small harvests to feed themselves and the other poor. They built their own houses and made, with their own hands, their own furniture and their own coarse clothing, and everything around them was simple and primitive and poor, because they were the least and the last of men, they had made themselves outcasts, seeking, outside the walls of the world, Christ poor and rejected of men.

Above all, they had found Christ, and they knew the power and sweetness and the depth and the infinity of His love, living and working in them. In Him, hidden in Him, they had become the "Poor Brothers of God." And for His love, they had thrown away everything, and concealed themselves in the Secret of His Face. Yet because they had nothing, they were the richest men in the world, possessing everything: because in proportion as grace emptied their heart of created desire, the Spirit of God entered in and filled the place that had been made for God. And the Poor Brothers of God, in their cells, they tasted within them the secret glory, the hidden manna, the infinite sweet exultancy of the fear of God, which is the first intimate touch of the reality of God, known and experienced on Earth, the beginning of heaven. The fear of the Lord is the beginning of heaven. And all day long, God spoke to them: the clean voice of God, in His tremendous peacefulness, spending truth within them as simply and directly as water wells up in a spring. And grace was in them, suddenly, always in more and more abundance, they knew not from where, and the coming of this grace to them occupied them altogether, and filled them with love, and with freedom.

And grace, overflowing in all their acts and movements, made everything they did an act of love, glorifying God not by drama, not by gesture, not by outward show, but by the very simplicity and economy of utter perfection, so utter that it escapes notice entirely.

In the years following World War II, Jewish Americans sought to come to terms with the atrocities of the Holocaust. In 1956 Elie Wiesel, a Holocaust survivor who had settled in the United States after the war, published Night, *a haunting memoir about life in the concentration camps of World War II. This passage describes the first night in camp, an experience that prompted him to call the existence of God into question. Wiesel, who dedicated his life to ensuring that humanity would never forget the horrors of hate and intolerance, was awarded the Nobel Peace Prize in 1986 for being a "messenger to mankind."*

The cherished objects we had brought with us thus far were left behind in the train, and with them, at last, our illusions. Every two yards or so an SS man held his tommy gun trained on us. Hand in hand we followed the crowd....

Never shall I forget that night, the first night in camp, which has turned my life into one long night, seven times cursed and seven times sealed. Never shall I forget that smoke. Never shall I forget the little faces of the children, whose bodies I saw turned into wreaths of smoke beneath a silent blue sky. Never shall I forget those flames which consumed my Faith forever. Never shall I forget that nocturnal silence which deprived me, for all eternity, of the desire to live. Never shall I forget those moments which murdered my God and my soul and turned my dreams to dust. Never shall I forget these things, even if I am condemned to live as long as God Himself. Never.

CHAPTER TWENTY-ONE

Religion in the New Frontier

R eligion played a central role in the 1960 presidential election. Only once before, in 1928, had a Roman Catholic run for president on a major party ticket, and Alfred E. Smith, the governor of New York, had lost resoundingly to Herbert Hoover. By 1960, however, with Roman Catholics having grown in numbers and having found their place in American society, the prospect of a Catholic president seemed less daunting, especially when the Democratic candidate, John F. Kennedy of Massachusetts, was so bright and charming and articulate—and young. His Republican opponent, Richard M. Nixon, had been Dwight Eisenhower's vice president. Nixon had forged close ties with the evangelist Billy Graham, who, over the course of a friendship that lasted several decades, probably came as close as anyone to being Nixon's soul-mate.

Although Graham publicly denied any preference in the presidential election, he took part in a secret meeting of American Protestant leaders in Montreux, Switzerland, in the spring of 1960, when it appeared likely that Kennedy would capture the Democratic nomination. The purpose of the gathering, which included Norman Vincent Peale, pastor of New York City's Marble Collegiate Church, was to discuss ways to deny Kennedy the presidency and thereby ensure Nixon's election. Although no specific action came from that meeting, the discussion itself drew on deep prejudices.

In April 1949 Paul Blanshard, a Congregational minister-turned-atheist, had published *American Freedom and Catholic Power*, which argued that Roman Catholics represented a threat to American democracy because of their loyalty to a "foreign" power, the Vatican. "Unfortunately the Catholic people of the United States are not citizens but *subjects* of their own religious commonwealth," he wrote. "They are compelled by the very nature of their Church's authoritarian structure to accept non-religious as well as religious policies that have been imposed on them from abroad." Blanshard's call to arms against the supposed threat of Catholicism went through eleven editions in as many months, reminding American Catholics that, despite their advances in American society over the previous decades, many Protestants remained deeply suspicious of their faith.

Kennedy addressed "the religion issue" directly at least three times during the 1960 campaign, responding to Protestant fears that he, as a Catholic, would be obliged to obey the pope on matters of public policy. "I want no votes solely on account of my religion," he declared to a meeting of the Society of American Newspaper Editors, and he reiterated that he was "dedicated to the separation of church and state, to the preservation of religious liberty, to an end to religious bigotry, and to the total independence of the officeholder from any form of ecclesiastical dictation." Later in the campaign, addressing the Ministerial Association in Houston, the Democratic nominee assured Americans that he would not be bullied by any pronouncement from the Vatican. Although some Protestants remained wary of a Roman Catholic in the White House, a majority of Americans—albeit a bare majority in one of the closest elections in U.S. history—voted to break with the past and entrust the nation, in the words of Kennedy's inaugural address, to "a new generation of Americans."

This new generation was more enamored of the future than the past, and Kennedy meant to lead America into that future, which he called the "New Frontier" and which included an enthusiastic embrace of science and technology. Ever since the Scopes trial back in 1925 many Americans had remained wary of science, which, in the wake of Charles Darwin's evolutionary theory, could no longer be counted on to shore up the claims of theology. When the Soviet Union launched *Sputnik*, a tiny satellite, on October 4, 1957, however, Americans' attitudes toward science, especially toward science education, began to change. In 1958 Congress passed the National Defense Education Act, which provided federal money for education in the sciences, and on May 25, 1961, Kennedy set before Congress the goal of a manned landing on the moon "before this decade is out."

Americans responded with a flurry of devotion to science and technology. Kennedy's vision carried Americans forward with a kind of inexorable force, and the future looked bright indeed—a world of interplanetary travel, a world of convenience, a world where science had eradicated hunger and disease. And if Americans needed a demonstration of this Brave New World that awaited them, they looked to a huge shrine in Flushing, New York, the New York World's Fair of 1964–65, with its whirring, futuristic exhibitions that extolled the virtues and the promise of the technological age.

For some Americans the dawn of this new era demanded a new theology, one that broke with the quaint suspicions and prejudices of bygone days. *Time* magazine placed the matter in the starkest terms with a 1966 cover, a black background with large red letters that asked: "Is God Dead?" The "death of God" theology, stated in various ways by a handful of theologians, represented a departure from old religious systems and an embrace of a new self-sufficiency on the part of humanity, which no longer needed the "crutch" of religion. That same year Richard Rubenstein, a rabbi, published *After Auschwitz*, which argued that religion as usual was no longer possible after the Holocaust.

But the rumors of God's death, to paraphrase Mark Twain, turned out to have been greatly exaggerated. Religious groups responded to the technological age by trying to retool for the new era, and no institution reshaped itself more profoundly in the 1960s than the Roman Catholic Church, an organization not often associated with change. On October 11, 1962, after Pope John XXIII had remarked that the leaders of the church were not meant to be "museum-keepers, but to cultivate a flourishing garden of life," more than 2,000 bishops from around the world gathered at St. Peter's Basilica for a meeting of Roman Catholic leaders known as the Second Vatican Council, or Vatican II. The council lasted more than three years, outlived its convener, John XXIII, and profoundly recast Catholic practice and teachings, from the nature of church authority to the conduct of the mass to the absolving of Jews from any responsibility for the death of Jesus. John XXIII, who was designated *Time* magazine's "Man of the Year" for 1962, resolved that the church should reach out to those he called the "separated brethren," by which he meant non-Catholics, and see them as engaged, knowingly or not, in the process of joining the church, either in this life or the next.

American Catholics saw the changes from Vatican II most clearly in everyday life. Mass was no longer said in Latin, but in the vernacular, the language of the local people, an innovation that soon led to "folk masses," or "guitar masses." Catholics no longer had to observe "meatless Fridays," when they could not consume meat. Nuns were no longer required to dress in habits, and priests forsook the cassock for more conventional trousers.

The Second Vatican Council brought a burst of energy and enthusiasm to the Catholic Church in America, which was now suddenly allowed to experiment with new forms of worship. Consistent with the reforms of Vatican II, the laity assumed a larger role in the affairs of the church, from the formation of parish councils and advisory boards for parochial schools to assisting at the mass. Some interpreted Vatican II as a license to press for further reforms, including the idea of married—or even female—clergy, but conservatives resisted, many using the Latin mass as a rallying point. The Catholic Traditionalist Movement, for example, was founded in 1964, insisting, in defiance of Vatican II, on the use of Latin in Roman Catholic services.

Still other changes racked the Roman Catholic Church in America in the wake of Vatican II. The council expressed a new openness to what the New Testament describes as "Spiritual gifts," ranging from love, joy, and peace to divine healing and even speaking in tongues, a phenomenon associated with Pentecostalism. These Spiritual gifts, "whether they be the most outstanding or the more simple and widely diffused," the council declared in its *Dogmatic Constitution on the Church*, "are to be received with thanksgiving and consolation, for they are exceedingly suitable and useful for the needs of the church." In 1967 four members of a lay faculty prayer group at Duquesne University, a Roman Catholic school in Pittsburgh, sought the gifts of the Holy Spirit. Having read *The Cross and the Switchblade*, which detailed the efforts of a Pentecostal pastor, David Wilkerson, to convert New York City gang members to Christianity, the Duquesne faculty group attended a Pentecostal prayer gathering held in the home of a Presbyterian lay woman. There they received the baptism of the Holy Spirit, including speaking in tongues, reminiscent of the Pentecostal revival that took place in Topeka, Kansas, at the beginning of the century.

Although such spiritual enthusiasm is more often associated with churches like the Assemblies of God, the Church of God in Christ, and various independent and storefront congregations, these spiritual expressions had begun to crop up in more established, formal settings. On a Sunday morning in January 1959, for instance, Dennis J. Bennett, an Episcopal priest and rector of St. Mark's Episcopal Church in Van Nuys, California, announced to his stunned parishioners that he had been baptized by the Holy Spirit and had spoken in tongues. The disclosure engendered a reaction in the parish—as Bennett was explaining his Spirit baptism before the congregation, one of his associates removed his vestments and resigned on the spot—a reaction that eventually led to Bennett's resignation. "We're Episcopalians," one relieved parishioner told *Time* magazine, "not a bunch of wild-eyed hillbillies." Bennett accepted an appointment as vicar of St. Luke's, a blue-collar mission in Seattle, which became a kind of beachhead for what became known as the charismatic renewal movement within the Episcopal church.

Similarly, the developments at Duquesne University reverberated throughout the Roman Catholic Church. A February 1967 retreat for faculty and students, which became known as the "Duquesne weekend," affected another thirty or so students, and by early March the movement had spread to the University of Notre Dame, where another weekend of prayer and reflection took place from April 7 to 9. By year's end the Catholic Charismatic Renewal had spread to Michigan State University and to the University of Michigan, and beginning in 1968

Catholic charismatics, those who claimed the gifts of the Holy Spirit, held the first of what became annual meetings at the University of Notre Dame.

By the late 1970s these gatherings, called the National Conference on Charismatic Renewal in the Catholic Church, attracted well in excess of 20,000 participants. At the parish level, the Catholic Charismatic Renewal succeeded in breathing new life into moribund congregations, although its spiritual ardor sometimes proved divisive. The Roman Catholic hierarchy in the United States viewed the renewal movement with some ambivalence. Although the Catholic Charismatic Renewal had revitalized many parishes, the expression of spiritual gifts could also be wildly enthusiastic and, therefore, unpredictable.

No one, however, could have predicted the firestorm of dissent that greeted the papal announcement from Rome on July 29, 1968. Pope Paul VI, John XXIII's successor, issued an official church encyclical, or teaching, on human sexuality called *Humanae Vitae*, "On Human Life." Although Paul VI had been regarded as something of a progressive prior to his elevation to the papacy in 1963, the pace of change unleashed by the Second Vatican Council alarmed him. He sought, for example, to amend some of the Vatican II documents before their publication in order to make the reforms less radical. On the matter of artificial means of birth control the church had long held the position that every act of sexual intimacy between husband and wife must be open to the possibility of procreation; the use of any artificial means of birth control, therefore, violated church teaching. Just as Vatican II had called other doctrines into question, so too the church established a commission to study the possibility of changes to its teachings on birth control.

Although the panel recommended overwhelmingly to allow contraception, Paul VI countermanded the commission and issued *Humanae Vitae*. He hewed to a conservative line and declared that all artificial means of birth control were contrary to church teaching; the pope allowed only the rhythm method, a natural means of birth control, which was quickly derided as "Vatican roulette." The effect of *Humanae Vitae* on American Catholicism was devastating. Catholic women, now primarily middle class and upwardly mobile, no longer wanted to be burdened with large families; fewer children, however, also meant fewer priests for the church because many devout families traditionally had designated one of their sons for the priesthood.

Although *Humanae Vitae* may have rested on solid theological ground, it undermined the Vatican's credibility in the eyes of many American Catholics. The pope was widely characterized as being hopelessly out of touch with everyday believers, and for perhaps the first time in history many Catholics could contemplate the possibility of disobeying the pope and still consider themselves good Catholics. For his part, Paul VI was so distressed at the reaction to *Humanae Vitae* that he issued no other encyclicals for the remainder of his papacy.

For the Roman Catholic Church in America, however, the damage had been done. Attendance at weekly mass fell precipitously, from 71 percent of Catholics in 1963 to 50 percent in 1974. Giving declined by almost $2 billion in that time, and parochial school enrollments dipped from 5.6 million in 1965 to 3.5 million a decade later. *Humanae Vitae*, of course, was not entirely to blame. There were other forces at work in the culture—feminism, the sexual revolution, social and political unrest, and a general distrust of authority structures—but there seems to be little reason to dismiss the conclusions of Andrew Greeley, a sociologist and Roman Catholic priest, who declared that, more than anything else, the encyclical accounts for "the disaster of American Catholicism."

Although American Catholics, with their middle-class attainments and with the election of one of their own to the presidency, had become full-fledged members of American society, African Americans still faced impediments. The 1954 *Brown* v. *Board of Education* decision may have provided the legal groundwork for equality, and the successful Montgomery bus boycott may have demonstrated the effectiveness of cooperation, but equality itself was slow in coming. On Monday, February 1, 1960, four black students from the local agricultural and technical college sat down at the F. W. Woolworth lunch counter in Greensboro, North Carolina. The waiters studiously ignored their requests for service, but the students nevertheless stayed until closing and reappeared the next morning with twenty-five others. Within two weeks lunch counter sit-ins had spread throughout the South, a direct challenge to Jim Crow laws.

The road to civil rights led from Montgomery to Selma to Birmingham, Alabama, to Albany, Georgia, to Philadelphia, Mississippi, where local Ku Klux Klan members murdered three civil rights activists, one African American and two Jews, and buried them in an earthen dam. The summons for civil rights had resonated with American Jews, who knew the sting of oppression and racism. Jews had made considerable strides in their quest to become full-fledged citizens, and some Jews had risen to prominence and visibility within American culture. Woodrow Wilson had appointed a Jew, Louis D. Brandeis, to the U.S. Supreme Court in 1916, for example, Hank Greenberg became a star player for the Detroit Tigers, and Americans danced to the big-band music of Benny Goodman.

American Jews, however, still fought against quotas limiting their entry into elite universities, and they struggled against the stigma of prejudice, which occasionally turned violent. On October 12, 1958, the same day that Dwight Eisenhower laid the cornerstone for the Interchurch Center in New York City, a handful of anti-Semites stuck several dozen sticks of dynamite into the wall of Atlanta's Hebrew Benevolent Society, the city's oldest and largest Reform congregation. The blast ripped a huge hole in the building on Peachtree Avenue, sending a message to Jews everywhere and especially to the congregation's rabbi, Jacob Rothschild, who had been a vigorous proponent of civil rights and racial equality.

Although the five suspects in the case, all of them associated with white supremacist groups, were acquitted, the incident only strengthened the resolve of Jewish and other religious leaders. In June 1963, for example, Abraham Joshua Heschel, a Polish-born rabbi who taught at Jewish Theological Seminary, sent a telegram to President Kennedy calling for an effort of "moral grandeur and spiritual audacity" to liberate America from the scourge of racism. Other religious leaders also joined the struggle. Archbishop Iakovos, head of the Greek Orthodox Archdiocese of North and South America, marched alongside Martin Luther King, Jr., demanding civil rights for all Americans.

Despite the cooperation of American Jews and others, the burden of the fight against segregation rested on the shoulders of King, the spiritual and symbolic head of the movement for civil rights. Throughout the struggle King advocated nonviolence, which he had learned from the teachings of Mahatma Gandhi. "The nonviolent approach does not immediately change the heart of the oppressor," King warned. "It first does something to the hearts and souls of those committed to it. It gives them new self-respect; it calls up resources of strength and courage that they did not know they had. Finally, it reaches the opponent and so stirs his conscience that reconciliation becomes a reality."

For blacks in the early 1960s, however, reality was segregation, beatings, the blast of fire hoses, and the assault of snarling police dogs unleashed against civil rights protesters by Bull Connor, the chief of police in Birmingham, Alabama. A sniper gunned down Medgar Evers, a black civil rights leader, outside his Jackson, Mississippi, home. "We will turn America upside down in order to turn it right side up," King promised. On August 28, 1963, King and other African-American leaders rallied a quarter of a million blacks (and some whites) for the March on Washington for Jobs and Freedom. The logistics of the demonstration had left King all but exhausted by the time he ascended the dais at the Lincoln Memorial to address the throng. He stumbled woodenly through his prepared remarks, when someone nearby shouted encouragement, "Tell 'em about the dream, Martin!"

In the best tradition of African-American call-and-response preaching, King unleashed an extemporaneous riff. "I have a dream," he cried, and the crowd began cheering. "I have a dream that one day on the red hills of Georgia the sons of former slaves and the sons of former slave owners will be able to sit down together at the table of brotherhood." The audience responded. "I have a dream," he continued, shouting down the thunderous waves of applause, "that even the state of Mississippi, a state sweltering with people's injustices, sweltering with the heat of oppression, will be transformed into an oasis of freedom and justice." The audience was electrified. "I have a dream," he cried again, "that my four little children will one day live in a nation where they will not be judged by the color of their skin but by the content of their character."

The March on Washington stirred the public conscience and prompted the Kennedy administration to draft legislation in support of civil rights. But real equality for African Americans remained a mirage. At 10:19 on Sunday morning, September 15, 1963, less than a month after King's "I Have a Dream" speech, a bomb ripped through the basement of the Sixteenth Street Baptist Church in Birmingham, killing four black children, injuring twenty others, and blowing the face of Jesus out of a stained-glass window. "I cannot sit idly by in Atlanta and not be concerned about what happens in Birmingham," King had written from the solitary-confinement jail cell in Birmingham several months earlier, where he was being held on charges of contempt. "Injustice anywhere is a threat to justice everywhere."

Noting that "we still creep at horse-and-buggy pace toward gaining a cup of coffee at a lunch counter," King, scribbling on the back of scrap paper, replied to his critics, many of them Protestant ministers, who counseled him to avoid confrontation. In so doing, he gave voice to the frustrations of people of color in a white America. "Perhaps it is easy for those who have never felt the stinging darts of segregation to say, 'Wait,'" King wrote, but the time for resistance had finally arrived. African Americans could no longer wait for equality. "There comes a time when the cup of endurance runs over," he concluded, "and men are no longer willing to be plunged into the abyss of despair."

As King mounted his nonviolent crusade for equality, based on his understanding of the Christian faith, other voices in the African-American community drew on other religious traditions. The Nation of Islam built upon such diverse sources as the Moorish Science Temple, the Jehovah's Witnesses, and Marcus Garvey's Universal Negro Improvement Association. Although the precise origins of the Nation of Islam are shrouded in mystery, in the summer of 1930 a light-skinned black man named Wallace D. Fard (also known as Farad Muhammad) circulated in a Detroit ghetto. Fard, who peddled exotic silks and artifacts, told blacks of their "true" heritage as Moors or Arabs and extolled the glorious history of black "Afro-Asia." The Qur'an, not the Bible, was the proper book for the Black Nation, he said, and Christianity had been used by the white man, the "blue-eyed devil," as a tool for the enslavement of blacks.

Fard organized meetings for his followers, and soon they assembled in what he called Temples of Islam. A young black man named Elijah Poole became Fard's most devoted follower and trusted lieutenant, and when Fard disappeared in 1934 Poole, who took the name Elijah Muhammad, assumed leadership of the movement and relocated to the South Side of Chicago. Muhammad declared himself "Prophet" and "Messenger of Allah" and proceeded to build a substantial following in Chicago and other cities. Taking a page from Garvey's teachings on economic self-sufficiency, Muhammad organized various business enterprises around the Chicago temple: a dry-cleaning plant, bakery, clothing stores, grocery stores.

Muhammad spread his teachings through a newspaper, *Muhammad Speaks*. He taught the virtues of hard work, thrift, and the accumulation of wealth. Blacks, he said, must stop looking to whites for jobs and justice, because the white man had conspired to keep the black man subservient. The Nation of Islam, however, was prepared to show blacks a better way. The original man, Muhammad taught, was black, not white. Light skin, in fact, had been the result of a perverse experiment conducted thousands of years ago, an experiment that had produced a pale-skinned race that was inferior physically, mentally, and morally and therefore unusually susceptible to evil.

Elijah Muhammad's teachings, though not standard Islam, had a powerful effect within the African-American community, especially among black urban males mired in poverty and hopelessness. The ideology of the Nation of Islam helped to explain their predicament, and it sought to replace the "magnolia myth" of black inferiority with the myth of black superiority. No one was affected more profoundly by Muhammad's teachings than a young inmate serving a ten-year sentence for burglary at the Charlestown State Prison in Massachusetts. Malcolm Little was born in Omaha, Nebraska, the son of a Baptist minister and his wife. One of Malcolm's earliest memories was seeing his house burn down as the firefighters stood around and watched; Malcolm's father, who had been a supporter of Marcus Garvey, disappeared under mysterious circumstances two years later. Malcolm went to school in Michigan and, after the eighth grade, found his way to Boston, where he "conked" his hair (straightened it, using lye), wore ghetto-style "zoot suits," dated white women, and became involved in drugs, alcohol, gambling, pimping, and burglary.

While in prison he came into contact with the ideas of Elijah Muhammad. "The very enormity of my previous life's guilt prepared me to accept the truth," Malcolm recalled of his prison conversion to the Nation of Islam. "Every instinct of my ghetto jungle streets, every hustling fox and criminal wolf instinct in me, which would have scoffed at and rejected anything else, was struck numb." Malcolm began to read voraciously and undertook to educate himself by copying the entire dictionary. Upon his release from prison in 1952 he became a zealous apostle for the Nation of Islam. Known as Minister Malcolm X, he quickly emerged as the Black Muslims' leading evangelist. "We Muslims believe that the white race, which is guilty of having oppressed and exploited and enslaved our people here in America, should and will be the victims of God's divine wrath," he told an interviewer in 1963; "white people who are also seeing the pendulum of time catching up with them are now trying to join with blacks, or even find traces of black blood in their own veins, hoping that it will save them from the catastrophe they see ahead. But no devil can fool God."

"The world since Adam has been white—and corrupt," he continued. "The world of tomorrow will be black—and righteous. In the white world there has been nothing but slavery, suffering, death and colonialism. In the black world of tomorrow, there will be *true* freedom, justice and equality for all." Malcolm reserved special contempt for those he called the "Negro preachers," the black Christian ministers who, he believed, had conspired in brainwashing the black man. Such rhetoric, of course, placed him at odds with Martin Luther King, Jr., and his nonviolent movement for racial integration. For Malcolm, following the teachings of Elijah Muhammad, desegregation was just another ploy on the part of whites, in partnership with the "Negro preachers," to keep blacks in servitude. "Christ wasn't white," Malcolm declared. "Christ was black. The poor, brainwashed Negro has been made to believe Christ was white to maneuver him into worshiping white men."

As Malcolm's influence grew in black America, he heard murmurings of sexual and financial improprieties on the part of his mentor, whom he unfailingly referred to as "the Honorable Elijah Muhammad." At first, Malcolm refused to believe the rumors, but as the evidence mounted he also detected that Muhammad was turning against him. In March 1964 Malcolm X broke with the Nation of Islam, and shortly thereafter he took a *hajj* (pilgrimage) to the Muslim holy city of Mecca, where he was exposed to representatives of worldwide Islam and was impressed by their lack of racial bias. By the time Malcolm returned to the United States he had renounced the black supremacist teachings of the Nation of Islam and had taken a new name, El-Hajj Malik el-Shabazz, which commemorated his pilgrimage and his conversion to mainstream Islam. He feared for his life, however, especially after his home on Long Island was firebombed, and on February 21, 1965, as he began a speech at the Audubon Ballroom in upper Manhattan, three gunmen in the front row stood and riddled him with sixteen bullets.

More than 22,000 people came to view the body of Malcolm X, the man who had given a voice and a theology to so many African Americans in the 1960s. Malcolm had inspired ideologies as diverse as black economic advancement and the radical Black Panther movement, which sought the overthrow of American social and political institutions. In 1969, for example, James Forman, on behalf of the National Black Economic Development Conference, a group of African Americans seeking economic justice, occupied the offices of the National Council of Churches in New York and issued a Black Manifesto "To the White Christian Churches and the Synagogues in the United States and to All Other Racist Institutions." The manifesto demanded $500 million in reparations "to the black people of this country." "Brothers and sisters, we are no longer shuffling our feet and scratching our heads," the manifesto read, echoing the sentiments of both Malcolm X and Martin Luther King, Jr., "We are tall, black and proud."

Born Malcolm Little in Omaha, Nebraska, Malcolm X lived the life of a street hustler before his arrest and conviction on burglary charges. While imprisoned in Massachusetts, he encountered the teachings of Elijah Muhammad, leader of the Nation of Islam. This passage, from the acclaimed Autobiography of Malcolm X, *recounts his powerful conversion to the Nation of Islam.*

"The true knowledge," reconstructed much more briefly than I received it, was that history had been "whitened" in the white man's history books, and that the black man had been "brainwashed for hundreds of years." Original Man was black, in the continent called Africa where the human race had emerged on the planet Earth.

The black man, original man, built great empires and civilizations and cultures while the white man was still living on all fours in caves. "The devil white man," down through history, out of his devilish nature, had pillaged, murdered, raped, and exploited every race of man not white.

Human history's greatest crime was the traffic in black flesh when the devil white man went into Africa and murdered and kidnapped to bring to the West in chains, in slave ships, millions of black men, women, and children, who were worked and beaten and tortured as slaves.

The devil white man cut these black people off from all knowledge of their own kind, and cut them off from any knowledge of their own language, religion, and past culture, until the black man in America was the earth's only race of people who had absolutely no knowledge of his true identity.

In one generation, the black slave women in America had been raped by the slavemaster white man until there had begun to emerge a homemade, handmade, brainwashed race that was no longer even of its true color, that no longer even knew its true family names. The slavemaster forced his family name upon this raped-mixed race, which slavemaster began to call "the Negro."

This "Negro" was taught of his native Africa that it was peopled by heathen, black savages, swinging like monkeys from trees. This "Negro" accepted this along with every other teaching of the slavemaster that was designed to make him accept and obey and worship the white man.

And where the religion of every other people on Earth taught its believers of a God with whom they could identify, a God who at least looked like one of their own kind, the slavemaster injected his Christian religion into this "Negro." This "Negro" was taught to worship an alien God having the same blond hair, pale skin, and blue eyes as the slavemaster.

This religion taught the "Negro" that black was a curse. It taught him to hate everything black, including himself. It taught him that everything white was good, to be admired, respected, and loved. It brainwashed this "Negro" to think he was superior if his complexion showed more of the white pollution of the slavemaster. This white man's Christian religion further deceived and brainwashed this "Negro" to always turn the other check, and grin, and scrape, and bow, and be humble, and to sing, and to pray, and to take whatever was dished out by the devilish white man; and to look for his pie in the sky, and for his heaven in the hereafter while right here on Earth the slavemaster white man enjoyed *his* heaven.

Many a time, I have looked back, trying to assess, just for myself, my first reactions to all this. Every instinct of the ghetto jungle streets, every hustling fox and criminal wolf instinct in me, which would have scoffed at and rejected anything else, was struck numb. It was as though all of that life merely was back there, without any remaining effect, or influence. I remember how, some time later, reading the Bible in the Norfolk Prison Colony library, I came upon, then I read, over and over, how Paul on the road to Damascus, upon hearing the voice of Christ, was so smitten that he was knocked off his horse, in a daze. I do not now, and I did not then, liken myself to Paul. But I do understand his experience.

CHAPTER TWENTY-TWO

Religion in an Age of Upheaval

Many Americans in the 1960s conducted a kind of courtship with science and technology, a romance that reached its symbolic zenith in the exhibitions of the New York World's Fair of 1964–65 and in Neil Armstrong's step onto the moon on July 20, 1969. But while science offered glimpses of a brave new world of technological advances, other Americans began to harbor second thoughts, and they used the language of religion and theology to express their discontent. By the mid-1960s the younger generation was becoming disillusioned with the war in Vietnam, with the burgeoning "military-industrial complex" of weapons production, with technology itself, and with their parents' religion, which they saw as tied into everything that was wrong with American society: too big, too impersonal, too authoritative, too unresponsive.

A period of unrest shook America to its very foundations as the younger generation took to the streets to demonstrate their impatience with the "establishment." Trust no one over thirty, they declared. Some burned their draft cards, some burned their bras, some burned their college campuses—all of which were seen as symbols of oppression. On August 15, 1969, more than 300,000 rock-and-roll fans descended on Max Yasgur's farm fields near Bethel, New York, for the Woodstock Music Festival, billed as "Three Days of Peace and Music." Bob Dylan's refrain "the times they are a-changin'" turned out to be not only the anthem of an entire generation but the understatement of the decade.

The war in Southeast Asia remained the flashpoint for dissent and bitterness. Philip and Daniel Berrigan, Roman Catholic priests and antiwar activists, broke into Defense Department offices, where they poured blood over files and sabotaged military hardware. Despite Richard Nixon's 1968 campaign promise that he had a plan to end the war in Vietnam, the battle continued, not only in Southeast Asia but also on the campuses and in the coffee shops of America. Dueling bumper stickers declared "AMERICA: LOVE IT OR LEAVE IT" and "AMERICA: CHANGE IT OR LOSE IT." Students erupted in protest across the country, from Berkeley, California, to New York City and also in Madison, Wisconsin, and Iowa City, Iowa. On May 4, 1970, twenty-eight Ohio National Guardsmen fired into a group of antiwar protesters at Kent State University in Ohio, leaving four students dead, permanently paralyzing another, and wounding eight others, thus reminding the nation yet again of its profound divisions.

"There is a revolution coming," Charles Reich, a social critic, warned in *The Greening of America*, published the same year. "It is now spreading with amazing rapidity, and already our laws, institutions and social structure are changing in consequence. It promises a higher reason, a more human community and a new and liberated individual. Its ultimate creation will be a new and enduring wholeness and beauty—a renewed relationship of man to himself, to other men, to society, to nature and to the land." Although the immediate reality looked rather different, many Americans, especially the younger generation, turned to the East for religious inspiration, in part out of disillusionment with Western religions and in part for the novelty of Hinduism, Sikhism, Buddhism, Zen Buddhism, Taoism, Hare Krishna, or even Transcendental Meditation.

"The various wisdoms of the West, religious, philosophical, and scientific, do not offer much guidance to the art of living," Alan Watts, a philosopher and popularizer of Zen Buddhism, explained, "and we find the prospects of making our way in so trackless an ocean of relativity rather frightening." The spirituality of the East, Watts declared, "has the speical merit of a mode of expressing itself which is as intelligible—or perhaps as baffling—to the intellectual as to the illiterate, offering possibilities of communication which we have not explored."

Perhaps so, but American culture has a way of leaving its unique stamp on every religious tradition, homegrown or exotic, it adopts. In North America, Buddhist practice, traditionally associated with the monastic life, emphasized meditation more than monasticism, making it more accessible to the middle classes, who were unlikely to exchange their suburban lives for the rigors of a Tibetan monastery. Hare Krishna devotees, who shaved their heads (except for a ponytail), wore saffron-colored robes, and espoused a variation of Hinduism, patrolled airports and street corners seeking converts. Transcendental Meditation (TM), a discipline of meditation developed by Maharishi Mahesh Yogi, who claimed the Beatles among his followers, offered lectures on American campuses. The saffron-robed evangelists and the clean-cut TM lecturers became the most visible practitioners of South Asian religions in America, despite the fact that they represented small minorities back in India.

Many Americans, in their time-honored tradition of openness to new religious ideas, simply absorbed these new religious forms alongside their more traditional involvement with Judaism or Christianity. Others, especially those identified with the counterculture, saw Eastern religions as a fitting complement to the dictum of Harvard-professor-turned-drug-advocate Timothy Leary: "Tune in, turn on, drop out."

By the early 1970s, however, the drug culture had taken its toll. "The center was not holding," Joan Didion, a perceptive social observer, warned in a haunting essay about the counterculture and life at the end of the 1960s. "Adolescents drifted from city to torn city, sloughing off both the past and the future as snakes shed their skins, children who were never taught and would never now learn the games that had held the society together. People were missing. Parents were missing. Those left behind filed desultory missing-persons reports, then moved on themselves."

About this time a preacher named Chuck Smith accepted an invitation to become pastor of Calvary Chapel, a small congregation of twenty-five contentious people in Costa Mesa, California. Smith's approach to Christianity was simply to open the Bible and begin teaching. People responded, and the congregation, which had been on the verge of disbanding, began to expand at the rate of 5 percent a week. The largest increase came from an unlikely source: the hippies roaming the beaches of southern California. "My wife and I used to go over to Huntington Beach and park downtown to watch the kids and pray for them," Smith recalled many years later. "We wanted somehow to reach them, but we didn't know how."

Smith confessed that "these long-haired, bearded, dirty kids going around the streets repulsed me," but he decided to try to lure them to his Bible studies. It worked. "At the time I learned about Calvary Chapel I was living down in Laguna Beach where there was a different representative of every faith on just about every corner," recalled Oden Fong, an early convert. "You could walk down the street and talk to a Zen Buddhist, walk a bit farther and see a Krishna, a little farther and see a Satanist." Fong and many others found, in his words, "compassion and love" at Calvary Chapel, and the word spread to other disenchanted hippies in southern California.

Some claimed instantaneous healing, both spiritual and physical, including release from drug and alcohol dependencies, when they converted to evangelical Christianity. Smith welcomed them, all of them, into his congregation, and, unlike many other churches, he accepted them with their long hair, beards, and Levi's. At about the same time that Judy Collins's recording of "Amazing Grace" rocketed to the top of the music charts, the "Jesus People" phenomenon began to attract notice, especially Calvary Chapel's large gatherings on the beach at Corona del Mar, near Newport Beach. Hundreds of reformed hippies, eager to recast their lives, participated in the ancient Christian rite of baptism, so rich in symbolism. Smith and what became known as the Jesus movement provided a kind of halfway house for these disillusioned radicals, easing them gently back onto the road of middle-class respectability.

As many hippies embraced various forms of Eastern religion and others gravitated back to Christianity in the early 1970s, the traditions they encountered were themselves being reshaped by the upheaval of the previous decade. African-American theologians, emboldened by the teachings of Malcolm X and Martin Luther King, Jr., challenged the racism of most religious institutions, invoking King's observation that eleven o'clock Sunday morning was the most segregated hour in America. On February

27, 1973, about 200 armed Native Americans occupied Wounded Knee, South Dakota, the site of a massacre of the Sioux by federal troops in 1890. The occupation, which lasted seventy-one days and led to two deaths and more than 300 arrests, nevertheless served to galvanize Native Americans. Many of them came to recognize that the "white man's religion" had deprived them of their own rich cultural and religious heritage and that the way to recover their cultural identity lay in reclaiming their religious practices, including such rituals as the Sun Dance and the sweat-lodge ceremonies.

An even larger revolution emanated from the women's movement and the sexual revolution. The 1963 publication of Betty Friedan's *The Feminine Mystique*, an attack on male domination in American society, touched off the feminist movement, as women began to challenge the strict—and confining—gender roles that had emerged after World War II. "There was a strange discrepancy between the reality of our lives as women and the image to which we were trying to conform," Friedan wrote. "These problems cannot be solved by medicine, or even by psychotherapy," Friedan concluded, adding that women needed to break free of the ties of the household and enter the academy and the workplace. "We need a drastic reshaping of the cultural image of femininity that will permit women to reach maturity, identity, completeness of self, without conflict with sexual fulfillment."

For many Americans, however, sexual fulfillment and sexual expression were fraught with danger, and despite the affinities between the women's movement and the sexual revolution, the two sometimes collided, especially over the issue of women's bodies. In December 1953, when Hugh Hefner founded *Playboy* magazine, which featured photographs of scantily clad women, he heard protests not only from religious leaders but from women, who accused him of exploitation. The sexual revolution itself can be traced to June 16, 1964, at a club called the Condor in the North Beach neighborhood of San Francisco. As the Republican National Convention was convening across town, Carol Doda, a dancer at the Condor, removed her brassiere and, in becoming a topless dancer, touched off the sexual revolution. The widespread availability—and increased reliability—of birth control and the hippies' defiance of the older generation's definition of morality gave rise to the "free love" and the sexual exhibitionism of the counterculture.

By the 1970s the old rules dictating gender roles and governing sexual behavior no longer applied for many Americans, even for those who considered themselves religious. Catholic women widely disregarded the pope's teaching against the use of artificial birth control, and the old taboos about sexual relations outside of marriage, especially premarital sex, were called into question. Rosemary Radford Ruether, a feminist theologian, identified sin with the "depersonalizing of women." The challenge facing women was to assert their independence from men and from religious institutions that had made them second-class citizens. "Salvation cannot appear save as the resurrection of woman," she wrote in 1973, "that is, in woman's self-definition as an autonomous person."

As women began their long struggle for acceptance and equality in education and commerce, some also began agitating for women to be ordained into the clergy. Since at least the late seventeenth century women have outnumbered men in the churches, often shouldering the burden of church work, especially religious education. Although Antoinette Brown had been ordained by the small Congregational church in South Butler, New York, in 1853, and Pentecostals ordained women as missionaries and pastors early in the twentieth century, women had generally been denied access to the ordained ministry.

In 1956 the northern Presbyterians approved the ordination of women to the ministry, and in the 1960s, falling before the juggernaut of the women's movement, the barriers to women's ordination tumbled in rapid succession. The formation of the United Methodist Church in 1968 (from the merger of the Methodist Episcopal Church and the Evangelical and United Brethren Church) guaranteed women access to ordination, and most Lutherans agreed to do the same in 1970. On June 2, 1972, Hebrew Union College, the seminary of the Reform branch of Judaism, generally considered the most liberal, ordained Sally Priesand the first female rabbi in the United States.

"For thousands of years women in Judaism had been second-class citizens," Priesand recalled later, "they were not permitted to participate fully in the life of the synagogue." As she sat in the historic Plum Street Temple in Cincinnati awaiting her ordination, Priesand took satisfaction in the knowledge that "one more barrier was about to be broken." Sandy Eisenberg became the first female rabbi in Reconstructionist Judaism two years later. In Philadelphia on July 29, 1974, three bishops of the Episcopal church, in a break with their denomination's teachings and tradition, ordained eleven women deacons to the priesthood, much to the dismay of conservatives within the denomination. In September 1976, the General Convention of the Episcopal Church approved the ordination of women to the priesthood, although conservatives continued their opposition for decades thereafter.

The women's movement even affected Mormons and Roman Catholics, two religious groups not known for feminist sympathies. The hierarchy of the Roman Catholic Church maintained its opposition to women's ordination, but the shortage of priests and nuns meant that the church relied more and more heavily on women for the operation of its schools, its social service agencies, and even its worship services, especially in rural areas. Among Mormons, Sonia Johnson, who billed herself as a housewife and mother, openly supported the proposed equal rights amendment (ERA) to the U. S. Constitution, a position that placed her at odds with the teachings of the Church of Jesus Christ of Latter-day Saints. Johnson's defiance of Mormon officials brought her a measure of notoriety and emboldened her to declare a largely symbolic candidacy for president. The church tried and excommunicated her for heresy in 1979; her presidential campaign, of course, was unsuccessful.

Someone else had his eyes on the presidency, a little-known one-term governor of Georgia who billed himself as a peanut farmer. When Jimmy Carter declared his candidacy for the Democratic nomination, few took him seriously. The presidential campaign of 1976 promised to be eventful, and it represented a ripe opportunity for the Democrats, who had lost the previous election by a landslide. The United States, still reeling from the chaos of the counterculture and struggling to extricate itself from the war in Southeast Asia, had endured the ordeal of the Watergate scandal and the resignation of Richard Nixon. Cynicism was rampant, and nothing made sense—as when the Nobel Committee awarded its 1973 Peace Prize to Henry Kissinger, who as Nixon's secretary of state was the man most responsible for widening the hostilities in Southeast Asia. Gerald Ford, a former congressman from Michigan who had ascended to the presidency on August 9, 1974, pardoned Nixon in the interest of putting the Watergate nightmare to rest, but that action provoked outrage and piqued public interest in a candidate who was not a Washington insider.

Carter fit that description. He campaigned tirelessly in the precincts of Iowa and the small towns of New Hampshire with his message that he would restore to the nation "a government as good as its people." Throughout the campaign Carter unabashedly declared that he was a "born-again Christian" and that he taught Sunday school at his Southern Baptist church back in Plains, Georgia. Although he faced a formidable field in the Democratic primaries and a spirited campaign from Ford, Carter's oft-repeated promise that he would "never knowingly lie to the American people" proved irresistible to an electorate wearied of Nixon's relentless prevarications.

The media were entranced by what they believed was the novelty of an evangelical Christian running for president, and they jumped on his statement in a *Playboy* interview that he had "looked on a number of women with lust" and had "committed adultery in my heart many times." That statement was rather unremarkable among evangelicals, who draw a careful distinction between temptation and sin, but the media treated it as newsworthy. In large measure because of Carter's self-description as an evangelical Christian, *Newsweek* magazine declared 1976 "the year of the evangelical," drawing attention to a movement that encompassed somewhere between 25 and 46 percent of the United States population, depending on the poll (the Gallup organization pegged the number at 50 million in 1976). The significance of the Carter campaign was not that an avowed evangelical was running for president; William Jennings Bryan had captured the Democratic nomination three times, to cite only one precedent. The significance lay in the fact that, for the first time in several decades, evangelicals—especially southern evangelicals—were participating in the political process.

The Scopes trial of 1925 had convinced American evangelicals that the larger world was corrupt and hostile to their interests, and they had responded by retreating from that world into a subculture of churches, denominations, Bible institutes, and colleges of their own making. They regarded politics as tainted, an arena unworthy of the true believer. In 1965, for example, Jerry Falwell, who would become one of the most prominent leaders of the Religious Right, declared that he "would find it impossible to stop preaching the pure saving gospel of Jesus Christ, and begin doing anything else—including fighting Communism, or participating in civil-rights reforms."

Carter's campaign for the presidency, half a century after the Scopes trial, began to change that. He lured evangelicals, many of whom were Southern Baptists like himself, into the political arena. He spoke their language and represented their values. Ironically, however, despite Carter's unequivocal stand for human rights and his brokering of the historic Camp David peace agreement between Israel and Egypt in 1978, many of the same evangelicals who had supported him in 1976 began to turn against him. Politically conservative evangelicals, emboldened by their influence at the polls, began to make more demands, but a little-known incident turned them against Carter. When his administration's Justice Department sought to enforce antidiscrimination laws at Bob Jones University, a fundamentalist school in Greenville, South Carolina, many evangelicals regarded this as governmental incursion into the evangelical subculture, which had been so carefully constructed in the decades following the Scopes trial. They became bitterly antagonistic toward the president.

Carter was, in a way, then, responsible for the rise of the Religious Right. Once politically conservative evangelicals had mobilized against what they regarded as federal interference at Bob Jones University, they cast about for other issues. According to Paul Weyrich, one of the architects of the Religious Right, the political agenda began to take shape during a conference call among evangelical political leaders in the late 1970s. After discussing their success in forming a coalition in the Bob Jones

case, someone asked for suggestions about other matters. Someone else said, "How about abortion?"

Throughout the 1980s and 1990s the leaders of the Religious Right were fond of saying that the Supreme Court's 1973
decision to legalize abortion was the catalyst for their political
activity. They also liked to cast themselves as the twentieth-
century counterparts to the abolitionist crusaders of the nineteenth century. The reality, however, was more complicated.
When the Supreme Court handed down the *Roe v. Wade* decision, which removed most legal barriers to abortion, on January
22, 1973, the bishops of the Roman Catholic Church protested,
but evangelicals offered nary a whimper. The Southern Baptist
Convention, in fact, endorsed the Court's ruling because it saw
abortion as a moral rather than a legal or a political matter; the
Southern Baptists also applauded the *Roe* decision because it
upheld the separation of church and state, a hallmark of Baptist
convictions dating back to Roger Williams in the seventeenth
century.

For the leaders of the Religious Right, busily cobbling
together a political agenda, however, opposition to abortion fit
perfectly. It allowed them to protest what they saw as a society that, dating back to the 1960s, had been far too permissive.
Despite the fact that evangelicals had been at the forefront of
social-reform movements and campaigns for women's suffrage
in the nineteenth century, evangelicals had resisted the feminist movement in the 1960s. They were uncomfortable with
the "free love" of the counterculture, and rising divorce rates
in the 1970s persuaded them that the family was imperiled. For
the overwhelmingly male leadership of politically conservative
evangelicals, moreover, abortion symbolized everything that was
wrong with America: women entering the workplace in large
numbers, expressing themselves sexually outside of marriage,

and then refusing to deal with the consequences, choosing abortion rather than responsibility.

As America headed into the 1980 elections the Religious Right, which included such organizations as Moral Majority and the Traditional Values Coalition, brought to the table a compelling message, one calculated to appeal to many Americans already fearful because of the economic woes of high oil prices and skyrocketing interest rates. Following the Iranian seizure of the United States embassy in Teheran in 1979, the evening news carried daily footage of Americans held hostage, taunted by their captors. In this climate of fear many evangelicals were prepared finally to shed their political indifference. "When I started Moral Majority, I was leading the evangelical church out from behind their walls," Jerry Falwell recounted in 1996. His 1980 book *Listen America!* warned that there was "no doubt that the sin of America is severe" and that the United States was "literally approaching the brink of national disaster." America must return to Jesus, the leaders of the Religious Right declared, many of them on their own television programs. They decried what they called moral decay in America—divorce, promiscuity, abortion, the Supreme Court decisions in the early 1960s outlawing prayer in public schools—and promised that "God will bless America when America blesses God."

For several weeks late in the summer of 1978 the eyes of the world shifted to the Vatican. Pope Paul VI, who had headed the Roman Catholic Church during the post–Vatican II years and who had issued the disastrous *Humanae Vitae* encyclical in 1968, died at Castel Gandolfo, the papal retreat, on August 6, 1978. The College of Cardinals assembled from around the world to select a successor, and eventually they chose Albino Luciani, the patriarch of Venice, who took the name John Paul I, in honor of his two immediate predecessors, Paul VI and John XXIII. The cardinals had barely returned home when word came that John Paul I himself had died only thirty-three days into his papacy.

Once again the cardinals assembled and, having just chosen an Italian, they felt free to search more broadly. They turned to a surprise candidate, the reluctant Karol Wojtyla, archbishop of Kraców, who became the first non-Italian pope since Hadrian VI had been elected in 1523. After considering the name Stanislaus, after the patron saint of Kraców, Wojtyla followed his predecessor's example and chose John Paul II. "To the See of Peter there succeeds today a bishop who is not Roman, a bishop who is a son of Poland," the pope declared at his investiture. "Pray for me! Help me to be able to serve you!"

The new pontiff, the first Slav ever elected to the papacy, was a remarkable man. He spoke a dozen or more languages and brought an unprecedented energy to the papacy. Having been reared under the communist regime in Poland, he understood firsthand the corruptions and the oppressions of Marxist-inspired government, which claimed to defend the people but which had degenerated into totalitarianism. John Paul II took a dim view of the "liberation theology" so popular among Roman Catholic priests in Latin America because that ideology relied on Marxism. In 1979 he made a return visit to his native Poland, then still under communist control, and prayed that the Holy Spirit might renew the face of "this earth," meaning Poland. As the Soviet empire teetered and then fell a decade later, John Paul could take satisfaction that his prayer had been answered.

More than any pope in history, John Paul II understood the value of public relations. Though conservative on matters of doctrine—he opposed abortion and artificial means of birth control and reasserted that priests must remain unmarried and celibate—his charisma came across well on television. He became the "traveling pope," trotting the globe as a goodwill ambassador for the church, drawing huge crowds to his open-air masses. Church attendance and seminary enrollments usually increased after his visit to a particular country. People around the world—Catholic, Protestant, or other—were enchanted by his warmth and humor. During John Paul's first visit to the United States, for example, he conducted an outdoor mass at Living History Farms, just outside Des Moines, Iowa. Standing toward the back of the crowd, an Iowa farmer, a Protestant, shook his head in admiration. "You've got a pope," he said, turning to his Roman Catholic neighbor, "who really knows how to pope."

Paul Weyrich, head of the Free Congress Foundation, a conservative lobbying organization, was one of the architects of the Religious Right. He recognized that politically conservative evangelicals represented a powerful voting bloc, and he sought to include them in a conservative political coalition. These remarks, presented at a conference in Washington, D.C., in 1991, shed light on the origins of the movement that became known as the Religious Right.

Most people who comment on the evangelical movement picture it as an offensive movement politically. It is not. It is a defensive movement. The people who are involved in it didn't want to get involved; they got involved very reluctantly. They had accepted the notion (which may have taken root historically at the Scopes trial) that a good Christian would raise his family in the proper manner and would not participate very much in public life. If you did that, you could avoid all the corruption that was manifest in politics....

What caused the movement to surface was the federal government's moves against Christian schools. This absolutely shattered the Christian community's notion that Christians could isolate themselves inside their own institutions and teach what they pleased. The realization that they could not then linked them up with the long-held conservative view that government is too powerful and intrusive, and this linkage was what made evangelicals active. It wasn't the abortion issue; that wasn't sufficient. It was the recognition that isolation simply would no longer work in this society.

CHAPTER TWENTY-THREE

Preachers, Politicians, and Prodigals

The large central building was ringed by bright colors. It looked like a parking lot filled with cars, " wrote *Time* correspondent Donald Neff. "When the plane dipped lower, the cars turned out to be bodies—hundreds of bodies—wearing red dresses, blue T-shirts, green blouses, pink slacks, children's polka-dotted jumpers. Couples with their arms around each other, children holding parents. Nothing moved. Washing hung on the clotheslines. The fields were freshly plowed. Banana trees and grape vines were flourishing. But nothing moved."

The scene was an obscure hamlet called Jonestown, deep in the rain forests of Guyana, a small country on the northern coast of South America. News of the mass murder-suicide at Jonestown, a heavily guarded colony founded by a California-based religious group called the Peoples Temple, stunned the world and prompted a flurry of questions about the dangers of religious charisma. The first Peoples Temple had been founded in 1956 by Jim Jones in Indiana, his home state. He moved the group to Redwood City, California, the following year and later set up branches in Los Angeles and San Francisco. The Peoples Temple became known for its interracial membership and its social-welfare activities, including job training, day-care centers, and nursing homes.

Although Jones was recognized for his humanitarian work, he also grew increasingly authoritative and paranoid. He cast himself as "Dad" to his followers and demanded submission, often resorting to physical and sexual abuse, threats, and blackmail. He also demanded that members turn over all their property and income to the Peoples Temple. After a series of newspaper and magazine articles brought these practices to light in 1977, Jones relocated his followers to Jonestown, the agricultural colony that his group had established in 1974. When a contingent of Americans led by U.S. representative Leo Ryan came to Guyana in November 1978 to investigate charges that some members were being held against their will, Jones's followers gunned down Ryan and four others. Retreating to the Jonestown compound, the remaining Peoples Temple members obeyed Jones's infamous order, issued November 18, 1978, to drink a deadly concoction of purple Kool-Aid laced with potassium cyanide. Armed guards enforced the order before obeying it themselves; Jones himself and some of his lieutenants apparently died of self-inflicted gunshot wounds.

As workers sifted through the carnage of 911 corpses—men, women, and children—shocked Americans worried about the destructive effects of religious charisma. At least since the counterculture of the 1960s, reports had circulated about the seductive power of religious personalities, especially those who preyed on young people and turned them against their families. The abduction of newspaper heiress Patty Hearst by an outlaw group calling itself the Symbionese Liberation Army—and Hearst's eventual cooperation with their activities—called further attention to the phenomenon of "programming," or "brainwashing." Groups such as Scientology, est, and Sun Myung Moon's Unification Church all faced criticism as "cults" as well as scrutiny about their beliefs and practices. None, however, faced questions as profound as those framed in the jungles of Guyana, but the dead could not answer.

America's evangelicals, who had been politically somnolent since the Scopes trial of 1925, began to awaken from their apolitical torpor in the 1970s. The presidential campaign of a Southern Baptist Sunday school teacher, Jimmy Carter, caught the attention of evangelicals, southerners especially, in the mid-1970s, and the Democratic candidate's message that he would never knowingly lie to the American people resonated with an electorate grown weary of Richard Nixon's endless prevarications. Ironically, however, many evangelical leaders turned against Carter during the course of his administration. Although these leaders of the fledgling Religious Right later struggled mightily to persuade their constituents that their activism was motivated by moral outrage over the Supreme Court's *Roe v. Wade* decision, which effectively legalized abortion, that argument was a creative work of fiction. While a few evangelicals registered mild dissent against the *Roe* decision, a larger number actually applauded the ruling as marking a proper delineation between personal morality and public policy, between church and state. Most evangelicals remained silent on the matter.

Leaders of the Religious Right eventually did mobilize in response to a court decision, but it was not *Roe v. Wade* in January 1973. Rather, they coalesced as a political movement in response to a lower court ruling, *Green v. Connally* (1971), which upheld the Internal Revenue Service's decision to deny tax-exempt status to any organization that engaged in racial discrimination or segregation. Decades earlier, many southern evangelicals had organized private religious schools, sometimes known as "segregation academies," in response to the Supreme Court's landmark *Brown v. Board of Education* ruling in 1954, which mandated the desegregation of public schools. Those schools stood to lose their tax exemption under the terms of *Green v. Connally*, as did the notoriously fundamentalist Bob Jones University, in Greenville, South Carolina.

Green v. Connally galvanized evangelical leaders who, at the behest of the conservative activist Paul Weyrich, united in defense of Bob Jones University—and in defense, they insisted, of the sanctity of evangelical institutions. Leaders of the Religious Right decided later to add other issues—prayer in schools, pornography, abortion—to their political agenda in preparation for the 1980 presidential campaign. Paradoxically, they anointed as their political savior Ronald Reagan, a divorced and remarried man who, as governor of California in 1967, had signed one of the nation's most permissive laws on abortion.

Although *Newsweek* had christened 1976 the "year of the evangelical," that designation may have been premature. All three major candidates in the presidential election of 1980— Jimmy Carter, John B. Anderson, and Ronald Reagan—claimed the mantle of evangelicalism. Carter had established his "born-again" credentials during the 1976 campaign; Anderson, a Republican turned Independent, had been reared in the Evangelical Free Church of America, a denomination with Scandinavian roots; and Ronald Reagan also tried to speak the evangelical language of personal piety.

With the formation of Jerry Falwell's Moral Majority in 1979 and the organization of politically conservative evangelicals as a voting bloc, it became clear that the Religious Right would become a potent force at the polls. While Moral Majority may have been the most visible eruption of Religious Right impulses, other organizations also fit beneath that umbrella, including the Religious Roundtable, Traditional Values Coalition, Focus on the Family, and Concerned Women for America. One of the defining moments of the 1980 presidential campaign occurred during the Religious Roundtable's first National Affairs Briefing, a rally of 15,000 conservatives in Dallas, Texas. After several stem-winding speeches by right-wing preachers, Reagan, who had been seated on the dais, walked to the podium and said, "I know this is a nonpartisan gathering, and so I know you can't endorse me, but I...want you to know that I endorse you and what you are doing." The crowd rose to its feet and shouted "Amen!" thereby all but ensuring that conservative evangelicals would turn their backs on Carter, a fellow evangelical, in favor of Reagan in the November election.

Changes in the telecommunications industry during the 1970s amplified the power of the television preachers, many of whom doubled as leaders of the Religious Right. In the 1950s and 1960s the major television networks, which controlled most of the stations, insisted—in compliance with the Federal Communications Commission (FCC) requirement that all television stations provide a certain amount of public-service time—that their affiliated local stations could not accept money for religious broadcasts they aired. With few exceptions, these stations looked to so-called mainstream religious groups—Protestants, Catholics, and Jews—to provide this programming. By the 1970s, however, when the FCC allowed local stations to accept money for religious programming and, later, with the expansion of cable television, a host of evangelical preachers eagerly took their messages to the airwaves, buying time at bargain prices late at night or during the programming "ghetto" of Sunday morning.

Just as evangelicals had jumped on radio as a means of spreading their message in the 1920s, so, too, they saw the potential for television, especially when coupled with increasingly sophisticated and computerized direct-mail fund-raising operations. No one exploited the medium to better advantage than a young preacher-businessman named Marion G. "Pat" Robertson. The son of a Democratic senator from Virginia and a graduate of Yale Law School, Robertson discerned a call to the ministry after failing to pass the bar exam. After graduating from seminary in 1959, Robertson considered becoming a pastor and applied to be a missionary in Israel. He mulled over the idea of a ministry in the Bedford-Stuyvesant slums of New York City, but nothing seemed to capture his interest until he heard that a defunct television station was for sale in Portsmouth, Virginia, for $37,000.

Robertson visited the station, climbing through a broken window and scaring away a large rat on the glass-strewn floors. He agreed to buy the station on an installment plan, grandly dubbed it the Christian Broadcasting Network (CBN), and by 1961, the same year he was ordained a Southern Baptist minister by the Freemason Street Baptist Church in Norfolk, Virginia, Robertson began broadcasting three hours of religious television per night.

Although the local clergy remained wary of the struggling enterprise, the station—featuring Robertson's smooth talk and his chatty preaching—began to catch on with viewers. In 1965 Robertson hired two young Assemblies of God evangelists, Jim and Tammy Faye Bakker, as additional talent. Fund-raising telethons fueled the growth of the station and eventually the network as the tentacles of the Christian Broadcasting Network stretched across the nation. An early telethon solicited 700 donors who would pledge $10 a month; in 1966 Robertson named his central program, a talk and entertainment format unabashedly based on the *Tonight Show*, the *700 Club*, and it was syndicated nationally in 1972.

By the 1980s the field of television evangelists, who came to be known as televangelists, was crowded. Preachers such as Jimmy Swaggart, Oral Roberts, Kenneth Copeland, James Robison, Robert Schuller, Falwell, and Robertson became household names, devouring millions of dollars annually in contributions. In 1987 *Time* magazine reported that Swaggart had taken in $142 million the previous year, while Falwell brought in about $84 million and Robertson $183 million.

No televangelists garnered more attention in the mid-1980s, however, than Jim and Tammy Faye Bakker, who had left Robertson's Christian Broadcasting Network to start their own operation in Charlotte, North Carolina. The *PTL Club*—variously known as "Praise the Lord," "People that Love," and, by cynics, "Pass the Loot"—featured both of the Bakkers and became the foundation for the PTL Network, which reported revenues of $129 million in 1986. The network soon moved into state-of-the-art production facilities at Heritage USA, the Bakkers' Christian theme park in Fort Mill, South Carolina, which included a hotel, a campground, a shopping mall, restaurants, condominiums, a water amusement park, and Billy Graham's boyhood home.

Jim and Tammy Faye Bakker careened recklessly along whatever line that remained separating preaching from entertainment. Both could send tears gushing at the drop of a hat—or, more likely, in response to a drop in contributions.

Tammy Faye was notorious for her goopy makeup—a popular T-shirt in the mid-1980s showed a massive blot of pastels and the legend "I RAN INTO TAMMY FAYE AT THE MALL"—and Jim was a tireless proponent of the so-called prosperity gospel, the "health-and-wealth" doctrine that God was eager to bestow worldly goods on anyone who contributed generously to God's work (read PTL). "We preach prosperity," Bakker said. "We preach abundant life. Christ wished above all things that we prosper." In his eagerness to raise money for Heritage USA, Bakker offered lifetime vacation accommodations to those who contributed substantial sums of money. That tactic would prove to be his legal undoing when it came to light that he had vastly oversold the timeshares and had no way of fulfilling his obligations.

Bakker's spiritual and moral undoing came in the person of Jessica Hahn, a church secretary from Long Island. On March 19, 1987, Bakker abruptly resigned as chairman of PTL. He spoke of a "hostile force" that was threatening him with black-mail in order to take over his religious empire. It later emerged that the "force" was fellow televangelist Jimmy Swaggart, who excoriated Bakker as a "pretty boy preacher" and a "cancer" on the Body of Christ. At issue was a 1980 tryst between Bakker and Hahn, which Bakker had attempted to conceal with hush money delivered by one of his aides, Richard Dortch. Bakker tried to save PTL by turning it over to another televangelist, Falwell. Still another televangelist, John Ankerberg, stepped forward with charges that Bakker was bisexual.

The drama was played out in the media—including *Good Morning America*, *Nightline*, and *Time* and *Newsweek* cover stories. The Bakkers' lifestyle of conspicuous consumption—gold-plated bathroom fixtures, Rolls-Royces, air-conditioned doghouses—soon came to light, along with a salary and bonus package that exceeded a million dollars annually, all the while that PTL and Heritage USA sank deeper and deeper into debt. PTL petitioned for bankruptcy, the Internal Revenue Service launched an investigation, and Bakker was defrocked by the Assemblies of God for sexual misconduct. In December 1988 Bakker was indicted on twenty-four counts of fraud and conspiracy relating to the financial improprieties surrounding PTL and Heritage USA. He was convicted the following year and initially sentenced to forty-five years in prison, a sentence later reduced to eight years.

Bakker's troubles were only the opening act of the televangelist drama that alternated between comedy and tragedy. Oral Roberts, a Pentecostal televangelist from Tulsa, Oklahoma, solemnly told his viewers that God had, in effect, taken him hostage and would call Roberts "home"—take him to heaven—unless God's people ponied up something on the order of $4.5 million. On February 21, 1988, more than 7,000 people jammed into Jimmy Swaggart's Family Life Center in Baton Rouge, Louisiana, to hear him confess his own shortcomings. "I do not plan in any way to whitewash my sin," Swaggart said in the wake of disclosures about having visited a motel room with a prostitute. "I do not call it a mistake, a mendacity. I call it sin." In a soliloquy that was baroque and eloquent at the same time, Swaggart apologized to his wife, his son, and his daughter-in-law. He apologized to the Assemblies of God, "which helped to bring the gospel to my little beleaguered town, when my family was lost without Jesus, this movement and fellowship that girdles the globe, that has been more instrumental in bringing this gospel through the stygian night of darkness to the far-flung hundreds of millions than maybe any effort in the annals of history."

Swaggart apologized, finally, to Jesus, "the one who has saved me and washed me and cleansed me." Swaggart's jaw quivered; rivulets of tears flowed down his cheeks. His eyes turned toward heaven. "I have sinned against you, my Lord, and I would ask that your precious blood would wash and cleanse every stain until it is in the seas of God's forgetfulness, never to be remembered against me anymore." The performance was vintage Swaggart—complete with anguish and tears and self-flagellation—but believers shuddered at the toppling of yet another televangelist, and the media, already in a feeding frenzy in the wake of Bakker's tryst with Jessica Hahn, had a field day lampooning the hypocrisy of the televangelists. Ratings—and contributions—for all the televangelists fell precipitously.

Despite the holier-than-thou attitude of the television preachers, it appeared that they were no different from the society at large in the 1980s, which had its own share of corruption. The Reagan administration, in direct violation of the law, had sold armaments to Iran and used the proceeds to fund anti-communist insurgents in Central America. Unscrupulous investors triggered a savings-and-loan scandal, which festered for most of the decade, costing taxpayers billions of dollars. Other investors gravitated toward "junk bonds," high-interest bonds of questionable legality that became the ticket to either quick wealth or financial ruin (or both). The Reagan government preached the virtues of "trickle-down economics," which provided tax cuts for the wealthy together with the hope that the less affluent might benefit as well. The fictional character Gordon Gekko, played by Michael Douglas in the movie *Wall Street*, captured the ideology of the 1980s when he proclaimed, "Greed is good!"

In this context of self-aggrandizement it was no coincidence that televangelists from Jim Bakker and Kenneth Copeland to Robert Tilton and Frederick Price extolled the virtues of something they called "prosperity theology." Simply put, prosperity theology, also known as "name it and claim it," guaranteed that Jesus would not only save your soul and, perhaps, mend your marriage, but he would also find ways to augment your bank account and get you a vacation home and that little red sports car you'd been coveting. The appeals were hardly subtle: Give your money to God—specifically, to whichever preacher was making the pitch—and God will make you financially prosperous.

Not everyone agreed. Many churches and synagogues saw the faces of poverty everywhere around them—on street corners, in soup kitchens, in homeless shelters and rehabilitation centers. Massive governmental cuts in social services in the 1980s (in an effort to help compensate for the tax breaks skewed toward the wealthy) heaped hardship on many Americans, and religious organizations stepped into the breach. In so doing they were reclaiming, though reluctantly, the role they had played a century earlier—running soup kitchens and employment bureaus and otherwise assisting the urban poor—until the massive social problems of the Great Depression overwhelmed them and they were forced to cede those duties to the government.

In one of the most remarkable religious mobilizations of the twentieth century, people of faith in the 1980s organized relief efforts on behalf of those less fortunate. They turned church basements into soup kitchens and homeless shelters. They also protested federal policies, which placed a higher priority on protecting capital gains and building "Star Wars" weapons systems than on feeding the hungry. For the most part these voices of dissent came from leaders of Roman Catholicism and mainline Protestantism, but others protested as well. People like Jim Wallis of Sojourners, a Christian community located in the ghetto of Washington, D.C., and Ronald Sider of Evangelicals for Social Action represented the political left wing of evangelicalism; while they generally shared the same theology with leaders of the Religious Right, their interpretation of the Bible led them to advocate more liberal political positions.

The approach of the 1988 Presidential campaign represented a challenge for the Religious Right. Although Ronald Reagan had spoken their language and had even appointed a few religious conservatives to positions in his administration, he had failed to prosecute their agenda as vigorously as they hoped he would. Abortion, the rallying issue for the Religious Right, was still legal, despite Reagan's promises to outlaw it; audible prayers, which they supported, were still banned in public school classrooms.

Several Republicans sought the blessing of the Religious Right, but one candidate in particular believed he could use the support of politically conservative evangelicals as a springboard to the nomination. On September 17, 1986, Pat Robertson capitalized on his media exposure, which had been enhanced by CBN's use of satellite technology, and announced that he would become a candidate for the Republican Presidential nomination if he could obtain three million signatures of support. Less than a year later he declared his candidacy on a far-right political platform. He took a leave from CBN, resigned his Southern Baptist ordination in September 1987, and studiously billed himself as a broadcasting executive, bristling when the media referred to him as a televangelist. Robertson's attempts to distance himself from his past were not always successful, however. Investigative reporters, for instance, found a tape of a 1985 broadcast of the *700 Club*, when Robertson ordered Hurricane Gloria to change course. "In the name of Jesus," he prayed, "we command you to stop where you are and head northeast, away from land, and away from harm. In the name of Jesus of Nazareth, we command it."

Despite these revelations and with the concerted efforts of politically conservative evangelicals at the grassroots, Robertson won a straw poll in Michigan and finished second to Bob Dole and ahead of George Bush, the eventual nominee, in the Iowa precinct caucuses. "It's almost, like we say, you've got to give God the credit," Robertson declared once the caucus results were in. "Satan has controlled politics for too long," a Robertson supporter remarked to a friend. In the face of increased scrutiny, however, Robertson faltered the following week in New Hampshire and eventually dropped out of the race, but his candidacy lured more evangelicals into the political arena. "Robertson brought out of the pew and into the process tens of thousands of new people, many of whom are still involved," anti-abortion activist Randall Terry said in 1991. "Their full impact will not be felt until the 1996 election, the 2000 election, 2004."

In January 1989, at the inaugural festivities for Bush, Robertson met a young political operative, Ralph Reed. Robertson solicited ideas for transforming the grassroots organizations he had assembled during his campaign into a political lobby for conservative evangelicals. Reed's long memorandum in response provided the blueprint for the Christian Coalition, which was formed later that same year. Robertson, as president of the organization (Reed was tapped as executive director), became a major force in American politics and especially within the Republican Party. With his embrace of such ideologies as Christian Reconstructionism, which seeks to replace American civil and criminal codes with the laws of Moses and ancient Israel, including "an eye for an eye, a tooth for a tooth," Robertson was often accused of wanting to collapse the First Amendment distinction between church and state. His excoriations of abortion, political liberals, feminists, and homosexuals earned him the label of intolerant, although such denunciations only served to endear him to many politically conservative evangelicals.

For the better part of three decades the most enduring symbol of the cold war was the Berlin Wall, a tangle of concrete, mines, barbed wire, and armed guards constructed hurriedly by the communists in 1961 to stanch the flow of East Germans fleeing to freedom in the West. President John F. Kennedy had endeared himself to Germans with his famous "Ich bin ein Berliner" (I am a Berliner) speech at the wall, and when Reagan visited there in 1987 he issued a direct challenge to Mikhail Gorbachev, the Soviet president and head of what Reagan once called the "Evil Empire": "Mr. Gorbachev, tear down this wall!" By that time communism itself was wheezing, crushed beneath the weight of its own failures, and the destruction of the wall itself in November 1989 represented its death rasp.

For nearly three-quarters of a century, since the Bolshevik Revolution of 1917, Americans more often than not had defined themselves in opposition to communism. America stood for goodness and truth, freedom and righteousness, whereas communism represented repression, tyranny, and atheism. These cold-war assumptions had dictated everything from military spending to churchgoing. The collapse of the Berlin Wall and the toppling of the Soviet empire may have ushered in what George Bush called the "New World Order," but it also robbed Americans of their most durable adversary. The decade ahead would be marked by an almost desperate casting about for new enemies. Economic and energy considerations suggested the Japanese or the Arabs for a time, but many Americans ultimately decided that enemies lurked closer to home—immigrants, homosexuals, and those they identified as enemies of all religion: "secular humanists."

CHAPTER TWENTY-FOUR

Religion for the New Millennium

If the New York World's Fair of 1964–65 symbolized Americans' unalloyed confidence in science and technology, the *Challenger* disaster arguably brought an end to that era of confidence. On the morning of January 28, 1986, a scant seventy-three seconds into its flight, the space shuttle *Challenger* exploded above the Atlantic Ocean, killing all seven crew members, including Christa McAuliffe, a social studies teacher from Concord, New Hampshire. Americans were transfixed as television played the tape again and again, searing the terrible beauty of that moment—the plumes of white smoke against an azure sky—onto the national consciousness of an entire generation.

Just as Black Thursday in 1929, D-day in 1944, and John Kennedy's assassination in 1963 had been defining moments for previous generations, the *Challenger* disaster—it was referred to almost universally as the "*Challenger* disaster," not "mishap" or "accident"—prompted questions about America's competence, its place in the world, and its reliance on technology, which might itself prove unreliable. Science, technology, and the information age may have made Americans' lives easier at some level—electric can openers and garage-door openers, microwave ovens and personal computers—but they were powerless to impart information on how to live, how to imbue everyday lives with meaning.

Despite the predictions of social scientists, who had warned for more than a century that as any society modernizes and industrializes religion would be pushed to the margins, Americans clung stubbornly to faith at the end of the twentieth century. Nationwide membership in the Ethical Culture Society, a secular organization founded in the nineteenth century to promote good works without religion, to cite one example, fell below 3,000 by the end of the twentieth century. More than 90 percent of Americans, on the other hand, professed a belief in God or a supreme being, a figure that had stayed constant since the advent of polling after World War II.

Americans remained religious, but the varieties of religious expression remained anything but constant, and the complexion of America itself was changing. In 1965, amendments to the Immigration and Nationality Act had ended quotas based on nationality, giving rise to major changes in the patterns of immigration to the United States. The number of immigrants from Canada and Europe dropped, whereas immigration from Asia and the West Indies grew dramatically.

Buddhists from Southeast Asia, Sikhs, Jains, and Hindus from South Asia, and Muslims from the Middle East brought their religions with them to the New World and, in so doing, reshaped the religious landscape of America. Sikh *gurdwárás* (temples), Buddhist and Hindu temples, Shinto shrines, and

Muslim mosques cropped up alongside churches, synagogues, and Mormon temples. Vodou and Santería shrines became commonplace in certain neighborhoods of Miami, New Orleans, and New York City, but the patterns of migration ensured that these changes in American religious life would not be confined to urban areas. The oldest mosque in continuous use in the United States, for example, is in Cedar Rapids, Iowa, and one of the major communities of Hare Krishnas, New Vrindavan, lies just outside of Moundsville, West Virginia.

The arrival of these immigrants had other effects. Clergy councils from small towns to big cities faced the prospect of expanding their ranks beyond Protestant ministers, Catholic priests, and Jewish rabbis to include Muslim imams. Many of these councils then mobilized to resist the stereotypical equation of Muslims with terrorism, although the terrorist bomb that ripped through the parking garage of the World Trade Center in lower Manhattan on February 26, 1993, made that task more difficult, especially when the act was traced to Omar Abdel-Rahman, an Islamic sheik and leader of a radical Muslim group.

Americans greeted new immigrants with attitudes ranging from hostility to indifference to enthusiasm. Tibetan Buddhism, for instance, became popular among various celebrities and Hollywood actors, and the movement's leader, the Dalai Lama, became something of a celebrity himself. Some Americans identified themselves as "Jew-Boos," those who readily combined Jewish ethnicity with Buddhist identity, and Robert A. F. Thurman, one of the Dalai Lama's most devoted acolytes and himself a Tibetan monk, maneuvered to secure an academic appointment at Columbia University, which he used as a platform to attain higher visibility for Tibetan Buddhism.

The resurgence of interest in Asian religions comported well with the fascination with New Age spirituality, a kind of spiritual smorgasbord that encompassed everything from astrology to Zen, various massage therapies, and (for some) belief in extraterrestrials. New Age became all the rage in the 1980s and 1990s. According to a 1987 survey, 67 percent of American adults read astrology reports, and 36 percent believed the reports were scientific. The survey indicated that 42 percent said they had made contact with the spirit of someone who had died; 30 million Americans believed in reincarnation. Nancy Reagan regularly consulted with an astrologer before finalizing her husband's White House schedule. Actress Shirley MacLaine published several best-selling books on New Age spirituality, and NBC aired a situation comedy featuring an alien named "Alf" (Alternative Life Form) from the planet Melmac. New Age music, a kind of dreamy jazz that provided the sensation of drowning in a sea of marzipan, became so popular that the Grammy Awards gave it a special category.

Americans incorporated hitherto "exotic" practices into their daily lives—yoga, tai chi, qi gong, shiatsu massage, all of which combined Eastern spirituality with some sort of physical activity—and saw no contradiction between an adherence to orthodox Christianity or Judaism and New Age practices. Many wore crystals, which were thought to have mysterious healing and spiritual powers, around their necks and worried about their *chakras*, the "energy points" in their bodies. A number of New Agers claimed to be able to "channel," to communicate with, ancient authorities, to speak their words of guidance and warning to a modern age that seemed so bereft of wisdom. Each "channeler" had his or her own character: the archangel Gabriel; Mafu; Zoosh; Soli, an "off-planet being"; or Ramtha, a 35,000-year-old denizen of Atlantis, channeled by J. Z. Knight, an ex-housewife from Yelm, Washington.

In August 1987, 20,000 people participated in a "harmonic convergence," a simultaneous New Age meditation at "sacred sites" from Central Park in New York City to Mount Shasta, California. The New Age had much in common with the environmental movement, believing that the Earth itself was sacred. Such places as Mount Shasta, Boulder, Colorado, Santa Fe, New Mexico, and Sedona, Arizona, became hives of New Age activity. An alternative newspaper in Santa Fe, for example, included advertisements for everything from massage to past-lives counseling (for those who believe in reincarnation and have lived previous lives) and Native American purification ceremonies. New Agers believed that Sedona lay at the intersection of four lines of spiritual energy located deep within the earth, an auspicious circumstance, and people in Sedona talked about the visit of extraterrestrials as casually as New Yorkers discussed traffic on the Gowanus Expressway.

The omnivorous New Age movement sought to appropriate Native American traditions and practices alongside its other conquests. While the sight of white middle-aged devotees sweating through a purification ceremony merely amused some Native Americans, others regarded them as interlopers and as yet another example of white cultural imperialism. In 1970 an act of Congress had finally restored Taos Blue Lake to the Pueblos, after a fight that lasted the better part of seven decades, and Native Americans, after the occupation of Wounded Knee, South Dakota, in 1973, had begun to reclaim their religious traditions at powwows, in kivas, or sweat lodges, or beneath the sacred sky. The Supreme Court, however, dealt another blow to Native Americans in 1990 when it ruled that there was no constitutional right to chew the hallucinogenic drug peyote in Native American religious practices. "We have never held that an individual's religious beliefs excuse him from compliance with an otherwise valid law prohibiting conduct that the state is free to regulate," the majority ruled in a 6-to-3 decision.

Native Americans quickly protested the ruling, pointing out that use of peyote in their religious ceremonies predated the Constitution. Religious groups and newspaper editorial pages across the country also decried the decision as a violation of the First Amendment guarantee of free exercise of religion. The *Des Moines Register*, for example, called the decision "awful" and characterized the Court's action as "a gratuitous swipe at its historic deference to religious freedom." A broad spectrum of religious leaders appealed to Congress for redress; Congress responded with the Religious Freedom Restoration Act, which argued that "governments should not substantially burden religious exercise without compelling justification." President Bill Clinton signed the bill into law on November 16, 1993, but the Supreme Court continued the tug-of-war by declaring the measure invalid in 1997, an indication to many of the fragility of First Amendment freedoms.

Other minorities faced threats as well, including threats from a motley collection of white supremacist "hate groups" bunched beneath the umbrella of Christian Identity, a reference to their belief that white Christians are God's chosen people. The ideologies driving these groups differed, but they generally directed their invectives against Jews, homosexuals, and minorities, especially African Americans. Some unabashedly claimed the legacy of Nazism, many were survivalists of various sorts (those who want to live without depending on the economic system—even grocery stores—for their existence), and almost all harbored deep suspicions of government. Inevitably, these groups clashed with federal officials, as when Randy Weaver, a survivalist wanted on weapons charges, faced off against law-enforcement officers in Ruby Ridge, Idaho; such confrontations stoked the paranoia and the hatred of Christian Identity groups toward the government.

Another confrontation, just outside of Waco, Texas, pitted the Bureau of Alcohol, Tobacco, and Firearms against a heavily armed colony of Branch Davidians, a religious sect led by David Koresh, who believed he was a messiah. After a standoff lasting fifty-one days and persistent reports about child abuse within the group, federal agents finally moved against the compound on the morning of April 19, 1993. The buildings erupted in a conflagration that killed at least eighty Branch Davidians, including Koresh. The most disastrous reprisal against the federal government occurred two years later to the day, on April 19, 1995, when a young vigilante named Timothy McVeigh and an unknown number of accomplices conspired to bomb the Alfred P. Murrah Federal Building in Oklahoma City, Oklahoma, leaving 168 dead, including nineteen children. The incident, at that time the most devastating terrorist act on American soil, traumatized the nation, but it also cast light into some of the darker corners of American religious life and exposed Identity and survivalist groups to public scrutiny and scorn.

Three decades after the Civil Rights Act black Americans were still struggling for their constitutional rights against the hoary vestiges of racism. California and other states sought to do away with affirmative action, a system of racial quotas that had helped minorities aspire to equal opportunity in education and employment. Dozens of African-American churches across the South, from Virginia to Louisiana, mysteriously caught fire in the 1990s, prompting a Justice Department official to call it "an epidemic of terror." The targeting of churches may have been significant because of the role that churches had played in the civil rights movement. Noting that the terrorists were not burning African-American businesses, Randolph

Scott-McLaughlin of the Center for Constitutional Rights said: "They're burning down black churches. It's like they're burning a cross in my front yard. They're burning symbols of resistance and community and hope and refuge."

Amid the embers of hate and destruction, however, some religious leaders saw signs of hope, even reconciliation. The arson of African-American houses of worship provoked ringing denunciations from Americans in all walks of life. "These attacks against African-American churches and other houses of worship are an affront to our most basic beliefs of religious liberty and racial tolerance," Bill Clinton said on July 2, 1996. "They pose a challenge to our entire nation." The Clinton administration established the National Church Arson Task Force, and Congress passed the Church Arson Prevention Act; within six months, nearly 150 people had been arrested. Individuals, congregations, corporations, even the players in the National Football League provided money for the rebuilding of churches; college students volunteered their labor, and the churches rose again. "We can never define ourselves as Americans by saying we are so good because we are not the other guy," Clinton remarked to a gathering of the Congressional Black Caucus on September 14, 1996, in response to the church burnings. "The other guys are us, too. We are all Americans."

Another challenge to racism in the 1990s came from an improbable source. On March 20, 1990, Bill McCartney, head football coach at the University of Colorado, and his friend Dave Wardell were traveling to a meeting of the Fellowship of Christian Athletes, in Pueblo, Colorado. In the course of their conversation, they came upon the idea of filling Colorado's Folsom Stadium with men dedicated to the notion of Christian devotion and discipline. This vision spread to a cohort of seventy-two men, who engaged in fasting and prayer in support of the notion.

More than 4,000 men showed up for the first gathering, and by July 1993 McCartney's original vision had been fulfilled. Fifty thousand men piled into Folsom Stadium for singing, hugging, and exhortations to be good and faithful husbands, fathers, and churchgoers. McCartney also insisted that his overwhelmingly white, middle-class audience bridge the barriers of racial hatred. By 1996 the organization, Promise Keepers, had an annual budget in excess of $115 million and offices in thirty-two states and provinces throughout North America. In 1995 more than one million men attended twenty-two rallies at sports stadiums across the country, and on October 4, 1997, Promise Keepers conducted a mass rally, called "Stand in the Gap: A Sacred Assembly of Men," on the Mall in Washington, D.C.

Promise Keepers was merely the latest manifestation of a phenomenon called muscular Christianity, a series of initiatives to make Christianity more attractive to men. At least since the late seventeenth century women have outnumbered men in religious adherence, a circumstance that has prompted these periodic attempts to lure men back to the churches. The Awakening of 1857–58, for instance, also known as the Businessman's Revival, appealed to men in the workplace with weekday noontime prayer meetings. At the turn of the twentieth century Billy Sunday, formerly a baseball player for the Chicago White Stockings, cajoled the men in his audiences to "hit the sawdust trail" and give their lives to Jesus.

"Many think a Christian has to be a sort of dishrag proposition, a wishy-washy, sissified sort of galoot that lets everybody make a doormat out of him," Sunday intoned. "Let me tell you the manliest man is the man who will acknowledge Jesus Christ." A few years later, at about the same time that Charles Sheldon's novel *In His Steps* portrayed Jesus as an astute businessman, an organization called the Men and Religion Forward Movement summoned men back to the churches with the slogan "More Men for Religion, More Religion for Men." The campaign held rallies in places like Carnegie Hall, rented billboards on Times Square, and placed display ads in the sports sections of newspapers.

Ever since the New Testament, Christianity has employed athletic metaphors to talk about the Christian life. St. Paul talked about the importance of running the race, and such organizations as the YMCA used sports as a means to lure men away from the temptations of the streets. In 1902 John Scudder, a Congregational minister in New York City, opened a gymnasium at his church in order to teach boys to box and thereby "inculcate virtues of highest moral value" because "manly sparring tends toward Christian growth." In the 1950s and 1960s James C. Hefley, an evangelical author, published edifying biographical sketches of professional athletes who professed to be Christians: Bobby Richardson, Dave Wickersham, Bill Glass, Al Worthington, among many others. A number of organizations emphasized the connection between sports and Christianity: Athletes in Action, the Fellowship of Christian Athletes, and Power Team for Christ, a weight-lifting troupe that traveled to various venues and interspersed evangelistic testimonies with spectacular feats of strength.

It should have come as no surprise, then, that Promise Keepers, the muscular Christianity of the 1990s, took on the trappings of athleticism. McCartney, founder of Promise Keepers, was a highly successful football coach who led the Colorado Buffaloes from obscurity to national rankings and the Associated Press National Championship in 1990. McCartney's rhetoric drew on athletic imagery; Promise Keepers rallies and publications most often featured athletes; and the gatherings themselves took place in sports arenas. Like evangelicals throughout American history before him, McCartney had found a way to speak the idiom of American men of a particular time.

Promise Keepers was the decade's Rorschach test, the exercise in which observers try to make sense of a random ink blot. Analysts of every stripe—and there was no shortage of analysts—saw in this men's mass movement almost anything, or at least whatever they wanted to see. Apologists regarded it as a religious revival, a moment of racial healing, and an important movement reminding men of their God-given responsibilities. Detractors saw Promise Keepers as frontal assault on homosexuality and feminism and as a tool of the Religious Right. Historians saw precedents in the ritual tradition of ancient Israel, in the religious awakenings of the eighteenth and nineteenth centuries, and in the camp meetings of the antebellum frontier. Marxists pointed to the movement's appeal to middle-class sensibilities and its commercialism, as evident in T-shirts, audiocassettes, books, and trinkets. Politically minded analysts identified Promise Keepers as yet another front in the so-called culture wars of the 1990s. Cultural historians cited precedents in fraternal orders, such as the Masons or the Elks Club, with the stadium replacing lodge rooms as a place to reaffirm one's masculinity.

Amid all the analysis, the detractors generally failed to notice that McCartney was delivering a message that few others dared to articulate. In an era of rampant divorce, phsical abuse of spouses (as illustrated in the O. J. Simpson case), and general male irresponsibility, McCartney enjoined men to be responsible husbands, fathers, and churchgoers. Although Promise Keepers offended feminists with its patriarchalism (men were told to return home and take charge of their households), it sought to mollify women by emphasizing the soft-breasted male, a man who was not afraid to admit his mistakes, to show his vulnerability, even to cry.

As with most eruptions of religious enthusiasm and as with previous incarnations of muscular Christianity, Promise Keepers faded almost as quickly as it had arisen. Within months of the Stand in the Gap rally, Promise Keepers announced that it would lay off most of its staff and rely on volunteer labor, although a modest infusion of contributions kept the organization alive, if only on life support.

With the approach of the year 2000 Americans were infected with millennial fever. An automobile company named one of its models Millenia, and a hotel in lower Manhattan took the name "Millenium" (although it is worth pointing out that both versions were misspelled: *millennium* has a double *n*). Lubavitch Hasidic Jews, those who practiced a strict form of Orthodoxy, believed that their rebbe, Menachem Schneerson, was the long-awaited messiah foretold by the Hebrew prophets, and his death in 1994 did little to dampen their ardor.

Many evangelical Christians, long preoccupied with the end of time because of their literal interpretation of the book of Revelation, detected a confluence between the calendar and their expectations of the return of Jesus. Most, however, were loath to make specific predictions because such claims in the past had proved false. In the early 1840s, for example, a farmer and biblical interpreter from Low Hampton, New York, calculated that Jesus would return sometime in 1843 or 1844. William Miller tirelessly publicized his predictions, and by the time the deadline arrived, October 22, 1844, more than 50,000 people had expressed sympathy for his teachings; so frenzied was some of the rhetoric about the imminent Second Coming that Horace Greeley felt obliged to publish a special edition of the *New York Tribune* to refute Miller's teachings.

Other religious groups in American history have fashioned their beliefs around the conviction that human history would soon come to an end. Joseph Smith taught (and Mormons still believe) that the center stake of Zion, the heavenly city, will be in Jackson County, Missouri. On Good Friday, 1878, Charles Taze Russell and a handful of his followers gathered on the Sixth Street Bridge in Pittsburgh to await their ascension into heaven; Russell's present-day followers, the Jehovah's Witnesses, still carry the message of apocalyptic judgment throughout the world.

Evocations of the end of time permeated countless sermons, motion pictures, and books. Billy Graham, for instance, often talked about the return of Jesus, and he wrote several books about the apocalypse predicted in the Bible. With the approach of 2000 and the turn of the millennium, moreover, speculation about the apocalypse reached a fever pitch. Clyde Lott, a fundamentalist and a cattle breeder from Mississippi, undertook a project to breed a Red Angus that would be available for the restoration of animal sacrifice when the Jewish Temple was rebuilt in Jerusalem. Such an animal would conform to the specifications spelled out in the book of Numbers in the Hebrew Bible: "Speak unto the children of Israel," the Lord said, "that they bring thee a red heifer without spot, wherein is no blemish, and upon which never came a yoke." The rebuilding of the Temple, of course, might indeed bring on the end of the world because the Temple Mount in Jerusalem already had a tenant, the Islamic Dome of the Rock, and any move by American fundamentalists or Jewish zealots to raze the Muslim holy place to make room for the Jewish Temple would certainly provoke a cataclysmic response.

Some evangelicals at the end of the second millennium even speculated about the identity of the Antichrist, a charismatic, devious person, according to the book of Revelation, who will lead many away from the truth. While Protestant speculation through the centuries had often centered on the pope (because of anti-Catholic bias), evangelicals in the twentieth century also suggested other candidates, ranging from Adolf Hitler to Mikhail Gorbachev to Ronald Wilson Reagan, who had six letters in each of his three names, corresponding to 666, the Mark of the Beast. In a missive widely distributed over the internet, someone asserted that if you convert the letters of his name to ASCII numbers, Bill Gates (3rd) totals 666. The posting also included the corroborating information that Windows 95, when parsed into ASCII numbers, also equals 666.

The mention of Gates, head of Microsoft and the world's wealthiest man, suggests another reason for anxiety as the year 2000 approached. The so-called Y2K computer bug, caused by the inability of the internal clocks in some computers to recognize the digits 00 as the year 2000 rather than 1900, led many Americans to fear all manner of calamities (including the loss of their retirement savings) at the stroke of midnight, December 31, 1999. Many became survivalists, buying generators and stockpiling provisions, even relocating to the wilderness, while others suggested that the Y2K crisis might be part of a larger apocalypse that would unfold at the turn of the millennium, thereby fulfilling biblical prophecies about the end of time.

As Americans faced a new millennium they could look back on a century full of contradictions. The 1900s witnessed the granting of legal equality to all Americans, regardless of religion, skin color, gender, or sexual orientation, even though the reality often fell short of that ideal. While some Americans finally attained full rights of citizenship, through the Civil Rights Act of 1964, for example, the twentieth century was arguably the genocidal century—two world wars, the

Holocaust, the dropping of the atomic bomb on Hiroshima, persistent ethnic conflict in Northern Ireland, the Middle East, and Bosnia—all providing ample evidence of human depravity. The technological revolution transported Americans from horse-and-buggy days to space travel, with several stops on the moon, but technology also proved destructive and unreliable, witness the environmental threat of industrialization and the *Challenger* disaster of 1986.

During the first year of the new millennium the frightful mix of depravity and technology came eerily to light on a crystalline September day when hijackers slammed passenger jets, gorged with fuel, into the Pentagon and into the twin towers of the World Trade Center in New York City. Americans rallied with relief efforts, many of them organized by religious groups. When it emerged that the hijackers were Arab extremists, many Arab Americans were subjected to prejudice and even violence, although other Muslims were quick to argue that the terrorists had betrayed the tenets of Islam. In the ensuing months, "September 11" or "9/11" became synonymous with fear and anger and determination, as Americans sought to understand the catastrophe. While some reasserted the familiar "America first" bravado, others began to consider America's place in a world of diverse cultures and non-Western sensibilities. Still others recognized that these cultures and sensibilities had become part of the United States itself, and if Americans meant to live peaceably with the rest of the world, they had better learn to understand their neighbors—their customs, their traditions, their forms of worship.

In the wake of 9/11, the people of the United States received expressions of sympathy and solidarity from the nations and peoples of the world. Many Americans, understandably, were consumed with a kind of blood lust against those who had perpetrated the attacks. President George W. Bush insisted that Saddam Hussein, the dictator of Iraq and the man responsible for all sorts of horrific acts against his own people, also shared responsibility for the terrorist attacks in New York and Washington. Though there was scant evidence to substantiate his claims, Bush also alleged that Iraq was developing nuclear weapons and that Hussein possessed weapons of mass destruction that represented an imminent threat to the United States.

Despite protests from the world community and from many religious groups in America, Bush, who claimed to be an evangelical Christian, dispatched American troops to Iraq, thereby brushing aside centuries of Christian thought on what constitutes a "just war." The invasion of Iraq toppled Hussein, but it also claimed thousands of casualties, including numberless civilians. As the war unfolded, it became clear that the U.S. government, in violation of the Geneva Conventions, engaged in the torture of political prisoners, either directly in places like Guantánamo Bay, Cuba, or indirectly by handing detainees over to third countries not averse to torture, a cynical policy called "extraordinary rendition."

Bush's management of the war, however, elicited nary a criticism from the leaders of the Religious Right, those who decades earlier had appointed themselves the arbiters of morality. They refused to call the justice of the war into question and even registered their support for the Bush administration's policies on torture. They preferred to focus their attention on such matters as the legality of same-sex unions, an issue that Bush and his operatives shrewdly used to their advantage in the election in 2004.

Bush rewarded his religious supporters with a program of so-called faith-based initiatives, which provided taxpayer funds for the administration of social services by religious organizations. Although this initiative never received even close

424

to the level of funding that Bush had promised, it represented a compromise of the separation of church and state mandated by the First Amendment to the Constitution: "Congress shall make no law concerning an establishment of religion or prohibiting the free exercise thereof."

In decades and centuries past, Americans could have relied on Baptists to patrol what the founder of the Baptist tradition in America, Roger Williams, called the "wall of separation" between church and state. Williams, a Puritan minister in Salem, Massachusetts, recognized the dangers to the integrity of the faith if it were to be identified too closely with the state. He wanted to protect what he called the "garden of the church" from the "wilderness of the world" by means of a "wall of separation." The Puritans, intent on constructing a theocracy in which church and state were coterminous, did not much care for Williams's ideas and expelled him from the colony. Williams decamped to Rhode Island, where he implemented his ideas about liberty of individual conscience and the separation of church and state. The founding fathers of the new nation enshrined these principles in the First Amendment, and throughout American history, from Williams and Isaac Backus and John Leland in the eighteenth century to George Washington Truett in the twentieth, Baptists have vigorously defended the separation of church and state.

Many Baptists began to retreat from their own heritage in the late 1970s, however, coincident with the conservative takeover of the Southern Baptist Convention and the rise of the Religious Right. They began to advocate public prayers in public schools, the use of taxpayer funds to support religious schools, and the posting of religious symbols and creeds in public places. In 2001 Roy S. Moore, chief justice of the Alabama Supreme Court, installed a 5,280-pound granite monument emblazoned with the Ten Commandments in the lobby of the Alabama

Judicial Building in Montgomery. Because Moore, who claimed to be a Baptist, had resisted all entreaties to represent other religious groups alongside of what he called the "Judeo-Christian tradition," the monument, which quickly became known as "Roy's Rock," clearly violated the establishment clause of the First Amendment. After Judge Myron Thompson issued his ruling to that effect, and as workers were preparing to remove the monument, one of the assembled protesters screamed, "Get your hands off my God!" Apparently, this poor soul had not considered the fact that one of the commandments etched into the side of that granite monument had something to say about the dangers of graven images.

After a lengthy review, Moore was dismissed from the Alabama Supreme Court for judicial misconduct, specifically for failing to obey a court order to remove the monument, whereupon he tried hard to make himself into a martyr for the Religious Right. Moore toured the country, addressing audiences of politically conservative evangelicals, and he ran for the Republican nomination for governor in 2006. Moore lost the Republican primary, however, to another evangelical, the incumbent governor. The saga of Roy's Rock admits many interpretations, but one lesson is that it attests to the resiliency of the Constitution and Americans' historic commitment to pluralism, even in the face of rapid and sometimes unsettling changes in American society.

The one constant, however, amid massive cultural changes, is that Americans remain incurably religious, however variously they define their religious lives, be it Protestant or Hindu, Jewish or New Age, Mormon, Buddhist, or Roman Catholic—or some wildly eclectic combination. Despite industrialization, modernization, even secularization, Americans clung stubbornly to religion and spirituality. This was the legacy they carried into the twenty-first century.

In 1906 the U.S. Forest Service seized Blue Lake, a sacred site for the Taos Pueblos of northern New Mexico, to include it in Kit Carson National Forest. After decades of fighting to reverse the action, which they considered an infringement on their religious freedom, a delegation of Taos Pueblos appeared before Congress in 1970 to make their case for returning the watershed to the Pueblos. The following year Congress restored the Taos Blue Lake region to the Pueblos. Taos Pueblos testified the following before Congress.

The entire watershed is permeated with holy places and shrines used regularly by our Indian people; there is no place that does not have religious significance to us. Each of the peaks or valleys, or lakes, springs, and streams has a time in our religious calendar when homage in one form or another must be given, or plants that we have studied and used for centuries gathered, or rituals performed. Our religious leaders and societies go regularly to perform these duties in accordance with this yearly calendar throughout the area. They also supervise, for a period of 18 months, the preparation of our sons for manhood....

Taos Pueblo has used and occupied the watersheds of the Rio Pueblo and Rio Lucero for 700 years or more. We have always practiced conservation of those watersheds; they yield clear water today because of our long-standing care. Today it is more important than ever that the natural conditions of those watersheds be preserved as the source of pure water in those streams.

Mario Cuomo, a devout Roman Catholic and governor of New York from 1983 to 1995, was an eloquent spokesman for the Democratic Party and for his faith, even though his generally liberal political views, especially on birth control and abortion, sometimes placed him at odds with more conservative Catholic bishops. On September 13, 1984, during the heat of the presidential campaign and during the height of the influence of the Religious Right, Cuomo spoke at the University of Notre Dame about the reponsibilities of an elected official in a pluralistic society.

[T]he Catholic who holds political office in a pluralistic democracy—who is elected to serve Jews and Moslems, atheists and Protestants, as well as Catholics—bears special responsibility. He or she undertakes to help create conditions under which *all* can live with a maximum of dignity and with a reasonable degree of freedom; where everyone who chooses may hold beliefs different from specifically Catholic ones—sometimes contradictory to them; where the laws protect people's right to divorce, to use birth control, and even to choose an abortion.

In fact, Catholic public officials take an oath to preserve the Constitution that guarantees this freedom. And they do so gladly. Not because they love what others do with their freedom, but because they realize that in guaranteeing freedom for all, they guarantee *our* right to be Catholics; *our* right to pray, to use the sacraments, to refuse birth control devices, to reject abortion, not to divorce and remarry if we believe it to be wrong.

The Catholic public official lives the political truth most Catholics, throughout most of American history, have accepted and insisted on: the truth that to assure our freedom we must allow others the same freedom, even if occasionally it produces conduct by them that we would hold to be sinful.

I protect my right to be a Catholic by preserving your right to believe as a Jew, a Protestant, a nonbeliever, or an anything else you choose. We know that the price of seeking to force our beliefs on others is that they might someday force theirs on us. This freedom is the fundamental strength of our unique experiment in government.

EPILOGUE

A t the beginning of the twenty-first century, religion in the United States seems to hold more questions than answers. If visitors from a distant country should first arrive in Washington, D.C., they might notice the words "In God We Trust" on the currency and the walls of some public buildings. But if they should hear an argument at the Supreme Court, watch a session of Congress, or observe the classical Greek influence on Washington's official architecture, they might form an impression that the United States is a wholly secular nation, with only superficial references to God in American public culture and perhaps equally few in Americans' private lives as well.

If the visitors should go on to view the immense, brooding statue of President Lincoln at the temple-like Lincoln Memorial, or the eternal flame burning at the tomb of President Kennedy, they might wonder if Americans venerated their dead leaders, much as the ancient Romans did.

And if the travelers should venture north to New York City, visit a board meeting at a Wall Street investment firm bent on maximizing profits, find themselves tossed about in Manhattan's Times Square by tourists seeking cheap souvenirs and limitless entertainment, or caught with angry commuters on a Queens subway stalled during a New York heat wave, they might conclude that venerable notions about the divine ordering of human affairs have been lost somewhere along the way. Passing by seedy bars and strip joints in Manhattan and later in other American cities and towns, the visitors might think that Americans mindlessly pursue immediate and surely irreligious pleasures that reject the seemingly strict morals of their more religious ancestors.

Yet in Manhattan, as well as in Cincinnati or St. Louis, the visitors also would encounter richly ornamented, well-attended synagogues of great beauty. In Milwaukee they would confront a skyline filled with the soaring steeples of Lutheran, Catholic, and Orthodox churches. Heading south, they would discover countless Baptist meeting houses marking the crossroads of just as many country roads. Moving west toward Salt Lake City, the travelers would see Mormon assembly halls jammed with well-scrubbed worshipers. Los Angeles in turn would present a spectacle of Pentecostal megachurches, gleaming with glass and steel, complemented by an ever-growing number of Buddhist temples tucked away on palm-lined streets.

In chain bookstores, they would find whole sections of religious books, not only by ministers, priests, and rabbis, but by spiritual writers fashioning new "traditions" or seeking to merge old ones. In Manhattan's Central Park, California's Yosemite, and in thousands of homes in between, they would find Americans following highly individualized religious inclinations that, at best, they share with just a few friends and neighbors.

Many of the visitors might scratch their heads. Which is the real America? The America that seems entirely secular? Or the many Americas that glow with treasured memories and sacred symbols? Clearly, one can make a case for either or both, depending on when and where one looks. Americans, like so many other humans, tend to busy themselves with the ordinary affairs through most of the day and seek the solace of faith as the morning dawns or the sun sets.

In all these respects, the early twenty-first century is not so different from the nineteenth or even the eighteenth or the seventeenth centuries. In none of these periods does religion occupy the attention of men and women all the time, or perhaps even most of the time. Americans have always ordered their lives around the challenges of making a living, rearing children, getting along with neighbors, and pursuing the simple (and sometimes not so simple) pleasures of life.

But Americans also demonstrate a remarkably common penchant to reflect on the meaning of their lives, individually and together. In a nation whose founders explicitly rejected any formal state religion, they mark the passage of time with symbols and ceremonies. They set apart holy sites for the worship of God, using many different forms. They measure their days by ethical standards derived from ancient scriptures, time-honored traditions, or fresh theologies that offer new light in new times. They check newspaper horoscopes and log pilgrimages to Salt Lake City or Santa Fe. And through prayer they make the fragile, flickering candle of life burn a bit brighter.

To be sure, in each century, religion bears its own distinctive features. But viewed from afar, each century also represents a single episode in the long drama of human aspiration, here played out on the vast stages of the North American continent. In America, men and women create and refresh astonishingly different means to comprehend themselves, each other, and their relationships to the divine. Their ability to sustain those engagements and to protect the right of others with similar missions— not perfectly amidst far too many resorts to bigotry, arrogance, and indifference—accounts not only for the uniqueness of religion in American life, but for the uniqueness of America.

CHRONOLOGY

1969

James Forman issues a "Black Manifesto" to the National Council of Churches demanding reparations for slavery

1970

An act of Congress returns the sacred Blue Lake to the Taos Pueblos

1971

In *Green v. Connally*, a federal court upholds the Internal Revenue Service's revocation of the tax-exempt status of any organization that engages in racial discrimination, including religious schools; this action becomes the catalyst for the rise of the Religious Right in the late 1970s

1972

Sally Priesand, a Reform Jew, becomes the first woman ordained as a rabbi

1973

The U.S. Supreme Court, in its landmark *Roe v. Wade* decision, strikes down laws banning abortion; "pro-life" Catholics denounce the decision, while many conservative Baptist leaders applaud it as marking a clear delineation between personal morality and public policy
A band of Native Americans occupies Wounded Knee, South Dakota, site of the massacre of Sioux by federal troops in 1890, to call attention to the plight of American Indians
Tenzin Gyatso, the fourteenth Dalai Lama, makes his first of many visits to the West; he becomes a kind of goodwill ambassador for Tibetan Buddhism

1974

    Chogyam Trungpa, a Tibetan Buddhist monk, establishes the Naropa Institute (now Naropa University) in Boulder, Colorado, which becomes the first accredited Buddhist-inspired liberal arts college in America

    Eleven female deacons are ordained to the Episcopal priesthood in Philadelphia on July 29

1976

    Jimmy Carter, a "born-again" evangelical Christian and former Democratic governor of Georgia, wins election to the presidency

1978

    Spencer W. Kimball, president of the Church of Jesus Christ of Latter-day Saints, announces on June 9 that men of color can enter the Mormon priesthood

    On November 18, members of the Peoples Temple obey their leader's instruction to commit mass suicide in Jonestown, Guyana

1979

    Jerry Falwell founds Moral Majority, a political organization intended to bring politically conservative evangelicals into the political process

    Conservatives (also known as fundamentalists) succeed in electing Adrian Rogers president of the Southern Baptist Convention, initiating what becomes a "takeover" of the denomination

1980

    Three candidates for president—Jimmy Carter, John B. Anderson, and Ronald Reagan—all claim to be evangelical Christians; the Religious Right throws its support to Reagan, helping to secure his election (as well as his reelection four years later)

    Pope John Paul II beatifies Kateri Tekakwitha

1985

    At the meeting of its general synod in Ames, Iowa, the United Church of Christ adopts a resolution calling its congregations to designate themselves as "open and affirming" to everyone, especially to "lesbian, gay, and bisexual people"

1986

    Elie Wiesel, Holocaust survivor whose life is dedicated to writing and speaking about the Holocaust, wins the Nobel Peace Prize

1987

A New Age "harmonic convergence" at sacred sites from New York to California takes place in August

Televangelist Pat Robertson, one of the leaders of the Religious Right, mounts a campaign for the Republican presidential nomination

1988

Pope John Paul II beatifies Junípero Serra

1989

Pat Robertson and Ralph Reed collaborate to form the Christian Coalition, a lobby group for politically conservative evangelicals

1993

Federal officials attack the Branch Davidian compound outside of Waco, Texas, on April 19, in which most of the inhabitants were killed

World's Parliament of Religions, a centennial observance of the first Parliament, meets in Chicago

President Bill Clinton signs the Religious Freedom Restoration Act

1994

Rebbe Menachem Schneerson, leader of the Lubavitcher group of Hasidic Jews, dies; most of his followers consider him to be the messiah, and some continue to look for his resurrection

1997

Promise Keepers, an organization of evangelical men, hold their "Stand in the Gap" rally in Washington, D.C., on October 4

1999

Popular fears about the Y2K "computer bug" and terrorism combine with apocalyptic predictions as December 31 approaches; the transition from 1999 to 2000 takes place virtually without a hitch

2001

Attack on the Pentagon and the World Trade Center mobilizes relief efforts, many by religious organizations

National Conference of Catholic Bishops requires theology professors at Catholic colleges and universities to obtain certification that they teach "authentic Catholic doctrine."

2002

Pope John Paul II canonizes Juan Diego at the shrine of Our Lady of Guadalupe in Mexico

United States Conference of Catholic Bishops establishes the National Review Board to develop policy on the sexual abuse crisis

Rick Warren publishes *The Purpose-Driven Life: What on Earth Am I Here For?* which sells 11 million copies

2003

The Episcopalian House of Bishops confirms Rev. Gene Robinson as the church's first openly gay bishop, creating a firestorm of protest and controversy within the Episcopal Church and the worldwide Anglican Communion.

2005

Evangelist Billy Graham conducts the final evangelistic "crusade" of his storied career, in Flushing, New York

Kansas State School Board endorses "intelligent design" in teaching science, which a newly elected board repeals in 2007

2006

Bishop Katharine Jefferts Schori becomes the first woman to head the Episcopal Church

2007

Keith Ellison, Democrat of Minnesota and the first Muslim ever elected to Congress, takes the ceremonial oath of office on a Qur'an once owned by Thomas Jefferson

FURTHER READING

GENERAL READING ON RELIGION IN THE UNITED
STATES

Ahlstrom, Sydney. *A Religious History of the American People*. 2nd ed. New Haven: Yale University Press, 2004.

Bays, Daniel H., and Grant Wacker, eds. *The Foreign Missionary Enterprise at Home: Explorations in North American Cultural History*. Tuscaloosa: University of Alabama Press, 2003.

Bednarowski, Mary Farrell. *The Religious Imagination of American Women*. Bloomington: Indiana University Press, 1999.

Butler, Jon. *Awash in a Sea of Faith: Christianizing the American People*. Cambridge, Mass.: Harvard University Press, 1990.

Butler, Jon, and Harry S. Stout, eds. *Religion in American History: A Reader*. New York: Oxford University Press, 1997.

Cherry, Conrad, ed. *God's New Israel* Rev. ed. Chapel Hill: University of North Carolina Press, 1995.

Gaustad, Edwin Scott, and Philip L. Barlow. *New Historical Atlas of Religion in America*. New York: Oxford University Press, 2000.

Gaustad, Edwin, ed. *Memoirs of the Spirit*. Grand Rapids, Mich.: Eerdmans, 1999.

——. *A Documentary History of Religion in America*. 2 vols. 2nd ed. Grand Rapids, Mich.: Eerdmans, 1993.

Gaustad, Edwin S., and Leigh E. Schmidt. *The Religion History of America*. Rev. ed. San Francisco: HarperSanFrancisco, 2002.

Gutjahr, Paul C. *An American Bible: The History of the Good Book in the United States, 1777–1880*. Stanford, Calif.: Stanford University Press, 1999.

Hill, Samuel S. *Encyclopedia of Religion in the South*. Macon, Ga.: Mercer University Press, 1984.

——. *Varieties of Southern Religious Experience*. Baton Rouge: Louisiana State University Press, 1988.

Holifield, E. Brooks. *A History of Pastoral Care in America: From Salvation to Self-Realization*. Nashville: Abingdon Press, 1983.

Kuklick, Bruce. *Churchmen and Philosophers: From Jonathan Edwards to John Dewey*. New Haven: Yale University Press, 1984.

Lindley, Susan Hill. *You Have Stept Out of Your Place: A History of Women and Religion in America*. Louisville, Ky.: Westminster John Knox, 1996.

Lippy, Charles H. *Being Religious, American Style*. Westport, Conn.: Greenwood, 1994.

Lippy, Charles H., Robert Choquette, and Stafford Poole. *Christianity Comes to the Americas, 1492–1776*. New York: Paragon House, 1992.

Marty, Martin. *Pilgrims in Their Own Land: 500 Years of Religion in America*. New York: Penguin, 1985.

McDannell, Colleen. *Material Christianity: Religion and Popular Culture in America*. New Haven: Yale University Press, 1995.

Mead, Sidney E. *The Lively Experiment*. New York: Harper and Row, 1963.

Miller, Perry. *Errand into the Wilderness*. Cambridge, Mass.: Harvard University Press, 1956.

Moore, R. Laurence. *Religious Outsiders and the Making of Americans*. New York: Oxford University Press, 1986.

——. *Selling God: American Religious in the Marketplace of Culture*. New York: Oxford University Press, 1994.

Morgan, David, and Sally Promey, eds. *The Visual Culture of American Religions*. Berkeley: University of California Press, 2001.

Mullin, R. Bruce. *Miracles and the Modern Religious Imagination*. New Haven: Yale University Press, 1996.

Niebuhr, H. Richard. *The Social Sources of Denominationalism*. New York: Meridian Books, 1957.

Noll, Mark A. *The Old Religion in a New World: The History of North American Christianity*. Grand Rapids, Mich.: Eerdmans, 2002.

Robert, Dana. *American Women in Mission*. Macon, Ga.: Mercer University Press, 1996.

Roof, Wade Clark, and William McKinney. *American Mainline Religion: Its Changing Shape and Future*. New Brunswick, N. J.: Rutgers University Press, 1987.

Sarna, Jonathan D., ed. *Minority Faiths and the American Protestant Mainstream*. Urbana: University of Illinois Press, 1997.

Tarasar, Constance, J., ed. *Orthodox America, 1794–1976*. Syosset, N.Y.: Orthodox Church in America, 1975.

Taves, Ann. *Fits, Trances, and Visions: Experiencing Religion and Explaining Experience from Wesley to James*. Princeton, N. J.: Princeton University Press, 1999.

Turner, James. *Without God, Without Creed: The Origins of Unbelief in America*. Baltimore; Johns Hopkins University Press, 1985.

White, James F. *Christain Worship in North America*. Collegeville, Minn.: Liturgical Press, 1997.

Williams, Peter W. *Houses of God: Region, Religion, and Architecture in the United States*. Urbana: University of Illinois Press, 1997.

Wilson, John F., and Donald L. Drakeman, eds. *Church and State in American History*. 2nd ed. Boston: Beacon, 1987.

RELIGIOUS TRADITIONS AND MOVEMENTS IN EARLY
MODERN EUROPE AND COLONIAL AMERICA

Albanese, Catherine L. *Sons of the Fathers: The Civil Religion of the American Revolution*. Philadelphia: Temple University Press, 1976.

Andrews, Dee E. *The Methodists and Revolutionary America, 1760–1800: The Shaping of an Evangelical Culture*. Princeton, N. J.: Princeton University Press, 2000.

Axtel, James. *The Invasion Within: The Conquest of Cultures in Colonial North America*. New York: Oxford University Press, 1985.

Bailyn, Bernard. "Religion and Revolution: Three Biographical Studies." *Perspectives in American History* 4 (1970): 85–169.

Balmer, Randall. *A Perfect Babel of Confusion; Dutch Religion and English Culture in the Middle Colonies.* New York: Oxford University Press, 1989.

Bloch, Ruth H. *Visionary Republic; Millennial Themes in American Thought, 1756–1800.* New York: Cambridge University Press, 1985.

Boles, John. *The Great Revival; 1787–1805.* Rev. ed. Lexington: University Press of Kentucky, 1996.

Bonomi, Patricia U. *Under the Cope of Heaven: Religion, Society, and Politics in Colonial America.* New York: Oxford University Press, 1986.

Bosher, J. F. *Business and Religion in the Age of New France, 1600–1760: Twenty-two Studies.* Toronto: Canadian Scholars Press, 1994.

Bossy, John. *Christianity in the West, 1400–1700.* New York: Oxford University Press, 1985.

Brekus, Catherine A. *Strangers and Pilgrims: Female Preaching in America, 1740–1845.* Chapel Hill: University of North Carolina Press, 1998.

Buckley, Thomas E., S.J. *Church and State in Revolutionary Virginia, 1776–1787.* Charlottesville: University Press of Virginia, 1977.

Bushman, Richard L. *From Puritan to Yankee: Character and the Social Order in Connecticut, 1690–1765.* Cambridge, Mass.: Harvard University Press, 1967.

Butler, Jon. *Awash in a Sea of Faith: Christianizing the American People.* Cambridge, Mass.: Harvard University Press, 1990.

——. *The Huguenots in America: A Refugee People in New World Society.* Cambridge, Mass.: Harvard University Press, 1983.

Christian, William A., Jr. *Local Religion in Sixteenth-Century Spain.* Princenton, N.J.: Princeton University Press, 1981.

Coalter, Milton J., Jr. *Gilbert Tennent, Son of Thunder: A Case Study of Continental Pietism's Impact on the First Great Awakening in the Middle Colonies*. New York: Greenwood, 1986.

Crawford, Patricia. *Women and Religion in England, 1500–1750*. New York: Routledge, 1996.

Curry, Thomas J. *The First Freedoms: Church and State in America to the Passage of the First Amendment*. New York: Oxford University Press, 1986.

De Jong, Gerald F. *The Dutch Reformed Church in the American Colonies*. Grand Rapids, Mich.: Eerdmans, 1978.

Demos, John Putnam. *Entertaining Satan: Witchcraft and the Culture of Early New England*. New York: Oxford University Press, 1982.

——. *The Unredeemed Captive: A Family Story from Early America*. New York: Knopf, 1994.

Dunn, Mary Maples. *William Penn: Politics and Conscience*. Princeton, N.J.: Princeton University Press, 1967.

Eire, Carlos M. N. *From Madrid to Purgatory: The Art and Craft of Dying in Sixteenth-Century Spain*. New York: Cambridge University Press, 1995.

Ellis, John Tracey. *Catholics in Colonial America*. Baltimore: Helicon, 1965.

Faber, Eli. *A Time for Planting: The First Migration, 1654–1820*. Baltimore: Johns Hopkins University Press, 1992.

Fiering, Norman. *Jonathan Edwards's Moral Thought and Its British Context*. Chapel Hill: University of North Carolina Press, 1981.

Frey, Sylvia R. *Water from the Rock: Black Resistance in a Revolutionary Age*. Princeton, N.J.: Princeton University Press, 1991.

Gaustad, Edwin Scott. *Faith of Our Fathers: Religion and the New Nation*. San Francisco: Harper & Row, 1987.

——. *The Great Awakening in New England*. New York: Harper & Row, 1957.

Ginzburg, Carlo. *The Cheese and the Worms: The Cosmos of a Sixteenth-Century Miller.* Trans. John and Anne Tedeschi. Baltimore: Johns Hopkins University Press, 1992.

Goen, C. C. *Revivalism and Separatism in New England, 1740–1800: Strict Congregationalists and Separate Baptists in the Great Awakening.* New Haven: Yale University Press, 1962.

Gollin, Gillian Lindt. *Moravians in Two Worlds: A Study of Changing Communities.* New York: Columbia University Press, 1967.

Goodfriend, Joyce D. *Before the Melting Pot: Society and Culture in Colonial New York City, 1664–1730.* Princeton, N.J.: Princeton University Press, 1991.

Gutiérrez, Ramón A. *When Jesus Came, the Corn Mothers Went Away: Marriage, Sexuality, and Power in New Mexico, 1500–1846.* Stanford, Calif.: Stanford University Press, 1991.

Hall, David D. *The Faithful Shepherd: A History of the New England Ministry in the Seventeenth Century.* Chapel Hill: University of North Carolina Press for the Institute of Early American History and Culture, 1972.

——. *Worlds of Wonder, Days of Judgment: Popular Religious Belief in Early New England.* New York: Knopf, 1989.

Hall, Timothy D. *Contested Boundaries: Itinerancy and the Reshaping of the Colonial American Religious World.* Durham, N.C.: Duke University Press, 1994.

Heimert, Alan. *Religion and the American Mind: From the Great Awakening to the Revolution.* Cambridge, Mass.: Harvard University Press, 1966.

Holifield, E. Brooks. *Theology in America: Christian Thought from the Age of the Puritans to the Civil War.* New Haven: Yale University Press, 2003.

Hutchison, William, R. *Religious Pluralism in America: The Contentious History of a Founding Ideal.* New Haven: Yale University Press, 2003.

Hutson, James, ed. *Religion and the New Republic.* Totowa, N.J.: Rowman and Littlefield, 1999.

Isaac, Rhys. *The Transformation of Virginia, 1740–1790*. Chapel Hill: University of North Carolina Press, 1982.

Juster, Susan. *Disorderly Women: Sexual Politics and Evangelicalism in Revolutionary New England*. Ithaca, N.Y.: Cornell University Press, 1994.

Lambert, Frank. *Inventing the "Great Awakening."* Princeton, N.J.: Princeton University Press, 1999.

Landsman, Ned. *Scotland and Its First American Colony, 1683–1765*. Princeton, N.J.: Princeton University Press, 1985.

Levy, Barry. *Quakers and the American Family: British Settlement in the Delaware Valley*. New York: Oxford University Press, 1988.

Marietta, Jack D. *The Reformation of American Quakerism, 1748–1783*. Philadelphia: University of Pennsylvania Press, 1984.

Marini, Stephen A. *Radical Sects of Revolutionary New England*. Cambridge, Mass.: Harvard University Press, 1982.

Middlekauff, Robert. *The Mathers: Three Generations of Puritan Intellectuals, 1596–1728*. New York: Oxford University Press, 1971.

Miller, Perry. *Errand into the Wilderness*. Cambridge, Mass.: Harvard University Press, 1956.

———. *The New England Mind: From Colony to Province*. Cambridge, Mass.: Harvard University Press, 1953.

———. *The New England Mind: The Seventeenth Century*. Cambridge, Mass.: Harvard University Press, 1954.

Morgan, Edmund S. *The Puritan Dilemma: The Story of John Winthrop*. Boston: Little, Brown, 1958.

Nelson, John K. *A Blessed Company: Parishes, Parsons, and Parishioners in Anglican Virginia, 1690–1776*. Chapel Hill: University of North Carolina Press, 2001.

Noll, Mark A. *America's God: From Jonathan Edwards to Abraham Lincoln*. New York: Oxford University Press, 2002.

———. *Christians in the American Revolution*. Grand Rapids, Mich.: Christian University Press, 1977.

Ozment, Steven E. *The Age of Reform 1250–1550: An Intellectual and Religious History of Late Medieval and Reformation Europe*. New Haven: Yale University Press, 1980.

——. *Protestants: The Birth of a Revolution*. New York: Doubleday, 1992.

Reff, Daniel T. *Plagues, Priests, and Demons: Sacred Narratives and the Rise of Christianity in the Old World and the New*. New York: Cambridge University Press, 2005.

Rhoden, Nancy L. *Revolutionary Anglicanism: The Colonial Church of England Clergy During the American Revolution*. New York: New York University Press, 1999.

Richey, Russell E. *Early American Methodism*. Bloomington: Indiana University Press, 1991.

Riforgiato, Leonard R. *Missionary of Moderation: Henry Melchior Muhlenberg and the Lutheran Church in English America*. Lewisburg, Pa: Bucknell University Press, 1980.

Roeber, A. G. *Palatines, Liberty and Property: German Lutherans in British North America*. Baltimore: Johns Hopkins University Press, 1993.

Rutman, Darrett B. *Winthrop's Boston: Portrait of a Puritan Town, 1630–1649*. Chapel Hill: University of North Carolina Press, 1965.

Schmidt, Leigh Eric. *Hearing Things: Religion, Illusion, and the American Enlightenment*. Cambridge: Harvard University Press, 2000.

——. *Holy Fairs: Scottish Communions and American Revivals in the Early Modern Period*. Princeton, N.J.: Princeton University Press, 1989.

Schwartz, Sally. *A Mixed Multitude: The Struggle for Toleration in Colonial Pennsylvania*. New York: New York University Press, 1987.

Sheridan, Thomas E., ed. *The Franciscan Missions of Northern Mexico*. New York: Garland, 1991.

Simpson, Patricia. *Marguerite Bourgeoys and the Congregation of Notre-Dame, 1665–1700*. Montreal: McGill-Queen's University Press, 2005.

Stein, Stephen J. *The Shaker Experience in America: A History of the United Society of Believers*. New Haven: Yale University Press, 1992.

Stout, Harry S. *The Divine Dramatist: George Whitefield and the Rise of Modern Evangelicalism*. Grand Rapids, Mich.: Eerdmans, 1991.

———. *The New England Soul: Preaching and Religious Culture in Colonial New England*. New York: Oxford University Press, 1986.

Thomas, Keith. *Religion and the Decline of Magic*. New York: Scribners, 1971.

Thornton, John. *Africa and Africans in the Making of the Atlantic World, 1400–1680*. New York: Cambridge University Press, 1992.

Tolles, Frederick B. *Meeting House and Counting House: The Quaker Merchants of Colonial Philadelphia, 1682–1763*. Chapel Hill: University of North Carolina Press, 1948.

Tracy, Patricia J. *Jonathan Edwards, Pastor: Religion and Society in Eighteenth Century Northampton*. New York: Hill and Wang, 1980.

Trinterud, Leonard J. *The Forming of an American Tradition: A Re-examination of Colonial Presbyterianism*. Philadelphia: Westminster, 1949.

Upton, Del. *Holy Things and Profane: Anglican Parish Churches in Colonial Virginia*. Cambridge, Mass.: MIT Press, 1986.

Walters, Kerry S. *Benjamin Franklin and His Gods*. Urbana: University of Illinois Press, 1999.

Westerkamp, Marilyn J. *Triumph of the Laity: Scots-Irish Piety and the Great Awakening, 1625–1760*. New York: Oxford University Press, 1988.

Woolverton, John F. *Colonial Anglicanism in North America*. Detroit: Wayne State University Press, 1984.

Ziff, Larzer. *The Career of John Cotton: Puritanism and the American Experience*. Princeton, N.J.: Princeton University Press, 1962.

AMERICAN RELIGIOUS TRADITIONS AND MOVEMENTS IN THE NINETEENTH CENTURY

Abzug, Robert H. *Cosmos Crumbling: American Reform and the Religious Imagination*. New York: Oxford University Press, 1994.

Arrington, Leonard J., and Davis Bitton. *The Mormon Experience*. 2nd ed. Urbana: University of Illinois Press, 1992.

Brekus, Catherine A. *Strangers and Pilgrims: Female Preaching in America, 1740–1845*. Chapel Hill: University of North Carolina Press, 1998.

Brereton, Virginia. *From Sin to Salvation: Stories of Women's Conversions, 1800 to the Present*. Bloomington: Indiana University Press, 1990.

Bushman, Richard Lyman, and Claudia Lauper Bushman. *Building the Kingdom: A History of Mormons in America*. New York: Oxford University Press, 2001.

Carter, Paul Allen. *The Spiritual Crisis of the Gilded Age*. DeKalb: Northern Illinois University Press, 1971.

Carwardine, Richard J. *Evangelicals and Politics in Antebellum America*. New Haven: Yale University Press, 1993.

Christiano, Kevin J. *Religious Diversity and Social Change: American Cities, 1890–1906*. New York: Cambridge University Press, 1987.

Cox, Robert S. *Body and Soul: A Sympathetic History of American Spiritualism*. Charlottesville: University of Virginia Press, 2003.

Croce, Paul Jerome. *Science and Religion in the Era of William James: Eclipse of Certainty, 1820–1880*. Chapel Hill: University of North Carolina Press, 1995.

Curry, Thomas J. *The First Freedoms: Church and State in America to the Passage of the First Amendment*. New York: Oxford University Press, 1986.

Dorrien, Gary. *The Making of American Liberal Theology: Imaging Progressive Religion, 1805–1900*. Louisville, Ky.: Westminster John Knox, 2002.

Fogarty, Robert S. *All Things New: American Communes and Utopian Movements, 1860–1914*. Chicago: University of Chicago Press, 1990.

Goen, C. C. *Broken Churches, Broken Nation: Denominational Schisms and the Coming of the American Civil War*. Macon, Ga.: Mercer University Press, 1985.

Gottschalk, Stephen. *The Emergence of Christian Science in American Religious Life*. Berkeley: University of California Press, 1973.

Guelzo, Allen. *Abraham Lincoln, Redeemer President*. Grand Rapids, Mich.: Eerdmans, 1999.

Grusfield, Joseph R. *Symbolic Crusade: Status Politics and the American Temperance Movement*. 2nd ed. Urbana: University of Illinois Press, 1986.

Hatch, Nathan O. *The Democratization of American Christianity*. New Haven: Yale University Press, 1989.

Hopkins, C. Howard. *The Rise of the Social Gospel in American Protestantism, 1865–1915*. New Haven: Yale University Press, 1940.

Johnson, Paul E. *A Shopkeeper's Millennium: Society and Revivals in Rochester, New York, 1815–1837*. New York: Hill and Wang, 1978.

Linenthal, Edward Tabor. *Sacred Ground: Americans and Their Battlefields*. Urbana: University of Illinois Press, 1991.

Maffly-Kipp, Laurie F. *Religion and Society in Frontier California*. New Haven: Yale University Press, 1994.

Mathews, Donald G. *Religion in the Old South*. Chicago: University of Chicago Press, 1977.

McDannell, Colleen. *The Christian Home in Victorian America, 1840–1900*. Bloomington: Indiana University Press, 1986.

Miller, Randall M., Harry S. Stout, and Charles Reagan Wilson, eds. *Religion and the American Civil War*. New York: Oxford University Press, 1998.

Moorhead, James H. *American Apocalypse: Yankee Protestants and the Civil War*. New Haven: Yale University Press, 1978.

Noll, Mark A. *The Civil War as a Theological Crisis*. Chapel Hill: University of North Carolina Press, 2006.

Numbers, Ronald. *Darwinism Comes to America*. Cambridge, Mass.: Harvard University Press, 1998.

Numbers, Ronald, and Jonathan M. Butler, eds. *The Disappointed: Miller and Millenarianism in the Nineteenth Century*. 2nd ed. Knoxville: University of Tennessee Press, 1987.

Schneider, Gregory. *The Way of the Cross Leads Home: The Domestication of American Methodism*. Bloomington: Indiana University Press, 1993.

Seager, Richard Hughes. *The Dawn of Religious Pluralism: Voices from the World's Parliament of Religions, 1893*. LaSalle, Ill.: Open Court, 1993.

Shattuck, Gardiner H. *A Shield and Hiding Place: The Religious Life of the Civil War Armies*. Macon, Ga.: Mercer University Press, 1987.

Shipps, Jan. *Mormonism: The Story of a New Religious Tradition*. Urbana: University of Illinois Press, 1985.

Smith, Timothy L. *Revivalism and Social Reform: American Protestantism on the Eve of the Civil War*. Nashville: Abingdon, 1957.

Stout, Harry S. *Upon the Altar of the Nation: A Moral History of the Civil War*. New York: Viking, 2006.

AMERICAN RELIGIOUS TRADITIONS AND MOVEMENTS IN THE TWENTIETH CENTURY

Alexander, Thomas G. *Mormonism in Transition: A History of the Latter-day Saints, 1890–1930*. Urbana: University of Illinois Press, 1986.

Ammerman, Nancy Tatom. *Bible Believers: Fundamentalists in the Modern World*. New Brunswick, N.J.: Rutgers University Press, 1987.

Balmer, Randall. *Thy Kingdom Come: How the Religious Right Distorts the Faith and Threatens America*. New York: Basic Books, 2006.

Bellah, Robert N. *Habits of the Heart: Individualism and Commitment in American Life*. Berkeley: University of California Press, 1985.

Boyer, Paul. *When Time Shall Be No More: Prophecy Belief in Modern American Culture*. Cambridge, Mass.: Harvard University Press, 1992.

Bruce, Steve. *Pray TV: Televangelism in America*. New York: Routledge, 1990.

Burns, Roger A. *Billy Sunday and Big-Time American Evangelism*. Urbana: University of Illinois Press, 2002.

Chidester, David. *Salvation and Suicide: An Interpretation of Jim Jones, the Peoples Temple, and Jonestown*. Bloomington: Indiana University Press, 1988.

Cox, Harvey. *Fire from Heaven: The Rise of Pentecostal Spirituality and the Reshaping of Religion in the Twenty-First Century*. Reading, Mass.: Addison-Wesley, 1995.

Gilbert, James. *Redeeming Culture: American Religion in an Age of Science*. Chicago: University of Chicago Press, 1997.

Griffith, R. Marie. *Born Again Bodies: Flesh and Spirit in American Christianity*. Berkeley: University of California Press, 2004.

Hauerwas, Stanley, William R. Herzog, and Christopher Hodge Evans, eds. *The Faith of Fifty Million: Baseball, Religion, and American Culture*. Louisville, Ky.: Westminster John Knox, 2002.

Larson, Edward J. *Summer for the Gods: The Scopes Trial and America's Continuing Debate over Science and Religion*. New York: Basic Books, 1997.

Lienesch, Michael. *Redeeming America: Piety and Politics in the New Christian Right*. Chapel Hill: University of North Carolina Press, 1993.

Marsh, Charles. *God's Long Summer: Stories of Faith and Civil Rights*. Princeton, N.J.: Princeton University Press, 1997.

Marty, Martin E. *Modern American Religion*. 3 vols. Chicago: University of Chicago Press, 1986–96.

McGirr, Lisa. *Suburban Warriors: The Origins of the New American Right*. Princeton, N.J.: Princeton University Press, 2001.

Meyer, Donald. *The Positive Thinkers: A Study of the American Quest for Health, Wealth and Personal Power from Mary Baker Eddy to Norman Vincent Peale*. Garden City, N.Y.: Doubleday, 1965.

Moore, Deborah Dash. *To the Golden Cities: Pursuing the American Dream in Miami and Los Angeles*. New York: Free Press, 1994.

Numbers, Ronald L. *The Creationists: The Evolution of Scientific Creationism*. New York: Knopf, 1992.

Orsi, Robert A., ed. *Gods of the City: Religion and the American Urban Landscape*. Bloomington: Indiana University Press, 1999.

Prothero, Stephen R. *American Jesus: How the Son of God Became a National Icon*. New York: Farrar, Straus and Giroux, 2003.

Reiser, Andrew Chamberlin. *The Chautauqua Moment: Protestants, Progressives, and the Culture of Modern Liberalism*. New York: Columbia University Press, 2003.

Shapiro, Edward S. *A Time for Healing: American Jewry Since World War II*. Baltimore: Johns Hopkins University Press, 1992.

Winston, Diane. *Red-Hot and Righteous: The Urban Religion of the Salvation Army*. Cambridge, Mass.: Harvard University Press, 1999.

Wuthnow, Robert. *The Restructuring of American Religion: Society and Faith since World War II*. Princeton, N.J.: Princeton University Press, 1988.

AFRICAN-AMERICAN RELIGIOUS TRADITIONS

Andrews, William L. *Sisters of the Spirit: Three Black Women's Autobiographies of the Nineteenth Century*. Bloomington: Indiana University Press, 1986.

Best, Wallace D. *Passionately Human, No Less Divine: Religion and Culture in Black Chicago, 1915–1952*. Princeton, N.J.: Princeton University Press, 2005.

Freedman, Samuel G. *Upon This Rock: The Miracles of a Black Church*. New York: HarperCollins, 1993.

Frey, Sylvia R., and Betty Wood. *Come Shouting to Zion: African American Protestantism in the American South and British Caribbean to 1830*. Chapel Hill: University of North Carolina Press, 1998.

George, Carol V. R. *Segregated Sabbaths: Richard Allen and the Rise of Independent Black Churches, 1760–1840*. New York: Oxford University Press, 1973.

Higginbontham, Evelyn Brooks. *Righteous Discontent: The Women's Movement in the Black Baptist Church, 1880–1920*. Cambridge, Mass.: Harvard University Press, 1993.

Morgan, Philip. *Slave Counterpoint: Black Culture in the Eighteenth-Century Chesapeake and Lowcountry*. Chapel Hill: University of North Carolina Press, 1998.

Murphy, Joseph M. *Santería: An African Religion in America*. Boston: Beacon, 1980.

Raboteau, Albert J. *Canaan Land: A Religious History of African Americans*. New York: Oxford University Press, 2001.

———. *Slave Religion: The "Invisible Institution" in the Antebellum South*. New York: Oxford University Press, 1978.

Salvatore, Nick. *Singing in a Strange Land: C. L. Franklin, the Black Church, and the Transformation of America*. New York: Little, Brown, 2005.

Sensbach, John F. *Rebecca's Revival: Creating Black Christianity in the Atlantic World*. Cambridge, Mass.: Harvard University Press, 2005.

———. *A Separate Canaan: The Making of an Afro-Moravian World in North Carolina 1763–1840*. Chapel Hill: University of North Carolina Press, 1997.

Sernett, Milton C. *African American Religious History: A Documentary Witness*. Durham, N.C.: Duke University Press, 1989.

Sobel, Mechal. *Trabelin' On: The Slave Journey to an Afro-Baptist Faith*. Westport, Conn.: Greenwood, 1979.

Weisenfeld, Judith. *African American Women and Christian Activism: New York's Black YWCA, 1905–1945*. Cambridge, Mass.: Harvard University Press, 1997.

ASIAN AMERICAN RELIGIOUS TRADITIONS

Fields, Rick. *How the Swans Came to the Lake: A Narrative History of Buddhism in America*. 3rd ed. Boston: Shambhala, 1992.

Tweed, Thomas A., and Stephen Prothero, eds. *Asian Religions in America: A Documentary History*. New York: Oxford University Press, 1999.

———. *The American Encounter with Buddhism, 1844–1912: Victorian Culture and the Limits of Dissent*. Bloomington: Indiana University Press, 1992.

Tworkov, Helen. *Zen in America: Profiles of Five Teachers and the Search for an American Buddhism*. Rev. ed. New York: Kodansha, 1995.

Williams, Raymond Brady. *Religious of Immigrants from India and Pakistan: New Threads in the American Tapestry*. New York: Cambridge University Press, 1988.

Yoo, David, ed. *New Spiritual Homes: Religion and Asian Americans*. Honolulu: University of Hawaii Press, 1999.

CATHOLICISM IN AMERICA

Abrahamson, Harold J. *Ethnic Diversity in Catholic America*. New York: Wiley, 1973.

Allitt, Patrick. *Catholic Intellectuals and Conservative Politics in America, 1950–1985*. Ithaca, N.Y.: Cornell University Press, 1994.

Carey, Patrick W., ed. *American Catholic Religious Thought*. New York: Paulist, 1987.

Carey, Patrick W. *People, Priests, and Prelates: Ecclesiastical Democracy and the Tensions of Trusteeism*. Notre Dame, Ind.: University of Notre Dame Press, 1987.

Dolan, Jay, and Allan Figueroa Deck, eds. *Hispanic Catholic Culture in the U.S.* Notre Dame, Ind.: University of Notre Dame Press, 1994.

Dolan, Jay P. *The Immigrant Church: New York's Irish and German Catholics, 1815–1865.* Baltimore: Johns Hopkins University Press, 1975.

——. *The American Catholic Experience: A History from Colonial Times to the Present.* Garden City, N.Y.: Doubleday, 1985.

Ellis, John T., ed. *Documents of American Catholic History.* Rev. ed. Chicago: Regnery, 1967.

Fisher, James T. *The Catholic Counterculture in America, 1933–1962.* Chapel Hill: University of North Carolina Press, 1989.

——. *Communion of Immigrants: A History of Catholics in America.* New York: Oxford University Press, 2002.

Gleason, Philip. *Keeping the Faith: American Catholicism Past and Present.* Notre Dame, Ind.: University of Notre Dame Press, 1987.

Kane, Paula. *Separatism and Subculture: Boston Catholicism, 1900–1920.* Chapel Hill: University of North Carolina Press, 1994.

Lynch, Christopher Owen. *Selling Catholicism: Bishop Sheen and the Power of Television.* Lexington: University Press of Kentucky, 1998.

Massa, Mark S. *Catholics and American Culture: Fulton Sheen, Dorothy Day, and the Nortre Dame Football Team.* New York: Crossroad, 1999.

McGreevy, John T. *Parish Boundaries: The Catholic Encounter with Race in the Twentieth-Century Urban North.* Chicago: University of Chicago Press, 1996.

Morris, Charles. *American Catholic.* New York: Times Books, 1997.

Nabhan-Warren, Kristy. *The Virgin of El Barrio: Marian Apparitions, Catholic Evangelizing, and Mexican American Activism.* New York: New York University Press, 2005.

Orsi, Robert Anthony. *The Madonna of 115th Street: Faith and Community in Italian Harlem, 1880–1950.* New Haven: Yale University Press, 1985.

Thwaites, Reuben G., ed. *The Jesuit Relations and Allied Documents: Travels and Explorations of the Jesuit Missionaries in New France, 1610–1791.* 73 vols. Cleveland: Burrows Brothers, 1896–1901.

Tweed, Thomas A. *Our Lady of the Exile: Diasporic Religion at a Cuban Catholic Shrine in Miami.* New York: Oxford University Press, 1997.

Vecsey, Christopher. *On the Padres' Trail.* Notre Dame, Ind.: University of Notre Dame Press, 1996.

———. *The Paths of Kateri's Kin.* Notre Dame, Ind.: University of Notre Dame Press, 1997.

Weber, David J. *The Spanish Frontier in North America.* New Haven: Yale University Press, 1992.

Weigle, Marta. *Brothers of Light, Brothers of Blood: The Penitentes of the Southwest.* Albuquerque: University of New Mexico Press, 1976.

ISLAM IN AMERICA

Abdo, Geneive. *Mecca and Main Street: Muslim Life in America after 9/11.* New York: Oxford University Press, 2006.

Gardell, Mattias. *In the Name of Elijah Muhammad: Louis Farrakhan and the Nation of Islam.* Durham, N.C.: Duke University Press, 1996.

Haddad, Yvonne Yazbeck. *The Muslims of America.* New York: Oxford University Press, 1991.

Haddad, Yvonne Yazbeck, and Jane Idleman Smith, eds. *Muslim Communities in North America.* Albany: State University of New York Press, 1994.

Kepel, Gilles. *Allah in the West: Islamic Movements in America and Europe.* Trans. Susan Milner. Stanford, Calif.: Stanford University Press, 1997.

Metcalf, Barbara Daly. *Making Muslim Space in North America and Europe.* Berkeley: University of California Press, 1996.

Smith, Jane I. *Islam in America.* New York: Columbia University Press, 1999.

Turner, Richard Brent. *Islam in the African-American Experience*. Bloomington: Indiana University Press, 1997.

Waugh, Earle H., Sharon M. Abu-Laban, and Regula B. Quershi, eds. *Muslim Families in North America*. Edmonton, Alberta: University of Alberta Press, 1991.

JUDAISM IN AMERICA

Barquist, David L., Jon Butler, and Jonathan D. Sarna. *Myer Myers: Jewish Silversmith in Colonial New York*. New Haven: Yale University Press, 2001.

Diner, Hasia R. *Lower East Side Memories: A Jewish Place in America*. Princeton, N.J.: Princeton University Press, 2000.

——. *A New Promised Land: A History of Jews in America*. New York: Oxford University Press, 2002.

Dinnerstein, Leonard. *Antisemitism in America*. New York: Oxford University Press, 1994.

Feingold, Henry L., ed. *The Jewish People in America*. 5 vols. Baltimore: Johns Hopkins University Press, 1992.

Hyman, Paula, and Deborah Dash Moore, eds. *Jewish Women in America; An Historical Encyclopedia*. 2 vols. New York: Routledge, 1997.

Jick, Leon A. *The Americanization of the Synagogue, 1820–1870*. Hanover, N.H.: University Press of New England for Brandeis University Press, 1976.

Joselit, Jenna Weissman. *The Wonders of America: Reinventing Jewish Culture, 1880–1950*. New York: Hill & Wang, 1994.

Kraut, Benny. *From Reform Judaism to Ethical Culture: The Religious Evolution of Felix Adler*. Cincinnati: Hebrew Union College Press, 1979.

Moore, Deborah Dash. *At Home in America: Second Generation New York Jews*. New York: Columbia University Press, 1981.

Sachar, Howard M. *A History of the Jews in America*. New York: Knopf, 1992.

Sarna, Jonathan, Benny Kraut, and Samuel K. Joseph. *Jews and the Founding of the Republic*. New York: Markus Wiener, 1985.

Sarna, Jonathan D. *The American Jewish Experience: A Reader*. 2nd ed. New York: Holmes & Meier, 1997.

——. *American Judaism: A History*. New Haven: Yale University Press, 2005.

——. *Jacksonian Jew: The Two Worlds of Mordecai Noah*. New York: Holmes & Meier, 1981.

Seltzer, Robert M., and Norman J. Cohen, eds. *The Americanization of the Jews*. New York: New York University Press, 1995.

NATIVE AMERICAN RELIGIOUS TRADITIONS

Bowden, Henry W. *American Indians and Christian Missions*. Chicago: University of Chicago Press, 1981.

Brandão, José António, ed. *Nation Iroquoise: A Seventeenth-century Ethnography of the Iroquois*. Trans. José António Brandão with K. Janet Ritch. Lincoln: University of Nebraska Press, 2003.

Capps, Walter H., ed. *Seeing with a Native Eye*. New York: Harper & Row, 1976.

Gordon-McCutchan, R. C. *The Taos Indians and the Battle for Blue Lake*. Santa Fe, N.M.: Red Crane, 1991.

Gutiérrez, Ramón A. *When Jesus Came, the Corn Mothers Went Away: Marriage, Sexuality, and Power in New Mexico, 1500–1846*. Stanford, Calif.: Stanford University Press, 1991.

Hultkrantz, Ake. *The Religions of the American Indians*. Berkeley: University of California Press, 1979.

Martin, Joel W. *The Land Looks after Us: A History of Native American Religion*. New York: Oxford University Press, 2001.

——. *Sacred Revolt: The Muskogees' Struggle for a New World*. Boston: Beacon, 1991.

McAlister, Elizabeth A. *Rara: Vodou, Power, and Performance in Haiti and Its Diaspora*. Berkeley: University of California Press, 2002.

McLoughlin, William G. *The Cherokees and Christianity: 1794–1870.* Athens: University of Georgia Press, 1994.

Merrell, James H. *The Indians' New World: Catawbas and Their Neighbors from European Contact Through the Era of Removal.* Chapel Hill: University of North Carolina Press, 1989.

Smith, Paul Chaat. *Like a Hurricane: The Indian Movement from Alcatraz to Wounded Knee.* New York: New Press, 1996.

PROTESTANTISM IN AMERICA

Abell, Aaron I. *The Urban Impact on American Protestantism, 1865–1900.* Cambridge, Mass.: Harvard University Press, 1943.

Ammerman, Nancy. *Baptist Battles: Social Change and Religious Conflict in the Southern Baptist Convention.* New Brunswick, N.J.: Rutgers University Press, 1990.

Balmer, Randall. *Blessed Assurance: A History of Evangelicalism in America.* Boston: Beacon, 1999.

——. *Grant Us Courage: Travels Along the Mainline of American Protestantism.* New York: Oxford University Press, 1996.

——. *Mine Eyes Have Seen the Glory: A Journey into the Evangelical Subculture in America.* 4th ed. New York: Oxford University Press, 2006.

Balmer, Randall, and Lauren F. Winner. *Protestantism in America.* New York: Columbia University Press, 2002.

Bendroth, Margaret L. *Growing up Protestant: Parents, Children, and Mainline Churches.* New Brunswick, N.J.: Rutgers University Press, 2002.

Blumhofer, Edith L. *Restoring the Faith: The Assemblies of God, Pentecostalism, and American Culture.* Urbana: University of Illinois Press, 1993.

Boylan, Anne M. *Sunday School: The Formation of an American Institution, 1790–1880.* New Haven: Yale University Press, 1988.

Brereton, Virginia. *Training God's Army: The American Bible School, 1880–1940.* Bloomington: Indiana University Press, 1990.

Carpenter, Joel A. *Revive Us Again: The Reawakening of American Fundamentalism*. New York: Oxford University Press, 1997.

Carpenter, Joel A., and Wilbert R. Shenk, eds. *Earthen Vessels: American Evangelicals and Foreign Missions, 1880–1980*. Grand Rapids, Mich.: Eerdmans, 1990.

Conkin, Paul K. *Cane Ridge: America's Pentecost*. Madison: University of Wisconsin Press, 1990.

Curtis, Susan. *A Consuming Faith: The Social Gospel and Modern American Culture*. Baltimore: Johns Hopkins University Press, 1991.

Finney, Charles G. *Lectures on Revivals in Religion*. Edited by William G. McLoughlin. Cambridge, Mass.: Harvard University Press, 1960.

Griffin, Clifford S. *Their Brothers' Keepers: Moral Stewardship in the United States, 1800–1865*. New Brunswick, N.J.: Rutgers University Press, 1960.

Hanley, Mark Y. *Beyond a Christian Commonwealth: The Protestant Quarrel with the American Republic, 1830–1860*. Chapel Hill: University of North Carolina Press, 1994.

Harvey, Paul. *Redeeming the South: Religious Cultures and Racial Identities among Southern Baptists, 1865–1925*. Chapel Hill: University of North Carolina Press, 1997.

Heyrman, Christine Leigh. *Southern Cross: The Beginnings of the Bible Belt*. New York: Knopf, 1997.

Hutchison, William R. *The Modernist Impluse in American Protestantism*. Cambridge, Mass.: Harvard University Press, 1976.

——. *Errand to the World: American Protestant Thought and Foreign Missions*. Chicago: University of Chicago Press, 1987.

Jones, Charles E. *Perfectionist Persuasion: The Holiness Movement and American Methodism, 1867–1936*. Metuchen, N.J.: Scarecrow, 1974.

Livingstone, David N. *Darwin's Forgotten Defenders: The Encounter Between Evangelical Theology and Evolutionary Thought*. Grand Rapids, Mich.: Eerdmans, 1987.

Magnuson, Norris. *Salvation in the Slums; Evangelical Social Work, 1865–1920*. Grand Rapids, Mich.: Baker Book House, 1990.

Marsden, George M. *Fundamentalism and American Culture: The Shaping of Twentieth-Century Evangelicalism: 1870–1925*. New York: Oxford University Press, 1980.

Martin, William. *With God on Our Side: The Rise of the Religious Right in America*. New York: Broadway, 1996.

Mathews, Donald G. *Religion in the Old South*. Chicago: University of Chicago Press, 1977.

May, Henry F. *The Enlightenment in America*. New York: Oxford University Press, 1976.

McCauley, Deborah Vansau. *Appalachian Mountain Religion: A History*. Urbana: University of Illinois Press, 1995.

McLoughlin, William G., ed. *The American Evangelicals, 1800–1900: An Anthology*. New York: Harper & Row, 1968.

Miller, Donald E. *Reinventing American Protestantism: Christianity in the New Millennium*. Berkeley: University of California Press, 1997.

Noll, Mark A. *American Evangelical Christianity*. Oxford: Blackwell, 2001.

———. *The Work We Have to Do: A History of Protestants in America*. New York: Oxford University Press, 2002.

Putney, Clifford. *Muscular Christianity: Manhood and Sports in Protestant America, 1880–1920*. Cambridge, Mass.: Harvard University Press, 2001.

Sack, Daniel. *Whitebread Protestants: Food and Religion in American Culture*. New York: St. Martin's Press, 2000.

Sizer, Sandra. *Gospel Hymns and Social Religion*. Philadelphia: Temple University Press, 1978.

Smith, Timothy L. *Revivalism and Social Reform*. 1957. Reprint, Baltimore: Johns Hopkins University Press, 1980.

Synan, Vinson. *The Holiness-Pentecostal Movement in America*. Grand Rapids, Mich.: Eerdmans, 1971.

Thuesen, Peter J. *In Discordance with the Scriptures: American Protestant Battles over Translating the Bible.* New York: Oxford University Press, 1999.

Wacker, Grant. *Heaven Below: Early Pentecostals and American Culture.* Cambridge, Mass.: Harvard University Press, 2001.

Weber, Timothy P. *Living in the Shadow of the Second Coming: American Premillennialism, 1875–1925.* Chicago: University of Chicago Press, 1987.

BIOGRAPHY

Angell, Stephen W. *Bishop Henry McNeal Turner and African-American Religion in the South.* Knoxville: University of Tennessee Press, 1992.

Arrington, Leonard J. *Brigham Young: American Moses.* New York: Knopf, 1985.

Berrigan, Philip. *Fighting the Lamb's War: Skirmishes with the American Empire: The Autobiography of Philip Berrigan.* Monroe, Me.: Common Courage, 1996.

Blumhofer, Edith L. *Aimee Semple McPherson: Everybody's Sister.* Grand Rapids, Mich.: Eerdmans, 1993.

——. *Her Heart Can See: The Life and Hymns of Fanny J. Crosby.* Grand Rapids, Mich.: Eerdmans, 2005.

Bordin, Ruth. *Frances Willard: A Biography.* Chapel Hill: University of North Carolina Press, 1986.

Bremer, Francis J. *John Winthrop: America's Forgotten Founding Father.* New York: Oxford University Press, 2005.

Brodie, Fawn McKay. *No Man Knows My History: The Life of Joseph Smith, the Mormon Prophet.* New York: Knopf, 1945.

Brown, Karen McCarthy. *Mama Lola: A Vodou Priestess in Brooklyn.* Berkeley: University of California Press, 1991.

Bushman, Richard L. *Joseph Smith: Rough Stone Rolling.* New York: Knopf, 2005.

Cunningham, Lawrence. *Thomas Merton and the Monastic Vision.* Grand Rapids, Mich.: Eerdmans, 1999.

Dorset, Lyle W. *Billy Sunday and the Redemption of Urban America*. Grand Rapids, Mich.: Eerdmans, 1991.

Findlay, James F. *Dwight L. Moody: American Evangelist, 1837–1899*. Chicago: University of Chicago Press, 1969.

Flood, Renee S. *Lost Bird of Wounded Knee: Heroic Spirit of the Lakota*. New York: Scribners, 1995.

Fox, Richard Wightman. *Reinhold Niebuhr: A Biography*. New York: Pantheon, 1985.

Frady, Marshall. *Billy Graham, a Parable of American Righteousness*. Boston: Little, Brown, 1979.

Friedman, Maurice S. *Abraham Joshua Heschel and Elie Wiesel: You Are My Witnesses*. New York: Farrar, Straus & Giroux, 1987.

Garrow, David J. *Bearing the Cross: Martin Luther King, Jr., and the Southern Christian Leadership Conference*. New York: Random House, 1986.

Gaustad, Edwin S. *Liberty of Conscience: Roger Williams in America*. Grand Rapids, Mich.: Eerdmans, 1991.

——. *Sworn on the Altar of God: A Religious Biography of Thomas Jefferson*. Grand Rapids, Mich.: Eerdmans, 1996.

George, Carol V. R. *God's Salesman: Norman Vincent Peale and the Power of Positive Thinking*. New York: Oxford University Press, 1993.

Gill, Gillian. *Mary Baker Eddy*. Reading, Mass.: Perseus, 1998.

Goff, James R., Jr. *Fields White unto Harvest; Charles F. Parham and the Missionary Origins of Pentecostalism*. Fayetteville: University of Arkansas Press, 1988.

Hambrick-Stowe, Charles E. *Charles G. Finney and the Spirit of American Evangelicalism*. Grand Rapids, Mich.: Eerdmans, 1996.

Harrell, David Edwin, Jr. *Oral Roberts: An American Life*. Bloomington: Indiana University Press, 1985.

——. *Pat Robertson, a Personal, Religious, and Political Portrait*. San Francisco: Harper & Row, 1987.

Kazin, Michael. *A Godly Hero: The Life of William Jennings Bryan*. New York: Knopf, 2006.

Malcolm X, with Alex Haley. *The Autobiography of Malcolm X*. New York: Grove, 1964.

Marsden, George. *Jonathan Edwards: A Life*. New Haven: Yale University Press, 2003.

Martin, Robert F. *Hero of the Heartland: Billy Sunday and the Transformation of American Society, 1862–1935*. Bloomington: Indiana University Press, 2002.

Martin, William. *A Prophet with Honor: The Billy Graham Story*. New York: William Morrow, 1991.

Middlekauff, Robert. *The Mathers: Three Generations of Puritan Intellectuals, 1596–1728*. New York: Oxford University Press, 1971.

Miller, Robert M. *Bishop G. Bromley Oxnam: Paladin of Liberal Protestantism*. Nashville: Abingdon, 1990.

———. *Harry Emerson Fosdick: Preacher, Pastor, Prophet*. New York: Oxford University Press, 1985.

Numbers, Ronald L. *Prophetess of Health: Ellen G. White and the Origins of Seventh-day Adventist Health Reform*. Rev. ed. Knoxville: University of Tennessee Press, 1992.

Polner, Murray. *Disarmed and Dangerous: The Radical Lives and Times of Daniel and Philip Berrigan*. New York: Basic Books, 1997.

Prothero, Stephen R. *The White Buddhist: The Asian Odyssey of Henry Steel Olcott*. Bloomington: Indiana University Press, 1996.

Raser, Harold E. *Pheobe Palmer, Her Life and Thought*. Lewiston, N.Y.: E. Mellen, 1987.

Reeves, Thomas C. *America's Bishop: The Life and Times of Fulton J. Sheen*. San Francisco: Encounter, 2001.

Rosen, Steven. *A Passage from India: The Life and Times of His Divine Grace A. C. Bhaktivedanta Swani Prabhupada*. New Delhi: Munshiram Manoharlal, 1992.

Scult, Mel. *Judaism Faces the Twentieth Century: A Biography of Mordecai M. Kaplan*. Detroit: Wayne State University Press, 1993.

Seaman, Ann Rowe. *Swaggart: The Unauthorized Biography of an American Evangelist*. New York: Continuum, 1999.

Silverman, Kenneth. *The Life and Times of Cotton Mather*. New York: Harper & Row, 1984.

Stout, Harry S. *The Divine Dramatist: George Whitefield and the Rise of Modern Evangelicalism*. Grand Rapids, Mich.: Eerdmans, 1991.

Stuart, Nancy Rublin. *The Reluctant Spiritualist: The Life of Maggie Fox*. Orlando, Fla.: Harcourt, 2005.

Sussman, Lance Jonathan. *Isaac Leeser and the Making of American Judaism*. Detroit: Wayne State University Press, 1995.

Watts, Jill. *God, Harlem U.S.A.: The Father Divine Story*. Berkeley: University of California Press, 1992.

Wright, Conrad, ed. *Three Prophets of Religious Liberalism: Channing, Emerson, Parker*. Boston: Beacon, 1961.

INDEX

herbs/plants for curing, 226
magic for curing, 67, 86–87, 107, 215
prayer for curing, 84
dispensationalism, 319–21
divination, augury and, 14–15
Divine, Father (Major Jealous), 333–34
divine nearness, 270
divorce, 390, 412
Dix, Dorothea, 167, 191
Doda, Carol, 385
Dogmatic Constitution on the Church, 364
dollar bill, 163–64, 167, 168
Dominican missionaries, 24, 26, 38
Dominic, St., 24
Dongan, Thomas, 71–72
Dortch, Richard, 402
Douglass, Frederick, 236–37, 244–45
dreams
Indians on, 1–2, 98, 215, 287
Moravians on, 98
visions and, 2, 14, 18–19
Drew, Timothy (Noble Drew Ali), 333
drugs, 198, 294, 295, 382
dry towns, 189
Duffield, George, Fr., 185
Dunkers, German, 77
Dunster, Henry, 59
Duquesne University, 364–65
Dutch Reformed Church, 71, 73, 74, 119, 122, 283
Dwight, Timothy, 174, 177, 179
Dylan, Bob, 380
d'Youville, Marguerite, 43

earthquake, San Francisco, 313
Eastern religions. *See* Asia; *specific religions*
Eclectic Readers (McGuffey), 188
Eddy, Mary Baker, 294–95, 306
Edict of Nantes, 73
The Education of Henry Adams (Adams, Henry), 261
Edwards, Jonathan, 121–22, 129, 174, 179
Eisenberg, Sandy, 386
Eisenhower, Dwight, 340, 355, 360, 368–69
El Camino Real (the King's Highway), 34
Eliot, John, 95–96
Elizabeth I, Queen (of England), 7–8, 10
Elks Club, 412
Elliott, Charlotte, 171

Emerson, Ralph Waldo, 167, 185, 262–64
encomienda, 35–36
encyclical, 366–67
England. *See also* Church of England; New England
Baptists in, 8, 116
Calvinism in, 52
Catholics *v.* Protestants and, 6–9, 46
Civil War of 1640s in, 8
Congregationalists in, 8–9
Jews in, 8–9
leadership modeled after institutions in, 116
Masons in, 167
Mormons in, 207
politics and religion in, 7
Presbyterians in, 8–9, 116
public worship in, 9
Puritans in, 8–9, 54, 55
Quakers in, 8–9, 81, 124–25
Virginia in, 22
Enlightenment, European, 220
environmental movement, 413
Episcopalians, 106, 142. *See also specific churches*
Civil War and, 239
culture of honor and, 187–88
High Church, 284
on ordination of women, 386
renewal movement and, 365
tradition and, 284
equal rights amendment (ERA), 387
est, 397
Ethical Culture Society, 410
Evangelical and United Brethren Church, 386
Evangelical Free Church of America, 398
evangelicalism, 171–84. *See also* healing, divine; missionaries; missions; reform; television evangelists; *specific churches/individuals/locations/religions*
Civil War and, 171–84, 319
democracy and, 183
politics and, 326
slavery and, 178, 180–81, 224, 226, 235–36
tradition and, 276–79
values/beliefs of, 188–89, 319–21, 342
after World War II, 293
Evans, Hiram Wesley, 331–32
Evening Light Saints, 312

471

ACKNOWLEDGMENTS

I am greatly indebted to many people for helping with *Religion in American Life: A Short History*, especially Nancy Toff of Oxford University Press. She taught me that clarity and vivid examples made good books, and she overlooked foibles and corrected errors with dispatch and grace.

I've leaned on plentiful histories written by wonderful scholars, only some of whose books can be listed in the bibliography. Without them, none of us could write anything else because we'd know so little.

And I'll always be indebted to the three people I've named at the beginning of this book. I couldn't have gone to graduate school with anyone more humane than Paul Lucas. With Judy, we laughed a lot, and I still feel privileged to have known people so smart and warmly kindhearted. Anita Rutman and Darrett Rutman were my first teachers at the University of Minnesota. They came from the east and pretended to be interested only in rigor. But we midwesterners found them out and discovered that they not only laughed but cared very, very deeply about students.

—Jon Butler

Many of the texts listed in the "Further Reading" section informed my thinking. I am especially indebted to four surveys: Catherine L. Albanese, *America: Religions and Religion* (1992); Mark A. Noll, *A History of Christianity in the United States and Canada* (1992); Peter W. Williams, *America's Religions: Traditions and Cultures* (1990); and *Eerdman's Handbook to Christianity in America*, edited by David F. Wells and others (1983), particularly the nineteenth-century section by Nathan O. Hatch and sidebar authors Stephen E. Berk, James E. Johnson, John B. Boles, Howard A.

Snyder, Sandra S. Sizer, Ronald L. Numbers, Lawrence Foster, Donald E. Pitzer, Wesley A. Roberts, Thomas A. Askew, Rockne McCarthy, Joseph M. White, Patrick Carey, Michael J. Roach, Thomas J. Schlereth, Jay P. Dolan, Ronald A. Wells, Ronald D. Rietveld, Donald Tinder, Susan B. Hoekma, Norris Magnuson, Anthony A. Hoekema, James W. Skillen, C. Norman Kraus, and David B. Wills. Two handbooks merit particular credit: *Dictionary of Christianity in America*, edited by Daniel G. Reid and others (1990), and Henry Warner Bowden, *Dictionary of American Religious Biography* (1977). Other particularly useful works include the Sound Editions audiotape *The Civil War*, by Geoffrey C. Ward with Ric Burns and Ken Burns; James H. Hutson, *Religion and the Founding of the American Republic* (1998); Ronald L. Numbers, *Prophetess of Health: Ellen G. White and the Origins of Seventh-day Adventism Health Reform* (1992); Catherine L. Albanese, *Sons of the Fathers: The Civil Religion of the American Revolution* (1976); Nell Irvin Painter, *Sojourner Truth: A Life, A Symbol* (1996); David Gollaher, *Voice for the Mad: The Life of Dorothea Dix* (1995); R. Laurence Moore. "What Children Did Not Learn in School: The Intellectual Quickening of Young Americans in the Nineteenth Century," *Church History* 68 (March 1999) 42–61; Charles Mann, "1491," *Atlantic Monthly*, March 2002, 41–53. Chapter 15, "Innovators in a World of New Ideas," contains several sentences from my essay in *Between the Times: The Travail of the Protestant Establishment, 1900–1960*, edited by William R. Hutchison (1989).

As always, individuals helped in special ways. Chris Armstrong, Joanne Beckman, Julie Byrne, Elesha Coffman, Russ Congleton, Susie Mroz, and Rosalee Velloso de Silva aided with the research and writing. Professors David Daily, William R. Hutchison, Joel Martin, Robert Bruce Mullin, and Harry S. Stout, as well as Oxford University Press editors Nancy Toff and Katherine Adzima, offered valuable criticisms of early drafts of the manuscript.

—*Grant Wacker*

My greatest inspiration, as always, is my family. Chris, Andrew, and Sara have enriched my life beyond measure, and life itself would be impoverished to the point of hopelessness without the love, humor, and companionship of Catharine, my wife.

ACKNOWLEDGMENTS

Only recently have I come to realize that my passionate interest in American religious history derives not only from my religious background but also from my childhood travels throughout North America. Every June my parents would pile all of us into the sedan—the last trip I remember was five kids, one in diapers—for a cross-country trip to attend my father's annual church convention, which took place in a different venue each year. I loved those excursions, and somewhere in the course of those travels I developed a lifelong fascination with American culture in all of its glorious and bewildering diversity.

I owe a debt of gratitude to my mother, my late father, and my four fellow passengers there in the back seat: Ken, David, Brian, and Mark.

—*Randall Balmer*

TEXT CREDITS

Sidebars

p. 74–75: *The Winthrop Papers*, vol. 2 (Boston: Massachusetts Historical Society, 1931).

pp. 89–90: Leo Hershkowitz and Isidor S. Meyer, eds., *Letters of the Franks Family (1733–1748)* (Waltham, Mass.: American Jewish Historical Society, 1968).

pp. 108–109: David Brainerd, *Mirabilia Dei inter Indicos; or, The Rise and Progress of a Remarkable Work of Grace Amongst a Number of the Indians in the Provinces of New Jersey and Pennsylvania, Justly Represented in a Journal Kept by Order of the Honourable Society (in Scotland) for Propagating Christian Knowledge* (Edinburgh, 1765).

pp. 129: John E. Smith, Harry S. Stout, and Kenneth P. Minkema, *A Jonathan Edwards Reader* (New Haven, Conn.: Yale University Press, 1995).

pp. 130–131: Mary Beth Norton, "'My Resting Reaping Times': Sarah Osborn's Defense of Her 'Unfeminine Activities,'" *Signs* 2 (1976).

pp. 150–151: *Records of the Presbyterian Church in the United States of America, 1706–1788* (Philadelphia: Presbyterian Board of Publication and Sabbath-School Work, 1904).

p. 170: Giles Gunn, ed., *New World Metaphysics: Religious Readings on the Religious Meaning of the American Experience* (New York: Oxford University Press, 1981), 129–31.

p. 184: Charles G. Finney, *An Autobiography* (Old Tappan, NJ.: Fleming H. Revell, 1908), 20–21.

p. 199: *Life, Letters, and Travels of Father De Smet* (1904), excerpted in *A Documentary History of Religion in America: Since 1865*, edited by Edwin S. Gaustad (Grand Rapids, Mich.: Eerdmans, 1983), 72–5.

p. 211: Joseph Smith, *The History of Joseph Smith, by Himself* (1838), excerpted in "Religion and Cultural Change in American History," edited by William R. Hutchison (readings for NEH Summer Seminar, 1986, Harvard University), u.p.

p. 230: Issac Mayer Wise, *Selected Writings* (1900), excerpted in *A Documentary History of Religion in America: Since 1865*, edited by Edwin S. Gaustad (Grand Rapids, Mich.: Eerdmans, 1983), 55–6.

pp. 244–245: Rosemary Radford Ruether and Rosemary Skinner Keller, eds., *Women and Religion in America*, 3 vols. (San Francisco: Harper & Row, 1981), II:126.

p. 260: Rosemary Radford Ruether and Rosemary Skinner Keller, eds., *Women and Religion in America*, 3 vols. (San Francisco: Harper & Row, 1981), II:126.

p. 290: Phoebe Palmer, *Promise of the Father* (New York: Garland, 1985), 329–30, 333–34.

p. 306: excerpted in "Religion and Cultural Change in american History," edited by William R. Hutchison (readings for NEH Summer Seminar, 1986, Harvard University), u.p.

p. 322: *Apostolic Faith*, September 1906, 1.

p. 339: *Christian Century*, December 27, 1917.

pp. 356–358: Thomas Merton, *The Seven Storey Mountain* (New York: Harcourt, Brace & World, 1948), 382–88, 396–405.

p. 359: Elie Wiesel, *Night* (New York: Hill & Wang, 1960), 44.

pp. 376–378: Malcom X, with Alex Haley, *The Autobiography of Malcolm X* (New York: Random House, 1964), 163–64.

p. 394: Michael Cromartie, ed., *No Longer Exiles: The Religious New Right in American Politics* (Washington, D.C.: Ethics and Public Policy Center, 1993), 25–26.

p. 427: *Congressional Record, 91st Congress, 2nd session.*

pp. 428–429: Mario M. Cuomo, "Religious Belief and Public Morality," *New York Review of Books*, October 25, 1984, 32.

Chapter epigraphs:

Chapters 8–10, 13–17: *The United Methodist Hymnal: Book of United Methodist Worship* (Nashville, Tenn.: United Methodist Publishing House, 1989).

Chapter 11: *The Hymnal: Reorganized Church of Jesus Christ of Latter Day Saints* (Independence, Mo.: Herald, 1956).

Chapter 12: *The Cokesbury Worship Hymnal*, C.A. Bowen, ed. (New York: Abingdon-Cokesbury, n. d.).

PICTURE CREDITS

Archives of the Billy Graham Center, Wheaton, IL: 3g; Courtesy of the Billy Graham Center Museum: 2d; Boston Athenaeum: 2e; Boston Public Library: 2c; Department of Special Collections, Charles E. Young Research Library, UCLA: If; Connecticut Historical Society, Hartford, CT: 1k; The Franciscan Friars of the St. Barbara Province: 3c; Glenbow Institute, Calgary, Canada: 2h; The Historical Society of York County, PA, Lewis Miller (1796–1882): 1e; © John T. Hopf: 1g; The Jacob Rader Marcus Center of the American Jewish Archives: 3d, 3k; Courtesy of the John Carter Brown Library at Brown University: Il; Courtesy John F. Kennedy Library (Pre-Presidential Papers, Box 1017): 3i; Library of Congress: 1a, 1b, 1c, 1d, 1j, 2b, 2g, 2k, 2l, 3a (LC-USZ62-63886), 3e (Pan Subject—Groups, no. 159 (E size)), 3h (NYWTS); Marquette University Archives: 3j; National Archives: 2a, 2j, 3f (306-PSC-63-4119); 3m (412-DA-13792); 3l (342-B-ND-064-12-115541); Pierpont Morgan Library: 1h; Archives and Museum of the United Methodist Church: 2f; Special Collections, J. Willard Marriott Library, University of Utah: 3n; Vedanta Society of St. Louis: 3b; Western History Collections, University of Oklahoma Libraries, Phillips Collection: frontispiece; Zeist, Evangelische Broedergemeente: li.

ABOUT THE AUTHORS

Jon Butler is Howard R. Lamar Professor of American Studies, History, and Religious Studies and Dean of the Graduate School of Arts and Sciences at Yale University. He received his B.A. and Ph.D. in history from the University of Minnesota. He is the author of *Power, Authority, and the Origins of American Denominational Authority*; *The Huguenots in America: A Refugee People in New World Society*; *Awash in a Sea of Faith: Christianizing the American People*; and *Becoming America: The Revolution Before 1776*, and, with Harry S. Stout, editor of *Religion in American History: A Reader*.

Grant Wacker is Professor of Christian History at Duke University. His publications include *Augustus H. Strong and the Dilemma of Historical Consciousness* (1985), and *Heaven Below: Pentecostals and American Culture* (2001). He has edited, with James R. Goff, Jr., *Portraits of a Generation: Early Pentecostal Leaders* (2002), and, with Daniel H. Bays, *The Foreign Missionary Enterprise at Home: Explorations in North American Cultural History* (2003). He is senior editor of *Church History: Studies in Christianity and Culture*.

Randall Balmer is Professor of American Religious History at Barnard College, Columbia University, and Visiting Professor of American Religion at Yale University Divinity School. He is the author of ten books, including *A Perfect Babel of Confusion: Dutch Religion and English Culture in the Middle Colonies* (1989); *Protestantism in America* (2002); and *Thy Kingdom Come: How the Religious Right Distorts the Faith and Threatens America* (2006). His second book, *Mine Eyes Have Seen the Glory: A Journey into the Evangelical Subculture in America*, now in its fourth edition, was made into an award-winning three-part documentary for PBS.